# Contentious Episodes in the Age of Austerity

Based on extensive data and analysis of sixty contentious episodes in twelve European countries, this book proposes a novel approach that takes a middle ground between narrative approaches and conventional protest event analysis. Looking particularly at responses to austerity policies in the aftermath of the Great Recession (2008–2009), the authors develop a rigorous conceptual framework that focuses on the interactions between three types of participants in contentious politics: governments, challengers, and third parties. This approach allows political scientists to map not only the variety of actors and actor coalitions that drove the interactions in the different episodes but also the interplay of repression/concessions/support and of mobilization/cooperation/mediation on the part of the actors involved in the contention. The methodology used will enable researchers to answer old (and new) research questions related to political conflict in a way that is simultaneously attentive to conceptual depth and statistical rigor.

Abel Bojar is a postdoctoral research fellow at the European University Institute.

Theresa Gessler is a postdoctoral researcher at the Department of Political Science and the Digital Democracy Lab at the University of Zurich.

Swen Hutter is Lichtenberg Professor in Political Sociology at the Free University of Berlin and Vice Director of the Center for Civil Society Research.

Hanspeter Kriesi is a professor at the European University Institute in Florence.

# Cambridge Studies in Contentious Politics

General Editor

David S. Meyer *University of California, Irvine*

Editors

Mark Beissinger *Princeton University*
Donatella della Porta *Scuola Normale Superiore*
Jack A. Goldstone *George Mason University*
Michael Hanagan *Vassar College*
Holly J. McCammon *Vanderbilt University*
Doug McAdam *Stanford University and Center for Advanced Study in the Behavioral Sciences*
Sarah Soule *Stanford University*
Suzanne Staggenborg *University of Pittsburgh*
Sidney Tarrow *Cornell University*
Charles Tilly (d. 2008) *Columbia University*
Elisabeth J. Wood *Yale University*
Deborah Yashar *Princeton University*

*(continued after the Index)*

# Contentious Episodes in the Age of Austerity

*Studying the Dynamics*
*of Government–Challenger Interactions*

Edited by

**ABEL BOJAR**
*European University Institute*

**THERESA GESSLER**
*University of Zurich*

**SWEN HUTTER**
*Freie Universität Berlin, WZB Berlin Social Science Center*

**HANSPETER KRIESI**
*European University Institute*

CAMBRIDGE
UNIVERSITY PRESS

Shaftesbury Road, Cambridge CB2 8EA, United Kingdom

One Liberty Plaza, 20th Floor, New York, NY 10006, USA

477 Williamstown Road, Port Melbourne, VIC 3207, Australia

314–321, 3rd Floor, Plot 3, Splendor Forum, Jasola District Centre, New Delhi – 110025, India

103 Penang Road, #05–06/07, Visioncrest Commercial, Singapore 238467

Cambridge University Press is part of Cambridge University Press & Assessment, a department of the University of Cambridge.

We share the University's mission to contribute to society through the pursuit of education, learning and research at the highest international levels of excellence.

www.cambridge.org
Information on this title: www.cambridge.org/9781009002011

DOI: 10.1017/9781009004367

First published 2021
First paperback edition 2023

*A catalogue record for this publication is available from the British Library*

*Library of Congress Cataloging-in-Publication data*
NAMES: Bojar, Abel, 1983– editor. | Gessler, Theresa, 1989– editor. | Hutter, Swen, 1978– editor. | Kriesi, Hanspeter, editor.
TITLE: Contentious episodes in the age of austerity : studying the dynamics of government-challenger interactions / edited by Abel Bojar, Theresa Gessler, Swen Hutter, Hanspeter Kriesi.
DESCRIPTION: Cambridge ; New York, NY : Cambridge University Press, 2021. | Series: Cambridge studies in contentious politics | Includes bibliographical references and index.
IDENTIFIERS: LCCN 2021025365 (print) | LCCN 2021025366 (ebook) | ISBN 9781316519011 (hardback) | ISBN 9781009002011 (paperback) | ISBN 9781009004367 (epub)
SUBJECTS: LCSH: Conflict management–European Union countries–Case studies. | Government, Resistance to–European Union countries–Case studies. | Global Financial Crisis, 2008–2009. | Recessions–European Union countries. | European Union countries–Politics and government–Case studies. | European Union countries–Foreign economic relations–Case studies. | European Union countries–Economic policy. | BISAC: SOCIAL SCIENCE / Sociology / General
CLASSIFICATION: LCC JN30 .C5795 2021 (print) | LCC JN30 (ebook) | DDC 320.94–dc23
LC record available at https://lccn.loc.gov/2021025365
LC ebook record available at https://lccn.loc.gov/2021025366

ISBN   978-1-316-51901-1   Hardback
ISBN   978-1-009-00201-1   Paperback

# Contents

# Figures

# Tables

# Contributors

ARGYRIOS ALTIPARMAKIS is a full-time Research Fellow in the Department of Political and Social Sciences at the European University Institute in Florence.

ABEL BOJAR is a full-time postdoctoral researcher in the Department of Political and Social Sciences at the European University Institute in Florence.

THERESA GESSLER is a postdoctoral researcher at the Digital Democracy Lab and the Department of Political Science at the University of Zürich.

SOPHIA HUNGER is a postdoctoral research fellow at the Center for Civil Society Research at the WZB Berlin Social Science Center.

SWEN HUTTER is Lichtenberg-Professor in Political Sociology at Freie Universität Berlin and Vice Director of the Center for Civil Society Research, a joint initiative of Freie Universität and the WZB Berlin Social Science Center.

HANSPETER KRIESI is a part time professor at the European University Institute in Florence. He is also affiliated with the Laboratory for Comparative Social Science Research, the National Research University Higher School of Economics, and the Russian Federation.

KATIA PILATI is Associate Professor in the Department of Sociology and Social Research (DSRS) at the University of Trento, Italy.

JULIA SCHULTE-CLOOS is Marie Curie Research Fellow at the Geschwister Scholl Institute of Political Science, Ludwig Maxmilian University of Munich.

# Preface

*Contentious Episodes in the Age of Austerity* is the final product of the project "Political Conflict in Europe in the Shadow of the Great Recession (POLCON)" funded by the European Research Council.[1] POLCON has previously studied the structuration of the European party-political space relying on election campaign data in *European Party Politics in Times of Crisis* (Hutter and Kriesi 2019) as well as the patterns of European protest activity relying on semi-automated protest event analysis in *Contention in Times of Crisis* (Kriesi et al. 2020). Both of these volumes focused on particular venues of political conflict: the electoral arena and the protest arena, respectively. A common intuition among many observers of the Great Recession (2008–2015) at the time was that it would turn out to be a watershed event in transforming European politics, possibly for the foreseeable future. Yet, the cautious conclusion we drew from our empirical works was the opposite: European politics, apart from a few noteworthy exceptions such as Greece or Hungary, was propelled forward by forces and mechanisms largely familiar from earlier times. It was business as usual, it would seem.

In some ways, our current study brings the two arenas – the electoral arena and the protest arena – together by studying a wide range of political actors and their action strategies in the wake of contentious policy proposals put forward by governments in their attempt to address the adverse consequences of the Great Recession. While some of the protagonists in our study coincide with the main actors driving the anti-austerity protest wave that we studied in our previous work – such as the Indignados movement in Spain or the traditional trade unions in Italy and France – others are party actors that came to prominence during this period either as government parties responsible for harsh

---

[1] The project was supported by the ERC-grant Nr. 338875.

austerity measures (e.g. Fianna Fail in Ireland) or as opposition parties aligning with challenger organizations to fight governments in parliaments, in the streets or in international forums (e.g. Syriza up until their rise to power in 2015). Still others are what we call 'third-party actors' (such as foreign governments, supranational institutions, constitutional courts etc.) because their functional role in the policy episodes we study was a form of mediation between governments and their challengers that often, however, meant a close alignment with one or the other.

Our approach to study political conflict in what we call 'policy episodes' follows in the footsteps of the *Dynamics of Contention* tradition (McAdam et al. 2001) that advocated a turn towards the middle ground between the narrative approach that traditionally dominated the field and the epidemiological approach of protest event analysis. Our main goal in this volume is to offer a solution to scholars who wish to implement this middle ground in a systematic fashion. Although the scope of our study is limited by the choice of the kind of episodes we study (mostly economic episodes, initiated by a government proposal), we hope our proposed method travels beyond what we show in the present volume and it will be used by scholars studying other forms of political conflict.

As any innovation in the social sciences, our approach had to overcome formidable challenges that we are acutely aware of. The empirical material we rely on in our analysis is exhaustive only to the extent that our keyword-based search from the national presses allows us to capture the full timeline of events in the respective political settings. The complexity of actions and actors needed to be condensed into a scheme that is amenable to interpretation and coding. The answers to where to begin and where to end the coding of a given episode were guided by operational rules that we laid down in the beginning, but at times the coding had to be adjusted to the empirical reality of episode-specific idiosyncrasies. Although we are optimistic that many of these limitations can be overcome and fine-tuned by future applications of our method, we regard some degree of simplification of a complex political world a necessary price to pay for the systematic scheme that we present to our readers.

Some of the choices in the way we structured our volume and the types of analysis we undertook were informed by the extremely useful feedback we have received along the way. We are particularly grateful to all the participants of our POLCON conference in October 2018, who highlighted some of the main problems that we could still address in time. Special thanks are due to Mark Beisinger and Mario Diani, who acted as discussants to individual papers and chapters that we presented at the conference. No less important were the comments we received at the discussion from Edgar Grande, Elisabeth Iversflaten, Zsolt Enyedi, Line Rennwald, Sofia Vasilopoulu, Herberth Kitschelt, Liisa Talving, Thomas Sattler, Silja Hausermann, Anton Hemerijck, Philip Manow, Ondrey Cisar and Stefaan Walgrave. Parts of our work have also been presented at the third LSE–Oxford-Sciences Po 'Young Doctors'

Political Economy Workshop, where we received equally helpful comments from Michael Zemmour, acting as discussant, as well as other participants, such as Tim Vlandas (conference organizer), Margarita Gelepithis, Charlotte Haberstroh, Sonja Avlijas, Angelo Martelli and David Hope, among others. Moreover, we greatly appreciated the opportunity to take part in the symposium organized by *Mobilization* with the conceptual summary paper of our project ("Contentious Episode Analysis"), where we received highly constructive remarks from David Meyer, Alex Hanna, Pamela Oliver and Sidney Tarrow.

Last but not least, none of this would have been possible without the painstaking effort to browse through and code thousands of articles by our research assistants at the European University Institute and beyond. In no particular order, we would thus like to express our gratitude for their coding efforts to Lola Guyot, Sophia Hunger, Anna Kyriazi, Argyrios Altiparmakis, Ieva Grumbinaie, Ieva Bloma, Zsofia Suba, Nodira Kholmitova, Gulzat Baialieva, Davide Morisi, Johannes Karremans, Radek Michalksi, Grzegorz Krzyzanowski, Frederico Ferreira Da Silva, Delia Radu, Nena Oana, and Mateus Alves. Likewise, the support we have received from our administrative staff, above all Maureen Lechleitner, proved crucial in the successful implementation of this project, and so we would like to extend our gratitude to her as well.

Let us conclude by pointing out that this volume is the result of intense cooperation between all of its contributors. The individual chapters have been written in the framework of the project and their authors have contributed not only to their own chapters but also to data collection, conceptual and methodological discussions, as well as data analysis.

PART I

A NEW APPROACH TO THE ANALYSIS
OF CONTENTIOUS EPISODES

I

# Introduction

## *A New Approach for Studying Political Contention – Contentious Episode Analysis*

Hanspeter Kriesi, Swen Hutter, Abel Bojar,
Argyrios Altiparmakis, Theresa Gessler,
Sophia Hunger, Katia Pilati, and Julia Schulte-Cloos

On 24 May 2011, in the middle of the parliamentary debate on the so-called mid-term adjustment plan, yet another round of austerity imposed by Greece's international creditors, a call for a demonstration at Syntagma Square in Athens and at the White Tower in Thessaloniki appeared on Facebook. By the next day at least 20,000 people assembled in the two squares, mostly chanting "thieves, thieves" at parliamentarians and cursing the Parliament. The movement of the Greek Indignados or Aganaktismenoi was born. It would prove to be massive, expansive, and innovative. Immediately after the initial demonstrations, the main squares in the two cities were occupied, and simultaneous protests began in almost all major urban centers of the country. Interest would focus on Syntagma Square, however, where the occupation was symbolically confronting Parliament, juxtaposing the public assembly and the symbolic seat of political power. In the following days, the occupation grew exponentially, eventually reaching almost 400,000 participants on June 5th. In our dataset, there is an event associated with the Aganaktismenoi on almost every single day until the end of the episode on June 30th.

At first, the Pasok government reacted to the movement in a mix of fear and embarrassment, but the original ambivalence soon gave way to growing anxiety. On the eighth day of the occupation, Prime Minister Papandreou addressed the ongoing mobilization, attempting to shift the blame to abstract "global powers" – to no avail. On the same day, the movement blocked all the exits from Parliament, effectively locking the M.P.s inside. Eventually, the M.P.s had to escape in the dark, with the help of the fire brigade, through the adjacent National Garden. Pasok M.P.s were becoming the main target, bearing the

Parts of this chapter are taken from: Hanspeter Kriesi, Abel Bojar and Swen Hutter. 2019. "Contentious Episode Analysis", *Mobilization* 24 (3).

brunt of the opposition to a policy about which they themselves had considerable reservations. They reacted by challenging the government, asking for explanations and for assurances that this austerity package would be the last one. On June 7th, in the parliamentary committee, the five ministers in charge of the bailout took fully thirteen hours to convince raging and fearful M.P.s of the need for new measures. The protestes in the squares, which were initially seen as a potential relief for Pasok, were by now fissuring the link between the government and its MPs.

At the same time, EU pressure on the government escalated, as did its pressure on the opposition leader to share responsibility for the new measures. The opposition, however, did not budge. On June 14th, when one Pasok M.P. resigned and another publicly declared that he would not vote for the midterm adjustment, the government majority shrank to only four M.P.s. At this point, the possibility of a lost vote and a subsequent chaotic default loomed large. At the same time, the unions entered the fray. On June 15th, the large strike demonstrations of the unions fused with the Syntagma Square occupation, gathering hundreds of thousands once more. The earlier blockade was repeated. For the first time after twenty days of protest, the riot police moved in forcefully to disband the blockade, and the new movement underwent its baptism of fire. Reports of police repression and brutality carried out on a crowd that was until then peaceful shocked the attending public.

On the evening of the same day, the prime minister called the opposition leader to ask for a government of national unity. The latter accepted, on the condition that the government's sole focus would be the renegotiation of the bailout and that elections would then be called. Papandreou first agreed but then withdrew his consent to such a program within a day and, instead, opted for a cabinet reshuffle, replacing his finance minister who had been the main target of the ire of the protesters and M.P.s. The new minister tried to open a dialogue with the movement and the unions. After the reshuffle, the government asked for a vote of confidence, which it received on June 21st. After having been finalized in the various committees, the midterm adjustment package was introduced in the plenary session.

The major unions responded with a forty-eight-hour general strike on June 28–29, the days of the plenary debate and the final vote on the program. The demonstration on June 29th, attended by both the unions and the Aganaktismenoi, proved to be one of the largest to date. While each organization had its own bloc, radical left parties, anarchists, a loose nationalist crowd, and Indignados united their forces in the first showing of an informal anti-bailout coalition. During the following night, while the midterm adjustment was legislated, a large group of hooded protesters clashed with riot police. As it turned out, the cabinet reshuffle and the signal of the new finance minister that he would consider social concerns sufficed to relieve the tension within Parliament and allowed the remaining Pasok M.P.s to vote compactly in order to pass the midterm adjustment program on June 30th. External pressure had vanquished the domestic threat from the new challengers. After the passage of the bill, the challenge subsided. The combination of repression and unresponsiveness by the elites deflated the movement.

This sequence of events, which has been told by Altiparmakis (2019: 143–154) in more detail, dramatically illustrates the patterns of interactions between challengers (Aganaktismenoi, unions, anti-bailout coalition), the government, and third parties (M.P.s of the governing party, opposition parties, foreign creditors) that had been triggered by austerity proposals by European governments during the Great Recession, one of the great economic crises in our time. In this book we shall study such patterns of interaction in twelve European countries. The Great Recession, which was unleashed by the breakdown of Lehmann Brothers in fall 2008 soon spilled over to Europe, where the initial shock of the financial crisis was to be followed by the Eurozone crisis, initiated in early 2010 with the sovereign debt crisis in Greece. While the worst of the crisis seemed to be over by fall 2012 after the head of the European Central Bank had declared that he would do "whatever it takes" to save the euro, the fallout from the crisis continued to haunt Europe at least until the conclusion of the third Greek bailout in summer 2015. It is hard to overstate the sheer magnitude of the impact the economic crisis has had on the lives of people in some, although not in all, parts of Europe. As Adam Tooze (2018: 5) has observed in the introduction to his account of "the first crisis of a global age," the combination of these crises and the economic and political responses to them are essential to understand the changing face of the world we are living in today.

Initially, governments countered the economic impact of the crisis by relying on some version of "liberal" (Pontusson and Raess 2012) or "emergency Keynesianism" (Hall 2013). Once the Greek crisis deepened, however, starting in early 2010, governments turned to austerity policies, which were the key sources of economic hardship in the most hard-hit countries. While the welfare states buffered the negative consequences of the crisis initially (Bermeo and Bartels 2014), especially in the countries of northwestern Europe, which had strong automatic stabilizers, the turn to austerity impeded the redistributive functions of the state and crucially contributed to the hardship of the populations. This aspect has focused the minds of the challengers on government policy and on the supranational constraints imposed on the national governments by agencies of the European Union, fellow governments of the Eurozone, and the I.M.F.

In the present volume, we focus on the interactions between the governments and their challengers in reaction to the governments' austerity proposals. We examine the austerity proposals and ask whether and how they have been challenged by social movements, unions, opposition parties, and other actors, and how the governments, in turn, have reacted to such challenges. We are trying to understand how it was possible that austerity came to pass in spite of popular resistance by investigating in detail the contentious episodes that were triggered by the austerity packages proposed by European governments. As we shall see in the subsequent analyses, the Greek episode that we used to illustrate the interplay between challenger actions and government reactions is an extreme case with regard to the contentiousness of the challenge and the intensity of the interaction between the two main protagonists. However, it proves to be rather typical with respect to its outcome. Even in a case of a very intense challenge such as this one, where the government was heavily shaken by the mobilization of the challengers, the authorities ended up imposing their austerity proposals. We shall try to make sense of the patterns of interaction by analyzing in detail the composition of the main protagonists, how they reacted to each other, and the extent to which their reciprocal reactions depended on contextual conditions.

In focusing on the patterns of interaction that developed during the contentious episodes unleashed by the austerity proposals of European governments during the Great Recession, we believe that we can achieve a better understanding of what happened during this crucial period of European politics. We already know that the crisis has been particularly deep in southern Europe, where it led to a wave of public economic protest against the government austerity programs, while protest remained much more limited in northwestern and centraleastern Europe (Kriesi et al. 2020). We also know that the southern European party systems have been profoundly transformed by the electoral consequences of the Great Recession, while the party systems in the other two European regions have been more resistant to change (Hutter and Kriesi 2019). However, our knowledge is based on a comparative-static analysis, and we have little understanding about the processes that have shaped the waves of protest and the electoral outcomes. It is the ambition of the present study to dig deeper into the dynamics of these processes in order to show the mechanisms that have driven the different outcomes at the macro level in the three European regions.

We have selected twelve countries to study the patterns of interaction underlying the macro-level outcomes – four countries each from the three regions of Europe: France, Germany, Ireland, and the United Kingdom in northwestern Europe; Greece, Italy, Portugal, and Spain in southern Europe; and Hungary, Latvia, Poland, and Romania in centraleastern Europe. In this selection we find several countries that have been particularly hard hit by the Great Recession, but there also countries such as Germany or Poland that have gotten much better through the crisis. For each country we study four austerity packages that were introduced by the respective governments during the Great Recession. For comparative purposes, we also include an institutional reform proposal for each country in our study. From the perspective adopted here, the austerity proposals (and possibly also the institutional reform proposals) of the governments constitute "proposals at risk," which are likely to be challenged by some actors mobilizing in the name of aggrieved groups in society. However, not all such proposals have been challenged, nor have all been challenged to the same extent. We shall not only describe how, by whom, and to what extent the different proposals have been challenged but also try to account for the differences in the contentiousness of the challenges and their outcomes.

For this study, we have developed what we call "Contentious Episodes Analysis" (CEA), a novel approach to the study of "contentious episodes" that aims at a more systematic analysis of the dynamics of interaction in such episodes. In this chapter, we shall introduce the broad outlines of our new approach, which is situated in the "middle ground" between the encompassing chronology of the episode, reproduced in narratives, and the micro level of the events, reproduced in simple event counts. Initially, we provide some arguments explaining why we have chosen to study the middle ground. Then we proceed to introduce the conceptual building blocks of our approach. Finally, we provide a brief summary and an overview over the contents of the present volume.

## WHY AND HOW TO STUDY "THE MIDDLE GROUND"

In his book on contentious performances, Charles Tilly (2008: 206) proposed to distinguish between *three levels of analysis* for studying contentious performances: the reconstruction of single events as one action or interaction after another (what he called the "narrative"), the count of contentious events (what he called "epidemiology"), and the close description of successive interactions within contentious episodes (what he called "the middle ground"). He advocated study at the middle ground, and suggested that from this level, we can move to either one of the other levels but also in a third direction – toward analytic sequences transcending any particular episode but identifying recurrent actions and relations. In this third vein, Tilly himself had aggregated verb categories (e.g. "attack," "control," "bargain") when comparing sets of episodes and then showed which sets of relations among claimants and objects of claims prevailed within different verb categories.

The "narrative" approach is the conventional storytelling of historians, where explanation takes the form of "an unfolding open-ended story fraught with conjunctures and contingency, where what happens, an action, in fact happens because of its order and position in the story" (Griffin 1993: 1099). In contrast, the "epidemiological" approach relies on conventional Protest Event Analysis (PEA). Here, the individual event constitutes the unit of analysis. According to this approach, we can describe an episode in terms of its aggregate *event* characteristics (e.g. the number of protest events in an episode, the number of events produced by different types of challengers) as well as in terms of the dynamic development of events over time (e.g. the weekly counts of protest events). The "middle ground," by contrast, focuses on the *interactions between challengers and authorities*.

Most notably, this middle ground has been the focus of the programmatic *Dynamics of Contention* (DoC) (McAdam et al. 2001). The goals of this seminal study were manifold. Among others, it aimed to (a) overcome the prevailing static approaches in social movement studies, (b) extend the field of study to include other types of actors, (c) introduce a new language to describe/reconstruct processes of contentious politics, and (d) explore the black box between independent and dependent variables, that is, to identify the mechanisms connecting the two. Reflecting on the book's impact ten years later, its authors (McAdam and Tarrow 2011) self-critically observed that they might have been trying to do too many things, that they had invoked too many mechanisms too casually,[1] that they had been too indifferent to measurement, and that theirs had still been a state-centric bias. We might add, most importantly, that they failed to provide a framework for the systematic study of interactions across a set of contentious episodes.[2]

Building on DoC, our goal is to further explore the "middle ground." We do so because we share Tilly's (2008: 21) view that this level of analysis offers the "opportunity to look inside contentious performances and discern their dynamics" without losing the opportunity to systematically analyze these dynamics. In other words, we suggest that CEA holds out the promise to go beyond the narrative approach by infusing it with the rigor and explicitness of PEA without losing its dynamic quality. At the same time, CEA aims to move beyond a narrow focus on protest activities by challengers (as in PEA-based research). In this it follows political claims-analysis (Koopmans and Statham 1999).

In addressing the middle ground, the challenge is to provide an analytical approach to the study of the dynamics of contention that allows for the systematic comparative analysis of causal patterns across single narratives. Instead of comparing entire narratives (as in sequence analysis), the strategy we propose in CEA is to break down the narratives into their component elements. This is in line with DoC, which insisted on the analysis of smaller-scale causal mechanisms that could then be concatenated into broader processes, that is into "causal chains," as Gross (2018) has proposed to call such sequences of mechanisms. As Gross points out (2018: 345), such causal chains have structures that may vary in the time period over which a mechanism sequence unfolds, in the number of mechanisms tied together, in the levels of social complexity spanned by actors, and in the abstract patterns formed by connections across mechanisms. CEA is designed to study such sequences of mechanisms systematically.

---

[1] Lichbach (2005: 228) has already pointed to the key problem of the introduction of mechanisms – multiplicity. As an antidote he proposed to embed causal mechanisms in theories and evaluate the mechanism by using stylized facts and historical narratives. He argued that generating mechanisms is easy but locating them is not. In his view, the real challenge is to embed mechanisms in larger and more organized structures of knowledge so as to deepen our understanding of interesting and important causal processes (Lichbach 2005: 233f).

[2] The same applies to Alimi et al. (2012), who adopt the mechanism approach but who use it in their narratives in a rather loose sense.

Generally, the goal of CEA is to specify the concepts of DoC in such a way that they can be applied to systematic comparative analyses across episodes.[3] Before introducing the building blocks of the proposed CEA in more detail let us highlight three more general points: First, in conceptual terms, CEA privileges the interaction between governments and their challengers. While this focus allows us to move away from the "starkly Ptolemaic view of social movements" that puts movements at the center of the political universe (McAdam and Boudet 2012), it keeps the state-centric perspective of DoC and its inherent limitations. It does so by largely drawing on the political process model, which has long since argued that social movements are sustained interactions between challengers and powerholders (Tilly 1978). In this perspective, challengers' actions can only be understood in relation to the actions by authorities. Relatedly, we shall only allow for a rather reductionist conceptualization of other participants in the episodes, and we shall limit the possible action repertoires of the various actors, too. In other words, there is a price to be paid for the systematic approach we propose here. In a way, the ontology we propose is rather "flat." That is, in line with the tradition of social movement research inaugurated by Tilly (1978), CEA adopts a structural-relational perspective focusing on interactions between challengers and authorities, neglecting other components of the mobilization process – in particular, the subjective dimension of contentious politics including processes of framing, the construction of collective identities, emotions, motivations, beliefs, and values. While focusing on interactions, CEA is distinguished from relational accounts of social movements focused on dynamics of interactions within social movements: that is, on interactions among challengers (see Diani 2015), thus excluding the analysis of groups, or "catnets" (Tilly 1978). In contrast, CEA aims to build the sequence of interactions within an episode by considering the actions by several types of actors – challengers as well as authorities and third parties – and it proposes a fairly parsimonious conceptualization of the action component on which it focuses.

Second, some details of the suggested approach are tailored to the examples that we shall study here – sixty contentious episodes that have taken place in Europe in the course of the great financial and economic crises that shook the continent from 2008 to 2015. However, we would like to insist that the approach is more flexible than it might seem at first. It is, for example, not restricted to interactions between the government and its challengers in the public arena. The type of arena and the type of actors studied may vary. For example, one might study the interactions between challengers and other types of authority – such as supranational or local political authorities, churches,

---

[3] In this respect, our approach differs from the one chosen by Griffin (1993), who relied on "event structure analysis," a procedure developed by Heise (1989) that allows reconstructing the causal structure of the narrative about an *individual* episode – in his case a lynching episode that took place in Mississippi in 1930.

business corporations, or media – or focus on the interactions between move-ments and countermovements. What we would suggest, however, is that one cannot do all these possible applications at the same time. In order to keep any analysis manageable, we have to make choices depending on the specific research questions.

As with classical PEA, we think that this flexibility might also be a major strength of the approach (see Beissinger 2002: 460f.). That is, CEA provides a common conceptual language and general guidelines for data collection and analysis, but ultimately researchers can and should adapt it to the specific research questions at stake. In our study, we ask questions about the variety of contention related to economic and institutional reforms in the Great Recession with regard to the intensity of conflict, the actors involved, the configurations of actor coalitions, and their action repertoires, as well as the outcome of the episodes. In addition, we ask about patterns of interaction in the course of the episodes – interactions between the two main contestants, gov-ernment and challengers, and between each one of them and potential third parties. We are also interested in identifying critical moments in an episode that decisively redirect the sequences of actions from one state of interaction dynam-ics to another.

Finally, let us point out that it is possible and, indeed, necessary to comple-ment the bare bones of an analysis based on the CEA framework we propose here with narratives (or process tracing) in order to get a more complete account of the dynamics of contention in the episodes in question. We would maintain that the skeleton of the structural-relational analysis we propose here will make it easier to put flesh on the bare bones in order to get to a full understanding of the episodes one is studying and to systematically compare the various cases. However, it only complements but does not replace a more qualitative and in-depth analysis.

## THE CONCEPTUAL BUILDING BLOCKS OF THE CONTENTIOUS EPISODE ANALYSIS

Our conceptualization of "contentious episodes" follows the tradition of DoC (McAdam et al. 2001), but we have adapted it to our specific purposes. McAdam et al. (2001: 5) defined *contentious politics* as

episodic, public, collective interaction among makers of claims and their objects when (a) at least one government is a claimant, an object of claims, or a party to the claims and (b) the claims would, if realized, affect the interests of at least one of the claimants.

They defined episodes as "continuous streams of contention including collective claims making that bears on other parties' interests" (p. 24). More than a decade later, Tilly and Tarrow (2015: 7) reiterated and clarified the notion of contentious politics:

contentious politics involves interactions in which actors make claims bearing on other actors' interests, leading to coordinated efforts on behalf of shared interests or programs, in which governments are involved as targets, initiators of claims, or third parties. Contentious politics thus brings together three familiar features of social life: contention, collective action, and politics.

For Tilly and Tarrow contentious claims making becomes political when the interaction involves agents of governments. Closely following these conceptions, but simplifying them, we define a *contentious episode* as a "continuous stream of interactions regarding policy-specific proposals between the government and its challengers, involving also some other actors." In other words, for us, the key defining element of a contentious episode is the *dyadic interaction* between two stylized types of actors – the government and its challengers – each making claims on behalf of its own interests and/or on behalf of some other actors.[4] Consequently, CEA examines the sequence of political claims making by different actors within broader episodes. In doing this, it goes beyond political claims making analysis (as for example proposed by Ruud Koopmans and Paul Statham 1999). Political claims making analysis indeed overcomes some problems related to PEA (protest event analysis), to the degree that it includes the investigation of political demands regardless of their form in which they are made and regardless of the nature of the actor (Koopmans et al. 2005: 254). However, the innovation of CEA lies in conceiving political claims within a sequence of ordered interactions – something that is missing from claims making analysis used in prior studies – thus enabling the possibility to engage fully in making inferences on causality and disentangle the mechanisms at work in interactions.

In the specific cases we study, the *government* is initiating the contentious episode by introducing a policy proposal into the public debate. Naturally, in the overall universe of cases, not all episodes need to be initiated by the government but our chosen focus on a subset of such episodes, namely *policy episodes*, entails that governments are the first movers. The *challenger* is an actor who opposes this proposal by means of "contentious performances" and other public claims making. A general account of such contentious performances should in theory allow for protest actions on behalf of the government, but in our selected cases of *policy episodes* this is rather unlikely, and we have in fact identified no such actions to warrant this concern.

In addition to the government and the challengers, we introduce a third set of actors who contribute to the sequence of interactions constituting the episodes – a heterogeneous category of *third parties*. Under this category, we aggregate all the other participants in the episode who intervene on behalf of

[4] Similarly, Ermakoff (2015: 96f.) distinguishes between two general "stakeholders" – challengers and target actors (the target of the challenge), while Biggs (2002) distinguishes between labor and capital, or workers and employers.

either the government or the challengers or who try to mediate between the two without being a member of either of the two camps that oppose each other in the contentious episode. In the example we presented at the beginning of this chapter, the category of third parties includes such diverse actors as the MPs of the governing party, opposition parties, and foreign creditors. The main reason for this simplification is that we are mainly interested in their relationships with the two main protagonists but not in the detailed relations between the various types of third parties.[5] Also, an important caveat for our definition for third parties above is that their role in a particular episode stays more or less unchanged. If an actor starts out as mediator but later gets directly involved in contentious challenges, we regard them as a challenger actor for the purposes of that particular episode.

Our conceptualization of the main actors in the contentious episode is closely related to the arena concept of Myra Ferree et al. (2002). We include all actors who are actively engaged in the conflict in the public sphere but exclude mere bystanders who do not get involved and who constitute the audience for the actors engaged in the public arena. Nor does our framework include the public as a specific actor,[6] but it does not exclude the addition of the public as a fourth actor depending on the research question one might have. We do not include it for the time being to keep the framework as parsimonious as possible.

Episodes then are composed of single *actions* by one of the three stylized actors interacting with the other actors. In protest event analysis, each action of the challenger constitutes an *event*. Instead, we shall reserve the term "action" for individual components of episodes. These actions are typically triggered by previous actions of some other participants in the episode. We call a *sequence* a series of actions in which each component action is triggered by a previous action. In adopting this terminology, we follow Tilly (2008: 10), who characterizes episodes very broadly as "bounded sequences of continuous interaction." The focal properties of sequences are order and convergence (Abbott 1983: 133). Order is crucial "for if the order of the sequence has no effect on its future development, there is no need to worry about sequences at all." Convergence refers to the end point of a sequence and is one possibility among others for a sequence to end (oscillation or divergence being possible alternatives).

Sequences can be of different length. They may range from short exchanges of verbal statements to a sustained series of interactions between the three types of actors. It is possible that an episode consists of a single sequence of

---

[5] In the real world, the boundary between the two camps and third parties is sometimes difficult to draw because members of either camp may distance themselves from their home turf during the episode-specific controversy, trying to operate rather as a third party.

[6] In specific instances, the general public is included in the analysis when there is a particular action that is attributable to it, with the referendum on Brexit being a prominent example.

interactions of variable length. More likely, however, an episode is composed of a set of partly overlapping sequences. These sequences may be triggered at different moments during the episode by successive actions of the protagonists. In the particularly complex episode of the midterm adjustment program with which we initiated this chapter, we counted no less than 216 partly overlapping sequences, with an average length of sixty-five actions. While the shortest sequence included only two actions, the longest sequence was composed of no less than 109 consecutive actions. Although the sequences were comparatively long in this episode, their pace was high, meaning one action followed rapidly upon the other. Thus, the average duration of a sequence was only eight days and the maximum duration of a sequence did not exceed three weeks.

As Tilly (2008: 10) suggests, "cutting the big streams into episodes" will usually allow us to get a better grip on the cause–effect dynamics. The question is, of course, how to cut. As already pointed out, we let an episode start at the moment when a government publicly announces the policy proposal that constitutes the focal point of the episode. This implies that the government is the first mover in our type of crisis episode and the challengers are in a situation where they can only react to the government's proposal. This situation is radically different from one where the challengers propose a reform, proactively attempt to put it on the agenda, and implement it against the opposition of the government (Walgrave and Vliegenthart 2012). There is nothing in CEA that prevents its application to this different kind of situation, however. Episodes can have different types of starting point, depending on the dynamics to be analyzed.

Episodes may also end in various ways. Our types of episode end in one of two ways. They typically end with the formal adoption of the (possibly modified) proposal by the government. The episode of the midterm adjustment program illustrates this type of ending. Alternatively, if the challenger continues to mobilize after the formal adoption of the proposal, the episode may end when the continuous stream of interactions between the government and its challenger related to the proposal breaks off.[7]

The focus on the actions by different types of actor does not come at the expense of focusing on *mechanisms*. However, it does clearly narrow down the type of mechanism under scrutiny. In CEA, we focus on what McAdam et al. (2001: 26) call "relational mechanisms," that is on mechanisms that "alter connections among people, groups, and interpersonal networks." For example, brokerage – a key mechanism introduced in DoC – is an action of a third party that mediates between two contestants that might change their relationship (into a more cooperative direction). Repression, to take another example, is an action by government that "raises the contender's cost of collective action"

---

[7] As a rule of thumb, we use a period of two months for assessing whether the interactions related to the proposal have indeed come to a halt before we can declare the episode to have ended.

(Tilly 1978: 100) and may thus trigger a violent reaction by challengers, and would be a sign of the further deterioration of the relationship between the perpetrator and the target actor. Radicalization by challengers, finally, is a mechanism that may threaten the government and induce it to step up its repression of the challengers' actions. In the way we conceive of mechanisms, they correspond to specific sets of interactions that concatenate into processes: that is, longer sequences of interactions.

To be sure, there are mechanisms that are not reducible to actions. In addition to relational mechanisms, DoC also distinguishes between environmental and cognitive mechanisms. We shall also rely on environmental mechanisms. They come into play once we introduce context characteristics that condition the interaction dynamics between the key actors (see Chapter 3). However, we largely neglect cognitive mechanisms. Our approach gives short shrift to the fact that politicians may be influenced by social movements in formulating their policy proposals, that they might anticipate movement protest, or that they might test policy before formal announcements in order to come up with a proposal that will find broad acceptance. As mentioned, our action-centered approach comes at the cost of neglecting beliefs and expectations. CEA is focused only on actions, the interrelationship between actions, and the patterning of these interrelationships. While it is true that a lot of what takes place within contentious episodes has to do with people's expectations and beliefs (not to mention emotions), our approach strips these considerations out of the equation in a way that the case study method does not. We concede this important point, but we would like to suggest that it is possible to use CEA to reconstruct the rough outlines of a given episode that are then taken as the starting point for a more detailed account of the development of this particular episode. We shall provide an example of this possible extension of our approach in Chapter 12, where we present the Greek episodes in more detail.

## Actors

According to our conceptualization, the *government* includes all public authorities linked to the government: that is, the head of government and other members of the cabinet as well as all national public officials. These actors are proposing the policy change. Usually, the political parties of the governing coalition are also part of the government. In some cases, however, a party of the governing coalition may be divided on the proposal and this division may have relevant repercussions on the overall conflict. In these cases, the dissenting voices from the governing party may be coded as third parties or even as part of the challenger coalition. Thus, in the episode of the midterm adjustment, the MPs of PASOK, the governing party, are considered as third parties because of their ambivalence with regard to the government's proposal.

The *challenger* includes all actors who oppose the government's proposal at least partly outside the routine, institutionalized arenas of interest articulation by means of sustained and coordinated collective action, possibly on behalf of other opposing groups. Note that this definition follows the general approach in social movement research and excludes actors who voice their opposition only in routine ways in institutionalized channels, such as national parliaments or tripartite bodies of interest representation (these actors are considered third parties). The challenger in a given episode can be (a) an individual organiza- tion – nonmainstream parties (such as a populist parties), mainstream oppos- ition parties, public interest groups (NGOs), unions, social movement organizations (SMOs) – or representatives of such organizations; (b) a social movement: that is a coalition of organizations or dense informal interorganiza- tional networks *with* a strong identity, or their representatives; or (c) a conflict coalition or alliance: that is, a network of organizations *without* a strong identity (see Diani and Bison 2004). Empirically, CEA can discern social movement dynamics from coalitional dynamics with no identity, given that the former involves sequences of sustained interactions within an episode (sustained interactions are the basis for the development of strong collective identities), while the latter relies on more contingent and less durable sequences of interactions.

All components of "the challenger" share the opposition to the government's proposal, but given that the proposal may be a package that includes diverse policy measures, they need not necessarily pursue the same targets, nor may they be part of the same coordinated effort to oppose the proposal. In other words, they form an "objective coalition" against the government (in the sense that they all oppose the same package of proposals) but not necessarily a "subjective" one (since they do not necessarily coordinate their efforts in one and the same collective action).

The challenger opposes the government by striving for the "expansion of conflict" to an ever larger public (Schattschneider 1975): that is, it seeks to politicize the proposal by drawing the public's attention to the proposal (to render it more salient), by mobilizing public resistance against it (to polarize public opinion on the proposal), and by expanding the number of actors opposed to it (see Hutter et al. 2016). Public claims making is designed to unleash a public debate, to draw the attention of the public to the grievances of the actors in question, to create controversy where there was none, and to obtain the support of the public for the actors' concerns. Controversial public debates and support by the general public are expected to open up access and increase the legitimacy of speakers and allies of the challenger with journalists and with decision-makers who tend to closely follow the public debates (Gamson and Meyer 1996: 288).

As already observed, third parties include all the other participants in the episode who intervene on behalf of either the government or the challengers or who try to mediate between the two without being a member of any one of the two camps. Just like challengers, third parties can cover a highly diverse group of actors in terms of their institutional characteristics: They can be supranational actors, foreign governments, independent regulatory state agencies, opposition parties, or even government coalition members. In the episode of the midterm adjustment, in addition to the MPs of the governing party, third parties also included opposition parties and supranational actors exerting pressure on the government.

As we alluded to above, we can treat the two adversaries and the third parties as unitary actors, but we can also distinguish the actors within the adversarial coalitions according to their *institutional characteristics*. The institutional taxonomy of actors will depend on the specific episodes. In our study, we coded a very large number of institutional actor types that we inductively reduced to more limited sets of actors. Chapter 6 will introduce more details in this respect.

Finally, note that this approach can also accommodate actors changing from positions of challengers or third parties to those of authorities and vice versa. An example would be the Democratic Party in the U.S.A. As shown by Heaney and Rojas (2015), when discussing the U.S. anti-war movement after 9/11, the Democratic Party initially allied with the anti-war movement in challenging the George W. Bush presidency in an effort to end the Iraq War: that is, it served as a third-party supporter of the movement. In this phase, leaders of the Democratic Party adopted the movement's issue and frames and worked together with movement activists to implement the movement's agenda. However, by 2009, after the presidential elections of 2008 won by Obama, synergies between the Democratic Party and the anti-war movement appeared to have largely vanished. "As the Democrats regained control of government ... rather than staying focused on their position on a single issue – such as their opposition to war – many partisans gave greater attention to other callings from the Democratic Party" (Heaney and Rojas 2015: 5).

## The Action Repertoires

The contentious politics scholars have focused their attention on the action repertoires. As Tilly and Tarrow (2015: 39; *emphasis in the original*) advise: "We can learn a lot from what activists say or later write about their activities. ...We will learn more by examining what activists *do* during major episodes of contention." Following this advice, we focus on the action component of the series of interactions constituting the episode. In following this approach, we suggest that the main problem of DoC is not so much the multiplicity of mechanisms it introduced but the fact that it too easily dropped the fine-grained analysis of single actions. As a result, the set of mechanisms it introduced was rather unsystematic. We argue that one needs to first focus on the level of the single action before one can systematically start to combine them into more complex sequences.

We conceptualize the action repertoire separately for each one of the three actors. Importantly, we suggest that the action repertoire of each has two

TABLE 1.1. *Detailed action repertoires of the three actor types*

|  | Government | Challenger | Third party |
|---|---|---|---|
| **Substantive** | | | |
| support of proposal | sticking | cooperation | support of government |
| rejection of proposal | concession | disruptive/non-disruptive action | support of challenger |
| **Procedural** | | | |
| conflictive | repression | disruptive/non-disruptive action | support of government/challenger |
| cooperative | concession | cooperation | mediation |

dimensions – a procedural one and a substantive one: that is, an actor can relate to another actor in procedural and in substantive terms. The *procedural* dimension refers to the relationship between two actors. This can range from conflictive to cooperative. The *substantive* dimension refers to the substance of the actors' claims that they address to each other. It can range from support to rejection of the government's proposal. In our proposed toolbox, each actor type has a specific action repertoire in terms of both dimensions. Table 1.1 presents an overview.

In the stylized world of CEA, each actor has three basic options. Once the proposal has been launched and challengers have reacted, the government's three options are repression, concessions (in procedural and substantive terms), and sticking to its policy. Tilly (1978) had originally also distinguished between three options (all conceived in procedural terms) – repression, facilitation, and toleration. Toleration was defined as a residual category in-between repression and facilitation that included inaction or disregard of protest. More recently, the term "toleration" has been criticized for its vagueness and value-laden implications (acceptance of the challenge). In her analysis of Egyptian protest against the Mubarak regime, Dina Bishara (2015) proposed to replace it with the term "ignoring," which ranges from passive to actively dismissive responses, and suggests that severe forms of ignoring can fuel protest by provoking moral outrage and indignation. Samson Yuen and Edmund Cheng (2017), analyzing the umbrella protest in Hong Kong, introduced yet another concept for government reactions to protest that lie between repression and concession – "attrition." In this case, toleration is only ostensible, while the government actually "uses a proactive action repertoire to discredit, wear out and increase the costs of protest" (p. 613). The proactive action repertoire in the case of the Chinese authorities in Hong Kong included maintaining elite cohesion, mobilizing countermovements, and using the courts for legal action against the protestors. From our perspective, both depreciating statements about the protestors by the Egyptian authorities and the more indirect proactive repertoire used by the Chinese authorities to counter the protests by challenging movements are all procedural reactions that would qualify as "repression" in the broader sense of the term. As a third category between repression and concession, we propose instead the phrase "sticking to the policy proposal," which means that the government reaffirms its support of the policy in substantive terms. This is, of course, equivalent to ignoring the protests and may have the effect of attrition as well, but it does not include proactive attempts to undermine the effectiveness of protest by dismissive statements or further-going acts of surveillance and under- cover repression.

The challengers react to the kind of proposals we study in our research. The challengers have first to decide whether they want to react at all. Given that the government proactively pursues policy reform, the challengers are in a situation where they can only react by rejecting the government's proposal in one way or another: that is, in our episodes we are dealing with threat-induced challenges. As argued by Almeida (2007: 125) against the background of the Latin American experience, "economic austerity policies (e.g. fuel price hikes, privatization of a public service or utility) that are expected to make popular sectors worse off if implemented are likely to set in motion defensive mobilization that focuses attention on the government and state managers." To put it differently, the challengers in our episodes constitute "movements of crises" (see Kerbo 1982) that attempt to fend off threatening policy measures. Threat is the cost that protestors will incur regardless of whether they act or not (Goldstone and Tilly 2001).

We assume that the challengers act rationally and that they adopt strategies that they expect to have the greatest chances of success at the lowest costs. Conventional politics is usually less costly than protest politics (Cunningham 2013: 293), but the costs of the threat posed by the government's proposal may be sufficiently high to induce the challengers to act outside of conventional politics. Once the challengers have decided to act, they have basically three options for action during the episode: They can launch a disruptive challenge, or a nondisruptive challenge (both in procedural and substantive terms), or they can cooperate (in the further course of the episode) with the government. Following the lead of claims making analysis, we extend the kind of communicative acts of challengers that we include in the analysis beyond protest events (see Koopmans and Statham 1999, 2010: 54f.): Non-disruptive actions such as verbal claims are included in the challengers' action repertoire as well. We distinguish nondisruptive from disruptive actions based on the extent to which they are conventional and institutionalized.

Finally, the three strategic choices of third parties include (a) siding (in substantive or procedural terms) with the government; or (b) siding with the challengers; or (c) attempting to mediate (in procedural terms) between the two. As already pointed out, we are not interested in the relationship between the third parties among themselves and we do not code neutral positions of third parties unless they proactively engage in mediation between the opposing actors. In general, we expect that third parties are more likely to react in substantive terms: that is, to participate in the debate on the proposal without entering into a debate about the mobilization process. Third parties that engage in favor of a given camp both in substantive and procedural terms can be considered to be stronger allies than those who engage in substantive terms only.

In the midterm adjustment episode, the predominant government strategy was to stick to its proposal. Given the external pressure, it did not have any other option. Subsidiarily, it attempted to fend off the challengers with repressive measures. The challengers on the other hand insisted that the government should withdraw the proposal, and they mobilized massively in demonstrations and strikes to support their claims. We counted no fewer than forty-three demonstrations and twenty-one strikes during the four-month period covered by the episode. The third parties were about evenly split: Half of their interventions supported the government, while half sided with the challengers.

Building on the action repertoire of the actors involved in an episode, we shall propose a summary measure of the *contentiousness* of each episode. The three types of actor each contribute to the contentiousness of an episode to the extent that they interact with each other and to the extent that their actions are disruptive (challengers), repressive (government), or one-sided (third parties).

## Sequences

The different types of action constitute the building blocks for the construction of the sequences within an episode. Recall that we define a sequence as a series of actions in which each component is triggered by a previous action: that is, the actions in a sequence are explicitly linked to each other. Sequences have properties of their own that can be studied in descriptive and explanatory terms. Sequence analysis occupies a well-established place among social science methodologies. The most prominent approach to study sequences rests on some assumptions that CEA does not fulfill, however. Moreover, this approach takes the whole sequence as the unit of analysis and attempts to find clusters of similar sequences, a goal that CEA does not try to pursue (see Chapter 6 for more details). Instead, CEA is interested in the overall sequence structure of an episode and in the dynamics of the sequences across episodes.

We shall analyze the overall sequence structure of entire episodes in temporal terms (referring to the duration and pace of the sequences), and in relational terms (referring to their length, breadth, and overall complexity), allowing us to get a first idea of the basic structural properties of the episodes and their determinants. In addition, the reconstruction of the sequence structure also allows us to identify specific important points in the development of the episodes, such as *turning points*. Turning points can be defined in two different ways. An action may be a turning point in the sense that it leads to a certain closure of the interaction process by closing alternatives and focusing the interaction on a single thread. Both Abbott (2001) and Ermakoff (2015) define turning points as closing points, but an action may also be a turning point in the sense that it opens up the interaction process by giving rise to a multiplicity of reactions of some consequence – that is, reactions each of which in turn trigger a series of further actions.

Based on the chronological order of the sequences, we shall analyze their interaction dynamics with the aim of uncovering general mechanisms that characterize the episodes triggered by austerity policies in the Great Recession. The gist of the interaction dynamics within an episode lies in the interdependence of the three types of actor. As Beissinger (2011: 27) has observed, "one of the defining features of mobilization – and its greatest challenge for causal explanation – is the high degree of inter-dependence of the actions and reactions involved, both within and across episodes of mobilization. While not a feature characteristic of mobilization alone, it figures so centrally in contentious politics that it is difficult to explain any protest episode without fundamentally addressing this issue." Our approach assumes that the actors involved act *retrospectively*: that is, they react to the actions of the other actors (see Moore 2000: 121).

The most elementary sequence is a *pair* of consecutive actions. We shall focus on pairs of actions that are chronologically following upon each other within a sequence, one being the trigger of the other. For example, we shall study the reactions of the government to disruptive actions of the challengers. Even with only three types of actor and a limited action repertoire of three types of action per actor, there are multiple patterns of possible interactions in any such pair of actions. In the example, the government can react in three ways to the disruptive challenger action, and one of the possible three pairs would be disruptive challenger action followed by government repression. Importantly, we shall generalize the approach based on pairs in two ways. First, we shall relax the restriction that the action triggering a given reaction must immediately precede the reaction in question: That is,. we shall allow for actions that are chronologically preceding the reaction in question by variable steps in the chain of the action sequence to have an impact on the reaction in question as well. In the example of government reactions to disruptive actions by challengers, we shall study the government's reaction to immediate challenger actions but also to such actions that are further removed in the sequence. Second, instead of studying specific pairs, for example a disruptive challenger action followed by government repression, we shall include in the analysis of the given type of reaction (for example, government repression) any possible trigger (for example, actions by third parties supporting the challengers, disruptive, and non-disruptive actions by challengers) of the reaction in question. In other words, we shall introduce the different action types of the three stylized actors into the multivariate analysis to explain a given reaction at one and the same time. These extensions will allow us to come up with a more detailed account of the interaction patterns in the various episodes.

## CONCLUSION AND OVERVIEW OVER THE VOLUME

In this introductory chapter, we have introduced a set of concepts and general guidelines of what we call Contentious Episode Analysis (CEA). In the footsteps of Dynamics of Contention (DoC), we are attempting to develop a conceptual framework that improves upon the concepts originally introduced by McAdam et al. (2001) and that allows us to study contentious episodes more systematically, in a nonnarrative mode. Our analytical strategy is similar to that of DoC: We also propose to decompose the episodes into their component elements – actors, actions, sequences of actions, pairs of actions – that can then be recombined in a systematic way to account for specific processes in the dynamics of contention. We suggest that CEA holds out the promise to go beyond the narrative approach by infusing it with the rigor and explicitness of PEA, without losing its dynamic quality. At the same time, following Koopmans and Statham's (1999) claim analysis, CEA aims to move beyond a narrow focus on protest activities by challengers (as typically done in PEA-based research) by incorporating into the analysis a broader set of action repertoires by a broader set of actors (as is typically done in claims analysis). In addressing the middle ground favored by Charles Tilly, we apply an analytical approach to the study of the dynamics of contention that allows for the systematic comparative analysis of causal patterns across individual narratives. We hope that the toolkit we introduce here will allow for a more systematic analysis of a wide variety of questions linked to the DoC.

In the subsequent chapters of this volume we shall elaborate these concepts in more detail and show how they can be operationalized and implemented in the analysis of specific questions. The volume is divided into three parts. In the remainder of the first part, we shall first present the methods we used to collect our data as well as the context conditions of the sixty episodes we study in this volume. In Chapter 2, we set out how we selected the sixty episodes and how we documented them. As for their selection, it is important to note that, following the lead of McAdam and Boudet (2012), we tried not to select on the dependent variable: Our selection procedure is not based on whether or not there was a serious challenge to the government's proposal. The documentation of the episodes involved the selection of articles in national quality newspapers and the manual coding of these articles. Chapter 3 puts our sixty episodes into their economic and political contexts. It clarifies that the actual decline in economic performance was much more strongly and sharply felt in the south than in the other two parts of Europe. Moreover, it shows that the governments in the hard-hit countries got under double economic and political pressure. In terms of the timing of the proposals, this chapter finds that it has been closely related to both the development of the economic crises and to strategic political considerations.

Part II elaborates the various key concepts, introduces their operationalization, and presents results at the level of the episodes. It provides an overview over the varieties of contention that we observed during the Great Recession. Building on the action repertoires, Chapter 4 introduces the multi-dimensional concept of contentiousness, describes the contentiousness of the individual episodes in the different countries, and provides a set of factors that contribute to the episodes' contentiousness. As it turns out, the Greek episodes (among them the midterm adjustment program that we introduced in this introductory chapter) have been the most contentious of all. In contrast, the German episodes were the least contentious ones. Of course, that is not so surprising given that Germany got through the Great Recession better than any of the other countries in our study. Chapter 5 presents the actors who have been involved in the various episodes, and characterizes them in institutional terms. Among other things, we find that labor unions have been the most important challengers during the contentious episodes in the Great Recession. The chapter also analyzes the actor coalitions and configurations in the various episodes. Chapter 6 introduces the analysis of the sequences. It characterizes the episodes according to the temporal and relational structure of the sequences. The chapter describes the overall sequence structure of the various episodes and makes an attempt to explain it. Thus, the episode types introduced in Chapter 3 turn out to be the best predictor of the temporal sequence structure, with structural and institutional reforms being characterized by a slower pace than I.M.F. bailouts, bank bailouts, and fiscal measures. The greater pressure associated with the latter episodes leads to a more intensive pace of interaction between the government and its challengers. Chapter 7 concludes Part II with an analysis of the outcomes of the episodes. The results of this chapter show that there was very little government responsiveness to challenger actions. Only exceptionally, in the case of episodes proposing extremely severe measures, did governments make some limited concessions to the challengers.

Part III presents various aspects of the dynamic interactions during the episodes. Chapter 8 sets the stage. It introduces the specific method we apply to studying the dynamic interactions between the three actor types, and it tests some general hypotheses concerning their interactions. For all action forms of both adversaries, it finds strong evidence for path dependence, with the pattern being somewhat stronger on the government side. By and large, government behavior appears to be independent of previous challenger actions. With respect to the impact of third parties, governments have a higher propensity to repress challengers when they are not supported by third parties. Most importantly, however, governments seem to honor mediation attempts with concessions. The analyses in this chapter do not take into account the context of the various episodes, however. It is the following two chapters that introduce context into the analysis: Chapter 9 focuses on government reactions to challengers, while Chapter 10 deals with the challengers' reaction to government repression. Both chapters indicate that context is very important. The results of these chapters are rather complex, and they tend to qualify the sweeping results of Chapter 8. Thus, the mediation effect which was uncovered in Chapter 8 appears to be limited to the least threatening episodes – the party-driven episodes, and even in these instances it has at best been marginal. In contrast, the intervention of international actors on behalf of either the government or the challengers tends to be more consequential, especially in party and movement-driven conflicts.

The last two empirical chapters adopt a somewhat different approach. Chapter 11 analyzes the two types of turning points in more detail and uses this concept to distinguish between different phases of the episodes – the opening phase, the main phase, and the closing phase. It shows that the government is mostly responsible for the turning points, and that it dominates in the opening phase, while the challengers play a much bigger role in the main phase and, above all, in the closing phase. There are signs of escalation in the closing phase of the episodes. Chapter 12, finally, shifts gears once again and shows how CEA can be used in a more qualitative way to analyze a series of episodes that have taken place in one country. The case studied in this chapter is Greece, the country that stands out for the extreme contentiousness of the episodes unleashed by austerity packages during the Great Recession. It treats the contentious episodes of this country not as separate units of analysis, as do the rest of the chapters, but as parts of a larger campaign that unfolded during the years Greek politics was dominated by the bailout. This chapter uses the contentious episodes as a guide to build a narrative account of Greek contention during the age of the bailout.

The final chapter 13, concludes. It draws together the various threads of the empirical chapters and presents our own assessment of the novel approach for the study of political contention that we introduce with this volume.

2

# Selecting and Coding Contentious Episodes

## Abel Bojar, Swen Hutter, and Sophia Hunger

INTRODUCTION

As we laid out in the introductory chapter of our volume, we propose a rather ambitious and innovative empirical strategy to study contentious politics – what we label as Contentious Episode Analysis (CEA). Having situated our approach in the intermediate meso-level between the "narrative approach" and the "epidemiological" approach exemplified by conventional protest event analysis (for reviews, see Hutter 2014; Koopmans and Rucht 2002), we aim to accomplish two tasks simultaneously. On the one hand, we wish to preserve the rich ontology and conceptual breadth of the "narrative approach" by distinguishing between a diverse set of actors, actions, and interactions in our empirical design. On the other hand, we aim to leverage the empirical scope and rigor of the "epidemiological approach" of protest event analysis by building a quantitative, cross-national dataset that allows for a variable-based analysis of the unfolding of interactions in contentious episodes. Therefore, in our efforts to preserve the strength (and avoid the weaknesses) of the two extant approaches, the main aim we set forth is to build a dataset that gives an accurate and fine-grained picture of the dynamics of political conflict condensed to a limited set of variables.

As the first step in this empirical strategy, however, we need to delimit the geographical and empirical scope of our universe. As the scholarly literature on social movements and contentious politics has spanned various geographical units, types of actors, and issue areas, we first need to locate our approach in these multiple dimensions. As for geography, our focus is on the domestic level of European Union (EU) member states. In particular, we aimed to select a manageable number of countries with two selection criteria in mind: first, to provide representative geographical coverage of the EU and, second, to ensure sufficient variation in the states' structural and institutional embeddedness in the European economy. Thus, we have chosen four member states from three broad geographical regions: France, Germany, Ireland, and the United Kingdom (a member of the EU during the period of our research) from north-western Europe; Greece, Italy, Spain, and Portugal from southern Europe; Hungary, Latvia, Poland, and Romania from centraleastern Europe. While some of these countries are members of the eurozone, others continue to use their national currencies. Some are creditor states in the international flow of financial capital. In contrast, others are debtors and found themselves in the center of the storm during the Great Recession as a result (for details on the economic and political contexts, see Chapter 3). Some are consolidated democracies with centuries of democratic history, while others are relatively recent democratizers or underwent democratic backsliding (Greskovits, 2015) during the period under scrutiny in this volume.

Regardless of geography and the political context we study, our central nexus is the interaction between two stylized types of political actors: governments and their challengers. To ensure that this nexus is indeed the central thread around which contention revolves, we decided to select policy episodes that are instigated by a government proposal[1] and, thus, likely to trigger reactions by challengers because of their inherently contentious nature (for instance, by confronting vested interests or imposing economic hardship on a broad segment of the population). More specifically and bringing us to the issue dimension, we prioritized economic policy episodes because the Great Recession and the ensuing Euro crisis provided fertile grounds for identifying a large number of proposals for austerity measures and economic reforms (at least four per country). As we know from an increasing body of scholarly work, the recent economic crisis and tide of austerity in Europe has also led to major political repercussions, particularly in the countries hardest hit.[2] However, we also allowed for our argument to travel beyond the economic domain as it is strictly understood. Of the sixty policy episodes we study overall, twelve (one per country) concern changes in the state's institutions, ranging from the organization of its legislative organs to rules governing the judiciary or changes in the media regime. Thus, as highlighted in the introductory chapter, we are interested in the dynamics of political conflict in episodes that have (a) occurred in twelve European countries during the Great Recession (from fall 2008 to the end of 2015) and (b) focused on relevant key policy proposals designed to come to terms with the consequences of the unfolding economic and political crises in most of these countries.

---

[1] That said, our general empirical strategy is applicable to episodes of contention initiated by challengers themselves or to ones beyond particular policy initiatives (such as against corruption or anti-democratic practices by state authorities).

[2] We refer the reader to our own previous volumes on electoral and protest politics in the Great Recession (Hutter and Kriesi 2019; Kriesi et al. 2020).

While a detailed description of the content of the episodes follows in Chapter 3, our goal in the current chapter is to outline how we get from these broad empirical ambitions to a functioning dataset that is readily amenable for empirical analysis. In the first part of this chapter, we introduce our selection strategy by answering the following questions: Based on what criteria did we identify the particular episodes in each country? How did we establish the time frame of the episodes and the main actors involved in the debate? What sources did we use to gather all relevant information for constructing the required variables for empirical analysis? How did we restrict a broad text corpus to a narrower one that is amenable for hand coding? In the second part of the chapter, we discuss the coding process itself. Given the fine-grained information that we need to filter out from a large text corpus, we relied on native-language coders, and we presented them with a set of detailed instructions to follow. The second part is thus dedicated to these instructions, followed by an overview of the variables we managed to assemble in the process.

Overall, we aimed for methodological innovation when developing CEA, meaning that we could not fall back on well-established routines but had to face trade-offs between setting out systematic rules at the start of the data gathering process and flexible adaptation throughout the process. As illustrated by the exchange with our critiques in the CEA symposium in the journal *Mobilization*, we are aware of the room for improvement in our data collection strategy and hope others will take up our approach and develop it further.

THE SELECTION PROCESS

## Selecting 'Policy Proposals at Risk' from the International Press

The selection procedure for the episodes studied in this volume follows McAdam and Boudet's (2012) advice that social movement research can only overcome its movement centrism by exploring a wider range of actions and actors (the key claim of the Dynamics of Contention program, see McAdam et al. 2001) and by no longer selecting on the dependent variable. In turn, McAdam and Boudet (2012) examine in their work "communities at risk," that is, communities confronted with controversial decisions about large-scale infra-structural projects. We translated this idea to study the dynamics of political conflict in the Great Recession by focusing on what we call "policy proposals at risk." As in McAdam and Boudet's work, we consider cases where resistance to political reforms is likely to emerge – but whether and to what extent remain open empirical questions.

More precisely, we only consider key policy proposals at a relatively high risk of being contested in the public sphere. To select these proposals systemat-ically and avoid selecting on the dependent variable (i.e., only taking proposals that led to the emergence of a strong challenger coalition in the streets), we have resorted to the international press as a radar for relevant events in the countries under scrutiny. A proposal appearing in the international media may be the result of its high public visibility and international relevance, which, in turn, may or may not be the result of the expansion of the conflict by some challenger in the national public sphere. To put it differently, key proposals are the most likely targets for overt mobilization, but such mobilization may not necessarily occur.[3] In operational terms, we define key proposals as proposals by national governments reported (more than once) in three international media sources: The *New York Times,* the *Financial Times*, and *Neue Zürcher Zeitung* (NZZ). All three sources have a fairly large high-quality network of international correspondents. The *New York Times* is one of the most prestigious international newspapers; the *Financial Times* is the leading European quality newspaper specializing in economic affairs; the Swiss NZZ is another important European quality newspaper published in German. Essentially, selecting episodes from the international press helped us identify a relatively limited number of episodes per country while minimizing the risk of selecting on the dependent variable. After an initial test run, we realized that the three sources tended to underreport the centraleastern European countries in our sample. Therefore, we decided to supplement the sample with additional English-language outlets specializing in covering the region for a broader international readership (these were the *Baltic Times* and *Warsaw Voice*).

Country experts from our ERC project *Political Conflict in Europe in the Shadow of the Great Recession* ((POLCON) Dataset) read all reports published in these newspapers from 2008 to 2015 that mentioned the respective country. They systematically coded events relating to social-economic and institutional policy decisions. The resulting database contains almost 4,200 such mentions of events (ranging from 104 for Romania up to 778 for the United Kingdom).[4] Around 45 percent were coded from the *Financial Times*, followed by the NZZ (29 percent) and the *New York Times* (21 percent). The two additional sources contributed 4.2 (*Warsaw Voice*) and 1.5 percent (*Baltic Times*), respectively.

Based on this event database, we selected the episodes for each country by first looking for (series of) months in which the international press reported on crisis-related economic and institutional policy measures in each country.

---

[3] In fact, since the international press is likely to report on the announcement of key policy packages right after or very close to the announcement date, whether mobilizations against the proposal materialized were typically unknown at the time of reporting.

[4] In the course of this exercise, we coded a larger set of events reported in the international press – from scandals, protests, election-related events, and government reshufflings to country-specific events (e.g., specific incidences such as the Smolensk disaster in the case of Poland) (N = 7,391). From the broader set of events, we can see that Romania is not less covered (N = 348), but the share of economic or institutional policy events is much smaller in comparison to the other countries in the sample. For empirical studies of how these different events shaped the electoral prospects of government and opposition parties, see Bojar et al. (2019) and Malet and Kriesi (2019).

Then we checked the specific proposals mentioned in these "windows of observation" and compiled a preliminary list of cases, usually covering five to ten cases.[5] From these lists, we selected four economic and one institutional proposal for each country, based on their attention in the international press and country-specific knowledge about potential overlaps and relations between the various proposals. The final set of episodes that we selected are listed in Table 2.1 by their names and the short labels assigned to them. In subsequent chapters of this book, we generally refer to the episodes by their full name, while in the descriptive tables, we indicate them via their short labels. Moreover, we offer a very detailed discussion of each proposal's content and timing as well its economic and political context in Appendix I. This information should be particularly helpful for readers not as familiar with the dynamics of European politics at the time.

## Selecting Relevant Articles from the National Press

While international media might be good radar for getting only important policy proposals, they are, of course, rather limited for tracing how the dynamics of conflict evolve over time. Therefore, we opted for national media as the primary source to collect that kind of information. This choice follows a long-standing tradition in protest event analysis (PEA) and its further developments, such as political claims or core sentence analysis (see Earl et al. 2004; Hutter 2014). In addition, we complemented the quantitative information provided by the systematic coding of national newspapers with available secondary material, such as online timelines, government reports, and the scholarly literature.

We have chosen newspapers as sources because we are most interested in the publicly visible interactions among the three stylized actors. This follows our general approach to regard media as a master arena to observe conflicts in present-day "audience democracies" (Manin 1997). However, as with PEA, the approach we propose here can be used to study different types of material that systematically document the actions of various actors involved in a policy-related conflict (such as governmental or parliamentary protocols or documentation produced by the challengers themselves). For the present study, we opted to only rely on one leading center-left national newspaper per country to

---

[5] For example, in the Italian case, we identify five windows of observation. The first one (June 2008 to December 2010) refers to Silvio Berlusconi's labor market reform, the second one (May 2011 to October) to his austerity package. The third and the fourth windows are contiguous with the second window, but they refer to different packages, since in November 2011 Mario Monti took over the position of prime minister. From our knowledge of Italian politics, we know that Monti introduced a new austerity package in November 2011, and that in March 2012, he added a labor reform to this package. Finally, the fifth window of observation refers to Matteo Renzi's labor market reform (September 2014 to December). In this last case, there are few mentions of the policy reform in the international press, but they form a contiguous sequence over three months.

TABLE 2.1. *List of policy episodes per country (episode names, short labels, and episode types in parentheses*)*

| Country | Eco1 | Eco2 | Eco3 | Eco4 | Inst |
|---|---|---|---|---|---|
| France | Sarkozy–Fillon austerity package France (s)* | Sarkozy's austerity package (b) | Hollande first austerity package (b) | Hollande–Valls budget cuts package France (b) | Decentralization |
| Germany | German bank-bailout (bo) | Bad banks (bo) | First Greek bailout (b) | Third Greek bailout (bo) | Constitutional debt brake |
| Greece | First bailout (imf) | Midterm adjustment (b) | Second bailout (imf) | Third bailout (imf) | TV shutdown |
| Hungary | I.M.F. bailout (imf) | 2010 austerity package (b) | Pension nationaliza-tion (s) | Internet tax (b) | Media law |
| Ireland | Bank guarantee (b) | 2009 austerity package (b) | I.M.F. bailout (imf) | Water tax (b) | Senate referendum |
| Italy | Berlusconi's job reform (s) | Berlusconi's austerity package (b) | Monti package (s) | Jobs act (s) | Judicial reform |
| Latvia | I.M.F. bailout (imf) | First 2009 austerity package (b) | Second 2009 austerity package (b) | 2010 austerity package (b) | Eurozone entry |
| Poland | 2009 crisis package (s) | Pension reform (s) | Tusk austerity package (b) | Labor code reform (s) | Constitutional court crisis |
| Portugal | PEC 1&2 (b) | PEC 3&4 (b) | I.M.F. bailout (imfl) | 2012 austerity package (b) | Municipal reform |
| Romania | I.M.F. bailout (imf) | First 2010 austerity package (b) | Second 2010 austerity package (b) | New labor regulations (s) | Impeachment |
| Spain | Zapatero first austerity package (b) | Zapatero second austerity package (s) | Rajoy austerity package (b) | Bankia (bo) | Constitutional amendment |
| U.K. | Bank bailouts (bo) | 2010 austerity package (b) | Tuition fees (b) | 2011 austerity package, welfare reform (b) | Brexit referendum |

* We also classified the economic policy proposals into four subcategories (indicated with the letters in parentheses): s = structural reforms, b = budgetary cuts, imf = I.M.F. interventions, bo = bailouts. Bailouts include recapitalizations and other forms of financial aid to domestic financial institutions as well as sovereign bailouts provided to other countries in the case of Germany (The first and the third Greek bailouts).

TABLE 2.2. *List of newspapers per country*

| Country | Newspaper |
|---------|-----------|
| France | *Le Monde* |
| Germany | *Süddeutsche Zeitung* |
| Greece | *Ta Nea* |
| Hungary | *Nepszabadsag* |
| Ireland | *The Irish Times* |
| Italy | *La Repubblica* |
| Latvia | *Latvijas Avize* |
| Poland | *Gazeta Wyborcza* |
| Portugal | *Publico* |
| Romania | *Ager Press* |
| Spain | *El Pais* |
| U.K. | *The Guardian* |

document the actions by the various actors. The underlying rationale for the selection has been that, on the margin, center-left media are more likely to focus on austerity-related challengers than their center-right competitors. The selected newspapers are shown in Table 2.2.

While we kept the source constant for all episodes in a country and aimed to select similar newspapers to allow for cross-national comparisons, the choice of only one newspaper per country was mainly due to pragmatic considerations. Thus, we must admit that our study falls short on a theoretically informed multi-source design. Here, we would like to note that PEA's advances in the last decades show potential avenues for further improvement of our novel approach in this respect. As Tilly (2002: 249) has emphasized in his essay on "event catalogues as theories," further elaborations of our CEA need to focus on both "a theory embodying explanation of the phenomenon under investigation, and another theory embodying explanation of the evidence concerning that phenomenon." In this book, we are careful in highlighting that what we establish as reoccurring features is based on a selective sample of media-represented actions and interactions only. However, as said before, we are not as concerned that we might not cover all types of events happening out there but rather that the newspapers we study might be biased compared to other media sources.

In practical terms, the selection of relevant articles[6] – that is, articles published in the selected newspaper that referred to the policy proposals and/or

---

[6] We focus on the "news" pages of the newspapers. We do not cover press commentaries and letters to the editors. However, we do include interviews. Furthermore, we only cover sections on national/international politics and economics. If possible, we excluded sections on local politics (if in a specific section), sports, and culture from our sample.

their potential elements in the case of policy packages – was made by a team of native-language-speaking coders[7] (a total of fifteen), who worked under the close supervision of the authors of this book. We organized weekly meetings to supervise their progress and resolve difficult selection and coding decisions that inevitably arise in such a detailed coding process. Special care was taken to apply these decisions for all episodes in a harmonized manner to make the final dataset as comparable across countries and episodes as possible.

The selection of articles was organized into two major steps. In the first step of the selection process, our coders were asked to establish the time frame of the data collection and a keyword list to search for relevant articles in the news-papers' electronic archives. For seven of the twelve countries, the newspapers were available in the international news archive Factiva so coders could use its search functionalities to enter a relatively simple Boolean combination of episode-related keywords to locate and download the relevant articles. However, for five countries – Greece, Hungary, Latvia, Poland, and Romania – the selected news sources were not listed in Factiva, so we had to download the articles directly from the newspapers' electronic archives. If the newspaper had no such archives, we looked for national databases that had access to the newspaper's archived articles. For instance, in the case of Hungary, we sub-scribed to the electronic database of EMIS (European Mathematical Information Service) to access needed articles from *Nepszabadsag*.

All in all, an episode timeline, as well as the final combination of search keywords, was established by an initial reading of selected articles from the news-papers as well as of other material that reported on the case (from Wikipedia, online reports, newspaper timelines, secondary scientific literature, etc.).

Regarding the time frame, the database from the international newspapers already provided some initial indications. Still, these were further refined in this step of the selection procedure and, if needed, at later stages. Note again that our episodes may end in one of two ways. They may end with the formal adoption of the (possibly modified) proposal by the government[8] or, if the challenger continues to mobilize after the formal adoption of the proposal, they may end when the continuous stream of interactions between the government and its challenger related to the proposal breaks off (see Chapter 1). As an operational rule of thumb, we used a period of two months for assessing whether the interactions related to the proposal had indeed come to a halt before we declared the episode to have ended.

---

[7] Note that our coders were PhD students from the European University Institute and, given their background, had a lot of country expertise. Moreover, they were trained in several sessions and constantly supervised by the authors of this book.

[8] The only exception to this was the Internet Tax proposal in Hungary that ended with an outright withdrawal by the government. After the withdrawal, since no further mobilization took place, establishing the end of that episode proved unproblematic.

Based on the reading of this material, we established a set of keywords in a Boolean combination. In cases where the policy proposal was consistently referred to under a certain label (e.g., the 2014 Jobs Act in Italy or the more prolonged Water Tax debate in Ireland), this task was relatively trivial. Given the importance of our selected policy proposals at risk (which served as selection criteria), most of the proposals were referred to in a rather systematic way in the press (e.g., the austerity budgets in Ireland or Portugal). In cases lacking such a concrete label or when the public debate only focused on specific aspects of broader packages, the content of the policy measures proposed by the governments served as a reference point for the selection of keywords (for instance, "austerity OR (pension AND reform)." We opted for rather broad keywords in such cases and for manually deselecting the many "false positive" hits. Thus, we invested a lot of effort into coming up with a comprehensive keyword-based selection strategy.

In the second step of the selection process, the coders downloaded all articles found using the keyword search. These articles were used to establish a timeline of media attention for each policy proposal. This timeline showed the weekly counts of articles over the selected period. The coders then wrote a short report of about two pages per episode and interpreted the ups and downs in the timeline. They were asked to read articles published during peaks in media attention and further consult the material collected in Step 1. Overall, they delivered a short report answering the following questions:

- What is the policy proposal's content?
- Which of its features became a matter of public controversy?
- How long did the controversy last?
- When were the critical moments of debate?
- What specific events were responsible for the peaks in the timeline (e.g., the proposal's initiation, parliamentary votes, major demonstrations, election campaigns)?

While the articles selected by the keyword search were the potential universe to be coded, some only referred to the policy proposals as contextual information or they did not report on actions that we were interested in (Examples read like "Amongst others, the election campaign focuses on the water tax." Or "Yesterday, the British Prime Minister attended the opening-night of the British fashion week. The visit took place in a period of growing resistance against his austerity bill."). To be more efficient in deselecting such false positive articles, we relied on the search functionalities of the news archives. We selected all articles that in the headline and the context of the keywords in the main text referred to the policy proposal and actions we were interested in. In the final step, coders were instructed to download all these potentially relevant articles once more as a single text corpus and use it for the subsequent coding process. This left the coders still with a range of 100–2,000 articles to fully read and code (847 on average across all 60 episodes).

## THE CODING PROCESS

As noted in the previous section, the basic building block of each contentious episode is identifying all actors that publicly interfered in the controversy related to the policy proposals under scrutiny. Since our theoretical framework is based upon the government–challenger–third party trichotomy, each episode coder was required to assign all of these actors to one and only one of the three categories. The main criteria for actor-type identification were laid out as follows:

- Government actors: all actors who are either part of the government narrowly understood – that is, cabinet members – or are affiliated with it through the party organizations of the ruling coalition or the institutions of the state and display a minimum level of unity with the government and broad agreement with the policy proposal.
- Challenger actors: all actors who display open opposition to the policy proposal at least once throughout the episode through contentious performances and protests and other public claims making that goes beyond routine verbal remarks.
- Third-party actors: all actors who do not openly challenge the policy proposal as per the definition provided above, nor do they form a part of the government either due to the absence of institutional links (e.g., a supranational actor) or because of their explicit opposition or at least skepticism vis-à-vis the policy proposal (e.g. dissenters within the ruling coalition).

One important caveat of our approach, but a necessary simplification for the coding process, was that the actor identity (as coded) does not change throughout the episode. For instance, if an opposition party is a mere bystander in the early phases of contention but later becomes a protagonist in the non-routine forms of mobilization, coders were instructed to code them throughout as challengers. To make the right decision, country coders were instructed first to give a preliminary reading of all actors' actions throughout the episode to decide to which stylized category they belong. Sometimes, however, coders had to recategorize actors during the coding process itself as their changing roles throughout the episode became clearer. In such instances, coders had to redo the coding in light of the new actor categories (this was necessary given that we coded more detailed information for the challenger and government actions as compared to the third-party ones).

To provide an example of the sort of decisions we had to take alongside the coders concerning actor categories, consider the I.M.F. bailout episode in Hungary in the fall of 2008. After the fallout with its liberal coalition partner SZDSZ a few months earlier, the ruling post-socialist MSZP party had to take full responsibility for resorting to institutional creditors' help and the resulting budgetary measures. Liberated from the yoke of government, SZDSZ now had a free hand to criticize the measures alongside the main opposition party at the time, FIDESZ. However, while FIDESZ occasionally engaged in nonroutine forms of opposition, such as boycotting the announcement of the measures in parliament as a personal affront to the prime minister, SZDSZ stayed at the conventional verbal forms of opposition (and occasional support). Hence, in this episode, SZDSZ was coded as a third party, while FIDESZ was coded as a challenger.

Importantly, each actor type can take on a variety of institutional forms. Therefore, coders were also instructed to place them in narrower institutional categories, noting the specific names of the organizations in the coding file. Overall, we categorized all the different actors into twenty such institutional forms, ranging from international actors through government institutions to parliamentary opposition and social movement organizations. Table 2.3 summarizes these institutional categories, some of which directly map onto our stylized actor types (e.g., by default, unions and social movement organizations almost always act as challengers). In contrast, others fall into more than one category. For instance, as the Hungarian example above shows, opposition parties can act both as challengers and third parties depending on their particular role in a specific episode (for a detailed analysis, see Chapter 6).

Having established who is undertaking the actions, the next task for coders was identifying various characteristics of the actions themselves. The first and most trivial aspect of the action was its timing, by calendar day. Most of the

TABLE 2.3. *Institutional actor categorization*

---

  1. EU actors (e.g., EU Comissioners, M.E.P.s etc.)
  2. Troika (European Commission, E.C.B., I.M.F.)
  3. Foreign governments
  4. Other international actors (e.g. foreign press, foreign opposition parties, foreign labor unions, etc.)
  5. National government
  6. National technocratic government
  7. President
  8. Local/regional authorities
  9. National central banks
 10. Other government institutions (e.g. Constitutional Court, councils, committees etc.)
 11. Government parties
 12. Business actors
 13. Experts, media (e.g., universities, think tanks)
 14. Mainstream opposition parties
 15. Radical-left opposition parties
 16. Radical-right opposition parties
 17. Nongovernmental organizations (N.G.O.s)
 18. Social movement organizations (S.M.O.s)
 19. Students
 20. Unions

---

time, newspaper articles provided direct reference to the day in question in relation to the publication day by such indicators as "yesterday" or "last Friday." In a minority of cases (around 2.5 percent of all actions), however, the references were vaguer and merely indicated a broader time frame, such as "last four days," "last week," or "January." In such cases, we coded the middle of that period as the action date.

Once the action's timing was defined, the next variable of interest was the form of the action. As indicated in Chapter 1, we differentiated two separate dimensions of each activity: the substantive aspect (the way actors relate to the policy proposal) and the procedural one (the form of action actors chose to express their position). In substantive terms, we can distinguish a range of actions from rejection to acceptance of a given demand/proposal. In procedural terms, the relationship between two actors can range from conflictive to cooperative. Along similar lines, Tilly and Tarrow (2015: 110f.) distinguish between three types of claims – identity, standing, and program claims. Actions related to the proposal's substantive aspects correspond to program claims that call the other side to act in a certain way (in our case, to withdraw or modify the policy proposal). In contrast, actions related to procedural aspects correspond to identity claims (related to the constitution of the actor) and standing claims (about recognition of the other).

For each day during the episode, we recorded the actions (in substantive and procedural terms) of each (component) actor of the three types of actor with respect to the (components of the) target actors. As a general coding rule, coders were instructed to code both aspects of the action. We distinguished between these codes for the respective actor types as summarized in Table 2.4.

To provide a few examples for the two aspects of action forms – substantive and procedural – take the negotiation between the Latvian government and the I.M.F. delegation regarding the second austerity package that the government had to implement in 2009. At one of the meetings (October 31, 2009), the government refused to comply with the creditors' request to replace the reduction of a nontaxable minimum threshold with a progressive tax schedule. The substantive code in this case, would be 1 – "government sticking to original plans." On the procedural front, however, it is the negotiation between the creditors and the government that we highlighted and, therefore, we assigned it a code of 6 – "government negotiates." Fast-forward a year to another epicenter of the austerity saga, and consider the example of the Portuguese Communist Party in the context of the first austerity episode in Portugal. The P.C.P. is coded as challenger because of its proactive role in the mass protests against the government's austerity package in summer 2010. On July 29, it called on the government to rescind the recent welfare cuts, and also announced several protest actions on the day throughout the country. In this case, the substantive challenger code is 1 – "challenger demanding withdrawal of proposal" and the procedural code is 4 – "challenger mobilizes."

TABLE 2.4. *Action forms and their codes*

|  | Government | Challenger | Third parties |
|---|---|---|---|
| Substantive | 1. Sticks to proposal<br>2. Adopts proposal<br>3. Raises doubts regarding proposal<br>4. Grants concessions on proposal to challengers<br>5. Withdraws proposal | 1. Demands withdrawal<br>2. Demands modification<br>3. Scale shift<br>4. Ready to accept proposal<br>5. Accepts modified proposal<br>6. Accepts original proposal | 1. Supports proposal<br>2. Opposes challenger's demands<br>3. Mediates<br>4. Opposes proposal<br>5. Supports challengers demands |
| Procedural | 1. Represses challenger<br>2. Deprecates challenger<br>3. Fails to recognize challenger<br>4. Circumvents legal barriers<br>5. Signals readiness to negotiate<br>6. Negotiates | 1. Constitutes itself<br>2. Threaten to mobilize<br>3. Announces mobilization<br>4. Mobilizes<br>5. Deprecates government<br>6. Stops mobilization<br>7. Signals readiness to negotiate<br>8. Negotiates<br>9. Demobilizes<br>10. Gives up | 1. Supports government action<br>2. Opposes challengers' actions<br>3. Mediates<br>4. Opposes government's actions<br>5. Supports challengers' actions |

Of course, at the heart of contentious politics are the procedural action codes of challengers – namely codes 2, 3, and 4 – the ones referring to mobilization. The voluminous literature on action repertoires (e.g., Tilly, 2006) has long dealt with the innovative tactics and their impact on how the events unfold after various forms of action by challenger organizations. As a third aspect of action forms, we instructed coders to differentiate between the various forms of protest mobilization that challengers announce or undertake. Importantly, we cover here not only actual mobilization but also threats and calls for action. Table 2.5 shows how we distinguish forms of mobilization. In the case of the Portuguese example considered earlier, for instance, the mobilization code of the Portuguese Communist Party is 4 – "demonstrative form."

Similarly to deciding on actor types, coding the right action form involved important decisions. On the government side, for instance, drawing the line

TABLE 2.5. *Forms of mobilization and their codes*

1. Direct democratic forms
2. Strikes and other forms of industrial action
3. Signature campaigns/petitions
4. Demonstrative forms
5. Confrontational forms
6. Violent forms
7. Other forms

between "government raising doubts" and government actually offering concessions was not always straightforward. Often it depended on the wording of the government's statement. As an example: In the second bailout episode in Greece, the government at that time was forced to make some partial concessions to taxi drivers and hospital staff, who were among the professions affected by the cuts. Among these concessions, however, many government officials indicated that they were *considering* rather than actually enacting these concessions. Such statements of consideration were therefore coded as "raising doubt" rather than as actual concessions. Likewise, on the challengers' side, what is considered as a "scale shift" depends on the particular episode. For example, the Indignados movement shifting its focus from Zapatero's austerity measures and pension reform to a more general and more scathing assault on the establishment as such ("La Casta") can be considered as a typical example of scale shift. Somewhat less straightforwardly, in the Tuition Fees' episode in the U.K., when representatives of three trade unions announced that they were joining the students and expected more people to participate in the protests against the government, we took this announcement as an indication of the unions' willingness to launch a more general challenge to the government beyond the particular policy proposal at hand, and hence coded it as a scale shift as well.

In view of the vast universe of actors in a highly diverse set of countries and episode types, as well as the theoretically unlimited variety of different action forms, our stylized ontology of contentious politics necessitates such case-by-case decisions for borderline cases. To ensure the maximum degree of comparability between coders and episodes, however, whenever such problematic cases arose, all coders were informed about the decisions we took and, if necessary, were required to update their codes.

Next, we also coded the *issue area* to which the various actions referred. In the case of episodes concentrated around a single thread, the coded issue was generally the episode label itself, such as in the Brexit referendum in the U.K. Other episodes, however, consisted of various elements, typically combining budget cuts with structural reforms. A case in point is the Sarkozy–Fillon

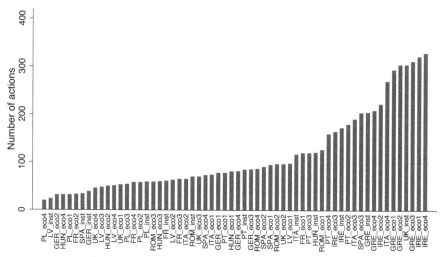

FIGURE 2.1. Total action count per episode

episode (see Table 2.1), consisting of a pension reform and a freeze in public spending. Another example is the austerity program introduced by the Rajoy government in Spain in late 2011 that consisted of budget cuts and a labor reform. The issue codes assigned by the coders thus proved essential in determining the central thread of the episode, helping us to place each episode into more detailed categories than the economic versus institutional distinction with which we had started out (for details on the classification, see Chapter 3).

All in all, the coders identified a total of 6,889 actions across the sixty episodes. However, the distribution of the total number of actions is heavily skewed with a few episodes – such as two of the Irish austerity episodes and three of the Greek episodes and the Brexit episode in the U.K. – containing significantly more action counts than the rest. We show the action count distribution in Figure 2.1.

Having specified who (actor) did what (action) when (timing) about which aspect of the policy proposal (issue), the final task for coders was to reconstruct the chain of interactions between all actions in an episode. This proved the most challenging aspect of the coding because unlike the substantive and procedural aspects of the actions – which news articles tend to report on at great length and depth – coverage tends to be less thorough on the causal antecedents, or the prior actions to which the contending parties are responding. Nevertheless, given our ambition to undertake a dynamic analysis in this volume (see the chapters in Part III of the book), we emphasized uncovering the chain of events that led up to any particular action. Therefore, once all relevant actions had been identified, and the coders had coded their forms, their task was to uncover the particular action that triggered the action at hand. In around one-third of the cases, the articles provided the necessary information. For instance, in a straightforward (but relatively rare) instance of police repression, the articles naturally report on both the repression and the mobilization that triggered the repression itself. In such cases, coders had no difficulties identifying which of the preceding actions served as a trigger and used the action ID assigned to the triggering action as the *trigger variable* of the current action. In the rest of the cases, however, the coders were required to revert back to the articles that reported on the preceding actions in reverse chronological order. This somewhat labor-intensive procedure, combined with the contextual understanding of the episode they had acquired at this point, allowed them to pinpoint the actions that served as the trigger for the original actions under analysis.

We can illustrate the importance of this recursive coding method via the first austerity episode in France, consisting of budget cuts and a pension reform raising the retirement age (the very first entry in Table 2.1 and see details in Chapter 3). Figure 2.2 illustrates the relationship between the actions via arrows that connect the chronologically preceding triggers with the actions they triggered. Black boxes stand for government actions, gray boxes stand for challenger actions, and white boxes stand for third-party actions. The chronology of the events starts from the top (G1), when the government announces the proposal in February 2010 and ends with an unsuccessful demonstration by unions in November 2010 after the adoption of the reforms. The chain of events indicates that identifying the triggers is not always straightforward, based on pure chronology alone. A recursive reading of previous events is necessary, short of explicit references in the articles. For instance, this last mobilization was indeed in response to the previous government action (G34, corresponding to the final adoption of the proposal). However, other activities, such as C33 by Force Ouvrière and other French unions, are responses to government actions that are not the ones immediately preceding in the chronological order (in the case of C33, it is a response to the draft legislation on pension reform, presented in July – G12). Thus, in our coding procedure, it proved essential for the coders to check back for all potential candidates as possible triggers and select the one with the highest substantive correspondence with the particular action under study.

We shall illustrate the importance of identifying the triggers and reconstructing the action sequences in more detail in subsequent parts of the book. Chapter 6 analyzes the characteristics of entire action sequences connected via the triggers: for instance, one running between G1 to C58 according to the action tree in Figure 2.2. Most importantly, we will use the trigger to construct lagged action variables, which form the backbone of the dynamic analysis we propose in Part III.

To sum up the coding process, we illustrate what the complete set of codes looks like using the examples of the Latvian and the Portuguese actions referred to in Table 2.6.

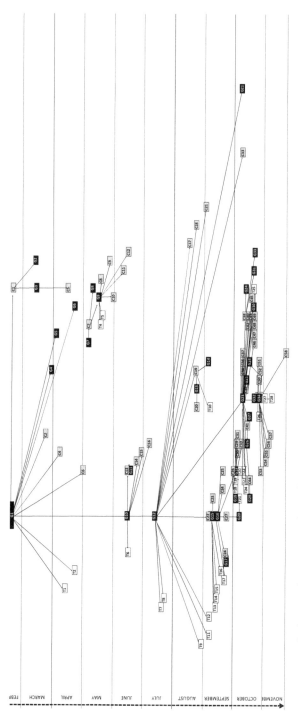

FIGURE 2.2. Actions and triggers in the Sarkozy–Fillon austerity episode.

TABLE 2.6. *Illustration of the complete code set*

| Episode | Action id | Actor type (3-way stylized) | Actor type (institutional) | Date | Substantive | Procedural | Mobilization | Trigger id | Issue |
|---|---|---|---|---|---|---|---|---|---|
| LV_eco3 | 9 | government | national govt | 31oct2009 | sticks | negotiates | – | 8 | 2010 budget |
| PT_eco1 | 538 | challenger | radical left opposition | 29jul2010 | Demands withdrawal | mobilizes | demonstrative | 15 | PEC II package |

CONCLUSION

In this chapter, we have introduced the main methodological building blocks of CEA. We hope CEA will be useful for scholars in the contentious politics tradition who aim for a systematic coding and analytical toolkit to examine and compare the course of contentious episodes.

In general, CEA shares many features with political claims-analysis (Koopmans and Statham 1999). Adding another extension of the original protest event analysis, claims-analysis considers action forms other than protest actions, an essential step in the direction of the method we propose. However, claims-analysis does not include the dynamic and interactive component that is characteristic of CEA and, consequently, its application has fallen short of adequately embedding protest and challenger activities in the stream of public claims making.

Similarly, CEA shares features with event structure analysis, which also aims to infuse narratives with "greater rigor and explicitness" (Griffin 1993: 1094). Generally, the goal of CEA is to specify the concepts of the DOC program in such a way that they can be applied to systematic *comparative* analyses across episodes. In this respect, our approach differs from the one chosen by Griffin (1993), who relied on event structure analysis (originally proposed by Heise 1989) as a procedure that allows reconstructing the causal structure of the narrative about an *individual* episode – in his case, a lynching episode that took place in Mississippi in 1930.[9]

While we did not cover all our methodological choices in this chapter – we shall discuss the statistical techniques we use for the dynamic analysis of action sequences in Part III – we have offered a detailed overview of the episode selection, article selection, and coding process that underpins CEA. As a brief recap, selecting the article corpus for hand coding involved two distinct steps. First, we identified the main "policy proposals at risk" based on reporting in the international press, followed by a careful time frame and keyword selection for each episode. In the second step, we downloaded all articles found with these keyword searches in the selected national news sources.

Once the episode-specific text corpus was established and downloaded, we instructed our trained coders and country experts to code the following characteristics of each action: the day of occurrence, the stylized type of actor undertaking it (according to the government–challenger–third-party trichotomy), the actor's institutional character, the substantive and procedural form of the action, the type of mobilization by challengers (if and when they occur), the narrower issue area of the action, and, finally, the trigger for the action. While we believe that relying on these codes allows us to capture the essence of contentious episodes, it is important to note that some forms of actions will

---

[9] For other insightful but single case applications, see also Bloom 2015; Ermakoff 2015; Isaac et al. 1994.

inevitably pass under the radar of our scrutiny. For instance, some actions (e.g., closed-door meetings without media access) are by construction beyond the reach of our research design. Other related stories may have been overlooked because our keyword choices might have failed to pick up every news article with tangential relevance for our purposes.

With these limitations in mind, the rest of the book builds on these codes and offers empirical analyses of the sixty contentious episodes from various angles. Part II takes episodes as units of analysis and describes them in terms of their contentiousness, actor configurations, the pace and complexity of the involved action sequences, and the governments' responsiveness to the challengers. As we shall show in the corresponding chapters, our detailed coding scheme offers a unique opportunity to operationalize systematically the concepts we introduce in this part. For instance, to understand the level of conflict – or in our terminology, the contentiousness of an episode – a detailed list of actor-specific action repertoires is necessary. Likewise, to provide a systematic mapping of coalition dynamics across the various episodes, the actor codes we outlined in Table 2.3 will prove essential.

Part III takes the process a step further by introducing a novel method to study the dynamics between the contending actors. This method is rendered feasible by our careful identification and coding of trigger events. With the help of these triggers, as we explain in detail in Chapters 6 and 8, we can provide a systematic test of many prominent themes in the contentious politics literature. Does government repression reduce or escalate conflict? Are overtures toward an adversary reciprocated by the latter? Does third-party involvement help to bring contenders to the negotiating table? To answer these questions based on many cases, one requires sequential data where individual actions are arranged in a causal chain. Relying on this sequential data, Part III aims to uncover the determinants of the action forms as a function of past actions, actor characteristics, and the contextual characteristics of episodes. Before we proceed to the empirical analysis, however, we shall discuss these contextual characteristics in the next chapter.

# 3

# The Economic and Political Contexts of the Episodes

Hanspeter Kriesi and Sophia Hunger

In this chapter, we put the sixty episodes into their economic and political contexts. As suggested in Chapter 1, we assume that the contentiousness of the episodes, the endogenous interaction dynamics that developed in the course of the episodes as well as their outcomes are crucially shaped by the economic and political contexts into which they are embedded. We shall introduce above all two aspects of the political opportunity structure of the challengers in a given episode – the economic problem pressure and the political problem pressure that the government were facing at the outset of the episode. We shall first take a closer look at the development of the economic crisis in the twelve countries and its relation to the severity of the episodes. The depth of the economic crisis has had an impact on the severity of the proposed policy measures. Next, we turn to the political context. In this respect, all of our countries are European democracies, but some of these democracies are of a higher quality than others – in terms of participatory structures and state capacity. The higher the democratic quality, the greater the capacity of the government to deal with economic pressure, and the greater the chance that challengers will get a fair hearing. We shall present some indicators for the quality of the democracy in the various countries under study. Our focus will, however, be on episode-specific aspects of the political context that are likely to have directly shaped the development of the episodes. First among these is the type of government – center-left, center-right, or technocratic – that proposed the policy measures, as well as the timing of the proposals with regard to the government's tenure. We know from Roberts (2013, 2017) that left-wing governments are much more vulnerable than right-wing governments when they are forced to adopt austerity measures. We shall identify the types of government that were responsible for the various episodes, and analyze their electoral vulnerability. Finally, we shall analyze the timing of the episodes with respect to the political context. We shall show that the timing depends on the combination of political pressure from international actors and strategic considerations of the government.

As we have pointed out in the previous chapter, forty-eight of the episodes deal with economic policy measures, while twelve episodes, one per country, refer to institutional reforms. The economic policy measures include above all fiscal austerity measures (twenty-four) but also structural reforms (eleven), and emergency measures – international bailouts (eight) and bank bailouts (five). Immediate emergency measures prevailed during the financial crisis that initiated the Great Recession, while the bulk of the austerity and structural reform measures followed during the first part of the eurozone crisis. In their first reactions to the financial crisis, governments focused on the stability of their national banking systems, and on the consequences for the real economy. They adopted bank rescue packages and they countered the economic impact of the crisis by passing modest fiscal expansionary measures (which are not part of our study), relying on some version of "liberal" or "emergency Keynesianism" (Armingeon 2012; Hall 2013; Pontusson and Raess 2012; Weber and Schmitz 2011). However, as the financial crisis turned into the eurozone crisis under the impact of the emerging Greek crisis in early 2010, governments changed their policies and generally turned to austerity measures. From then on, austerity policies, including deep cuts in government expenditures, tax increases and structural adjustment programs (above all labor market reforms, deregulations of some selected sectors, and pension reforms) became the only game in town. TINA – "there is no other alternative" – became the catchphrase of economic policy.

Figure 3.1 gives an idea of how the episodes in the different countries were distributed over time. While the institutional reforms are spread out over the whole period covered, most of the economic episodes are clustered during the financial crisis (Fall 2008–2009) and the early phases of the eurozone crisis (2010–2011). Thus, roughly one quarter of the packages were introduced in the financial crisis, and about one half in the early phases of the eurozone crisis, which roughly lasted from the beginning of 2010, when the problems of the Greek budgetary deficit became known, to the end of 2011, when the eurozone leaders adopted the Treaty for Stability, Coordination and Governance to reinforce the Stability and Growth Pact (SGP) in December 2011. Only about one fifth of the economic episodes were initiated after 2011. In northwestern Europe, three of the four countries – Germany, the U.K., and Ireland – had to bailout their banks early in the financial crisis, and the bulk of the austerity measures followed rather quickly in the first part of the eurozone crisis. Only in France are austerity measures more stretched out over time. Similarly, the economic policy measures in eastern Europe cluster in the financial crisis and the early part of the eurozone crisis. Latvia is the country where the crisis started particularly early, with three of the four economic episodes clustering in the financial crisis. In contrast, southern European countries reacted to the economic crisis mostly during the eurozone crisis.

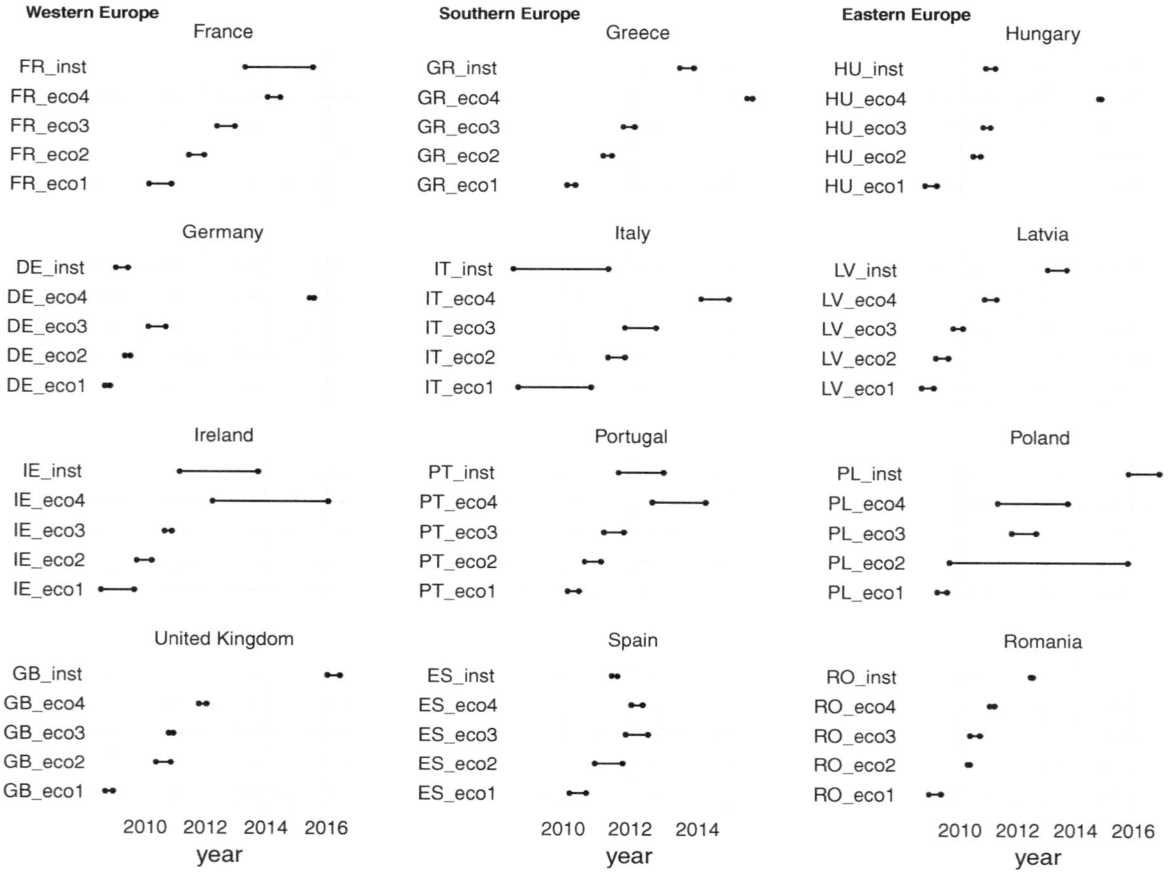


FIGURE 3.1. The timing of the episodes, by country and type

## THE ECONOMIC CRISES

For the characterization of the economic context we use six indicators – three objective indicators and two subjective ones. Our objective indicators are the seasonally adjusted unemployment rate, which probably provides us with the best overall measure of the depth of the economic crisis in a given country, the year-on-year GDP-growth rate, and the debt level. In addition, we use three subjective economic measures – the shares of the population that are satisfied with the current and with the future state of the national economy, and the Economic Sentiment Indicator (ESI).[1] The ESI is a composite indicator made up of five sectoral confidence measures with different weights: industrial, services, consumer, construction, and retail trade confidence measures. These confidence measures are based on surveys conducted within the Joint Harmonized EU Program of Business and Consumer Surveys. ESI is calculated as an index with a mean value of 100 and a standard deviation of 10 over a fixed standardized sample period. ESI refers to the prospects for economic development. Just like the other subjective indicators, ESI is a socio-tropic measure that assesses the situation of the national economy. Each indicator tells a somewhat different story, but we shall try to treat these stories as complementary rather than contrasting.

Table 3.1 presents the average state of the economy at the outset of the episodes per country. The countries are ordered according to their average level of unemployment. Greece and Spain top the table. While Greece's episodes are marked by slightly less unemployment than Spain's, Greece is performing worse than Spain on all the other objective and subjective indicators. Latvia, Ireland, and Portugal come next, followed by France, Hungary, and Italy. Surprisingly, Romania is closing the list, together with Germany, the U.K., and Poland. According to the objective indicators, Romania had been doing comparatively well at the moments when its government launched the episodes. However, in subjective terms the share of Romanians satisfied with the current state of the economy is as low as it is in the hard-hit southern European countries that top the table. Moreover, as we shall see in the next section, at the time when it was adopting the policy proposals that led to our episodes, Romania was in poor shape politically. To some extent the same can be said of Italy, while the opposite applies to Ireland and to some extent to Latvia, which were both in comparatively poor economic shape, although politically they did fare better than Romania or Italy.

The country-specific economic development throughout the financial crisis (September 2008 to December 2009) and the eurozone crisis (January 2010 to August 2015) is presented next in two graphs that group the countries by

---

[1] Source for the share of the population that is satisfied with the current and expected future national economy: Eurobarometer (half-yearly measures); source for ESI: Eurostat (http://ec .europa.eu/eurostat/web/products-datasets/-/teibso10).

TABLE 3.1. *Economic indicators, country averages for the five episodes*

| Country | Unem- ployment rate | GDP- growth rate | debt level | ESI | Satisfaction with national economy current | Satisfaction with national economy expected |
|---|---|---|---|---|---|---|
| Spain | 21.6 | −1.1 | 66.0 | 92.4 | 0.03 | 0.22 |
| Greece | 20.1 | −4.6 | 159.6 | 87.0 | 0.02 | 0.09 |
| Latvia | 14.9 | −5.5 | 30.7 | 88.9 | 0.08 | 0.19 |
| Ireland | 13.4 | 0.7 | 77.9 | . | 0.03 | 0.15 |
| Portugal | 13.1 | −0.8 | 105.3 | 89.2 | 0.07 | 0.08 |
| France | 9.7 | 1.2 | 90.7 | 96.8 | 0.10 | 0.23 |
| Hungary | 9.7 | 0.8 | 78.4 | 102.0 | 0.11 | 0.22 |
| Italy | 8.7 | −0.4 | 113.5 | 96.6 | 0.13 | 0.22 |
| Poland | 8.6 | 3.7 | 51.2 | 92.4 | 0.37 | 0.21 |
| United Kingdom | 7.0 | 0.6 | 72.7 | 93.5 | 0.25 | 0.23 |
| Germany | 6.8 | −1.8 | 69.5 | 88.5 | 0.44 | 0.14 |
| Romania | 6.7 | −1.6 | 26.8 | 88.9 | 0.08 | 0.16 |
| Average | 11.7 | −0.7 | 78.5 | 92.4 | 0.14 | 0.18 |

region. We distinguish between northwestern, southern and eastern Europe. Figures 3.2 and 3.3 present the developments of the Economic Sentiment Indicator (ESI) and unemployment levels, respectively. The dashed vertical lines in the two figures indicate the beginning of the financial crisis with the fall of Lehman Brothers in September 2008 and of the eurozone crisis in early 2010, as well as the end of the eurozone crisis, which we locate at the time of the adoption of the third Greek bailout in summer 2015. As Figure 3.2 shows, all countries across the three regions experienced a sharp drop in the subjective assessment of the national economy as Europe entered into the financial crisis.[2] In all the countries, the economic sentiment also recovered rather rapidly in the aftermath of this event, but we nevertheless observe two important regional differences. After a brief recovery, the southern European countries entered into a deep double-dip recession in summer 2011 from which they only started to recover again in summer 2013. Greece was even hit by a triple recession, the third of which started in early 2015, when the radical-left Syriza government took office, and reached its trough at the time of the Greek referendum on the memorandum in July 2015. In northwestern and eastern Europe, the recovery was more stable, even if the northwestern European countries as well as Hungary and Poland also experienced a milder second dip. Overall, the actual decline in economic performance was much more strongly and sharply felt in

[2] Unfortunately, we do not have data on Ireland for this indicator.

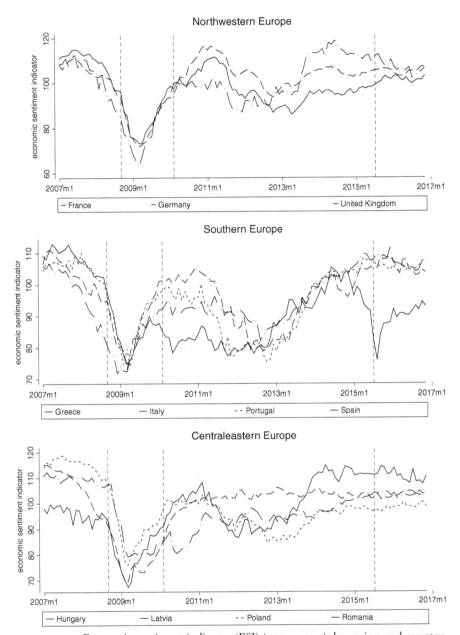

FIGURE 3.2. Economic sentiment indicator (ESI) (2007–2015), by region and country

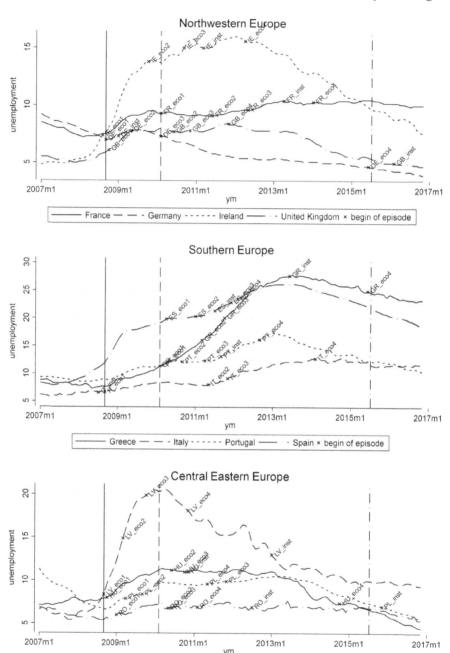

FIGURE 3.3. Development of unemployment (2007–2015) and the timing of the episodes, by region

the south than in the other two parts of Europe. This becomes most apparent from the development of the share of the population that was dissatisfied with the current state of the national economy (not shown in detail): Throughout southern Europe, the economic mood of the public has remained very morose since the beginning of the eurozone crisis.

Figure 3.3 presents the development of unemployment levels, seasonally adjusted, again by country and ordered regionally. In contrast to the subjective indicator in the previous figure that focuses on the ups and downs of the economic development, the unemployment levels serve to indicate the cumulative impact of the economic crisis. In this figure, we have also included the starting points of the sixty episodes to situate their timing with respect to the economic development in the different countries. Let us first comment on the variations in the development of the unemployment rates within regions. Thus, the countries in northwestern Europe experienced quite different developments in their unemployment rates, reflecting the variation in the extent to which they were hit by the economic crisis. In Ireland, the hardest-hit country of the region, the unemployment rate tripled from 5 to 15 percent in the course of the financial crisis, but, in line with the generally rather rapid recovery of the region's economies, Irish unemployment has sharply declined since the beginning of 2013. In the U.K. and France, the unemployment rate also increased during the financial crisis but only modestly. In the U.K. it returned to low levels after the second dip, while in France, it stabilized at around 10 percent and there is no indication of a further decline. In Germany, finally, the unemployment rate, which was the highest in this part of Europe before the crises, continued to decline throughout the economic crisis period to reach record low levels at the end of the eurozone crisis.

In southern Europe, the first country to be hit by the economic crisis was Spain. Already early on during the financial crisis, unemployment in Spain rose to very high levels and it continued to grow until the end of the double dip to 26 percent. The other three countries took their greatest hit later during the eurozone crisis. While Greek unemployment only started to grow during the eurozone crisis, it ended up at even higher levels than unemployment in Spain. In Portugal and Italy, however, unemployment rose more slowly and to more moderate levels (up to 17 percent in Portugal and 13 percent in Italy). After the double dip, unemployment started to decline across southern Europe, but it remained at comparatively high levels in all four countries throughout the period covered – an indication of the stagnating economies in this region. In southern Europe, external adjustment was ruled out because of eurozone membership, and internal adjustment policies were either blocked domestically or – via conditional bailout packages – externally forced upon these countries.

In eastern Europe, unemployment generally rose early during the financial crisis. It reached extreme levels in Latvia, easily the hardest hit among eastern European countries. However, unlike southern Europe, Latvian unemployment decreased rapidly during the eurozone crisis and declined to roughly 10 percent by the end of the period covered. Moreover, the other three countries did not experience such rampant unemployment at all. Thus, in Hungary and Poland unemployment only increased up to a level of 10 percent, and since the end of the double dip, it has decreased in these countries, too. In Romania, finally, unemployment hardly increased at all. In general, the countries of eastern Europe show a relatively quick recovery with declining unemployment rates, as a reaction to painful measures of external (Poland) and internal devaluation (Hungary, Latvia, and Romania) implemented by national governments (Walter 2016).

SEVERITY OF THE POLICY PROPOSALS

We have tried to assess the severity of each proposal based on a series of criteria that we formulated for each one of the five types. Table A3.1 in the appendix to this chapter specifies these criteria and the coding rules for the severity assessment. We eventually coded the proposals into three categories of severity – low, medium, and high. While rather rough, this assessment still provides a first impression of the harshness of the economic measures and of the depth of the institutional reforms.

Table 3.2 presents the country-specific means for the severity of economic and institutional measures, respectively. The countries are ordered according to the mean severity of the economic measures. As is immediately apparent and not at all surprising, the countries hardest hit by the economic crises are also the ones that had to adopt the harshest economic policy measures: On average, Greece and Portugal took the harshest measures, followed by Ireland, and a group of countries that includes Latvia, Romania, Spain, and the U.K. Poland

TABLE 3.2. *Mean severity by country and episode type*

| Country | Economic | Institutional |
|---|---|---|
| Greece | 3.0 | 2.0 |
| Portugal | 3.0 | 2.0 |
| Ireland | 2.8 | 2.0 |
| Latvia | 2.5 | 2.0 |
| Romania | 2.5 | 2.0 |
| Spain | 2.5 | 1.0 |
| United Kingdom | 2.5 | 3.0 |
| France | 2.3 | 2.0 |
| Hungary | 2.0 | 2.0 |
| Italy | 2.0 | 2.0 |
| Germany | 1.8 | 1.0 |
| Poland | 1.5 | 3.0 |
| Average | 2.4 | 2.0 |

and Germany, which managed comparatively well through the crisis, adopted economic proposals that were comparatively benign. In France, Italy, and Hungary the economic policy proposals linked to our episodes were also of comparatively low severity. This may be surprising, especially in the case of Hungary, because this is a country that was among the first to feel the full impact of the financial crisis in 2008. As early as October 2008, the socialist Hungarian government had to turn to the EU and the I.M.F. for help. In return, the government had to adopt harsh austerity measures. However, the policy proposals adopted subsequently by the Fidesz government, which came into power in 2010, turned out to be less severe than one might have expected given the original depth of the crisis. The case of Italy may also be surprising, but as we have already seen, the country slid into the crisis more slowly and, as it appears now, reacted less decisively to overcome the economic predicament than other countries. The institutional reforms were, on average, less severe than the economic policy proposals, but there have been two institutional reforms of great severity – the Polish reform of the Supreme Court and the British Brexit referendum.

Overall, the severity of the economic (but not of the institutional) proposals is likely to depend on a combination of problem pressure and type of measure. We use the seasonally adjusted unemployment rate as the objective indicator of problem pressure, as well as two measures for the public perception of the state of the country's economy – the share of the public satisfied with the current state of the national economy and the corresponding share satisfied with the expected future state of the economy.[3] We expect that the severity of the measures is the more pronounced, the higher the unemployment rate and the worse the perceived state of the economy: that is, the lower the share of the public that is satisfied with the current and future state of the national economy. For the type of measure, we use dummy variables for the types of measures that we have distinguished – fiscal austerity measures, structural reforms, international bailouts, bank bailouts, and institutional reforms, with structural reforms constituting the reference category.

Table 3.3 presents the results for the prediction of the severity of policy proposals. The first model includes only the four dummies for the policy types. The analysis indicates that international bailouts are on average most severe, while fiscal austerity measures also tend to be more severe than the other types of policies (bank bailouts, structural reforms, and institutional reforms). The second model introduces the seasonally adjusted unemployment rate. It is interacted with institutional reforms so as to test whether economic problem pressure is, indeed, only relevant for economic policy proposals. Unemployment does have the expected effect on economic policy proposals: the greater the unemployment rate, the more severe the measures

---

[3] The source for the subjective indicator: biannual Eurobarometer surveys.

TABLE 3.3. *Determinants of severity of proposed measures*

|  | 1 | 2 | 3 | 4 |
|---|---|---|---|---|
| international bailout | 1.182*** | | | 0.585 |
| | (3.883) | | | (1.981) |
| bank bailout | 0.182 | | | |
| | (0.515) | | | |
| fiscal measures | 0.640** | | | 0.426* |
| | (2.684) | | | (2.120) |
| institutional | 0.182 | 0.620 | -1.316 | -0.986 |
| | (0.665) | (1.243) | (-1.099) | (-1.359) |
| unemployment | | 0.045* | 0.005 | |
| | | (2.342) | (0.259) | |
| institutional#unemployment | | -0.081* | -0.008 | |
| | | (-2.206) | (-0.194) | |
| share satisfied with current economy | | | -2.036** | -1.539* |
| | | | (-3.130) | (-2.629) |
| institutional#share satisfied current economy | | | 4.448** | 4.002** |
| | | | (2.936) | (3.073) |
| share satisfied with future economy | | | -3.990** | -3.475* |
| | | | (-2.812) | (-2.329) |
| institutional#share satisfied future economy | | | 2.348 | 1.971 |
| | | | (0.534) | (0.502) |
| Constant | 1.818*** | 1.813*** | 3.256*** | 2.850*** |
| | (9.207) | (7.190) | (7.958) | (8.574) |
| Observations | 60 | 60 | 60 | 60 |
| AIC | 124.27 | 131.75 | 119.16 | 112.94 |
| BIC | 134.74 | 140.12 | 135.91 | 129.70 |
| r2 | 0.27 | 0.14 | 0.39 | 0.45 |

proposed.[4] However, as expected, the unemployment rate does not increase the severity of institutional reforms (direct + interaction effect = .045 − .081 = −.036). Model 3 adds the subjective indicators of problem pressure to the unemployment rate, again in interaction with institutional reforms. Its $R^2$-value shows that the subjective indicators provide a better summary of the problem pressure than the objective unemployment rate. Moreover, once we introduce these subjective indicators, the unemployment rate no longer has any effect at all on the severity of the proposed measures. Similar to the previous model, the interaction effects with institutional reforms indicate that the problem pressure only affects economic policy proposals but not institutional reforms. Model 4 combines the

---

[4] Unemployment is only one among several indicators of "objective" problem pressure. We have tested other indicators as well. Year-on-year GDP growth rates have a comparable effect. Inflation rates and debt levels, however, do not register any effect at all.

significant effects of the previous models. Adding the subjective indicators for problem pressure to the dummies for international bailouts and fiscal austerity measures considerably attenuates the latter's effect but scarcely changes the effects of the former. This is to suggest that it is, indeed, the greater problem pressure that imposed the severe measures in the case of the international bailouts and the fiscal austerity measures accompanying them.

## THE POLITICAL CONTEXT

We distinguish between the general and the issue-specific political context. We measure the *general political context* during the period covered by two indicators of the quality of democracy – an indicator for state capacity for the output side of democratic quality, and one for the strength of participatory democratic structures for the input side of democratic quality. These characteristics of a given country are likely to be rather stable over time. To be on the safe side, we measured the strength of both state capacity and participatory structures at the beginning of the episodes and provide the country averages across episodes. For the coding of the two dimensions of the democratic quality we rely on the Varieties of Democracies (VDem) Project (Coppedge et al. 2018). On the output side, we arrive at an indicator for state capacity by taking a country's score on the factor composed of the clientelism index, the rule of law index, and the political corruption index. On the input side, we rely on the participatory democracy subindex as it directly speaks to our theoretical interest. Figure 3.4 presents the country averages for the combination of the two indicators.

As the figure shows, the strength of the state capacity and of democratic participation are quite closely correlated with each other and vary considerably across Europe. At the one end, we find the northwestern European countries, which all have rather strong states and high scores on participatory democracy. They are joined by Portugal and Spain from southern Europe, and by Latvia and Poland from eastern Europe. At the other end, there is Romania, where both indicators are rather weak. Hungary and Greece are situated somewhere in between the extremes, while Italy is close to the bulk of the countries, although somewhat weaker in terms of state capacity. The upshot of this comparison is that Romania clearly stands apart from the rest of the countries in terms of the quality of its democratic institutions, and that Greece and Hungary (and Italy) also have institutions that do not quite live up to the usual European standards of democracy. This means that the capacity of the Romanian government, but also of the governments of the other three countries, to deal with economic pressure is generally more limited. It also means that the chances for the challengers to get a fair hearing is much more limited in Romania than in the other countries, and somewhat more limited in Greece and Hungary as well.

The key aspect of the *episode-specific context* to be considered refers to the composition of the government that announced the proposal giving rise to the

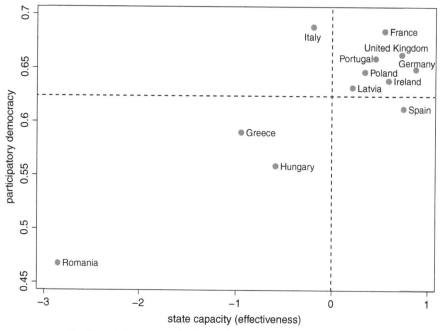

FIGURE 3.4. Quality of democracy in the twelve countries

episode. Table A3.2 in the Appendix presents the list of the fifty-nine governments that were in power in the twelve countries during the Great Recession (fall 2008 to summer 2015).[5] The stability of the governments clearly varies from one country to another. While there were no less than ten governments in Romania and seven in Latvia during this seven-year period, we count only two in Ireland, and three in Germany, the U.K., and Spain. The governments launching an economic policy proposal were both from the left (twelve out of twenty-nine) and the right (fifteen out of twenty-nine), one was a technocratic government (Monti in Italy), and one was a grand coalition (CDU–SPD in Germany). Importantly, in three of the southern European countries – Greece, Portugal, and Spain – the first austerity proposals were introduced by governments from the center-left; and even in Italy, the key austerity proposals were introduced by a technocratic government that was supported by a broad coalition including the center-left. As already mentioned, Roberts' (2013) analysis of Latin-American austerity episodes has shown that left-wing governments that introduce austerity measures are particularly vulnerable in electoral terms. Their adoption of such measures contradicts their programmatic positions, leading to program dilution and eventually to the destabilization not

---

[5] We built this list based on the cabinet data from parlgov.

TABLE 3.4. *Government electoral vulnerability: standardized vote intentions for the cabinet parties at the start of the episodes, by country*

| Country | Econ I | Econ II | Econ III | Econ IV | Institutional |
|---|---|---|---|---|---|
| Greece | 2.1 | 0.0 | −2.2 | 0.6 | −1.0 |
| Romania | 1.9 | −0.7 | −1.0 | −1.1 | 1.3 |
| Ireland | 0.9 | −0.9 | −1.2 | 1.0 | |
| Italy | 0.5 | −0.9 | −1.6 | −0.8 | 0.3 |
| Spain | 0.2 | −0.7 | −1.3 | 1.3 | −0.6 |
| Portugal | −0.2 | −0.7 | −1.0 | −0.6 | 3.3 |
| Latvia | −0.7 | −0.4 | −0.7 | 1.2 | −0.7 |
| France | 0.1 | −0.7 | 0.6 | −0.8 | −0.3 |
| UK | −1.0 | 2.8 | 1.7 | 1.0 | |
| Hungary | −1.0 | 2.4 | 2.1 | 1.1 | 2.0 |
| Germany | 0.6 | 0.6 | −0.9 | 0.9 | 0.5 |
| Poland | 0.7 | 1.0 | 0.9 | 0.3 | −2.4 |

only of the left-wing parties in government but of the whole party system. As a matter of fact, the heavy involvement of left-wing incumbent parties in the austerity episodes decisively contributed to undermining the center-left main-stream parties in southern Europe (see Hutter and Kriesi 2019; Roberts 2017). It is equally important that, in the other regions, the majority of the economic austerity proposals were introduced by governments from the right (or grand coalitions), for whom the adoption of such proposals is more in line with their programmatic stance and, therefore, less threatening.

The government's electoral vulnerability at the time it introduced the economic policy measures is reflected in its electoral vulnerability score, which corresponds to the standardized vote intentions for the governing parties. This indicator measures to what extent vote intentions at a given point in time are below or above the country-specific average: Negative values indicate high vulnerability, positive values low vulnerability. Table 3.4 presents this measure for the starting month of each episode. The table groups the episodes by country and the economic episodes in chronological order from left to right. The chronological order is important because the government's electoral vulnerability crucially depends on its past record of economic policy making. The countries are grouped by different patterns of government vulnerability. The first five countries in the table – Greece, Romania, Ireland, Italy, and Spain – are all characterized by increasingly electorally vulnerable governments as we progress from one economic episode to the next. Greece is the paradigmatic case: The series of episodes starts with an electorally very robust government

(the newly elected Papandreou government) that initiates episode I in early
2010. As we move to episodes II and III, the government's electoral viability
deteriorates massively, until, in episode IV, a new government (the Tsipras
government) has recovered some electoral standing. The other four countries
in this group follow a similar pattern. In Ireland and Spain, but not in Romania
and Italy, new governments (the Fine Gael and the Rajoy governments, respectively) also eventually recovered electoral standing by the time of episode IV. As
we have seen, these five countries have all been hard hit by the crisis. The
governments that happened to be in power when the crisis hit were all severely
punished in the course of the events. The next set of countries – Portugal and
Latvia, two equally hard-hit countries – follow a similar trajectory, with the only
difference that the governments were already in dire straits at the start of episode
I. In both countries, the economy had already slowed down prior to the fall 2008.
While, by episode IV, new governments recovered electorally in Latvia, this did
not occur in Portugal. In the case of Portugal, the center-right government that
took over after the bailout in summer 2011 was rapidly hit by the public ire as
well. France is a special case to the extent that the four episodes are divided into
two sets, for which two different presidents were responsible. Both become
electorally weaker as we move from the first to the second episode.

However, not all governments were equally vulnerable to electoral punishment for their economic policy measures. Thus, the Hungarian and U.K.
governments both follow an opposite trajectory: In these countries, the governments were electorally very vulnerable in episode I, that is early in the crisis, but
were rapidly replaced by new governments that proved to be electorally much
more robust throughout the rest of the episodes. Finally, the governments of
Germany and Poland were only little (Germany) or hardly at all (Poland)
affected by the episodes of economic policy making during the crisis. This is
not at all surprising, given that these two countries managed comparatively well
through the crisis, as we have seen in the previous section.

We can test more formally to what extent a government's electoral vulnerability at the time it has launched its economic proposals depends on the
severity of the economic measures proposed, on its composition, and on the
preceding record of economic policy making. For this test, we use the measure
for the severity of the proposals that we introduced previously. We distinguish
between highly severe proposals (1) and the rest (0). With respect to the incumbents, we distinguish between left-wing governments and right-wing governments (reference category), as well as a category for grand coalitions and
technocratic governments, which are typically supported by a large coalition
including established center-left and center-right parties. Third, we distinguish
between the chronological order of the economic episodes by introducing three
dummies (the first episode being the reference category).

Table 3.5 presents the results of this analysis. Model 1 only includes the
measure for the severity of the government policy proposals (plus country-fixed
effects). It shows what we would have expected: The more severe the proposals,
the more the government's popularity suffers. Although it does not reach

TABLE 3.5. *The correlates of government vulnerability (vote intention, standardized): OLS regression coefficients, t-values, and significance levels[1])*

|  | (1) | (2) | (3) |
|---|---|---|---|
| severity_high | −0.571 | −0.597 | −0.656 |
|  | (−1.413) | (−1.525) | (−1.742) |
| left govt. |  | −0.799 | −1.028* |
|  |  | (−1.688) | (−2.224) |
| grand coalition/ |  | −1.244 | −1.049 |
| technocratic govt. |  | (−1.646) | (−1.454) |
| economic II |  |  | −0.296 |
|  |  |  | (−0.693) |
| economic III |  |  | −1.083* |
|  |  |  | (−2.474) |
| economic IV |  |  | −0.281 |
|  |  |  | (−0.648) |
| country-fixed effects | yes | yes | yes |
| Constant | 0.035 | 0.448 | 1.007 |
|  | (0.059) | (0.713) | (1.466) |
| Observations | 48 | 48 | 48 |
| aic | 158.35 | 156.41 | 152.49 |
| bic | 182.68 | 184.47 | 186.17 |
| r2 | 0.29 | 0.37 | 0.49 |

[1] +.10, *=.05, **=.01, ***=.001

conventional levels of significance, the effect is substantial: If the proposal includes highly severe measures, the government's popularity decreases by roughly half a standard deviation. Model 2 suggests that governments from the left and grand coalitions/technocratic governments, which adopt austerity proposals and/or institutional reforms, indeed, suffer more than governments from the right. These effects are again not significant, although in substantive terms they are even more substantial. Adding the order of the proposal in the sequence of economic austerity proposals in Model 3 enhances the previous effects of severity and the impact on left-wing governments. The latter now becomes significant: The popularity of a left-wing government that launches an austerity package decreases by roughly one standard deviation in the month when it launches that package, independently of the severity of the measure in question. For right-wing governments, no such popularity loss takes place. Model 3 also corroborates the notion that additional austerity measures become increasingly costly for governments in general. The third measure is the one that is most costly, as has already been suggested by the previous table. This may be somewhat of a chance outcome, given that by the time of the fourth episode in several countries new governments had taken over and consequently did not suffer from a cumulation of punishments for austerity packages adopted previously.

THE POLITICAL CONDITIONS FOR THE TIMING
OF THE EPISODES

The governments were, of course, not free to adopt these austerity packages. In the first place, these packages were forced upon them by the dire economic circumstances. However, the governments of the hard-hit countries were also put under pressure to adopt such packages by international actors. Table 3.6 presents the minimum, mean, and maximum of international pressure on a country's government in the month when the episode was launched. We measure the international pressure by the share of international actors among all actors intervening during the start month of the episode. In the table, the countries are ordered by the average international pressure across all episodes.

Surprisingly, Germany is the country that experienced the greatest international pressure, both on average and in terms of the maximum. This result points to an aspect of the eurozone crisis that is often overlooked: It is not only the debtor countries that were hard pressed internationally but also the creditor countries that had to decide about supporting the bailouts of the debtor countries. As a matter of fact (see Appendix A2), two of the German episodes dealt with the Greek bailouts – that is, with the ratification of the respective German shares of the economic adjustment programs for Greece – which goes a long way to explain this unexpected result. France, too, experienced a lot of international pressure at the start of its episodes, although it is generally perceived as a creditor country. In line with expectations, Greece and Portugal, two of the hardest-hit debtor countries, were heavily pressured by international agencies at the outset of their episodes, as were the other bailout countries at least in some of their episodes. In contrast, Poland experienced no

TABLE 3.6. *Pressure from above: share of international actors among all actors intervening during the starting month of the episode, by country – minimum, mean, and maximum*

| Country | Min | Mean | Max |
|---------|-----|------|-----|
| Germany | 0.09 | 0.44 | 1.00 |
| Greece | 0.11 | 0.19 | 0.33 |
| Portugal | 0.09 | 0.17 | 0.33 |
| France | 0.00 | 0.16 | 0.33 |
| Hungary | 0.06 | 0.14 | 0.23 |
| Italy | 0.00 | 0.10 | 0.40 |
| Latvia | 0.00 | 0.08 | 0.19 |
| Romania | 0.00 | 0.05 | 0.14 |
| Ireland | 0.00 | 0.04 | 0.18 |
| Spain | 0.00 | 0.02 | 0.10 |
| UK | 0.00 | 0.02 | 0.05 |
| Poland | 0.00 | 0.00 | 0.00 |
| Total | 0.00 | 0.12 | 1.00 |

international pressure at all, and this kind of pressure also remained very limited in the U.K.

A closer look at the changing political context suggests that the timing of the episodes was not completely exogenously determined; it was also influenced to some extent by endogenous political considerations. Figure A3.1 in the Appendix presents the development of the vote intentions for the incumbent parties (their vulnerability) per country from 2007 to 2015 and situates the start of the episodes with respect to this development. Strikingly, the start of the episodes is often located close to major or minor peaks in the country-specific vote intentions for the incumbents. These peaks mark elections of new governments or changes in the cabinet between elections. Thus, the incoming Conservative–Liberal coalition under David Cameron in the U.K. launched its spending review immediately after having won the elections. Similarly, French President Hollande embarked on his first austerity package immediately after having come to power. The Italian technocratic government that came to power without elections – the Monti government – introduced major austerity packages immediately after taking office. Similarly, the new Dombrovskis government in Latvia – that replaced the Godmanis cabinet in spring 2009 in a reshuffle among the Latvian parties – embarked on its extremely ambitious austerity program immediately after having taken power. The second Tusk government in Poland presented its most severe austerity proposal right after having been reelected and the new Orban government in Hungary also set in motion its train of reform measures immediately after the elections. There are, of course, also counter-examples, such as the Portuguese bailout that was approved by the caretaker government that had called for early elections. The bailout memorandum was approved right before the June 2011 elections, with the joint support of the Socialist Party (PS), the Social Democratic Party (PSD), and the People's Party (CDS-PP). Also, while the second Greek bailout was eventually signed by the technocratic Papademos government, negotiations for the bailout had already started before the new cabinet took office in fall 2011 and it was actually the failure of the Papandreou government to resolve the issue of the second bailout that led to its replacement by the technocratic government. In spite of these counter-examples, it is quite striking that many of the crucial proposals were introduced by newly elected governments or by governments explicitly set up to introduce such measures.

This reminds us of the electoral and partisan cycles in economic policies and outcomes that have been the object of a voluminous literature (for overviews see Franzese 2002, Franzese and Jusko 2006, and de Haan and Klomp 2013). As the more recent work of this literature suggests, electoral cycles seem to be highly context conditional (Franzese and Jusko 2006: 550). In line with this literature, we expect that the introduction of austerity measures by newly elected or newly formed governments during the Great Recession was conditioned by the severity of the economic crisis. Under conditions of a severe crisis, we expect such new governments to be particularly likely to introduce austerity measures.

TABLE 3.7. *Determinants of the timing of the economic policy episodes (September 2008–2015): OLS and fixed effects regressions – regression coefficients, t-values, and significance levels*[1]

|                                              | Model 1   | Model 2  | Model 3  |
|----------------------------------------------|-----------|----------|----------|
| D.vote intention                             | 0.442*    | 0.189    | 0.160    |
|                                              | (2.426)   | (0.984)  | (0.830)  |
| Cabinet change                               |           | 1.120*   | 1.067*   |
|                                              |           | (2.225)  | (2.073)  |
| Honeymoon                                    |           | 0.540    | 0.605    |
|                                              |           | (1.368)  | (1.523)  |
| D.unemployment                               |           |          | 1.561**  |
| seasonally adjusted                          |           |          | (2.807)  |
| country-fixed effects                        | yes       | yes      | yes      |
| Observations                                 | 978       | 978      | 978      |
| AIC                                          | 335.97    | 331.29   | 325.56   |
| BIC                                          | 340.86    | 345.95   | 345.10   |

[1] ***=.001, **=.01, *=.05, +=.10

We can test these expectations using monthly data for the period September 2008–2015. The dependent variable is a dummy indicator that takes the value of 1 if one of our economic policy episodes was launched in the respective month, and 0 otherwise. Our first independent variable is the change in electoral vulnerability (standardized vote intentions). We presume that the governments introduce austerity packages when they enjoy a boost in popularity. This increase in popularity may be the result of elections or cabinet reshuffles (see Table A3.2). These events are represented by a dummy indicator that takes the value of 1 for the months when either elections or cabinet changes occurred and 0 otherwise. For all new governments, irrespective of whether they were created by elections or by cabinet changes between elections, we also introduce a honeymoon, which is assumed to last for three months (including the election month or the month of cabinet change). For the changing problem pressure we use the change in the unemployment rate. We estimated three fixed-effects logit models for economic policy proposals. Table 3.7 presents the results for the three models.

Model 1 confirms that governments tend to introduce economic austerity packages when they enjoy increasing popularity. Model 2 specifies that this increasing popularity is a result of cabinet change, either following elections or involving a reshuffle during a legislative period, but the effect of cabinet change is greatest in the month when the cabinet change takes place. The honeymoon period also enhances the likelihood of an economic policy proposal somewhat, but the effect is not significant at conventional levels. Model 3 confirms that economic problem pressure is, of course, also highly important for the launching of economic austerity proposals. However, the introduction of economic problem pressure does not modify the effect of cabinet change, suggesting that strategic considerations by the governments also contribute to the launching of our episodes, independently of the economic problem pressure.

CONCLUSION

In this chapter, we have presented the development of the economic and political pressures in the twelve countries during the period covered as well as the timing of the episodes with respect to the two types of pressure. Overall, the actual decline in economic performance was much more sharply felt in the south than in the other two parts of Europe. The development of the economic sentiment and of unemployment rates for the different countries indicate that the southern European countries were not only more heavily affected in the first place but that they also recovered less rapidly than those in the other two regions. However, the development of the crisis indicators also varies within regions. Thus, Latvia took a much stronger hit in terms of unemployment than the other eastern European countries, and the same applies to Ireland in north-western Europe. Two countries, Germany and Poland, survived the crises exceptionally well.

The economic problem pressure forced the governments to adopt the policy measures that have given rise to the economic episodes under study. The greater the economic problem pressure, the more severe the economic policy proposals proved to be. In addition, governments that introduced such measures also came under political pressure. Their electoral vulnerability increased – a more or less direct result of the severity of their economic policy proposals. Moreover, the adoption of early measures contributed to the electoral vulnerability of those governments that had to introduce additional measures later on. As we progress from one episode to the next in the different countries, governments were either replaced by new governments or became increasingly vulnerable as they had to adopt additional measures. This progression applies especially to the southern European countries but also to the hard-hit countries in the east (Latvia and Romania) where governments changed frequently, as well as to hard-hit Ireland. France experienced the repeat of a similar pattern under two successive presidents.

In contrast, governments in Germany and Poland that felt less economic pressure to begin with – but also governments in Hungary (the Orban government) and the U.K. (the Cameron government) – were less affected by these dynamics. Still, this does not mean that the governments of these countries did not experience any pressure. Thus, as we have seen, even the government of a creditor country like Germany underwent strong foreign pressure. The stronger the cumulated pressure on the governments – economically, electorally, and otherwise, the more likely they were to launch an economic policy proposal that was at the origin of one of our episodes. However, the occasion for launching such a proposal was not entirely the result of exogenous pressure, but, to some extent, it was also influenced by endogenous political considerations. Strikingly, the start of the episode is often located close to major or minor peaks in the country-specific popularity of the incumbents: that is, to moments of reduced electoral vulnerability. These peaks mark elections of new governments or changes in the cabinet between elections. In line with the literature on electoral cycles, it is quite significant that many (albeit not all) of the crucial proposals were introduced by newly elected governments or by governments that were set up explicitly to introduce such measures.

PART II

VARIETIES OF CONTENTION

# 4

## Conceptualizing, Measuring, and Mapping Contentiousness

### Theresa Gessler and Swen Hutter

INTRODUCTION

Portugal and Spain were among the countries hardest hit by the global financial crisis that led to the eurozone's near collapse after the revelation of Greek public debt in late 2009. Both countries experienced a massive economic shock, as revealed by objective and subjective indicators (Chapter 3). Faced with a dire economic situation and increasing European pressure, the mainstream left in government – PS in Portugal and PSOE in Spain – announced severe austerity measures throughout 2009 and 2010 (Bremer and Vidal 2018). Consequently, the two countries saw union-organized protests against the measures early in the crisis (Accornero and Ramos Pinto 2015; Della Porta et al. 2017a; Kriesi et al. 2020; Portos 2019). Both countries experienced a turning point in 2011 when further noninstitutional actors entered the scene: Geração à Rasca [Screwed generation] in March 2011 in Portugal and 15M (named after the first large-scale protests on May 15, 2011) in Spain. According to some estimates, almost 5 percent of the Portuguese population took to the streets on March 12, 2011 (Carvalho 2018: 98).[1] 15M and the battle cry of the central organizing network Democracia Real, Ya! [Real democracy now] led, after the first demonstration with about 20,000 participants on Puertas del Sol, to weeks of mass protests across the country.

Protest event data highlights the similar dynamics in Portugal and Spain up to early 2011 and the strongly diverging trends after that first period. Portuguese protest, as Carvalho (2018) puts it, "deflates and follows a stop-and-go pattern, while in Spain it escalates into an unceasing and sustained wave

---

[1] The Portuguese mobilization not only preceded the Spanish, it also served as a more general precursor in terms of action repertoires and discourse for the protests that followed across southern Europe (see Baumgarten 2013; Flesher Fominaya 2017).

of contention until the end of 2013" (see also Portos and Carvalho 2019). As is
well documented, the massive protest wave in Spain spilled over into electoral
politics, giving rise to a new party, Podemos, and leading to a significant
restructuring of Spanish politics (Della Porta et al. 2017b; Vidal and Sánchez-
Vítores 2019). In Portugal, the follow-up protests were mainly organized by
institutionalized actors, especially the major unions and left-wing opposition
parties, but no new party emerged (Da Silva and Mendes 2019). Thus, the two
cases underscore that similar grievances and starting points of mobilization can
lead to starkly different outcomes. As the insightful paired comparison by
Carvalho (2018) shows, these differences were due to factors endogenous to
the challengers' activities on the streets (such as their action repertoire and
coalition strategies) and exogenous ones (such as the responses of institutionalized actors).

In this chapter, we build upon such detailed case studies but innovate in two
respects. First, we move beyond an exclusive focus on the most well-known
cases of anti-austerity mobilization during the Great Recession. Instead, we
look at all sixty episodes covered in this book and ask: How contentious are the
interactions of the actors involved in the public conflicts over austerity and
institutional reforms? Which factors drive the level and type of contestation in
an episode? At the core of our endeavor is the idea that the economic and
institutional reforms proposed to cope with the Great Recession vary in the
level and type of conflict they sparked. While some policy proposals made their
way through the political decision-making process smoothly, others were met
with strong public opposition.

Second, we move beyond the exclusive focus on (aggregates of) protest
events to compare conflict levels systematically. More specifically, we innovate
by developing the concept of the *contentiousness* of an episode. That is, we aim
to turn the dichotomous distinction of "routine" and "contentious politics" –
the core of the Dynamics of Contention (DOC) program by McAdam et al.
(2001) – into an empirically observable matter of degree. Based on DOC's focus
on the interactions of actors in a conflict, our guiding assumption is that the
contentiousness of an episode is the product of the behavior of all three stylized
actor types: The more all actors (the government, challengers, and third parties)
contribute to the public conflict over the policy proposal, the more contentious
the episode. To construct our indicators, we combined insights from classical
protest event analysis (focusing on the actions staged by the challengers) with
research on agenda setting and the politicization of issues in the public sphere
(focusing on broader classes of claims making).[2]

Note that we adopt an "aggregative" approach in this part of the book.
Later parts consider the relational aspects of the data (for the aggregative versus

---

[2] See Baumgartner et al. (2019); Baumgartner and Jones (1993); Green-Pedersen and Walgrave
(2014); Hutter et al. (2016); Koopmans and Statham (1999).

relational distinction, see Diani 2013; 2015). In our opinion, such a systematic "lumping" of the data is essential for at least three reasons: First, it helps us answer whether and under what conditions fully fledged contentious episodes emerge. Second, it permits the identification of critical cases for more in-depth analyses. Third, it puts well-known cases, such as the briefly sketched 2011 mobilizations in Spain and Portugal, in a broader comparative perspective.

The chapter is structured in four parts. First, we introduce our new explication of the concept of contentiousness. Second, we outline the full range of coded actions and the construction of our indicators. Third, we map the contentiousness of the sixty episodes before we finally shift to factors that might explain the uncovered variation. We follow classical approaches in social movement studies, distinguishing grievances, mobilizing structures, and political context. We also systematically distinguish general from episode-specific explanatory factors.

## CONTENTIOUSNESS: A MULTIDIMENSIONAL CONCEPT

We propose to define contentiousness as a multidimensional concept and to use the action repertoire available to the three stylized actors as building blocks. Following Schattschneider's (1975) understanding of politics, we are interested in who aims to increase the "scope of conflict" and by what means. We ask how each stylized actor may reinforce the conflict over the proposals at risk. In doing so, we consider both the frequency and the type of action as crucial "ingredients" of what makes an episode contentious. We follow Tilly and Tarrow's (2015: 39; emphasis in the original) approach by prioritizing "what activists *do* during major episodes of contention" in comparison to "what activists say or later write about their activities." We also aim to link the DOC program with two related strands in political sociology: the scholarly literature on agenda setting and politicization that both build on Schattschneider's foundational work.

The core dimension for each actor type is the *intensity of adversarial actions* (see Figure 4.1). Here, we take up the idea from Chapter 1 that each actor has three central options at its disposal. The government – who initiates the episode by launching the proposal – could concede to the challenger's demands, stick to its request, or repress the challenger (ordered from most to least cooperative), while the challenger is the second mover in the threat-induced conflict we study in this book. It can opt to cooperate with the government, launch a nondisruptive or a disruptive action against the proposal.[3] Finally, the third parties also

---

[3] To repeat, the distinction of nondisruptive versus disruptive refers to contestation purely by verbal opposition or by fairly institutionalized actions, such as petitioning, direct democracy, or industrial conflict in the form of strikes as nondisruptive; with unconventional and non-institutionalized forms of contentious performances, including demonstrative, confrontational, and violent protest events regarded as disruptive.

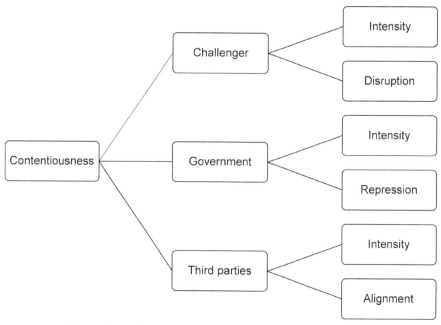

FIGURE 4.1. Dimensions of contentiousness

have three broad options: They can mediate between the government and the challenger by suggesting a compromise or offering to be brokers; alternatively, they can side with the government or side with the challenger. To assess how intensely each one fuels the conflict, we consider each actor's second and third options as adversarial, while we regard the first options (concession by the government, cooperation by the challenger, and mediation by the third parties) as conflict-dampening actions that are not part and parcel of contentiousness. To what extent such accommodative measures co-occur with contentious interactions is an empirical question (see Chapter 7).

The intensity of publicly visible actions mirrors the emphasis put on issue salience in the agenda-setting literature that ultimately regards politics as a fight over attention (e.g., Baumgartner and Jones 1993; Baumgartner et al. 2019; Carmines and Stimson 1993; Green-Pedersen and Walgrave 2014).[4] As the agenda-setting literature typically does not study position-taking, our emphasis

---

[4] It is important to note that we only consider *publicly visible actions*. To explain what we mean here, let us refer to Meguid (2005, 2008), who has aptly summarized the three strategies that mainstream parties have when faced with a challenger: ignore, attack, or accommodate. We list these options here as it is important to highlight that our conceptualization of publicly visible actions only covers strategies of ignorance by the government if they were linked explicitly to declaring to stick to the proposal. Thus, our conceptualization of contentiousness covers

on *adversarial* action as the basic element of contentiousness sets our approach apart. Consequently, our multidimensional understanding of conflict comes closer to works on the politicization of issues in the public sphere.[5] An emerging consensus in this field conceptualizes politicization as a three-dimensional concept. Salience or visibility of an issue is combined with polarization and the range of actors involved in public contestation (de Wilde et al. 2016; Hutter et al. 2016). Ultimately, the most politicized constellation refers to a highly salient conflict in which a broad range of actors adopts strongly diverging positions.

We build on such a multidimensional understanding of political conflict in our attempt to conceptualize contentiousness. Furthermore, we bring in the distinct action repertoires at the core of social movement studies and the DOC program by McAdam et al. (2001). To do so, we complement the intensity dimension with a second, actor-specific dimension: *disruption, repression, and alignment* (see Figure 4.1). The second dimensions for each actor indicate that the interactions in a contentious episode may range from a barely visible public exchange of verbal arguments between the different actors to an intense public controversy in which a coalition of actors stages a fully fledged contentious campaign that might be met with repression by the authorities and a clear alignment of the third parties.

On the part of the challenger, such a fully fledged contentious campaign involves a broad range of tactics (including protest mobilization) to produce a sustained challenge to the government's proposal (Almeida 2014). As highlighted before, we define a disruptive action in terms of noninstitutionalized and unconventional forms of protest. In operational terms, we consider two central aspects of protest events as indicating their disruptiveness: the logics of damage and numbers (Della Porta and Diani 2006: 171ff.). Similarly, the government may also further escalate the conflict by adopting a more repressive action repertoire toward the challenger and its actions, covering activities from depreciating statements about the protestors, to legal acts, to the use of the police. Finally, third parties can also fuel a dispute by sending out signals supporting either the challenger or the government (this is what the "intensity" dimension covers). Additionally, we suggest that third parties render a public debate most contentious if their actions show a clear-cut alignment with one of the two contestants. In that case, they take a clear-cut position in the configuration of allies and adversaries (on the distinction, see Rucht 2004 and Chapter 5, this volume).

To sum up, episodes may be contentious due to both the intensity and the types of actions of each stylized actor. In our understanding, an episode is most

"ignorance by insistence and non-recognition of the challenger as a relevant actor," but it does not cover "ignorance by pure silence and non-atttention to a given issue/demand."

[5] The concept of politicization has become particularly important in the study of conflicts over European integration. For the question of why EU studies have turned to study the phenomenon, see the programmatic article on a post-functionalist theory of integration by Hooghe and Marks (2009).

TABLE 4.1. *Types of contentious episodes*

|  |  | Contentiousness by challenger | |
|---|---|---|---|
|  |  | Low | High |
| Contentiousness by government and third parties | Low | Low-intensity episode | Bottom-up dominated episode |
|  | High | Top-down dominated episode | Fully fledged episode |

contentious if all three actors become intensively involved: the challenger moves beyond verbal opposition by staging more disruptive protests; the government moves beyond "sticking to its proposal" verbally to forms of repressive behavior; and the third parties add fuel to the fire by clearly aligning with either the challenger or the government. In the end, these actors bring together what Tilly and Tarrow (2015: 7) see as essential features of contentious politics: contention, collective action, and politics.

The combination of the challenger's contentiousness and the other two types of actors can be used to construct a simple two-by-two table. As shown in Table 4.1, this exercise allows for the differentiation of types of contentious episodes: from what we call "low-intensity episodes," in which all actors keep their activity to a minimum, to fully fledged contentious episodes marked by a distinct and robust presence of all three actors. The resulting typology is a first step in moving from the quantity of contentiousness to assessing its quality.

## CONTENTIOUSNESS: AN ACTION-BASED MEASURE

Before we detail how we measure contentiousness, it is helpful to consider the distribution of the full set of coded actions (see Chapter 2). For this purpose, Table 4.2 shows the frequencies of the different codes by actor type. Note that we coded a total of 6,841 distinct actions. As discussed in Chapter 2, the coders were instructed to note each action's substantive and procedural aspects. In practice, the articles often only provided information on one of the two elements, with the substantive part being more widely available and, thus, more frequently coded (N = 6,293 substantive codes versus N = 3,209 procedural codes).

Starting with challengers' actions, it is readily apparent from Table 4.2 that a considerably greater diversity characterizes their procedural repertoire than their substantive one. The substantive dimension is heavily skewed, with most challenger demands in favor of the proposal's withdrawal. Only a relatively small share corresponds to challengers accepting the policy either in the original or a modified form (less than 4 percent). This finding is hardly surprising. By the

TABLE 4.2. *Frequency of procedural and substantive actions, by actor type*

| Actor | Action type | Action | N | Share |
|---|---|---|---|---|
| Challenger | Substantive | *Demands withdrawal* | 1,641 | 72.2 |
| | | Demands modification | 421 | 18.5 |
| | | Scale shift | 124 | 5.5 |
| | | Ready to accept the proposal | 49 | 2.2 |
| | | Accepts modified proposal | 22 | 1.0 |
| | | Accepts original proposal | 17 | 0.8 |
| | Procedural | Constitutes itself | 46 | 2.5 |
| | | Threatens to mobilize | 177 | 9.4 |
| | | Announces mobilization | 318 | 16.9 |
| | | *Mobilizes* | 866 | 46.1 |
| | | Deprecates government | 303 | 16.1 |
| | | Stops mobilization | 21 | 1.1 |
| | | Signals readiness to negotiate | 80 | 4.3 |
| | | Negotiates | 55 | 2.9 |
| | | Demobilizes | 5 | 0.3 |
| | | Gives up | 6 | 0.3 |
| Government | Substantive | *Sticks to proposal* | 1,375 | 74.9 |
| | | Adopts proposal | 105 | 5.7 |
| | | Raises doubts about the proposal | 245 | 13.4 |
| | | Grants concessions to challengers | 96 | 5.2 |
| | | Withdraws proposal | 14 | 0.8 |
| | Procedural | Represses challenger | 43 | 7.2 |
| | | *Deprecates challenger* | 190 | 32.0 |
| | | Fails to recognize challenger | 42 | 7.1 |
| | | Circumvents legal barriers | 31 | 5.2 |
| | | Signals readiness to negotiate | 122 | 20.5 |
| | | Negotiates | 166 | 28.0 |
| Third parties | Substantive | *Supports proposal* | 878 | 41.2 |
| | | Opposes challenger's demands | 53 | 2.5 |
| | | Mediates | 173 | 8.1 |
| | | *Opposes proposal* | 987 | 46.3 |
| | | Supports challengers demands | 39 | 1.8 |
| | Procedural | *Supports government action* | 250 | 33.9 |
| | | Opposes challenger actions | 57 | 7.7 |
| | | Mediates | 123 | 16.7 |
| | | *Opposes government actions* | 261 | 35.4 |
| | | Supports challenger actions | 47 | 6.4 |

*Note*: We ordered the coded action forms for the challenger and the government from adversarial to accommodative; action forms with a share higher than 30 percent by actor and action type are highlighted in italics.

very definition of being challengers, their raison d'etre is demanding changes to the policy proposal. We can discern more variation on the procedural dimension and the form of mobilization they launch (if they decide to do so). A little less than half of all coded procedural actions correspond to actual mobilization. In addition, a nontrivial share covers preparatory steps to mobilization (i.e., threats and announcements, around 25 percent) and verbal attacks (depreciating or demonizing governments, 16.4 percent). This result highlights the added value of our coding approach, which focuses not only on actual protest events but covers a broader set of both substantive and procedural actions. Less than 10 percent of all procedural codes correspond to forms of negotiation or demobilization by challengers.

Similarly, the governments' substantive actions indicate an unwavering pursuit of the proposal, and only a relatively minor share (around 20 percent) corresponds to different forms of compromising tactics (raising doubts, granting concessions, or withdrawing the proposal altogether). On the procedural dimension, the two most common government actions are verbal attacks (depreciating/demonizing the challengers) and negotiation. In contrast, outright repression and circumvention of legal barriers are relatively rare forms of government actions during our period of observation (for a detailed assessment of when they occur, see Chapter 9).

Regarding the final actor type, third parties, the different codes indicate how they relate to the contending parties, either on the substantive domain (to the proposal/demands) or on the procedural one (their actions). On the substantive dimension, third parties tend to relate to the proposal *itself* rather than the demands of challengers. They either support or oppose the proposal in roughly equal proportions. As shown in Table 4.2, the corresponding shares amount to somewhat more than 40 percent. On the procedural dimension, there is a greater diversity of action forms. Attempts to mediate between the challengers make up a little less than 17 percent of third parties' procedural codes. However, most third-party actions relate to government actions rather than to challenger responses (less than 15 percent). Third parties are roughly evenly split between supporting and opposing government actions (33.8 versus. 35.4 percent). Overall, this first aggregate analysis suggests that the third parties have sided equally with governments and challengers. At the same time, they hardly ever directly engage with the challengers' demands or activities.

After this first look at all actions in our dataset, we now turn to how we measure the contentiousness of a given episode based on these codes. As outlined before, our guiding assumption is that contentiousness is a product of all three actors' behavior. Thus, we propose to measure the contentiousness induced by each actor and combine the three actor-specific measures into a joint one (see Figure 4.1 for an overview of the dimensions). Next, we detail each dimension and its indicators outlined in Table 4.3, which also presents summary statistics.

For each actor, we consider the *intensity* of the actor's involvement in the episode by measuring the absolute frequency of adversarial actions. In the case

TABLE 4.3. *Dimensions, indicators, and descriptive statistics for contentiousness*

| Actor | Concept | Indicator | N | Mean | Std. dev. | Min | Max |
|---|---|---|---|---|---|---|---|
| **Challenger** | Intensity | Frequency of adversarial actions | 60 | 0.28 | 0.22 | 0.00 | 1.00 |
| | Disruption | Mean of weighted frequency of disruptive protest actions and number of participants involved in such events | 60 | 0.31 | 0.27 | 0.00 | 1.00 |
| | Contentiousness by challenger | Sum of the above indicators | 60 | 0.37 | 0.27 | 0.00 | 1.00 |
| **Government** | Intensity | Frequency of adversarial actions | 60 | 0.26 | 0.22 | 0.00 | 1.00 |
| | Repression | Weighted frequency of repressive actions | 60 | 0.17 | 0.21 | 0.00 | 1.00 |
| | Contentiousness by government | Sum of the above indicators | 60 | 0.27 | 0.24 | 0.00 | 1.00 |
| **Third parties** | Intensity | Frequency of adversarial actions | 60 | 0.19 | 0.22 | 0.00 | 1.00 |
| | Alignment | Abs. position of adversarial codes | 60 | 0.39 | 0.32 | 0.00 | 1.00 |
| | Contentiousness by third party | Sum of the above indicators | 60 | 0.32 | 0.21 | 0.00 | 1.00 |

*Note:* All frequency measures are standardized by the number of weeks that saw at least one action to account for the varying length of the episode. Moreover, all measures were standardized to range from 0 to 1 so that they can be directly combined in an additive way. N = number of episodes.

of the challenger, adversarial actions refer to launching a nondisruptive or disruptive action against the proposal (omitting cooperation). We use the following codes to operationalize the distinction between purely verbal opposition (code 1), threats (code 2), and actual mobilization (codes 3 to 5).

1. Sticking to opposition (substantive, verbal only)
2. Threats/announcements to organize actions classed as 3 to 5
3. Nondisruptive mobilization (petitions, direct democracy, and strikes)
4. Demonstrative protest forms
5. Confrontational or violent protest forms

For the intensity measure, we give all codes the same weight and calculate a simple sum. To operationalize disruption, we follow the general approach in protest event research and consider two features as central: the capacity to cause damage and to mobilize large numbers of participants. First, we calculated the weighted frequency of demonstrative and confrontational/violent protest forms (weighting codes 4 and 5 in the list above as 1 = demonstrative and 2 = confrontational/ violent). Second, we produced a categorical variable based on the number of participants involved in any kind of protest (codes 3 to 5).[6] We recoded both indicators to range from zero to one, and we combined them into a summary indicator for the challenger's disruptiveness. The resulting measure is then combined with the intensity: *Contentiousness by the challenger = intensity + disruption.*

For the government, adversarial actions refer to continued verbal support for the proposal (including refusal to accept the challengers' suggestions) and repressive behavior in procedural terms. Thus, we include the following action forms in the intensity measure (giving the same weight to all of them).

1.    Sticking to the proposal (substantive, verbal only)
2.    Depreciate/denounce/demonize or explicitly refuse to recognize the challenger as a relevant interlocutor (repression "light")
3.    (Violent) repression of the challenger (repression "heavy")

To assess how repressively the government acted, we calculated the weighted frequency of the government's repressive actions by considering only codes 2 and 3 listed above. We assigned a weight of 1 to light repression and a weight of 2 to heavy repression. To combine intensity and repression, we again recode both indicators using the range from zero to one and add them in a simple combination, giving equal weight to both: *Contentiousness by the government = intensity + repression.*

---

[6] Our variable ranges from zero to four, based on country-specific thresholds. Given that we only have data for large events, we have opted for a categorical variable. This is also a better way to address outliers with a vast number of participants. We decided for the following cut-off points (differentiating small and big countries): 0 < 10,000 (small countries) or 20,000 (big countries); 1 > 10,000 or 20,000; 2 > 50,000 or 100.000; 3 > 100,000 or 200,000; 4 > 250,000 or 500,000.

As highlighted before, the third parties may add to the conflict if they get publicly involved with statements that side with one of the two contestants (i.e., the government or the challenger). This indicator again omits neutral or mediating positions.

-1    Side with the government's proposal or actions
1     Side with challenger's proposal/and or actions

We calculated the absolute number of both codes to measure the intensity of third-party involvement. For the second dimension "alignment," we recoded the absolute average positions per episode into a categorical variable that ranges from 1 to 4 (from ambiguous to clear-cut, regardless of the direction).[7] We again standardized both indicators (ranging from zero to one) and combined them in a straightforward additive way: *Contentiousness by the third parties = intensity + alignment*

Finally, we added up the contentiousness induced by the three actor types to get a joint measure of the contentiousness of the entire episode. In the spirit of the DOC approach, we suggest that the challengers' actions are essential to talk about high(er) levels of contentiousness. Without the emergence of a challenger coalition, the government might still take its default option of sticking to its proposal. The third parties (usually institutional "insiders") might agree or disagree. Yet, they cannot turn a routine verbal conflict into a fully fledged contentious episode. Therefore, we give the challengers a double weight, resulting in a measure ranging from 0 (least contentious) to 4 (most contentious):

*Overall contentiousness: 2\*contentiousness by the challenger + contentiousness by the government + contentiousness by the third parties*

## MAPPING CONTENTIOUSNESS IN THE GREAT RECESSION

Having outlined how we turn the "routine versus contentious" distinction into a quantitative scale, we now map the extent to which the different proposals at risk have been challenged in the public sphere. Starting with the challengers' contribution to the conflict, Table 4.4 shows that the Greek challengers were, on average, substantially more contentious than any others in Europe during the period under scrutiny. Challengers in Portugal were also very contentious, followed closely by Ireland, Spain, Italy, and Romania, while challengers in Germany were the least contentious. The similarities between Portugal and Spain as shown in Table 4.4. are instructive because protest event data tends

---

[7] The four categories are based on the absolute averages: $<0.25=1$; $>0.25=2$; $>0.5=3$; $>0.75=4$. We opted for this fourfold measure as extreme positions of -1 and 1 are empirically only observable with very few observations, which renders the alignment measure highly correlated with the intensity measure.

TABLE 4.4. *Country averages for contentiousness*
*(sorted by challenger contentiousness)*

|            | Challenger | Government | Third parties | *Overall* |
|------------|-----------|-----------|--------------|-----------|
| Greece     | 0.79      | 0.64      | 0.50         | 2.72      |
| Portugal   | 0.54      | 0.11      | 0.25         | 1.45      |
| Ireland    | 0.48      | 0.31      | 0.43         | 1.70      |
| Spain      | 0.47      | 0.20      | 0.32         | 1.46      |
| Italy      | 0.46      | 0.26      | 0.28         | 1.46      |
| Romania    | 0.41      | 0.50      | 0.28         | 1.61      |
| Hungary    | 0.38      | 0.39      | 0.38         | 1.53      |
| UK         | 0.32      | 0.25      | 0.41         | 1.31      |
| France     | 0.22      | 0.09      | 0.25         | 0.79      |
| Poland     | 0.17      | 0.07      | 0.20         | 0.61      |
| Latvia     | 0.16      | 0.14      | 0.21         | 0.66      |
| Germany    | 0.08      | 0.25      | 0.38         | 0.78      |

*Note:* The contentiousness measures for each actor have been standardized to a range from 0 to 1. Given that the overall measure gives a double weight to the challenger's contribution, its potential range runs from 0 to 4.

to lead to a different conclusion: "more contentious in Spain than Portugal" as remarked upon in the introductory section.

The country averages, however, hide significant variance within countries. As shown in Figure 4.2, in Greece and Germany the challenger's contentiousness is fairly similar across the five episodes, whereas Portugal, Ireland, Spain, and especially Romania and Hungary, exhibit a much wider spread regarding how strong a challenge materialized as a response to the proposed reforms. Although in several countries the institutional episodes are less contentious than the economic ones, this is not a general pattern (We return to this point in the section "Why Do Episodes Become Contentious?")

Is the challenge particularly intense or disruptive? To answer the question, Figure 4.3 shows the two dimensions used to measure challenger contentiousness. Overall, the figure indicates that the challengers' intensity and disruptiveness mostly align: The more frequently the challenger coalition intervenes in the conflict, the more likely it relies on disruptive actions (correlation coefficient $r=0.56$). There are, however, insightful deviations from that pattern. The strongest difference between intensity and disruption can be observed in the case of Zapatero's second austerity package (labeled as ES_eco2).[8] This episode, which spans the early phase of the sustained Spanish protest wave, is hugely disruptive. The Spanish challengers (including the Indignados) were able to mobilize frequently and bring masses to the streets (Portos 2019; Portos and Carvalho 2019). In comparison, the Portuguese episode from early 2011

---

[8] A list of all sixty proposals and the respective abbreviations can be found in Chapter 2.

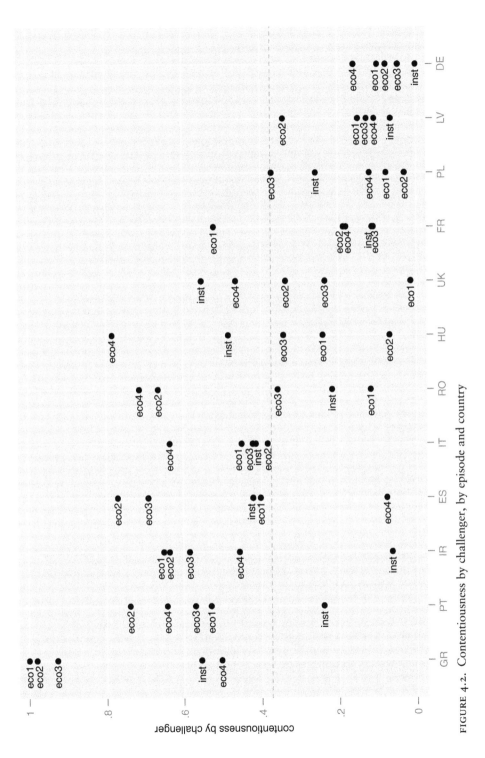

FIGURE 4.2. Contentiousness by challenger, by episode and country

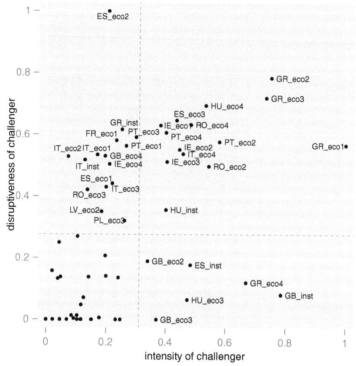

FIGURE 4.3. Intensity and disruptiveness of the challenger

(PT_eco2) shows a lower although still above-average disruptiveness but a far higher intensity of challenger actions. The latter indicates a considerably higher share of verbal activities and engagement in a sustained public controversy beyond moments of protest mobilization. In short, our new measure of challenger contentiousness captures crucial differences between the Portuguese and Spanish cases, as emphasized in the chapter's introduction. It allows comparing the extent and type of protest (as in classical protest event analysis) and the broader action repertoire at the disposal of those aiming to challenge the government's austerity programs.

Outliers in the direction of relatively high involvement but low disruptiveness come mainly from the United Kingdom. The Brexit episode (GB_inst) – with its direct-democratic campaign – is exemplary here as it involved intense struggles but had neither significant mass mobilization nor disruptive action during the period we examine. At a much higher level of disruption, the first Greek I.M.F. bailout (GR_eco1) exhibits a similar pattern of "intensity exceeding disruptiveness." This episode is very intense, but the challengers' actions are less disruptive than those throughout the second and third economic episodes in Greece (on the episodes' interrelatedness, see Chapter 12).

## Contentiousness by the Government and Third Parties

So far, we have only discussed challenger contentiousness, but the government and third parties also influence the conflict levels during an episode. Table 4.4, which we have presented earlier, already includes the summary measures for the two actor types per country. While Greece is also most contentious on these dimensions (followed by Romania), other countries' rank ordering differs. Notably, government and third-party contentiousness in Germany are about average, although the country had the fewest bottom-up challenges to the proposed measures.

Figure 4.4 maps each episode on the two dimensions of government and third-party contentiousness. As we can see, the relationship between government and third-party contentiousness is relatively close (r = 0.41), with a few important exceptions. At one extreme, we again have the Brexit referendum, where third-party contentiousness was much higher than government contentiousness. At the other extreme, we find the Romanian impeachment referendum, in which the government added much more fuel to the conflict than the third parties. Both cases are symptomatic of the kind of atypical actor

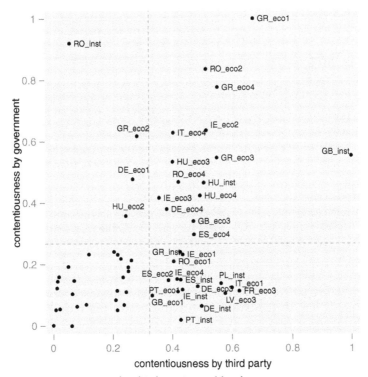

FIGURE 4.4. Contentiousness by third parties and by the government

constellations that may alter the dynamic of an episode. In the Romanian case, the government took a legally controversial decision to impeach the sitting president, Traian Basescu. In pushing the charge against Basescu, the government was much more active than average and was the most repressive among all episodes we study; in contrast, third parties were more conflicted. Although very active in the episode, they did not uniformly side with either the government or the challenger. We observe the opposite pattern in the case of Brexit. The government had won the 2015 general election with a promise to hold a referendum on EU membership. As the government was divided, government action was limited, and its contentiousness is only slightly above average, with the involved third parties clearly aligned with the government. Third-party actors included a range of domestic and international actors, most of whom took a strong position in favor of staying in the EU.

However, beyond these outliers, the pattern of variation shown in Figure 4.4 suggests a systematic relation. We may suspect that a government gets involved in a contentious episode to the extent that third parties are also involved and take sides (or vice versa). This findings supports Schattschneider's (1960: 1–2) maxim, "Nothing attracts a crowd as quickly as a fight." Notably, the link between government and third-party activities is particularly strong when we look at the intensity of their actions and not so much whether the third parties get involved in opposing or supporting the government's plans.

## Overall Contentiousness and Types of Contentious Episodes

Referring to Table 4.4, we can see that government and third-party contentiousness matter a great deal for overall contentiousness. They explain the singular position of Greece in our study: Not only did challengers act more contentiously in the Greek episodes, but government activity was also very intense and, in many cases, more repressive than the average. Third parties were also extremely active with up to 8.6 actions per week compared to an overall average of 1.7. All in all, this makes the Greek episodes by far the most contentious. Greece stands out with an average of 2.7 for overall contentiousness (on a range from 0 to 4), whereas the second-most "rebellious" country Ireland follows with 1.7 (see the last row in Table 4.4). Interestingly, we observe almost identical average values for Portugal and Spain – the two countries we used to introduce our approach.

Figure 4.5 shows the relationship between challenger contentiousness and third party/government contentiousness as included in our overall contentiousness measure. It is the empirical counterpart to the theoretical Table 4.1. As shown in the figure, in many episodes we observe a systematic relation between the contentiousness of all actors (r = 0.45). Thus, there are many "full-fledged episodes," most clearly illustrated by the Greek economic episodes 1–3 (N = 15), whereas most episodes in which challenger contentiousness is below or close to the average also show below-average contentiousness for the

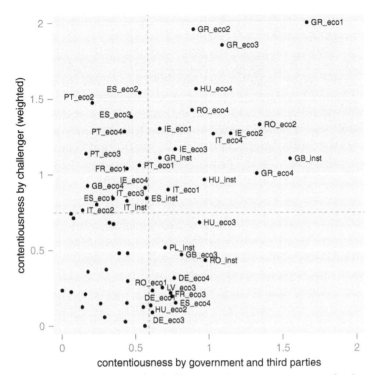

FIGURE 4.5. Contentiousness by the challenger and by the government/third parties
*Note*: The contentiousness by the challenger is weighted double for the overall measure of contentiousness (range 0–2).

government and third parties. We called them "low-intensity episodes" with primarily standard forms of verbal claims making (N = 20).

At the same time, we also find a few of what we called "top-down dominated episodes" (located in the bottom-right quadrant) with third-party and government activity exceeding challenger activity (N = 11). Examples are the German discussions surrounding the Greek bailout that tend to show very little challenger activity. Here, the contention was mostly introduced by the international debate on the topic and related to institutionalized conflicts and debates between the government and third parties. Finally, there are also several cases where high challenger contentiousness does not go together with high values on the third-party and government measure, leading to what we have called "bottom-up dominated episodes" (located in the upper-left quadrant) (N = 14). Particularly in the Portuguese cases, both government and third-party contentiousness were far lower than the contentiousness by the challenger. The same applies to the Spanish episode in 2011 (ES_eco2). As indicated previously, the reforms proposed by Zapatero faced one of the most forceful challengers in the street. As our data points out, this did not lead to an equally strong public engagement of other, more institutional actors. This contrasts sharply with the externally imposed I.M.F. bailouts in Greece, in which the government and third parties were involved at a comparable level to the challenger activity. Therefore, the figure visually confirms our observation that Greece has a singular position due to the high level of contentiousness for all actor types. At this point, we may only suspect that the stake of international actors and the extraordinary pressure they exerted on the Greek government could explain the division between fully fledged contentious episodes (as in Greece) and bottom-up dominated episodes (as in Portugal and some Spanish cases).

WHY DO EPISODES BECOME CONTENTIOUS?

In the following, we take a first step at explaining why certain episodes have seen more contentious interactions than others. While later chapters in this book will answer the question by studying the interaction dynamics at play more closely, we rely on two key insights from the classical social movement agenda. On the one hand, we have learned from the classical literature on social movements and protest that political mobilization depends on the combination of three sets of factors: grievances, mobilizing structures, and opportunities (McAdam et al. 1996). Grievances constitute the starting point: A shock like the financial and economic crisis in Europe and the harsh policy measures implemented to cope with it create a tremendous amount of popular discontent. People with grievances seek to express them, and they do so by raising their voices in different political arenas or by exiting from politics (Hirschman 1970). However, as the second and third set of factors highlight, they may only raise their voice to the extent that they have mobilizing capacity and face a favorable political context. Without these additional factors, we can hardly expect a fully fledged contentious episode involving a strong challenger and repeated interactions between the government and its challengers, with third parties being drawn into the conflict as well.

On the other hand, later work in the political process tradition has emphasized that scholars should move beyond too general, institutional, and static political opportunities. Instead, those in the field should examine issue-specific, discursive, and more dynamic elements of the political context (Giugni 2009; Koopmans et al. 2005; Meyer and Minkoff 2004). We adopt this idea and suggest distinguishing general factors from episode- or policy-specific factors systematically. Importantly, we suggest incorporating such a differentiation not only for the political context (the main focus of the cited literature) but also for grievances and mobilizing structures.

To operationalize the different features, we build upon Chapter 3, which introduced the episodes and embedded them in their economic and political context. We shift now from explaining a government's initial decision to launch a proposal to explaining the level of conflict sparked by it. To keep the analysis simple, we work with three measures that indicate the general and episode-specific *grievances*. First, we have combined the adjusted unemployment rate, GDP growth, and the items on respondents' satisfaction with the current and expected state of the national economy using factor analysis. Second, we also consider that in the countries hardest hit by the Great Recession, particularly in southern Europe, the economic problems triggered or amplified a political crisis (Della Porta 2015; Kriesi 2015). We constructed a factor based on trust in the national government, trust in the national parliament, and satisfaction with national democracy (again, relying on Eurobarometer data and combining the three with factor analysis). Finally, to measure the grievances directly related to the severity of the economic and institutional reform proposals, we rely on the checklist approach introduced in Chapter 3.

Regarding general *mobilizing structures*, we expect that countries with a tradition of economic protests and resistance are more likely to see the emergence of a strong challenger to proposed policy reforms in- and outside of the protest arena. This is because a history of contention and waves of protest typically leave behind dormant mobilizing structures and organizational capacities that may become reactivated in later phases (Taylor 1989). As Almeida (2003) highlights in the case of El Salvador, "such enduring organizations provide a fungible resource infrastructure from which protest waves may emerge in different political environments. One such political context is that of threat, whereby a set of *unfavorable* environmental conditions pushes groups into collective claims making." All the selected policy proposals at risk constitute such negative conditions that may reactivate preexisting mobilizing structures. To operationalize this aspect, we use the average number of days not worked due to strikes per 1,000 employees in the years before the crisis (2000–2009) (Vandaele 2016). As a more episode-specific type of mobilizing structure, we consider the range of organizations that opt to get involved in the struggle over a proposal. While a broader coalition might face more challenges regarding collective identity formation, we expect that, at least in the short run, it might be more likely to increase the contentiousness of an episode. Broad coalitions might mobilize a larger share of the population and draw on more (and more diverse) additional resources. Moreover, the government and potential third parties might also be more likely to respond to (at least parts of) a broad challenger coalition.[9]

Finally, the general *political context* is measured by combining a state's capacity (effectiveness) and its participatory quality (for details, see Chapter 3). The two aspects resemble Kitschelts' (1986) emphasis on the input and output sides of political systems as factors that shape the level and type of social

---

[9] To measure this aspect, we rely on the breadth of the challenger coalition (for a detailed discussion of the concept and measurement, see Chapter 5).

movement actions.[10] The general thrust of Kitschelt's argument is that challengers face the worst of all constellations in states that tend to be closed on the input side and lack capacity on the output side. In addition to state structures, we rely in this chapter on Kriesi et al.'s (1995) argument about the legacy of the political left as another factor that may (still) boost present-day conflicts over economic reforms due to pre-existing networks and historical reference points. For the episode-specific features, we rely on the electoral vulnerability and the ideological composition of the government at the launch of the proposal (for the measures, see again Chapter 3). Many of the harshest economic reforms during the Great Recession were proposed and implemented by left-wing governments. Thus, it is likely that they are met with strong resistance from their former allies in the streets, who contest the "betrayal" and "brand dilution" on the political left (for the case of Latin America, see Lupu 2014; Roberts 2013).[11]

Given the small number of cases (N = 60 episodes) and the fact that some of our contextual variables are related, we first present simple bivariate correlations and t-tests in Table 4.5 before showing some regressions to assess the impact of our independent variables in a multivariate framework. We present results for both challenger contentiousness and the episode's overall contentiousness in line with our interest in the challengers and the interactions between all actor types.

As evident from the correlations in Table 4.5, we observe a positive relationship between the level of grievances and the contentiousness of an episode. All our general and episode-specific indicators of grievances are positively related to challenger contentiousness and overall contentiousness. This finding supports previous research highlighting that the severity and accumulation of crises are important factors in explaining the political consequences of the Great Recession in Europe (e.g., Bernburg 2015; Burden and Wichowsky 2014; Grasso and Giugni 2016; Hernández and Kriesi 2016; Hutter et al. 2018; Kriesi et al. 2020). Except for the relationship between political crisis and overall contentiousness, these relations are statistically significant. Resources or rather a history of contention also seem to matter as the level of strikes during the pre-crisis period and the breadth of the challenger coalition are both positively related to our two variables of interest. The strong correlation of pre-crisis strikes is most notable.

---

[10] The focus on both sides of political systems is also prominent in recent studies on the quality of democracies (e.g., Dahlberg and Holmberg 2014).

[11] Importantly, such a reasoning goes against another prominent interpretation in the social movement literature that traditionally expected stronger protests in the streets when the mainstream left is in opposition as it can then act as an ally of ideologically close social movements, while, it needs to respond to broader societal demands and political constraints when in government (see Kriesi 1995; Meguire 1995).

TABLE 4.5. *Bivariate correlation table (N = 60)*

|  | Challenger contentiousness | Overall contentiousness |
|---|---|---|
| Economic crisis | 0.40[***] | 0.27[**] |
| Political crisis | 0.33[**] | 0.21 |
| Crisis overall (economic and political) | 0.39[***] | 0.27[**] |
| Severity of proposal | 0.32[**] | 0.28[**] |
| Level of strikes (precrisis) | 0.51[***] | 0.53[***] |
| Breadth of challenger coalition | 0.34[***] | 0.33[**] |
| Quality of democracy[1] | −0.34[*** 2] | −0.46[*** 2] |
| Tradition of split left | 0.40[*** 2] | 0.26[** 2] |
| Electoral vulnerability | 0.14 | 0.05 |
| Left in power | 0.12 | 0.11 |

[*] $p < 0.10$, [**] $p < 0.05$, [***] $p < 0.01$
[1] operationalized as a dummy (1= weak state capacity and weak participatory democracy)
[2] t-test (reported are the differences of the groups' means)

For the features of the political context, our results are mixed. There seems to be a strong negative relation between contentiousness and the quality of a democracy. Though we operationalize the democratic quality with an indicator that considers both input and output, the relation is driven primarily by the input dimension. This finding suggests that the more citizens and other actors can influence policy making through institutional means, the less they turn to contentious actions to make their voices heard. Our measure for the overall contentiousness of an episode is also negatively related to the quality of democracy. In addition, our results indicate a statistically significantly higher degree of contentiousness in countries with a traditionally split left (France, Greece, Italy, Portugal, and Spain), while the two more episode-specific political factors – electoral vulnerability and the government's ideological composition – do not seem to have a strong effect.

Next, we assess these variables in a multivariate framework and introduce the indicators for grievances, resources, and political context in a stepwise fashion (see Table 4.6). We do so to avoid introducing a high number of (often related) predictors given our small sample size. Overall, the results for challenger contentiousness (Models M1–M4) and overall contentiousness (Models M5–M8) confirm the bivariate analyses. For the challenger, the only change in the grievance model (M1) is that proposal severity is no longer a significant predictor when we control for the extent of the crises in a given country. This makes sense as proposals are frequently linked to the severity of the Great Recession in a country (as shown in Chapter 3). Notably, neither the severity of

TABLE 4.6. *Impact of general and episode-specific factors on challenger and overall contentiousness (OLS regressions)*

| | Challenger contentiousness | | | | Overall contentiousness | | | |
|---|---|---|---|---|---|---|---|---|
| | M1 | M2 | M3 | M4 | M5 | M6 | M7 | M8 |
| Extent of crises | 0.06** | | | 0.03 | 0.10 | | | 0.03 |
| | (2.33) | | | (1.20) | (1.31) | | | (0.06) |
| Proposal severity | 0.07 | | | | 0.22 | | | |
| | (1.50) | | | | (1.54) | | | |
| History of strikes | | 0.00*** | | 0.00 | | 0.00*** | | 0.00** |
| | | (4.92) | | (1.23) | | (5.14) | | (2.46) |
| Breadth challenger | | 0.23*** | | 0.23** | | 0.65*** | | 0.58*** |
| | | (3.32) | | (3.32) | | (3.22) | | (2.94) |
| Democratic quality | | | -0.25*** | -0.15** | | | -0.92*** | -0.55*** |
| | | | (3.50) | (2.18) | | | (4.45) | (2.73) |
| Split left (=1) | | | 0.24*** | 0.16** | | | 0.51*** | 0.14 |
| | | | (3.82) | (2.1) | | | (2.85) | (0.64) |
| Elect. vulnerability | | | -0.03 | | | | -0.00 | |
| | | | (-0.68) | | | | (-0.05) | |
| Left in government | | | -0.02 | | | | -0.06 | |
| | | | (-0.81) | | | | (-0.86) | |
| Constant | 0.19* | 0.09 | 0.35** | 0.05 | 0.80** | 0.52*** | 1.16*** | 0.47** |
| | (1.77) | (1.44) | (2.45) | (0.83) | (2.42) | (2.87) | (2.78) | (2.50) |
| N | 60 | 60 | 60 | 60 | 60 | 60 | 60 | 60 |
| r² | 0.18 | 0.38 | 0.32 | 0.47 | 0.11 | 0.39 | 0.32 | 0.46 |

* $p < 0.10$, ** $p < 0.05$, *** $p < 0.01$

the political and economic crisis nor proposal severity are significant in the overall contentiousness models. Note that we have also tested the effects of the type of proposal. The only statistically significant impact is that bank bailouts face less contentiousness by the challenger (compared to the reference category of structural reforms). In the resource model for challenger and overall contentiousness (M2 and M6), we observe a significant effect for the historical legacy of strike activities and the breadth of the challenger coalition. The model for political context for challenger contentiousness (M3) again shows a significant negative effect for democratic quality and a positive effect for a history of a split left. Both results hold for overall contentiousness (M7) as well. When introducing all previously significant variables into a joint model (M4 respectively M8), the most notable effects are that (a) a broad challenger coalition tends to correlate with more contentious conflicts and (b) bad democratic quality seems to have a mobilizing effect. The effect of grievances, however, appears to be entirely mediated by resources and the political context.

## CONCLUSIONS

This chapter has set out to conceptualize, measure, and map how contentious the sixty episodes covered by this book have been. The chapter's main contribution consists of developing a multidimensional understanding of contentiousness and introducing a way to observe it empirically. We have conceptualized contentiousness by the combined behavior of all three stylized actor types (challenger, government, and third parties). More specifically, we have outlined how the intensity and specific action repertoire of each actor may increase conflict levels in the public sphere. In a nutshell, an episode is most contentious if all three actors become intensively involved; the challenger moves beyond verbal opposition by staging more disruptive protests; the government moves beyond verbal claims making to forms of repressive behavior; and third parties add fuel to the fire by clearly aligning with either the challenger or the government

In discussing our empirical results, we first focused on challenger contentiousness, which is typically the object of social movement studies. We highlighted the complex relationship between the intensity of challenger actions and their disruptiveness. Second, we highlighted the relation between the contentiousness induced by the different actor types. Strong interaction dynamics are particularly evident in the case of Greece, where all actors show elevated levels of contentiousness, leading to so-called fully fledged contentious episodes. The Greek story contrasts with the Portuguese and Spanish cases in 2011 that we introduced at the beginning of the chapter. Based on our new measure, we label these Spanish and Portuguese episodes as "bottom up-dominated" with a comparatively strong presence of challengers. Importantly, our measure also captures differences in the form of the challenge at the time. The Spanish resistance to Zapatero's second austerity package in 2011 trumps all other episodes in terms of the challengers' capacity to mobilize massively in the streets. In contrast, the Spanish challengers were comparatively weak regarding representation in the public debate with less-disruptive action forms. In this regard, the analogous Portuguese episode with the emergence of Geração à Rasca [Screwed generation] is different, already hinting at the starkly different trajectories that the political conflict over austerity have taken in the two Iberian countries (Carvalho 2018; Portos and Carvalho 2019).

Finally, we have taken the first step in explaining why some episodes have been more contentious than others. The results indicate that general and episode-specific grievances, mobilizing structures, and political contexts all affect an episode's overall contentiousness, particularly challenger contentiousness. That said, in the full model, the most substantial effects refer to the scope of the challenger coalition and the quality of democracy. We observe the most contentious struggles when the challenger coalition is broad and in contexts with lower democratic quality. The helpful distinction between general and episode-specific explanatory factors draws upon one of CEA's key contributions: its ability to draw upon time-variant context while pursuing a systematic comparative analysis.

Further chapters will move beyond our aggregative approach and account for the dynamics *within* each episode to better understand how the interactions ultimately shaped the conflict and its outcome. However, before that, we will disentangle the actors lumped together under the broad headings of governments, challengers, and third parties to uncover who has actually been engaged in contentious struggles in the age of austerity.

# 5

## Actor Configurations and Coalitions in Contentious Episodes

Theresa Gessler and Swen Hutter

INTRODUCTION

So far, we have mapped what the three stylized actors did in the (more or less) contentious episodes, treating all three actors as unitary entities. This chapter takes the analysis a step further by describing features of the coalitions and actor configurations. In doing so, we answer who the actors involved in the conflicts over austerity and institutional reforms were and how they are typically related to each other. Available protest event studies on the Great Recession indicate at least three organizational features of the recent protest wave in Europe (e.g., Carvalho 2019; Diani and Kousis 2014; Hunger and Lorenzini 2019; Portos 2016, 2017; Portos and Carvalho 2019). First, they highlight the crucial role of institutionalized actors, particularly labor unions, in bringing the masses to the streets early on when the crisis hit the European continent in 2008 and 2009. Second, newly established and loose networks played an essential part in the southern European countries hit hardest by the crisis – the Portuguese Geração à Rasca, Democracia Real, and the Indignados in Spain as well as their Greek counterpart Aganaktismeni are illustrative of this dynamic. Third, the moment of such noninstitutionalized players who entered the protest scene tended to be relatively short lived, but, remarkably, even in Spain, there are indications of a process of institutionalization as formal organizations (trade unions and political parties) became more important in later phases of the protest wave.

CEA's methodological toolkit allows us to go beyond descriptions (like those in classical protest event research) of the actors that had called for, taken part in, or organized a protest. It enables us to breakdown and relate a challenger coalition to the other parties involved in the conflict. While such an encompassing and relational view of claim makers and their objects is central to the DOC program (McAdam et al. 2001), we also make use of previous concepts from the political process approach. Its application has been criticized for being overly static and institutional (e.g., Goodwin and Jasper 1999), but its conceptual apparatus has always incorporated features of the actor configuration and even interaction dynamics (for an overview, see Kriesi 2004). A crucial distinction is between the configuration of allies and the configuration of adversaries (e.g., della Porta and Rucht 1995; Kriesi 1985; Kriesi et al. 1995). In our case, the former refers to the actors who publicly intervene on behalf of the organizations and the networks that oppose a proposal through contentious performances – while the latter refers to the actors who engage on behalf of the government and its stance.

As Rucht (2004: 199) aptly noted, such a dualistic view of actor configurations comes at the expense of "neglecting the role of additional (and important) reference groups of movements: bystander publics, third parties, and mediators." While CEA does not consider the role of bystanders, it systematically incorporates the function of third parties – the umbrella term under which all actors who publicly engage in the conflict over a policy proposal without being a member of any one of the two opposing coalitions, that is, the government and the challenger, are subsumed.[1] In this regard, CEA follows more relational approaches in social movement research (e.g., Diani 2013, 2015). Our approach allows us to answer the question empirically regarding the extent to which third parties act as mediators, or whether they clearly side with the government or the challenger. Apart from uncovering the diversity and institutional character of the main contestants, this chapter thus considers the different functions played by third parties in the sixty episodes, thereby improving our understanding of actor coalitions in contentious politics during the Great Recession.

We follow Rucht's (2004: 202) caveat that such an interactionist conceptualization of social movements and contentious politics becomes "quite complicated," and ultimately, "complex relationships and processes can only be grasped step by step in a process of gradual disentangling." Therefore, we structure the analysis as follows: Initially, we introduce the institutional character of all coded actors before we focus on the challenger coalitions and then clarify the functions and nature of third parties. Finally, we combine all information on the actors and their relations to map the differing actor configuration across countries and episodes.

## INSTITUTIONAL CHARACTERISTICS OF THE ACTORS IN CONTENTIOUS EPISODES

To get an overview of the actors who have been the most active in the contentious episodes covered by our research, the first three columns in Table 5.1

---

[1]  As defined in Chapter 1, the government category includes all public authorities that propose the policy change and are linked to the government: the head of government and other members of the cabinet as well as all public officials. The challenger category includes all actors who oppose the government's proposal, at least partly, outside the routine, institutionalized arenas of interest and articulated by means of sustained and coordinated collective action.

TABLE 5.1. *Institutional character of all actors, by percentages*

| | N | Overall share | Share among government | Share among challengers | Share among third parties |
|---|---|---|---|---|---|
| **International actors** | | | | | |
| EU actors | 205 | 3.0 | – | – | 8.9 |
| Troika–E.C.B.–I.M.F.–Eurozone | 198 | 2.9 | – | – | 8.7 |
| foreign governments | 129 | 1.9 | – | – | 5.6 |
| other international actors | 110 | 1.6 | – | 0.2 | 4.6 |
| **National governmental actors** | | | | | |
| government | 1,865 | 27.3 | **88.9** | 1.4 | 0.8 |
| technocratic government | 104 | 1.5 | 5.0 | – | – |
| president | 89 | 1.3 | 0.3 | 0.6 | 2.9 |
| local/regional authorities | 121 | 1.8 | – | 1.9 | 3.2 |
| national bank | 53 | 0.8 | – | – | 2.1 |
| other government institutions | 187 | 2.7 | 1.8 | 1.8 | 4.6 |
| government parties | 506 | 7.4 | **3.8** | 5.7 | 12.5 |
| **Business, experts, media** | | | | | |
| business | 244 | 3.6 | – | 2.8 | 7.6 |
| experts/media | 125 | 1.8 | – | 0.8 | 4.6 |
| **Opposition parties** | | | | | |
| mainstream opposition | 868 | 12.7 | – | 15.5 | 20.9 |
| radical-left opposition | 276 | 4.0 | – | 8.7 | 2.5 |
| radical-right opposition | 87 | 1.3 | – | 1.3 | 2.4 |
| **Civil society** | | | | | |
| nongovernmental orgs | 137 | 2.0 | – | 2.2 | 3.5 |
| social movement orgs | 364 | 5.3 | – | 11.8 | 2.9 |
| student orgs | 66 | 1.0 | – | 2.5 | – |
| **Unions** | | | | | |
| unions | 1,107 | 16.2 | – | **42.5** | 1.6 |
| Total | 6,841 | 100.0 | 100.0 | 100.0 | 100.0 |

*Note*: The table shows the distribution of twenty actor categories in the overall dataset (N = 6,841 actions). The top three categories per actor type are highlighted in bold.

present twenty actor categories, the total number of observations for each category, and their share across all episodes. As with the first cut at the action categories in Chapter 4, we disregard the division into sixty episodes and instead treat each action equally. The actor categories refer to the institutional characteristics of actors, ranging from international bodies through national government institutions to parliamentary opposition, social movement organizations (SMOs), and unions. The categories are based on a first aggregation, given that we coded the actors in great detail (see Chapter 2).

As is apparent from Table 5.1, national governments and their members (27.3 percent) are the most active group across all episodes. At some distance, they are followed by unions (16.2 percent) and parties from the mainstream opposition (12.7 percent). Most of the other specific actor categories shown in the table account for only a small share of the actions coded for all sixty contentious episodes, including individual governing parties (7.4 percent) and social movement organizations (SMOs) (5.3 percent).

Table 5.1 also presents the share of each category among the three stylized actors (we highlight the three most prominent categories per actor type in bold). As expected, there are apparent differences in the composition of each of the stylized actors. Unsurprisingly, the government almost exclusively consists of national governments and their officials – heads of government or cabinet ministers – strictly understood (88.9 percent). The figure becomes even higher if we consider the 5 percent of so-called technocratic governments, mainly referring to the Italian Monti and the Greek Papademos government, which came into office within days of each other in November 2011. Less than 4 percent of all government actions are attributed to what we call "governing parties," that is, members of governing parties that do not hold an executive office (e.g., leaders of parliamentary groups).

In contrast to the government, the challengers' institutional characteristics are more diverse, although labor unions are by far the largest group, with 42.5 percent of all challenger actions. This finding mirrors previous results based on protest event analysis (e.g., Hunger and Lorenzini 2019; Portos and Carvalho 2019), and it also reflects our emphasis on economic policy proposals. The second most important challengers are political parties, both mainstream and radical-left opposition parties (15.5 and 8.7 percent, respectively). Note that parties from the radical right hardly appear in the contentious episodes studied in this volume. SMOs, by contrast, constitute a bigger group, making up 11.8 percent of the challenger actions. The first cut at the dataset supports claims about the crucial role of labor unions in challenging the national governments during the Great Recession.

The category of third parties is most diverse in terms of its institutional characteristics. The mainstream opposition is relatively important in this group (20.9 percent), just like speakers from governing parties (12.5 percent). In contrast to the other two stylized types of actors, there is also a significant share of international actors, including EU institutions, Troika and Eurozone actors, other national governments, and other international actors (each constituting between 4.6 and 8.9 percent of third-party actions). Using the terms suggested by Koopmans and Statham (2010), we observe both horizontal and vertical Europeanization/internationalization. Moreover, the data suggests that the third parties are mainly composed of conventional institutional actors rather than more peripheral actors. The share of civil society actors, unions, and the two types of radical opposition parties add up to roughly 13 percent across all episodes. The overrepresentation of institutional "insiders" complements the finding from Chapter 4 that most actions by third parties referred to the governments' proposals and actions, and not to the challengers.

WHO IS CHALLENGING THE GOVERNMENT?

Having outlined the broad picture, we now focus on the two most diverse stylized actor categories – the challengers and the third parties. At first we reveal which actors launched the challenge to the reform proposals in the Great Recession. We use two characteristics to describe a challenger coalition (understood as "objective" coalitions).[2] First, we look at its *diversity*: Is it a narrow set of actors that aims to challenge the government's proposal in a given episode, or is the challenger coalition composed of a diverse group of actors? Second, we analyze its dominant *institutional character*: Which types of actors dominate the challenger coalition? Were the governments faced with a more conventional institutional challenge or a more grassroots one? Are there cross-actor-alliances at play?

As we break our analysis down to the level of individual episodes, and given the small shares of many of the categories shown before, we summarize the organizations in a reduced set of four groups: (1) *Unions*, as the most critical category among the challengers; (2) *civil-society organizations* (CSOs) (including S.M.O.s, N.G.O.s, students as well as business actors, experts, and media representatives); (3) *opposition parties* of all kinds; and (4) *governmental actors* (mainly referring to members of governing parties that joined forces with the challengers). These four groups encompass the spectrum of the institutional character of the challenger coalition. The diversity of the challenger coalitions is assessed by their distribution across the four groups: The more equal the representation of these four groups, the more diverse the alliance. To construct an indicator, we followed the agenda-setting literature (e.g., Boydstun et al. 2014). We calculated Shannon's diversity measure, ranging from zero to the natural logarithm of the number of categories.

In Table 5.2, we show the average diversity of the challenger coalition and the share of each of the four actor groups per country. Note that we now focus

---

[2] Objective coalitions refer to actors that are bound together by a common objective but not necessarily by common actions.

TABLE 5.2. *Diversity and institutional character of challenger by country*

| Country | Average diversity | Labor unions | Opposition parties | Civil society | Governmental actors |
|---------|-------------------|--------------|--------------------|---------------|---------------------|
| PT      | 1.03              | **34.2**     | **31.1**           | 16.2          | 18.6                |
| IE      | 0.97              | **28.0**     | **33.8**           | 25.7          | 12.5                |
| GR      | 0.91              | **51.6**     | 11.0               | 17.2          | 20.1                |
| HU      | 0.85              | 15.6         | **34.4**           | **43.1**      | 6.9                 |
| LV      | 0.78              | **44.2**     | 6.5                | **41.8**      | 7.6                 |
| U.K.    | 0.78              | **35.8**     | 18.5               | **31.6**      | 14.1                |
| ES      | 0.76              | **41.2**     | **44.5**           | 13.1          | 1.2                 |
| RO      | 0.73              | **38.6**     | **32.7**           | 0.0           | **28.7**            |
| PL      | 0.69              | **48.2**     | 12.1               | 24.4          | 15.4                |
| DE      | 0.66              | 3.3          | **26.6**           | 13.3          | **36.8**            |
| IT      | 0.43              | **74.9**     | 13.2               | 10.8          | 1.1                 |
| FR      | 0.24              | **68.0**     | 0.3                | **31.7**      | 0.0                 |
| *Average* | *0.74*          | *40.3*       | *22.1*             | *22.4*        | *13.6*              |

*Note:* The table shows the average diversity of the challenger coalition (Shannon's diversity measure) and the proportion by actor category. The numbers are calculated as an overall average (N = 60 episodes) and by country (N = 5 episodes). Categories with more than 25 percent highlighted in bold.

on episodes as our units of analysis (N = 60 overall, 5 for each country). Compared to the theoretical maximum, the average challenger coalition is not that diverse, with a value of 0.74 compared to the possible maximum of 1.38. Interestingly, the Portuguese episodes stand out with the broadest coalitions, followed by Ireland and Greece. In contrast, the challenger coalitions in France and Italy are most limited in terms of diversity.

As already visible from our previous analysis in Table 5.1, the low diversity within the challenger coalition is due to the strong presence of unions. Unions account for 68 percent of all coded challenger actions in France and almost 75 percent in Italy. On average, 40.3 percent of challenger actions are by unions, although they are mostly absent in Germany (3 percent) and Hungary (16 percent). In Hungary, the challenge has been launched by civil society actors and opposition parties. In Germany, the most important actors who challenged the government's proposal have come from within its party ranks. As the last column in Table 5.2 indicates, the strong presence of governmental actors is exceptional for the German episodes and – to a lesser extent – the Romanian and Greek cases. In contrast, the most common challenger coalition type has been unions plus opposition parties (Portugal and Spain) or unions plus civil society organizations (Latvia, the U.K., and France).

Moving from country averages to the level of individual episodes, we reduce the complexity of the available measures further by indicating whether one of the four types of actors (unions, opposition parties, C.S.O.s, or governmental

TABLE 5.3. *Types of challenger coalitions*

| Unions >25% | Opposition >25% | C.S.O. >25% | Government >25% | Number of episodes | Average contentiousness by challenger |
|---|---|---|---|---|---|
| ✓ | ✓ | ✗ | ✗ | 16 | 0.50 |
| ✓ | ✗ | ✗ | ✗ | 14 | 0.41 |
| ✓ | ✗ | ✓ | ✗ | 6 | 0.39 |
| ✗ | ✓ | ✓ | ✗ | 6 | 0.31 |
| ✗ | ✗ | ✗ | ✓ | 5 | 0.33 |
| ✗ | ✗ | ✓ | ✗ | 3 | 0.32 |
| ✗ | ✗ | ✓ | ✓ | 3 | 0.11 |
| ✗ | ✓ | ✗ | ✗ | 3 | 0.20 |
| ✓ | ✗ | ✗ | ✓ | 1 | 0.66 |
| ✗ | ✓ | ✗ | ✓ | 1 | 0.08 |
| ✗ | ✓ | ✓ | ✓ | 1 | 0.07 |
| 37 | 27 | 19 | 11 | | |

*Note*: The number of cases in the second last column indicates the number of episodes with a particular challenger coalition. For example, sixteen episodes are characterized by a strong presence of unions plus opposition parties. The number of cases in the last row indicates the number of episodes in which a certain type of actor is represented with more than 25% regardless of what the share of the other actors is. For example, unions are represented with more than 25% in thirty-seven of the sixty episodes.

actors) are represented with more than 25 percent, that is, overrepresented as compared to equal representation. Table 5.3 shows the distribution of the eleven empirically observed combinations. The second to last column shows the frequency of the respective challenger coalition among the sixty cases. The bottom row lists the number of episodes in which the particular actor type has been a central part of the challenger coalition regardless of its varying allies.

Again, the findings in Table 5.3 underscore that labor unions were central in challenging austerity and institutional reforms in Europe since the onset of the Great Recession. Unions formed a fundamental part of the challenger coalition in more than 60 percent of all episodes (37 out of 60 cases). The two most common coalitions were unions with a strong presence of opposition parties (N = 16) or unions alone (N = 14). The other three patterns that are present in at least five episodes are (a) unions with CSOs (N = 6), (b) opposition parties with CSOs (N = 6), and (c) opposition from within the government (N = 5). All other potential combinations, particularly those involving governmental actors, are far less common.

The aggregate numbers shown in Table 5.3 qualify the findings from the previous chapter that suggested that a more diverse coalition implies a more serious threat as it is associated with higher levels of challenger contentiousness. On the one hand, the focus on the characteristics of the challenger coalitions underlines that this is a positive but weak association. Several types of challenger coalitions can result in highly contentious conflicts. To illustrate, we can draw a useful contrast between the two episodes with the broadest coalitions in our study: the events surrounding the first bailout in Germany and the midterm adjustment in Greece. With a challenger diversity of around 1.3, both episodes are sustained by far more diverse coalitions than the average episode. However, in Germany, this coalition was mostly inactive despite the inclusion of various actors (challenger contentiousness = 0.04). The Greek coalition, however, was among the most active with 4.96 adversarial actions per week, mobilizing masses in its wake and resulting in a very high level of contentiousness (0.98).

On the other hand, the results indicate that union presence, especially in alliance with opposition parties, is associated with a slightly higher contentiousness level. Apart from the one case in which unions and government actors joined forces (this was the first austerity-related episode in Romania), the highest average value of 0.50 reported in Table 5.3 refers to cases when labor unions and opposition parties joined forces to challenge a government proposal. Above-average challenger contentiousness characterizes twelve of the sixteen episodes in this group: all four economic episodes in Portugal, two Spanish cases (the ones centered around Zapatero's first austerity package and the one introduced by his successor Rajoy in 2012; ES_eco1 and ES_eco3) but also the Irish conflicts over the I.M.F. bailout and the related first and second austerity budgets (IE_eco1 to IE eco_3). The exclusively union-dominated episodes have a slightly lower average of 0.41. Highly contentious examples from this group are all four economic episodes in Italy, three of the Greek episodes (the first two bailout episodes – GR_eco1 and GR_eco3 – and GR_inst, the one related to the closure of the public broadcaster) as well as the conflicts around the 2010 pension reforms and freezing of the budget proposed by then French President Sarkozy and Prime Minister Fillon (FR_eco1).

The constellation most often examined in social movement research is when civil society forces either align with unions or opposition parties. The most contentious cases for the former dynamic are the episodes around the Greek midterm adjustment program (GR_eco2) and around the second austerity program of the Spanish Zapatero government in 2011 (ES_eco2) that ultimately triggered the Indignados movement. Thus, our CEA-based measures confirm the crucial difference in the organizational makeup of the challengers in the streets of Spain and Portugal in 2011: much more union-dominated in Portugal in comparison to Spain (Carvahlo 2019; Portos 2016, 2017). Regarding the alliance of C.S.O.s and opposition parties, the episodes with above-average contentiousness are the institutional one in Hungary, the water tax in Ireland (IE_eco4), and the U.K.'s 2011 welfare reform (UK_eco4). As shown in Table 5.2, civil society organizations were highly active in the Hungarian episodes more generally. In the institutional reform episode, which concerned a law that increased state regulation of independent media, they succeeded in bringing together a coalition of opposition parties from all sides, with civil society actors representing the media and loose networks on Facebook to reach an unusually high conflict level.

Figure 5.1 illustrates the main findings on the relationship between the institutional characteristics and a coalition's ability to intensively and disruptively challenge the government proposal. First, we do not find a strong association between the institutional makeup of the challenger coalition and its contentiousness, indicating that several types of alliances may lead to the same outcome. Second, although we do not find a relation overall, union-dominated coalitions are linked to higher levels of challenger contentiousness (as indicated

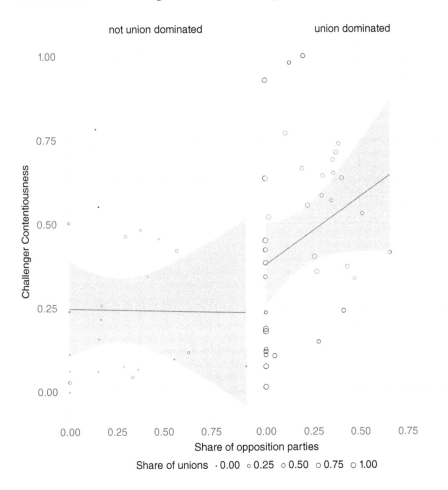

FIGURE 5.1. Types of challenger coalition and contentiousness by the challenger unions plus opposition parties

*Note*: Episode classified as more, respectively, less than 25% involvement of unions.

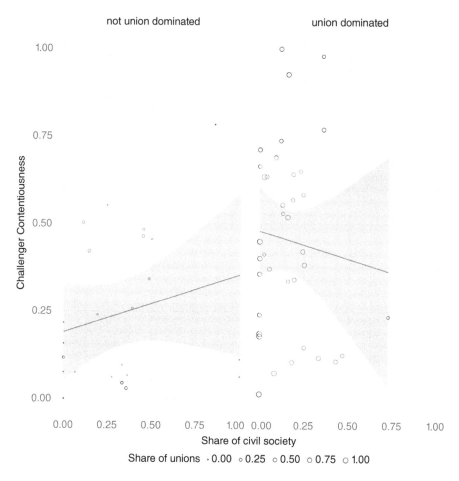

FIGURE 5.1. (*cont.*)

by the much higher values in the graphs on the right). Finally, the upper-level graphs show that the more unions joined forces with opposition parties, the stronger the challenge they posed (note that the direct effect of union presence and its interaction with an opposition dummy are also statistically significant in a simple OLS regression).

## WHAT ROLE DO THE THIRD PARTIES PLAY? AND WITH WHOM?

Having described the diversity and institutional characteristics of the challenger coalition, we turn to the third parties that also engage publicly in an episode without being a member of either the government or the challenger coalition. As posited in the introductory section, the third parties may vary in institutional

TABLE 5.4. *Positioning of third parties by country*

| | Average position | Proportion with target government | Weekly number of adversarial actions | Weekly number of mediation actions |
|---|---|---|---|---|
| Ireland | 0.44 | 0.97 | 2.1 | 0.2 |
| Hungary | 0.39 | 0.82 | 1.3 | 0.3 |
| U.K. | 0.33 | 0.92 | 2.5 | 0.1 |
| Portugal | 0.28 | 0.89 | 1.1 | 0.2 |
| Poland | 0.25 | 0.91 | 0.3 | 0.0 |
| Italy | 0.25 | 0.93 | 1.6 | 0.3 |
| Germany | 0.21 | 0.99 | 2.5 | 0.6 |
| Latvia | 0.20 | 0.94 | 0.4 | 0.1 |
| France | 0.18 | 0.96 | 1.2 | 0.0 |
| Greece | −0.05 | 0.95 | 6.8 | 0.2 |
| Romania | −0.10 | 0.78 | 1.4 | 0.3 |
| Spain | −0.42 | 0.86 | 1.0 | 0.1 |
| Average | 0.16 | 0.91 | 1.8 | 0.2 |

*Note*: The table shows the average position of the third parties, the proportion of actions targeting the government as well as the weekly standardized numbers of adversarial actions (siding clearly with one of the main contestants), and mediating actions (aiming for a compromise and negotiations between the two). The numbers are calculated as overall (N = 60 episodes) and country averages (N = 4 episodes).

character and play different roles – ranging from mediators to players with a firm place in either the configuration of allies (when visibly siding with the challenger coalition without being engaged in contentious performances themselves) or the configuration of adversaries (when visibly siding with the government without being a member of the governing coalition or any state institution). Therefore, we are first interested in the positioning of the third parties before considering their diversity and institutional character.

To understand the positioning and roles of the third parties in the sixty episodes, Table 5.4 presents another set of indicators by country. As in the previous chapter, we analyze the average position taken by the third parties when looking at what we labeled there as "adversarial actions," that is, actions that side with one of the two major contestants. As the results show, the average position across all sixty episodes is 0.16 (on a scale from −1 = full support of the government to +1 = full support of challenger). This means that the third parties did indeed occupy varying positions in the actor configurations across episodes. Moreover, we find clear-cut country differences. In most countries, the third parties lean towards the challengers' side and thus belong to the configuration of allies (most strongly in Ireland and Hungary). In contrast, we observe a relatively strong bias towards the government's side in Spain, with an average position of −0.42, that might be another reason for the sustained protest mobilization that Spain experienced in the period under scrutiny (for a comparative assessment, see Kriesi 2020).

While their place in the actor configuration varies across countries, the third-party actions mainly target the government and not the challenger. As shown, the average proportion of statements by third parties that target the government amounts to more than 90 percent (see the second column in Table 5.4). The high numbers underscore that third parties mainly interacted with the government, positively or negatively. The strong government focus reflects that episodes under scrutiny in our study were triggered by the threat induced into the political debate by the government's reform plans, not by mobilization from below.

As discussed in Chapter 4, the absolute number of coded adversarial actions by third parties varies considerably across countries and episodes – once more indicated by their weekly counts as shown in Table 5.4. The numbers are an instructive benchmark when judging how frequently third parties acted as mediator, either by suggesting the proposal's modification or acting as a broker in negotiations between a challenger and the government. Mediation is an exception. We only observe an average of 0.2 mediating actions per week as compared to 1.8 adversarial actions. In both absolute and relative terms, the third parties in Germany have most strongly acted as mediators – often mediating among the opposing factions from within the governing parties, but we observe hardly any mediation in France and Poland.

In sum, the country averages already suggest that the so-called third parties mainly targeted the government and hardly intervened as mediators in the contentious episodes around austerity and institutional reform we analyze here. Before delving into episode-level differences, we first analyze the actors' institutional characteristics included under the broad third-party label. To do so, we use a slightly modified grouping, following the distribution of actors that we have previously analyzed (see Table 5.1). Unlike our categorization of challengers, we do not single out unions but instead introduce a distinction between other governmental actors and government parties. Specifically, we distinguish between four groups: (a) governing parties (members of the governing party); (b) other governmental actors (including what we have labeled "international actors" and "national executive actors"); (c) opposition parties; and (d) civil society plus unions. Table 5.5 outlines the diversity and institutional character of the third parties overall and by country.

The third parties were not more diverse than the challengers, with an average diversity of 0.81 compared to 0.74 for the challenger coalition. Generally, the overview shows that governmental actors were the most prominent group among the third parties (with almost 50 percent), followed by opposition parties (25 percent). C.S.O.s (including unions) and governing parties are responsible for less than 20 percent of all actions across all episodes. If we consider that the opposition category is mainly composed of mainstream parties, it is fair to conclude that the third parties are institutional insiders. The most diverse countries with third parties actively engaged in the

TABLE 5.5. *Diversity and institutional character of third parties, by country*

|  | Diversity | Governing parties | Other government actors | Opposition parties | Civil society/ unions |
|---|---|---|---|---|---|
| GR | 1.02 | 0.11 | **0.47** | **0.34** | 0.07 |
| IT | 1.01 | **0.36** | **0.30** | **0.26** | 0.09 |
| PT | 1.00 | 0.15 | **0.59** | 0.13 | 0.13 |
| FR | 0.97 | 0.12 | **0.35** | **0.49** | 0.04 |
| RO | 0.92 | 0.05 | **0.57** | 0.13 | **0.26** |
| DE | 0.89 | 0.10 | **0.45** | 0.08 | **0.36** |
| IE | 0.89 | 0.04 | 0.20 | **0.28** | **0.47** |
| U.K. | 0.85 | 0.21 | **0.28** | 0.17 | **0.34** |
| ES | 0.80 | 0.00 | **0.37** | **0.47** | 0.16 |
| HU | 0.55 | 0.02 | **0.77** | 0.15 | 0.06 |
| LV | 0.40 | 0.15 | **0.83** | 0.00 | 0.02 |
| PL | 0.39 | 0.14 | **0.31** | **0.55** | 0.00 |
| *Average* | *0.81* | *0.12* | *0.46* | *0.25* | *0.17* |

*Note*: The table shows the average diversity of the third parties (Shannon's diversity measure) and the proportion of each of the four categories. The numbers are calculated as overall (N = 60 episodes) and country averages (N = 4 episodes). Categories with more than 25 percent highlighted in bold.

contentious episodes were in southern Europe (Greece, Italy, and Portugal), followed closely by France, while a single type of actor dominated the third parties in three eastern European countries (Poland, Latvia, and Hungary).

The share for each actor included in Table 5.5 shows the origins of low diversity in eastern Europe; the third parties in Hungary and Latvia were dominated by governmental actors, which make up roughly four out of every five third-party actions. In contrast, Polish third parties were dominated by the partisan opposition and other executive actors. The latter combination is also characteristic of the third parties in Greece, France, and Spain. In Romania, Germany, and the U.K., the most visible third parties are other government actors joined by actors from civil society. Interestingly, Italy is the country having by far the highest share of actors from governing parties listed among the third parties, indicating that the governing parties did not fully embrace the government's position. Instead, they aimed to mediate or even oppose the government's proposal (critical instances have been the conflicts over Monti's reform proposal and the Jobs Act – IT_eco3 and IT_eco4); next in line is the U.K., where governing party involvement was mainly due to the Brexit episode.

Table 5.6 identifies the most common combinations of third-party actors in the sixty episodes. Overall, those with a large share of other governmental actors dominated (forty-two out of sixty cases). The most frequent configurations are either other governmental actors (both domestic and European/ international) alone (N = 16) or in combination with opposition parties

TABLE 5.6. *Types of third-party configuration*

| Gov. parties >25% | Other Gov. >25% | Oppo- sition >25% | CSO/ unions >25% | Number of episodes | Conten- tiousness by TP | Average position | Share target govern- ment |
|---|---|---|---|---|---|---|---|
| ✗ | ✓ | ✗ | ✗ | 16 | 0.29 | 0.15 | 0.87 |
| ✗ | ✓ | ✓ | ✗ | 13 | 0.29 | 0.09 | 0.90 |
| ✗ | ✗ | ✓ | ✗ | 8 | 0.31 | 0.38 | 0.93 |
| ✗ | ✓ | ✗ | ✓ | 7 | 0.47 | −0.35 | 0.92 |
| ✓ | ✓ | ✗ | ✗ | 5 | 0.25 | 0.30 | 0.94 |
| ✗ | ✗ | ✗ | ✓ | 4 | 0.38 | 0.44 | 1.00 |
| ✓ | ✗ | ✓ | ✗ | 2 | 0.24 | 0.53 | 0.97 |
| ✓ | ✗ | ✗ | ✗ | 2 | 0.26 | 0.03 | 0.93 |
| ✗ | ✗ | ✓ | ✓ | 2 | 0.46 | 0.60 | 0.92 |
| ✗ | ✓ | ✓ | ✓ | 1 | 0.36 | −0.03 | 0.95 |
| 9 | 42 | 26 | 14 | | | | |

*Note*: The number of cases in the fifth column indicates the number of episodes with a specific third-party configuration. For example, sixteen episodes are characterized by a strong presence of other government actors only. The number of cases in the last row indicates the number of episodes in which a certain type of actor is represented with more than 25%, regardless of the share of the other actors. For example, governing parties are represented with more than 25% in nine of the sixty episodes.

(N = 13). All other combinations are represented fewer than ten times in our sample. In general, the table indicates no pronounced differences regarding the third parties' contribution to the contentiousness of the conflict, their average position, or targeting. There tends to be no systematic relationship between *who* the third parties are and *what they do* in a contentious episode. We observed only one deviation from this pattern: When governmental actors and civil-society organizations (including unions) acted as third parties (N = 7), they tended to intervene more in the conflict and were more likely to side with the government's position. It is important to note that three of these cases are from Germany: the institutional episode around the constitutional debt brake (DE_inst) and the debates around the bank bailout and the establishment of a bad bank (DE_eco1 and DE_eco2). However, this group's most illustrative case is the Brexit episode, when the coded third parties mainly sided with the majority position within the government and opposed the challenger coalition, which favored leaving the European Union.

## ALLIES AND ADVERSARIES: THE OVERALL ACTOR CONFIGURATION

In the final section, we put the three stylized actor categories back together and present the actor configuration in an integrated way. We adopt the distinction between the four types of contentious episodes introduced in Chapter 4: fully fledged, bottom-up, top-down, and low-intensity episodes. We distinguish the cases according to the involvement of challengers and governments as well as third parties. We do not consider the twenty "low-intensity episodes" character-ized by a relatively weak involvement of all stylized actors, while so-called fully fledged and bottom-up episodes (N = 15 and 14, respectively) are what McAdam et al. (2001) have relied upon to illustrate their approach. These are episodes characterized by the emergence of a strong challenger who relies on contentious performances. The key difference between the two types is that in fully fledged cases we also observe a comparatively active involvement of the government and third parties, whereas these institutional insiders are much less involved in bottom-up episodes. The final type, top-down episodes, is characterized by the relative absence of challengers, with the government and third parties being actively engaged in conventional forms of public claims making (N = 11).

The following figures identify the typical patterns of these configurations. The key aspects are the involvement of each actor type and their positioning toward the two other actors. To show these aspects, Figure 5.2 is based on all actions of the three actor types, varying the size of the label as a function of the total number of actions attributable to the actor in question. The arrows show the relations of support and opposition between each pair of actors. Their width reflects the total number of actions addressed to the other actor in the corresponding pair. Support is portrayed by arrows in light gray, opposition by arrows in dark gray. Finally, we show the third-party alignment in a simplified fashion (alignment with government, challenger, and no alignment) by pos-itioning the third-party label.

Among the fully fledged episodes, we can identify three typical patterns. The first pattern corresponds to an intense conflict between government and chal-lenger, with the third parties siding with the government. We observe such a configuration in six of the fifteen fully fledged episodes. Four of them center on bailouts and involve a substantive share of international actors: the three Greek bailout episodes (including the first one used to illustrate the configuration in Figure 5.2) and the Irish one in late 2010. The remaining two cases with this configuration are the Brexit episode in the U.K. and the Romanian episode related to the labor market reform (RO_eco4).

The second type of configuration also shows an intense conflict between highly unified challengers and the government. The difference is that the third parties took on a more neutral or even negative position toward the govern-ment. This pattern is the most common configuration among the fully fledged episodes (eight out of fifteen). The Greek midterm adjustment episode (GR_eco2) serves as a prototype for this pattern.[3]

---

[3] We observe a similar pattern in the institutional episodes around the closure of the public broadcaster in Greece (GR_inst) and the controversial media law in Hungary (HU_inst) and five additional economic episodes: the conflicts over the bank guarantee and the 2009 austerity package in Ireland (IE_eco1 and IE_eco2); labor market reforms in Italy (IT_eco1 and IT_eco4), and the 2010 austerity package in Romania (RO_eco2).

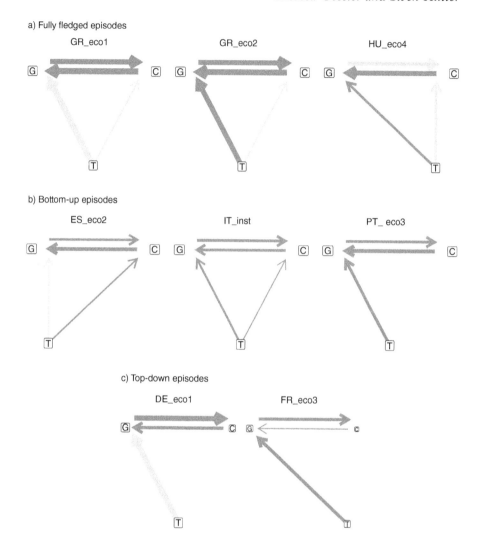

FIGURE 5.2. Types of actor configurations

*Note*: The graph shows illustrative examples for the configurations among the three stylized actors. Examples are presented for the three most relevant types of contentious episodes identified in the previous chapter, omitting the twenty cases of "low-intensity episodes."

For the final configuration shown in Figure 5.2a, we could only identify one case, the so-called internet tax episode in Hungary. This exceptional case is one of the few in which a government gave in to the challengers' demands and completely withdrew its reform proposal (see Chapter 7).

Among the bottom-up episodes, there are also three types of actor configurations. First, there are several episodes, mainly from southern Europe, that are characterized by a strong challenger–government conflict and third parties that side with the government (five out of fourteen). As the example of the second austerity package by Zapatero (ES_eco2) in Figure 5.2b indicates, unlike the fully fledged episodes, the challenger coalition is much more visible, while the government's engagement is lukewarm – at least on the public sphere's front stage.[4] Second, five episodes are characterized by a similarly high level of conflict but include a third-party coalition that opposes the government. These cases include the Portuguese bailout episode (PT_eco3), in which the third parties do not positively relate to the challenger but strongly disagree with the government. We show this episode in Figure 5.2, but two other Portuguese episodes (PT_eco1 and PT_eco2), the French Sarkozy–Fillon episode (FR_eco1), and the 2011 austerity episode in the U.K. also belong to this group. Finally, four cases among the bottom-up episodes stand out because of a division within the third parties that oppose the government and the challengers alike. We present the example of the Italian institutional episode (IT_inst), a controversial judicial reform promoted by Berlusconi. Three other cases of mutual third-party opposition exist in our dataset: the water tax in Ireland (IE_eco4), the first austerity package in Spain (ES_eco1), and the 2012 austerity package in Portugal (PT_eco4).

Finally, we identify two actor configurations among the top-down episodes. In these episodes, where the challenger is far less active, there is either a government–third party controversy or a government–third party consensus. The former pattern occurs more frequently (eight out of eleven cases): In Figure 5.2c, we present the first austerity package of the Hollande government (FR_eco3) as an example.[5] Importantly, these episodes usually boil down to a conflict between institutional insiders, as shown when focusing on third-party composition. The final configuration of consensus is far less frequent, occurring in a total of three cases. As illustrated in Figure 5.2c by the German bank bailout episode (DE_eco1), the challenger is somewhat invisible. Instead, the actor configuration reflects broad support for the government's decision to bail out the German banks by the involved third parties. Similar arrangements emerged in the Polish episode triggered by the constitutional court reform (PL_inst) and the Romanian IMF bailout episode (RO_eco1).

[4] Similar dynamics emerged when Zapatero aimed to amend the Spanish constitution (ES_inst) and when his successor Rajoy presented his major austerity package (ES_eco3). Other cases in point are our prime example from Portugal (PT_eco2) and the Italian episode triggered by Monti's austerity plans (IT_eco3).
[5] The other episodes were the German ones around the first and third Greek bailout (DE_eco3 and DE_eco4), the Hungarian ones around austerity and pension reforms (HU_eco 2 and HU_eco3), the only Latvian one among the contested ones (LV_eco3 – the second austerity package in 2009), and finally the institutional episode from Romania (RO_inst on the impeachment referendum).

CONCLUSION

This chapter has provided answers about the actors involved in the sixty contentious episodes and how they are typically related to each other. CEA allows us to go beyond classical protest event research and describe how challenger coalitions are embedded in a broader actor configuration. To do so, we examined the institutional characteristics, diversity, and configuration of the three stylized actor types at CEA's core in four steps.

First, we described the set of actors in the overall dataset. This step already revealed the strong presence of government actors, unions, and the mainstream opposition. These three categories were far more visible in the conflicts over austerity and institutional reform than parties from the fringes and civil society organizations (including N.G.O.s and S.M.O.s). The analysis also indicated that the challengers and third parties were much more diverse in their institutional characteristics than the government (mainly covering national governments and their officials).

Second, we also examined the challenger coalition – defined as an objective coalition with shared goals but not necessarily joint actions. We described the diversity of the actors challenging the governments' proposals by unconventional means. Furthermore, we identified the dominant institutional characteristics and potential cross-actor alliances. From this perspective, the challenger coalitions were not that diverse, given the significant role of labor unions. Labor unions were by far the most visible opponents of the reform proposals. More than 40 percent of all challenger actions in this period of austerity could be attributed to labor unions, while only around 20 percent were due to opposition parties or civil society actors. Analyzing the patterns across episodes, we showed that unions formed a fundamental part of the challenger coalition in more than 60 percent of all episodes: the two most common alliances were unions with a strong presence of opposition parties or unions alone. Any other combinations were far less common. While this mirrors previous research relying on protest event analysis (e.g., Carvalho 2018; Diani and Kousis 2014; Hunger and Lorenzini 2019; Portos 2016, 2017; Portos and Carvalho 2019), our CEA-based measures reveal the role of unions in politicizing austerity in even more detail.

There is no strong link between the type of coalition and the contentiousness of an episode. Still, our findings suggest that union activism, particularly in alliance with opposition parties, leads to more contentious interactions. Simultaneously, some of the most controversial episodes show the pattern most studied by social movement research: that is, coalitions of civil-society organizations with unions. Among these cases, we find the Spanish episode linked to the rise of the Indignados movement in 2011 and the highly contested midterm adjustment program in Greece that saw the emergence of Aganaktismenoi, the Indigandos counterpart in Greece, a few months later. The Portuguese episode around that time, however, is classified as a "unions plus parties" coalition.

This interpretation differs from research based solely on protest event analysis. The latter tends to underestimate the role of opposition parties in Portugal because they were not as visible as protest sponsors (Portos and Carvalho 2019: 8). They relied on more conventional actions to contest austerity as our CEA approach highlights.[6]

Third, we honed in on the third parties, the actors who publicly engaged in the conflict without being a member of either the government or the challenger coalition. Our results are instructive as they show that third parties were mostly institutional insiders. Most visible are actors belonging to government institutions, both national and international, followed by actors from the mainstream opposition. In more than two thirds of all contentious episodes, government actors dominated the category of third parties. The most frequent constellations were other government actors alone or in combination with opposition parties. Third parties mainly targeted governments (instead of directly targeting the challenger), and they rarely intervened as mediators. However, we did not find systematic differences between third-party composition and their positioning, their focus on the government, and their contribution to public controversy. Finally, combining all the elements, we showed the varying actor configurations across the types of episodes identified in the previous chapter. We reduced the complexity to eight configurations. Analysis revealed the crucial but variable role played by third parties. They tended to target the government, either supporting or opposing it, depending on the episode. Challengers vary in intensity but were hardly ever the direct target of third parties. In some cases, we observed conventional public debates involving institutional insiders, where the challengers played a marginal role at best. In other cases the challengers were embedded in very different actor constellations depending on the third parties, highlighting the benefit of an integrated approach to the study of government–challenger interactions.

Overall, this chapter has taken advantage of CEA to summarize such interaction patterns throughout a full episode and to distinguish different configurations. The chapters in the third part of the book will focus more closely on the dynamics of government–challenger interactions and the contextual factors that influence them.

---

[6] Note that Carvalho (2019) and Portos and Carvalho (2019) also emphasize this point when they consider why Spain saw a sustained protest wave during the Great Recession but Portugal did not.

# 6

# Action Sequences and Dynamic Indicators of Contention

## Abel Bojar and Argyrios Altiparmakis

### INTRODUCTION

As the reader may have noted, in the previous two chapters we have treated contentious actions largely in isolation from each other. Our contentiousness indicators, for instance, relied on the relative frequency count of disruptive or repressive action types by the contending adversaries without any explicit consideration of how these actions relate to each other beyond their clustering in time. Likewise, we studied the coalition patterns of contentious episodes by considering the institutional characteristics and action forms of each actor and derived the episode-specific actor configurations from the relative numerical frequencies of these actions.

The current chapter marks an important next step in our study of contentious episodes because for the first time we turn toward an explicit operationalization of interdependence between actions. While in the previous chapters we focused on the static characteristics of episodes, here we focus on their dynamics, setting the stage for Part III of this volume. As we made it earlier, we build on Tilly and Tarrow's (2015) definition and conceptualize contentious politics as a "continuous stream of interactions regarding policy-specific proposals between the government and its challengers, involving also some other actors." The main methodological contribution we provide in this chapter is a systematic operationalization of those streams of interactions. While the narrative approach can provide a fine-grained snapshot of these interactions at particular junctures of the debate, it does not provide a systematic and replicable tool for connecting the entire causal chain of individual actions throughout a whole policy episode. At the same time, although epidemiological approaches are better suited to identifying all the relevant actions in the debate, their capacity for introducing a dynamic account of how these actions link together is rather limited. We thus consider that our method for reconstructing action sequences is an example of the "middle ground" in the study of contentious politics that we outlined in the introductory chapter to this volume: a move from an action-centered to an *inter*action-centered perspective while preserving the rigor and explicitness of protest event analysis (PEA).

Additionally, we do not merely stop at the level of action sequence reconstruction, we also aim to infuse these sequences with substantive content. A systematic mapping of sequences allows us to describe entire policy episodes by the characteristics of its main constituent parts. Our second main contribution therefore is to increase the descriptive accuracy of the study of contentious politics by offering a set of comparable indicators that strike at the heart of political conflict. In particular, we describe sequences by their pace (the average time lapsed between two actions in the sequence) and their complexity (the degree of concentration of contention in a limited number of threads).

The main building block we use to operationalize action sequences and construct our indicators is the concept of *action triggers*. Action triggers are defined here as actions that causally precede a given action, embedded in a chain of events involving any combination of stylized actors, as developed in chapters 1, 2, and 5. Action sequences are the complete set of such chains of actions and their responses/reactions ordered chronologically. Our goal in this chapter is to utilize these building blocks to construct indicators that can describe the dynamics of an episode: namely, the average lags between the actions, as well as the length and "thickness" of sequences over time. We then construct indices for pace and complexity of episodes – indicators that trace an episode's dynamics throughout time. While our pace indicator is intended to capture whether sequences in an episode tend to involve a fast or slow alternation of actions, our complexity measure gauges whether these sequences tend to overlap or, alternatively, whether the episode moves forward on separate sequences for an extended period of time. Before we get there, however, we have to discuss the basic concepts and data required to construct these indices.

Note that the study of sequences occupies a well-established place among social science methodologies. The most prominent method to study them rests on the assumption that sequences are identical in length and are composed of a finite number of elements that, in turn, are characterized by their states (see an overview of applications by Abbott, 1995 and a methodological overview by Blanchard, 2011).

In the way we conceptualize action sequences, however, conventional sequence analysis cannot be applied because our sequences vary greatly in length. Once a contentious action triggers no further action, a given sequence comes to an end although simultaneously occurring actions in the same episode may evolve into other, longer sequences. Also, as Figure 6.1 illustrates, sequences can (and typically do) have significant overlaps in contrast to sequence analysis applications where the units (usually individuals) are strictly and fully separate from each other. For our purposes, it is thus preferable to

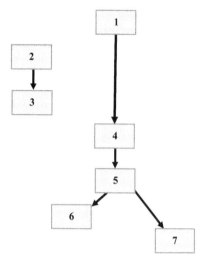

FIGURE 6.1. Stylized illustration of sequences with and without overlaps
*Note*: The actions are ordered chronologically from the top to the bottom and arrows indicate the action-trigger pairs. In this illustration, we have a total of three sequences: 2–3, 1–4–5–6, and 1–4–5–7. Note that while the first sequence is fully separate from the other two, the second and third sequences share three quarters of the actions (1, 4, and 5).

think of sequences in terms of tree structures and, accordingly, to derive a set of conceptual tools to characterize sequences and their entire structure.

Our main questions in this chapter are therefore the following: How are actions and reactions distributed over time, and how and why does this differ between episodes? How can we link these actions and reactions to each other and what sort of substantively meaningful indicators can we derive to characterize action sequences? In particular, by analyzing episode action sequences, we can examine whether the type of policy episode, the economic and political contexts in which it is embedded, as well as other episode characteristics analyzed in previous chapters, influence the pace and complexity of sequences as they evolve over time.

This chapter aims to answer these questions by first offering a descriptive overview of actions along with their triggers to give a sense of the basic building blocks of sequences. This descriptive overview is then complemented by a similar overview of the sequences themselves and their relative distribution per episode. In the next section, we derive a set of sequence characteristics, namely their length and duration, and from those we construct further indices that capture the dynamic characteristics of episodes, namely episode pace and complexity. In the third section, we use these indicators as dependent variables to be explained in a multivariate analysis. The final part of this chapter offers a detailed illustration of sequences in action by focusing on one particular context of interest, Ireland, followed by our concluding remarks.

## ACTIONS, TRIGGERS, AND SEQUENCES

In this section, we guide the reader through our conceptualization of sequences and the method of constructing our indicators, necessarily dealing with some technical aspects of our coding. To begin with, we would like to remind the reader of the idea of action triggers as discussed in detail in Chapter 2. In the first coding round, coders were instructed to identify explicit references to previous actions in the downloaded news articles that the actor at hand responds to. Such explicit mentioning can take a variety of forms, but a typical case would be the police confronting protestors against the policy proposal. If the previous action (in this example, the protest itself) had already been coded, the coder would simply use the code for the previous action as the action trigger. In the majority of the cases, however, such explicit references were not forthcoming; therefore, in a second round of coding, coders were required to check back for each preceding action as a potential trigger and select the one that was most consistent with the overall storyline of the episode. Having familiarized themselves with the main actors and critical actions involved in the episode, coders were able to assign an action trigger to a predominant share of all contentious actions. The remaining actions without a trigger (around 3 percent) either constitute the beginning of the episode (i.e. typically the policy proposal itself) or are responses to non action-related events (such as rising bond yields).

With this brief methodological reminder, we are now ready to offer a first mapping of action-trigger pairs. The first natural question to ask is whether sequences tend to resemble a chain: that is, actions continuously triggering and following each other. Or are they rather structured like a tree: that is, action sequences tend to have some "central thread," a trunk, from which most of the other actions, the "branches" and "leaves" branch off at a later moment in the sequence.

A brief answer is that the trigger distribution is extremely skewed. Indeed, action sequences tend to resemble a tree, with a limited number of actions being highly central to the whole episode. As Table 6.1 shows, more than two thirds

TABLE 6.1. *Frequency distribution of actions in terms of the number of further actions they trigger: percentages*

| Number of actions triggered | Frequency, % | Share of government action, % |
|---|---|---|
| 0 (leaves) | 70.2 | 10.3 |
| 1–5 (branches) | 22.6 | 67.8 |
| 5–10 (branches) | 4.4 | 97.3 |
| 11–20 (trunk) | 1.6 | 100.0 |
| 20+ (trunk) | 1.2 | 98.8 |
| Total | 100.0 | 29.7 |

of all actions (around 70 percent) trigger no further actions. Using the tree metaphor for the episodes, these actions can be conceptualized as leaves. A further 22.6 percent of actions trigger between one to five further actions, implying that they either constitute the trunk/branches of the tree or they are points where the tree bifurcates into a relatively limited number of further branches or sub-branches. From then on, the frequency of actions, in terms of the number of further actions they trigger, steadily drops. These actions constitute the critical points, the "trunk" of the tree (see more about them in Chapter 11), the locations where the stream of interactions branches off in multiple directions. A small minority of actions (1.2 percent of total, or eighty-three actions) branch off in more than twenty directions.

Once the leaves of the trees have been identified, we are well equipped to recursively trace back all preceding actions to derive the entire action sequence. Of course, since actions in the tree trunk can be the triggers of different branches, it is evident that different branches share some (nontrivial) overlap. That said, for analytical purposes, we still treat these sequences as separate even if only one action separates them. Such a scenario would arise from a branch that ends up in two separate leaves at the end, like the second and third sequence shown in Figure 6.1. In total, therefore, the number of sequences equals the total number of leaves of all episode-specific trees. We end up with a total of 4,834 sequences or just above eighty per episode on average. The number of sequences, however, depends on the overall structure of the episodes and as a result they are highly unevenly distributed across them.

## SEQUENCE CHARACTERISTICS

One of the primary interests for scholars studying contentious politics is the nature of interaction that follows the initial action (in our case, a policy proposal by the government). This interaction, to an extent that it unfolds at all, can take a simple action–reaction form, it can extend to a triadic type of action–reaction–counterreaction, or it can actually resemble the sort of "continuous stream of interactions" that really puts the flesh onto the bones of contentious episodes. Therefore, arguably the most important characteristic to describe sequences is how many component actions they include: that is, how long they are or how long they last. We distinguish between sequence length – the number of components (actions) in a sequence, and sequence duration – its extension over time. The two aspects, while possibly related, provide different information about the nature of interaction between actors. Table 6.2 summarizes the distribution of all sequences according to these two different aspects of length.

As apparent from the table, the distribution of sequence length is considerably more skewed than that of duration. Close to half of all sequences end after a relatively limited number of actions (five). A further 19.5 percent end after ten actions and another 16.7 percent end within twenty actions. Only less than

TABLE 6.2. *Summary of length and duration of sequences*

| Sequence length | Frequency, % | Duration | Frequency, % |
|---|---|---|---|
| <5 | 49.1 | Less than a month | 35.6 |
| 6–10 | 19.5 | 1 month–3 months | 29.6 |
| 11–20 | 16.7 | 3 months–6 months | 17.8 |
| 21–40 | 8.4 | 6 months–1 year | 9.1 |
| 40+ | 6.4 | 1 year+ | 7.9 |
| Total | 100.0 | Total | 100.0 |

15 percent of sequences extend beyond twenty actions, but a nontrivial 6.4 percent of sequences show considerable length, extending beyond forty actions. Comparatively speaking, the duration of sequences is more evenly distributed, with the most typical sequence lasting somewhat less than a month (35.6 percent of all sequences). However, relatively large shares (29.6 percent and 17.8 percent) last between one and three months or between three months and six months, respectively. Sequences longer than six months are comparatively rare, but the tail of the duration distribution is still somewhat thicker than the tail of the sequence length distribution.

These two different aspects of length speak to different features of the sequences, and one does not mechanistically follow from the other. As is to be expected, the correlation between the two features is positive with a Pearson's correlation coefficient of 0.38: After all, the more actions that make up a sequence, ceteris paribus, the longer it is expected to last overall. However, the correlation between them is relatively weak, showing that these two features are not just two sides of the same coin. While as would be expected, some sequences that contain many actions last longer, others contain the same number of actions in a much shorter time interval. There are, therefore, episodes with all kinds of combinations of long/short sequences in terms of length and duration. We will use both these aspects of sequence length as the fundamental measures – namely episode pace and complexity – from which we will produce composite indices in order to characterize episodes.

Combining these aspects of sequence dynamics therefore, we can readily derive an indicator that shows the average speed at which a sequence (or by aggregation, the whole episode) moves forward. We shall refer to this characteristic of contentious episodes as their *pace*, which we define simply as the ratio of the average duration over the average length of its component sequences. We should note here that a high value of this indicator signifies a relatively slow pace because the sequences either take longer in time (long duration) or contain fewer actions within a given amount of time (short length), while low values of the indicator signify a fast pace. Episodes characterized by a fast pace resemble a sort of "ping-pong match" between the adversaries: Actions tend to be followed up soon by reactions and there is little deliberation time in between.

In contrast, episodes that move forward at a slow pace are more akin to a "chess game," implying long periods of breaks and deliberations during which no actor intervenes.

We can now readily calculate the overall mean pace in our sample. It is around fifteen days. This implies that in a typical sequence, it takes around two weeks for an action to take place after its trigger. However, it is important to note that this average is biased upward by two aspects of our data structure. First, because of the significant overlaps between sequences, those actions that constitute the trunks and branches of the tree get counted multiple times and they tend to have longer lags than the overall average, biasing the mean pace towards a slower pace. Second, there are some clear outliers in multi-year episodes with action lags longer than a year. When disregarding these outliers and counting each action only once (or in other words, departing from sequences as the units of analysis), the average number of days elapsing between two actions is reduced significantly to 9.7 days. Overall, it is still fair to characterize the evolution of the typical action sequence as rather slow.

Beyond the actual lags at which contending parties react to each other, the typically slow evolution of sequences is also rooted in methodological and substantive reasons. One methodological reason may be due to the fact we only looked at newspapers, which only report public reactions. Behind the scenes, unions and other civil society associations might have been pulling strings and reacting to government announcements in ways that we do not capture in our data. It is also likely that newspapers mostly report and emphasize the most newsworthy aspects of the interactions – that is, strikes and breakdowns in negotiations. Additionally, the slowness of the reactions may also have to do with the resources required to muster a reaction. Unions need time and resources to decide to strike and organize to do so. In different countries, union procedures and resources may also vary, and this factor could be an additional source of variation of sequence length and duration.

Our second indicator measuring sequence characteristics is that of *complexity*, which aims to capture the extent to which episodes are characterized by multiple sequences running parallel to each other for an extended period of time or by interactions that tend to be concentrated in a few central sequences of limited length. The intuition behind the complexity measure is that episodes can be regarded as complex due to two different structural characteristics of sequences, one of which we have already discussed – sequence length. Longer sequences, ceteris paribus, indicate a more complex set of interactions compared to sequences that come to a halt after a limited set of actions. However, another important aspect of complexity is the number of sequences that simultaneously unfold at any given point in time or, in other words, the extent to which an episode is dominated by a limited number of central threads of interactions. To measure this second aspect of complexity, we constructed an auxiliary measure of *width*, which is simply the average number of actions per week that belong to separate, nonoverlapping sequences, indicating the

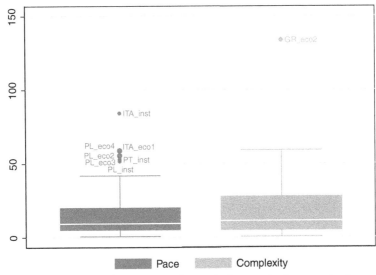

FIGURE 6.2. Distribution of our pace and complexity metrics in our episodes

"thickness" of our sequence "trees." Averaging the sequence length and sequence width indicator for the entire episode and taking their product thus provides a two-dimensional measure of episode complexity. The higher the complexity, therefore, the more events occur and the more they tend to occur concurrently. A box plot showing the distribution of pace and complexity for our episodes is provided in Figure 6.2, showing that the episodes tend to be condensed around their central values but with some prominent outliers. For instance, the judicial reform in Italy and four out of the five Polish episodes stand out for their slow pace, while the midterm adjustment episode in Greece is by far the most complex episode in our sample.

Additionally, and more importantly, when we plot the episodes with regard to their pace and complexity, (Figure 6.3), we can see how the two indicators relate to each other. The correlation is negative, suggesting that more complex episodes, on average, tend to have faster pace (fewer average number of days having elapsed between actions and their triggers). However, the correlation is far from overwhelming (r = –0.37) and the episode space is populated by different combinations of pace and complexity, although extremely slow episodes are never complex.

That said, we can cluster episodes according to their combination of pace and complexity by relying on a clustering algorithm based on distances from the median of the two variables in each cluster.[1] As Figure 6.3 shows, with the

---

[1] Because of the outliers on both dimensions shown in Figure 6.3, median-based clustering provides a more accurate composition of groups than means-clustering.

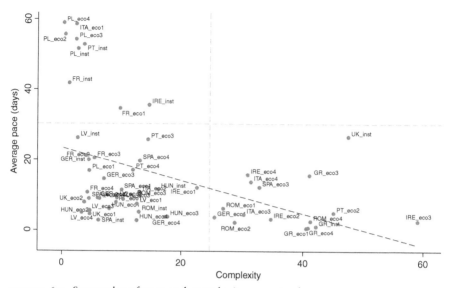

FIGURE 6.3. Scatterplot of pace and complexity per episode
*Note*: The dashed lines signify the cluster boundaries based on the result of the splitting algorithm.

two most extreme outliers (ITA_inst and GR_eco) removed for visualization, the slow-complex combination is practically absent from the sample, making a three-cluster solution satisfactory for our purposes. Accordingly, the clustering solution provides the following episode clusters: a slow-simple cluster including episodes with low pace and low complexity; a fast-simple cluster including episodes with high pace and low complexity; and a fast-complex cluster including episodes of high pace and high complexity. The list of episodes in the three clusters, along with the median values of the two dimensions within each cluster, is provided in Table A6.1 in the Appendix.

The main purpose of this visualization is to understand how episodes can differ across time and to supplement our more static concepts of contentiousness and diversity from the previous chapter with these dynamic characteristics. However, what we ultimately want to examine are the empirical correlates of these indicators – that is, the factors that create the circumstances for complex or rapid interactions (or the opposite). In other words, we shall probe the determinants of whether sequences in an episode tend to evolve more rapidly and in a "decentralized" manner or move forward slowly and along a central thread of conflict.

## THE EMPIRICAL CORRELATES OF THE DYNAMIC CHARACTERISTICS OF SEQUENCES

In this section, we aim to uncover the determinants of sequence characteristics that we have derived thus far. The overarching questions are what makes

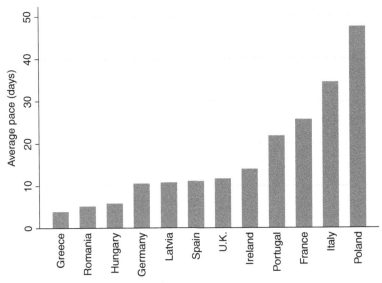

FIGURE 6.4. Average sequence pace, by country

certain episodes sprawl over time or generate quicker or denser interactions between actors. First, we will describe the relationship between the different pace-complexity combinations for different countries and episode characteristics.

We start with the country in contention. Different countries have different contentious legacies, which, for multiple reasons, may affect the speed with which actors interact for multiple reasons. The unions/challengers might have fewer/more resources and thus be able to respond correspondingly slower/ faster. The media might press for a government response faster in some countries than others, or more entrenched traditions of protest might urge the government to do so regardless.

Figure 6.4 confirms that, in terms of the country rankings, Greece stands out as particularly fast paced and Poland as particularly slow paced, again closely related to the specific episodes that occurred in these countries. In addition to Greece, two other countries, Hungary and Romania, also belong to the "fast" type of countries with an average pace below ten days while at the other extreme, Italy is an another country with slowly moving episodes, with an average pace of over one month. This makes sense both in terms of protest legacy, of which Greece has a particularly tumultuous one but also in terms of economics: Greece was the country that experienced the deepest crisis in the Great Recession, while Poland was the country that did not record any recession throughout these years. Italy did experience a recession, but it came slowly and insidiously, meaning that it was not perceived as such for a long time. Other than that, while episode pace varies considerably among countries, there is no obvious reason, geographical or institutional, for this particular ranking.

Similar patterns seem to apply for complexity – Polish episodes are the least and Greek episodes are the most complex. A clear outlier, for example, is the midterm adjustment program in Greece that uniquely scores above a hundred in our multiplicative complexity measure. The other four Greek episodes are also high up in the complexity distribution, whereas three of the five Polish episodes constitute the least complex ones in our sample. That said, other countries show a larger spread in their complexity distribution. For instance, while the British institutional episode (Brexit) has the third-highest score overall, the first British austerity measure, announced by the new coalition government in 2010, is among the least complex. The order of the rest of the countries, however, shows considerable differences compared to their pace ranking. Irish episodes, for instance, have typically slow pace but high complexity. Vice versa, Hungarian episodes tend to evolve at a rapid pace but score comparatively low in the complexity measure.

As the juxtaposition of Greece and Poland suggests, one obvious explanation for these different patterns is the type of episode that occurred in different countries. Perhaps I.M.F. interventions and bank bailouts, rather than country characteristics, are the main determinants of the fast-complex type of episode, as suggested by the Greek and Romanian cases. Aggregating by episode types, we can indeed discern important differences in the average pace of the episodes. As shown in Figure 6.6, there is a clear difference between three types of episode that evolved relatively rapidly (budgetary consolidation measures, external bailouts, and bank bailouts) with an average pace of less than ten days, and those that move forward at a much more measured pace (structural reforms and institutional reforms), with an average pace of around a month.

Figure 6.7 reveals that with regard to complexity, only I.M.F. bailout episodes stand out from the rest since they are on average characterized by a considerably higher level of complexity (>thirty on average), followed by austerity episodes (around twenty), with the other three episode types (structural reforms, bank bailouts, and institutional reforms) being roughly equal at an average complexity score of thirteen.

Episode type therefore seems to be an important predictor of episode pace and complexity, in particular I.M.F. episodes. There are multiple explanations why this might be the case, and we collectively refer to these as the set of macro-constraints that the government faces. The first is the urgency of these policy episodes. As episodes involving the I.M.F. typically involve an emergency situation that has to be diffused under tight constraints, the government actions are more temporally constrained and the challengers may also need to reckon with the imperative to act. There is little time for deliberation and the I.M.F.-imposed measures are typically voted on within a matter of weeks. Contrasting this are the typically slow-paced institutional episodes, some of which may take up multiple years to complete, underscoring these patterns as presented in Figures 6.4–6.7. Bank bailout episodes, and to a lesser degree budgetary consolidations, also have relatively stringent timelines that need to be adhered

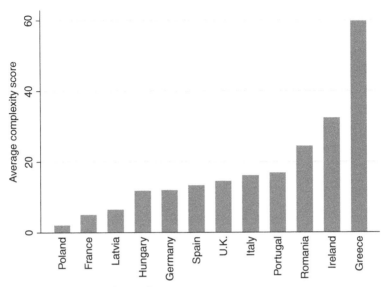

FIGURE 6.5. Average complexity, by country

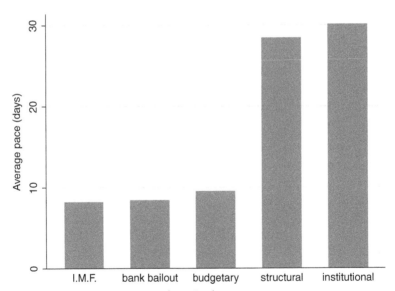

FIGURE 6.6. Average sequence pace, by episode type

to – timelines that are considerably less binding, if they exist at all, for structural or institutional reforms.

An alternative but related explanation is that in bank bailouts, and more generally, time-constrained episodes, the government has less control over the

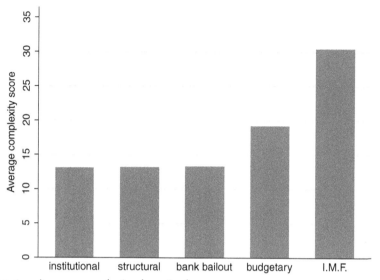

FIGURE 6.7. Average complexity, by episode type

policy process. Whereas structural reforms can always be initiated, halted, and resumed at the government's will and according to strategic considerations, bailout packages cannot. The Hungarian government famously reversed its plans to introduce an "internet tax" in response to protests – a paradigmatic "fast-simple" episode – while the same luxury could not be afforded to the Greek government in its bailout battles. The Irish government, as will be seen in the final section of this chapter, could afford to take its time with senate reform, deliberating and conversing with social partners to diffuse criticism. The same options are typically not available in a bailout episode, where the government has much less control over the policy process and its timing.

A third characteristic rooted in the idea of macro-constraints that might explain the differences among episode types is the presence of external actors. The presence of foreign parties is likely to increase the complexity of episodes because the number of simultaneously running threads of contention is probably higher compared to scenarios where the major battle lines are fought only among domestic actors. International actors are likely to engage with very different aspects of the debate (e.g. overall fiscal targets) compared to domestic stakeholders (e.g. how particular policy details afflict particular social groups). Additionally, the involvement of third-party actors could not only put pressure on the government to respond to their demands but also intensify pressure to act among the challengers when they see external actors intervening in their internal affairs.

We operationalize *urgency* simply as a variable based on the type of episode. In particular, we code episodes as urgent when it is a bank bailout or an I.M.F.

episode and not urgent in the other cases. For government control, we propose to take the share of actions where the government sticks to its proposal or utilizes repression as a sign of the government controlling the agenda. If more challenger actions were present as a response to such government actions, government control would decrease, whereas if fewer are present, it should be an indication that the government is proceeding uncontested or challenged only by fringe opponents it feels it can repress without many repercussions. Finally, we define external pressure as the share of actions by international third parties in an episode, to see how they affect their dynamic characteristics.

Furthermore, episode type is also linked to the contextual characteristics of the episodes ( see Chapter 3). I.M.F. bailouts tend to take place when the economy is already in dire straits. From this perspective, higher pace and complexity of the episodes might be a result of the underlying economic malaise as challengers react more intensively to a government's austerity plans. In particular, we use an objective (the national unemployment rate) and a subjective (Consumer Confidence Index – CCI) indicator as a proxy for the state of the national economy at the time of the policy debate. Alternatively, economic grievances might result from the nature of the policy response itself. In particular, episodes that we coded as "high severity" (see Chapter 3) are likely to aggravate the sense of economic insecurity among the populace and intensify the mechanisms that give rise to fast and complex sequence structures. We thus include a dummy variable for high-severity episodes to test this channel.

In addition to economics, higher pace and complexity might be expected where there are wider grievances with the political system, leading to quicker reactions to government plans. Following Easton's distinction (1975), these grievances might have resulted from the withdrawal of either specific or diffuse support for the political system. While the former is targeted against particular governments, the latter refers to a more generic attitude vis-a-vis the political regime of the day. We operationalize the former concept via the share of the population expressing trust in the government, while the latter as the share of the population satisfied with the way democracy works in their country. We derive both indicators from Eurobarometer surveys as presented in Chapter 3.

Finally, we examine the role that actor configurations might play in the course of contention. First, we propose that the diversity of the challenger coalition, as operationalized in Chapter 5, is positively related to complexity because a wider challenger coalition implies more stakeholders who are likely to engage simultaneously with multiple parts of the policy package, giving rise to a more complex sequence structure. At the same time, we expected that the partisan leaning of the government matters for the type of action sequences that occurred in the wake of the policy proposal. In particular, because of their historically closer links to some prominent challenger organizations, such as unions, and their general policy preferences being opposed to the overall direction of these austerity packages, center-left governments might be seen as more likely targets for concessions by challenger organizations. As a result, when center-left governments are in power, they might create a more hospitable environment for quick "ping-pong"-like exchanges between the government, challengers, and third parties, who might perceive that more is at stake. Therefore, faster and more sustained engagement with the policy debate is likely to ensue from the policy proposal.

We ran multinomial logit regressions with the three clusters of episodes as the dependent variable, the results of which are shown in the Appendix Table A-2. We introduced one group of variables at a time, starting with the economic variables (Model I), macro-political sentiments (Model II), actor characteristics (Model III), and the macro-constraints we outlined in this section (urgency, external pressure, and government control) (Model IV). In Model V, we repeated the exercise with the variables in the model that attained statistical or high substantive significance in Models I–IV. We specifyed the dependent variable with the slow-simple cluster as the omitted reference category, so all coefficient estimates are relative to this reference cluster. In any event, since interpreting the substantive impact of these coefficients is far from straightforward in a logistic framework, we provided predicted probability plots for selected explanatory variables below (with other covariates in the model held at their sample mean), and we showed the coefficient estimates from the models in the chapter in the Appendix (Table A6.2*)*.

Starting with the economic variables (Model I), although the underlying economic conditions (unemployment and CCI) have the expected sign, only episode severity emerges as a significant predictor of episode clusters. When calculating the predicted probabilities from the merged model (Model V), Figure 6.8 shows that high-severity episodes are associated with a significantly higher probability of belonging to the fast-complex cluster, with the estimated difference in the point estimate compared to episodes of lower severity amounting to 0.26. In line with our expectations, therefore, economic insecurity triggered by the material impact of policy responses to the Great Recession appears to be associated with faster-moving sequences and more complex sequence structures.

Turning to political grievances, our measure for the diffuse type of political support emerges as the stronger predictor of sequence structures. Although in the restricted model (Model II) both the trust in government and satisfaction with democracy coefficients produce the expected signs, only the latter achieved statistical significance and only at the 0.1 level. However, as evidenced by the merged model (Model V) and the calculated probabilities in Figure 6.9, the substantive impact of this variable was quite large, with a high level of satisfaction with democracy (sample maximum) being associated with −0.44 lower estimated probability of being in the fast-complex cluster compared to low levels of satisfaction (sample minimum).

Concerning the model on actor characteristics, Model III flagged up both challenger breadth and center-left governments as significant and substantively important predictors of episode clusters. When including these variables in the

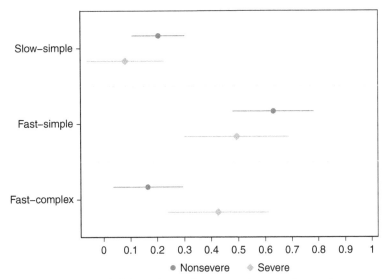

FIGURE 6.8. Predicted probability of episode clusters, by episode severity

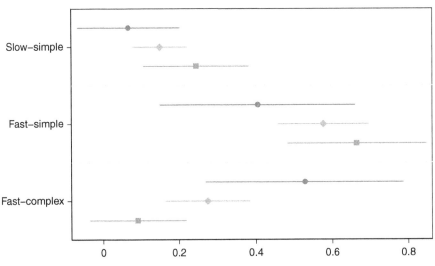

FIGURE 6.9. Predicted probability of episode clusters, by satisfaction with democracy

merged model (Model V), however, only the coefficient for the center-left government dummy survived as significant at the 0.1 level and the coefficient for challenger breadth was considerably reduced. Figure 6.10 illustrates the predicted probabilities of belonging to the three episode clusters as a function of whether the government is center left or not (ie. center right or technocratic).

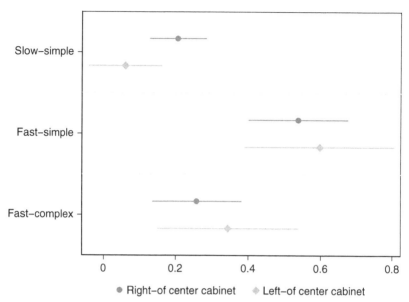

FIGURE 6.10. Predicted probability of episode clusters, by government type

Unlike the previous variables, the center-left dummy had the greatest impact on the probabilities of belonging to the slow-simple cluster. In particular, under center-left governments, episodes were extremely unlikely to take the slow-simple structure (p = 0.06) as opposed to settings under noncenter-left governments (p = 0.2). This is, again, in line with our expectations: Under center-left governments, the course of contention appeared to speed up and/or give rise to increasingly complex sequence structures.

Finally, of the three new variables we introduced in this chapter that are all related, in one way or another, to the type of policy episode under consideration, all the coefficients point to the expected positive direction but only external involvement showed up as a significant predictor of episode clusters. Figure 6.11 illustrates these patterns for this last variable, as calculated from the merged model. The most marked differences appeared with regard to the slow-simple cluster. As external pressure increases from low to high, the probability of an episode belonging to this cluster was reduced from an estimated 0.42 to just above 0. At the same time, the impact of external involvement greatly increased the probability of belonging to the middle (fast-simple) cluster, while the probability of episodes taking the fast-complex form was more or less constant across the values of external involvement – around 0.2–0.3.

Of course, these somewhat rough measures of theoretically interesting aspects of contentious episodes can only tell us so much about the particular mechanism linking cause and effect. In the next section, we aim to go a step further by focusing in more depth on particular case studies where some of the

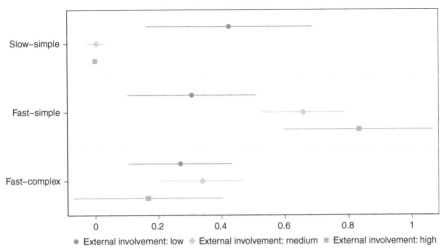

FIGURE 6.11. Average complexity by episode clusters entailing external involvement

relevant episode characteristics introduced and operationalized quantitatively can be illustrated in action.

## CASE STUDY: SEQUENCE CHARACTERISTICS IN IRELAND

To fill our measurement indices with substantive meaning, we now analyze them by focusing on two cases in Ireland: the I.M.F. bailout and the senate reform. The first of these episodes is among those with the fastest pace and highest complexity overall in the entire sample, an archetypical "fast-complex" episode. The senate reform, however, is a slow-moving episode with low complexity. What does this actually mean in practice, and why is it so? Concepts like episode severity and external intervention and their effects can be better understood by juxtaposing these cases.

Let us first look at the Irish I.M.F. bailout episode. It covers the agreement between the Irish government and I.M.F./Europeans to stave off a government default, under strict conditionality attached to fiscal adjustment and structural reforms. This aspect already provides some clues to the reasons for the rapid pace and high complexity observed in this episode. The length of the average action sequence was high because international third parties absent in more "domestic" episodes, a key component of what we termed external involvement, were omnipresent and operating within strict time constraints. Each of the Irish government's reassurances, reminders, and amendments to its proposed legislation was praised, commented on or criticized by international actors, resulting in ever longer lengths of action sequences.

The second reason for the long sequences characterizing the episode lies in its very nature (episode type). Being a product of the infamous Troika's

intervention, the proposed legislation incorporated a battery of fiscal measures
and more general structural reforms, augmenting the range of actors that had
"skin in the game." Indeed, in addition to international actors, the Irish episode
had a relatively high number of N.G.O.s, namely the Irish Church, civil-society
unions, research foundations, and think tanks reacting positively or negatively
to the proposed bailout. Hence, the severity of the episode, in terms of the reach
and significance of the bailout for Irish society, triggered many more responses,
in a shorter timespan than in other episodes.

That said, the episode is not particularly contentious. The eleven demonstrations recorded throughout the entire period pale in comparison to the level of
contentiousness that Greek, French, and Spanish episodes experienced, particularly given the highly conflictual context. However, Ireland does not have a
legacy of protest similar to those other countries, nor were the actors traditionally engaged in conflictual modes of interaction. Even compared to other Irish
cases, this episode ranks fairly low in terms of challenger mobilization, with the
second-lowest level of mobilization observed among the Irish episodes.

Instead, what drives the high pace are two additional factors. The first is that
the scathing impact of the Irish bailout mobilized opposition parties into action,
in particular Labour and Fine Gael, prompting them to sharpen their critique of
the government. Opposition parties were the actors that appeared most frequently among the rather diverse challenger coalition, missing no opportunity
to chastise the government over its bailout plans. The political opportunity
space available for opposition parties thus contributes to the long action
sequences, allowing them to capitalize on the government's constrained room
for maneuver vis-a- vis the bailout.

This also highlights the role political grievances can play. Between the first
instance of austerity, the first economic Irish episode, and the Irish bailout,
satisfaction with democracy dropped by 10 percentage points. Suddenly, the
entire system of government over which Fianna Fail had presided over the past
twelve years came under attack and took the blame for the unprecedented
economic collapse. Fianna Fail's bank bailouts, which imposed an unsustain-
able debt burden on the Irish state, were widely blamed for their coziness with
important financial actors in the country, causing a wider and deeper disillu-
sionment with Irish democracy.

The second reason for the high pace is the emergency nature of the episode,
given the already-mentioned external involvement. Due to the dire economic
straits the Irish government was trapped in, coupled with market pressure and
Troika exigencies, the whole process had to be concluded in a short time frame.
The episode spans the period from mid-September 2010 to the conclusion of
the bailout vote in the Irish parliament in mid-December. However, the bulk of
the action was concentrated in the later days of the episode. From the moment
the agreement was reached on November 21, and presented in Parliament on
November 25, the pace of events quickened. There were 2.2 actions per day,
compared to 1.6 before November 21. Additionally, sequence width, and hence

complexity, also dramatically increased after the introduction of the bill into parliament. This largely follows from the fact that the government's bill was heavily criticized by the combined forces of opposition parties, civil society, and unions, while international actors kept supporting the Irish government's effort to conclude the bailout legislation. Hence, any government action was met with numerous contemporary reactions. This period, however, is also associated with increased pace as the duration of sequences shortened; considering that the bailout had to be approved by the parliament within a specific time period, reactions to it had to be instantaneous and there was no time for delay. Even in Ireland, where mobilization is comparatively rare, there was a spectacular increase in contentious actions in the period between the introduction of the bill and its vote, both in the streets and in parliament. Pace and complexity were therefore high in the Irish bailout case because of the diversity of actors involved, the strict time constraints imposed on actors, and the limited agenda-setting power of the government, which had to navigate tight deadlines, but they were also heavily dependent on the "phases" of the episode. In particular, both pace and complexity increased when the policy legislation process began in earnest.

It is useful to juxtapose this case with another Irish episode, the one involving the proposed reform of the senate, the Irish "institutional" episode. The average sequence length of this episode is approximately the same as in the Irish bailout case. However, complexity and pace are considerably lower, due to the low width of the sequence structure – in other words, the limited number of sequences running parallel to each other – and high duration.

The Irish senate reform case has a similar number of sequences as the I.M.F. bailout, but they tend to overlap much more with each other, reducing the average width of sequences in the episode. This is because the Irish senate case was a much more conventional type of government–opposition conflict than the Irish bailout. Most sequences were of a "ping-pong" variety, adversarial interactions between government and opposition parties, without any international involvement or any particularly contentious action for that matter. Most of the third-party actions, other than those of opposition parties, were embedded in the sequences originating from opposition parties, hence overlapping with them and reducing complexity. There was no separate government–Troika chain of interactions, nor was there any government–challengers chain of interactions, as in the bailout case. However, even in the bailout case, contention was relatively low compared to other bailout episodes, in Greece for example. Nevertheless, the lack of external involvement, the lack of urgency this factor creates, and the lower severity of the episode all contributed to make the Irish senate case a slow-simple episode type, in stark opposition to the bailout.

Similarly, the pace is lower in this episode because of the longer duration of sequences (in fact, the highest in the whole sample). While average sequence length is fairly similar to the bailout episode, events unfolded at a glacial pace.

This may be partly due to the fact that the government dominated the chain of events, with 47 percent of all actions attributable to it. Despite government control not emerging as a statistically significant predictor of episode type, in this particular case we can see that it might have played a role. Arguably, it is precisely the lack of external involvement and the lack of procedural constraints that allowed the government to control the policy agenda via setting the timing and deciding on the content of the senate reform. This factor allowed the government to strategically constrain the opportunity for contention and minimize the toll the episode would take on its popularity. It neither had the obligation to introduce any legal text into parliament nor to vote for it within a specific time after its announcement. Instead, since the issue was clearly domestic, it could gauge reactions, take its time to talk to social partners, and proceed through the different stages of legislation at its own pace. It is highly indicative that this is one of the least contentious episodes, despite its temporal length, with only one demonstration occurring throughout. In short, compared to the bailout case, the lack of a challenger coalition beyond institutional actors, the government's grip on the agenda, and the absence of external pressure rendered this episode much slower and less complex compared to the bailout episode.

Alhough earlier in this chapter we tried to explain the pace and complexity of the episodes, in the foregoing discussion we also exposed them as potential explanatory factors of some broader features of contention. The Irish bank and I.M.F. bailouts had wide repercussions on Irish political life, upending the country's political system. The senate reform did not. We can speculate on whether pace and complexity can serve as useful meso-level indicators in the tunnel of causation, capturing dynamic aspects of contention that emerge from static variables such as the diversity of social movement coalitions, political opportunities, and a government's agenda-setting power. Therefore, not only may they eventually determine the degree of government coherence and its persistence to persevere with its proposal in the face of political challenges but they may also indicate a more general propensity to disrupt a country's institutional makeup and political life.

CONCLUSION

In this chapter, we have offered the first conceptualization of the link between contentious actions, taking the first step from a static towards a dynamic analysis. We have introduced the basic link between actions via the concept of triggers and offered an empirical mapping of how a chain of actions tied together via their triggers comes together in an action sequence. Thinking of episodes in terms of sequences, we relied on a tree metaphor whereby the main line of early interactions (the trunk) branches off in various branches and leaves. We then derived various indicators for sequences and aggregated these indicators across episodes. In this fashion, episodes can be described in terms of their average pace (the ratio of the sequences' duration and their length), and their complexity (the product of the average length and the width of the episode to approximate the "area" of the sequence tree).

Having defined and operationalized our concepts, we presented descriptive patterns and undertook a multivariate analysis to predict in which cluster episodes were likely to fall in the combination of average pace and complexity, depending on the underlying economic and political grievances, actor characteristics, and the macro constraints that a government faces. To reiterate the main patterns we have found, high episode severity, lower levels of satisfaction with democracy, center-left governments, and external third parties' involvement tended to "push" episodes towards the high pace–high complexity end of the spectrum. It appears, therefore, that certain aspects of the external environment that collectively have the greatest potential to upset the status quo are likely to shape the course of contention by speeding up actors' reactions to preceding actions and by triggering multiple threads of contention and prolonging them in time.

In addition to our statistical results, we also illustrated how these sequence characteristics play out in two Irish episodes: the I.M.F. bailout and the senate referendum. A deeper analysis of these particular cases reveals that the sequence characteristics were closely related to the types of actors involved in the episode and that the time dimension must also be taken into account; for instance, the 2010 November bailout agreement marked a clear shift from a slower to a more rapid evolution of contention in Ireland.

In sum, both the quantitative analysis and Irish case study have highlighted time as a crucial aspect of contention that is contingent on various aspects of the external environment as well as on key events in the policy debate. More generally speaking, the importance of time will be the main subject of analysis in Part III of the book, where we explicitly model contention in dynamic terms.

# 7

## Outcomes: Government Responsiveness

### Sophia Hunger and Julia Schulte-Cloos

INTRODUCTION

Shortly after his reelection in 2014, Hungarian Prime Minister Orbán proposed a new bill that would charge private internet users and enterprises alike for each gigabyte of data usage. Trusting that he enjoyed broad support among the Hungarian public, he may have not expected that this proposal would unleash a massive wave of protests across the country. Starting to organize their collective action in social media outlets on the very day of the government proposal, the protesters quickly spread in masses on to Hungarian streets, sparking broad international media coverage, and even attracting the support of an EU commissioner. While the ruling Fidesz party initially tried to tame the protesters by slightly modifying the proposal in response to the vivid and vocal opposition all across the country, the various challenger actors kept protesting relentlessly against the introduction of the so-called internet tax. Only ten days after having proposed the bill, Prime Minister Orban, in a widely transmitted radio interview, decided to back off. The government proposal was withdrawn, and the internet tax never became part of Hungarian legislation. In a very short period of time and in a country where a political tradition of mass mobilization is largely absent, the Hungarian citizens managed to be heard. The government took their demands seriously and fully responded to their opposition.

In contrast to the case of the Hungarian internet tax, most governments scarcely responded to contention during the Great Recession. This chapter shows that governments rarely met the challengers' demands and, if so, their reaction was merely symbolic in nature as they did not make substantive concessions toward the core demands of challengers. We draw on Gamson's (1975) seminal piece on social protest to develop our theoretical framework, distinguishing between different qualities and degrees of responsiveness to study the implications of substantive as opposed to procedural government responsiveness.

We first review the most important theoretical concepts of government responsiveness proposed in the literature and present our own operationalization, which allows us to capture different degrees of both procedural and substantive responsiveness. Subsequently, we present the related manifestations of government responsiveness in our sixty contentious episodes, providing evidence that substantive responsiveness is indeed a rather rare event in our sample. Above all, substantive government responsiveness seems to originate in specific circumstances, such as the involvement of supreme courts or popular votes. Furthermore, we show that governments overproportionally responded in procedural terms. Hence, they attempted to *appear* responsive rather that making actual substantive concessions. Building on the descriptive presentation of the cases at hand, we integrate these findings with accounts on external government constraints during the financial crisis that will play a key role in our discussion of government responsiveness – and lack thereof – during the contentious episodes studied in this book. We then move to analyze whether the predictors derived from existing accounts can systematically explain the variation in government responsiveness that we observed during the European financial crisis. The results show that the variation in government responsiveness did not relate to the breadth of protests, the polarization of contention in a given episode, or the action repertoire of challengers. It appears that in times of heavy austerity measures and external economic constraints, governments mostly responded to their domestic challengers when the economy was not at stake. We found that the type of episode is the most powerful predictor in explaining the variance observed in our data.

## GOVERNMENT RESPONSIVENESS: DEFINITION AND DISTRIBUTIONS

Our approach to measuring government responsiveness carries several advantages. Studying single episodes and the success of challengers within these episodes allows us, first, to present a more fine-grained and clearer picture of government responsiveness – especially when compared to approaches that look at the success of entire movements. Second, as we included procedural responsiveness in addition to substantive responsiveness in our analysis, we could study the more "symbolic" side of protest politics: that is, situations in which governments try to *appear* responsive rather than actually giving in to challengers' demands. Third and most notably, as we included various characteristics of our respective policy episodes, our approach enabled us to compare how the features of different challengers (e.g. their radicalness, breadth) and governments (e.g. their vulnerability or the level of polarization within the cabinet) might drive the outcome of a policy episode. Finally, our approach allowed us to include context variables in our analysis, a feature that is critical for understanding how external factors that were beyond the control of all involved actors (e.g. the economic situation, pressure from external actors) helped to shape government responsiveness.

The majority of existing studies propose two approaches to conceptualizing government responsiveness and the outcomes of political contention of policy

TABLE 7.1. *Categorization of government responsiveness by Gamson (1975)*

|  |  | Acceptance | |
|---|---|---|---|
|  |  | Full | None |
| New | Many | Full response | Preemption |
| Advantages | None | Cooptation | Collapse |

proposals through challengers. On the one hand, scholars conceive rather broadly of such outcomes by looking at the general success or failure of an entire movement. Movements are, however, often very heterogeneous and lack a clearly stated and specified goal in terms of policy change or implementation. Thus, the success or failure of a movement may not always indicate whether governments have proven to be responsive to their demands. On the other hand, scholars perceive of outcomes in a narrower way and study specific policy outcomes and the role of protest movements in the realization (or prevention) of these policy proposals. As our sample consisted of episodes covering a very specific time frame – the time from the announcement of a policy proposal until its adoption or final rejection – our approach has been situated within the latter strand of scholarly work. Thus, focusing on these episodes has provided us with a clearer picture regarding both the challengers' goals as well as the governments' reactions to their demands in a clearly defined period. Our set of challengers comprised various subtypes of actors, including interest groups and social movement organizations (Burstein 1999). We also took various characteristics of both governments and challengers into account.

In addition to substantive responsiveness, we included a second type of responsiveness that refers to the relationship between challengers and governments. Our approach is inspired by Gamson's seminal work on social protest. He distinguished between two dimensions of movement success – acceptance and new advantages. In Gamson's terminology (see Table 7.1), a movement could be successful on both dimensions ("full success"), it could lack success on both dimensions ("collapse"), it could obtain new substantive advantages without procedural success ("preemption"), or it could obtain only procedural success ("co-optation'"). His distinction between acceptance and new advantages is closely related to our distinction between procedural and substantive actions of governments.

Gamson's concept of "acceptance" as a dimension of possible outcomes refers to the "acceptance of a challenging group by its antagonists as a valid spokesman for a legitimate set of interests" (Gamson 1975: 28). To acknowledge the interests of challengers, at times, may be a powerful political symbol, which can be sufficient to pacify the mass public by means of gestures more than real political action (Edelman 1985: 172). In emphasizing the change in the relationship between challengers and governments, Kitschelt's (1986) concept of procedural responsiveness is very similar. As a result, we have the coding scheme (see Table 7.2) that differentiates between substantive and procedural responsiveness:

TABLE 7.2. *Operationalization of substantive and procedural responsiveness*

| Substantive responsiveness | Procedural responsiveness |
|---|---|
| Government makes concessions | Government ready to negotiate |
| Government withdraws proposal | Government considers concessions |
| | Government negotiates |

We introduced binary variables that measure these concepts, with zero denoting no substantive or procedural responsiveness from the government's side. Our approach, thus, also took those cases into account that were characterized by a lack of government responsiveness, in line with the theoretical arguments proposed by Giugni (1999) as we were also studying cases in which movements were unsuccessful.

This classification allowed us to cluster our episodes into four distinct groups, depending on whether they were characterized by both procedural and substantive responsiveness, by at least one type of responsiveness, or by no government responsiveness at all. Table 7.3 indicates to which of these categories the single episodes belonged. We provided examples for all four fields in Gamson's two-by-two typology, starting with episodes in which governments were both substantively and procedurally responsive. These cases amount to a total of thirty-six (60 percent) in our sample, thereby representing more than half of our cases. At first sight, this suggests that the challengers obtained considerable success in the episodes under study. However, this impression is quite misleading: Only in a single case did the challengers obtain full success. This single case is the Hungarian internet tax proposal that we discussed above that was fully withdrawn by the government. The proposed policy to tax internet traffic first sparked several demonstrations with tens of thousands of participants, online protest, and a strong negative reaction by international actors: for example, from the European Commissioner for Digital Agenda. Subsequently, the proposal was entirely withdrawn. Only ten days passed from the announcement of the government's proposal to Victor Orban's statement not to follow up on the initiative. The fact that we only found a single case of full government responsiveness among all of the sixty contentious episodes under study indicates that full responsiveness was an exception during the Great Recession.[1] In most of the other cases of both substantive and procedural responsiveness, the government made only some limited substantive concessions. For instance, in the German Bad Bank Scheme, the government made substantive changes regarding the involvement of regional banks in the

---

[1] Note, however, that the Irish institutional episode on the Abolishment of the Senate also ended with the proposal not entering into force. This case is highly particular, however, as the proposal was not withdrawn by the government but only after a successful referendum in which 52 percent of the electorate voted against the abolishment.

TABLE 7.3. *Categorization of episodes*

| | | Procedural responsiveness | |
| --- | --- | --- | --- |
| | | Yes | No |
| Substantive Responsiveness | Yes | France: Sarkozy–Fillon austerity<br>Germany: Bank bailout, Bad banks, First bailout, Third bailout<br>Greece: Second and Third bailout<br>Hungary: I.M.F. bailout, 2010 austerity, Pension nationalization, Internet tax, Media law<br>Ireland: Bank guarantee, 2009 austerity, Water tax, senate<br>Italy: Berlusconi 1st austerity, Monti package, Jobs Act<br>Latvia: I.M.F. bailout, 2009 austerity, 2009 2nd austerity, 2010 austerity<br>Poland: 2009 crisis package, Pension reform<br>Portugal: PEC 1 and 2, PEC 3 and 4, I.M.F.bailout, 2012 austerity, Muncipal reform<br>UK: 2011 austerity/Welfare reform<br>Spain: Zapatero 1st and 2nd austerity<br>Romania: I.M.F. bailout, 2010 2nd austerity, Labor regulations | France: Decentralization |
| | No | France: Sarkozy 2nd austerity, Holland–Valls cuts<br>Greece: First bailout, Midterm adjustment, TV shutdown<br>Italy: Berlusconi 2nd austerity, Judicial reform<br>Latvia: Eurozone entry<br>Poland: Tusk austerity, Labor code<br>Romania: 2010 1st austerity<br>Spain: Rajoy austerity, Bankia<br>UK: Bank bailouts, 2010 austerity, Tuition fees, Brexit | France: Holland 1st austerity<br>Germany: Debt brake<br>Ireland: I.M.F. bailout<br>Poland: Constitutional court<br>Romania: Impeachment<br>Spain: Constitutional amendment |

scheme. This happened after hearings with banks and management organizations – that is, after procedural concessions.

Second, in seventeen of the cases (roughly 30 percent), substantive concessions did not follow at all after procedural responsiveness. Thus, in these
episodes the governments only granted procedural responsiveness without a
follow up. In the French episode regarding the reduction of government
spending by 50 billion Euros carried out by the French President Hollande
and Prime Minister Valls, the government repeatedly promised concessions
and organized hearings; however, it did not change the policy proposal. This
set of actions was related to a new railway law that sparked a series of
strikes. In reaction to these strikes, the government negotiated with the
Confédération Générale du Travail (CGT) (the French confederation of
labor), but these meetings remained inconsequential in not leading to substantive government responsiveness.

While full substantive responsiveness, the withdrawal of the proposal, is
extremely rare in our sample, governments were more responsive in procedural
terms. In fifty-three of our sixty episodes the governments either demonstrated
some readiness to negotiate, engaged in actual negotiations, or even considered
concessions. This gap between substantive and procedural responsiveness further suggests that governments tried to *appear* responsive despite their lacking
leeway to give in substantively to challengers' demands.

Third, in a single case in our sample, the government was substantively
responsive without taking procedural action beforehand. In the French
decentralization episode, which is the institutional episode for this country
and characterized by its very short duration of five months, several concessions were made, including the rejection of the first part of the draft law as a
reaction to a strong opposition from local representatives, such as mayors
and presidents of regions, who were fearing to lose their independence
and competences.

Finally, in six of our episodes, the respective governments were not responsive – neither in procedural nor in substantive terms.[2] Interestingly, four of
these episodes concern institutional reforms. Both during the Spanish
Constitutional Reform and in the course of the Polish reform of the
Constitutional Court, challengers were highly active in taking their opposition
to the streets. In contrast, during the German debt brake episode, even though
some academics, the Trade Union Confederation, and several individual left-
leaning politicians voiced harsh critique, challengers did not become active. The
other two cases of government nonresponsiveness during the Great Recession
are the I.M.F. intervention in Ireland in 2010, and President Hollande's first

---

[2] The Romanian case of the impeachment of President Basescu is another example: Basescu stayed
president after the Constitutional Court ruled the referendum invalid. He also embodies the only
challenger in this episode.

austerity package in 2012 that was mostly about the ratification of the Treaty on Stability, Coordination and Governance in the Economic and Monetary Union (short name: Fiscal Stability Treaty or TSCG). Both episodes are characterized by a broad array and large number of active challengers. Another common characteristic of these episodes is the significant involvement of international actors, the I.M.F. in the first case, and the EU and the German government in the latter.

GOVERNMENT RESPONSIVENESS DURING THE GREAT RECESSION: THE ROLE OF COURTS AND REFERENDA

Some of the few successful episodes share common characteristics and patterns, which we shall highlight in the following section. First, the role of constitutional courts is noteworthy. Second, we shall discuss how referenda might have served several functions: Sometimes, they provided governments with "an easy way out," while in other cases challengers could use referenda as a vehicle to accomplish their demands. The role of constitutional courts is ambiguous in the cases characterized by government concessions. Many of the policy proposals under study were heavily debated and their constitutionality was highly contested. In several episodes the courts ruled in favour of the governments, declaring the proposed policies and laws as being in conformity with the constitution, for instance in the Polish pension reform, in the French decentralization reform, or in the case of a new pension law during the Sarkozy–Fillon austerity measures. In other cases, however, the constitutional courts declared the policy proposals void that had been contested by the challengers. This happened, for instance, during the Latvian austerity measures in 2009, when the constitutional court ruled that cuts in retirement pensions contradicted the principle of legal certainty, forcing the government to pay back the reduced benefits retrospectively. Similarly, the French constitutional court declared the 75 percent income tax, which was proposed as part of the first austerity package by Francois Hollande, as being unconstitutional.

Second, many of the institutional episodes were marked by referenda, such as Brexit, the abolishment of the Irish senate, and the impeachment of Romanian President Basescu. While these institutional proposals often required popular votes, referenda were also used in the economic episodes. The 2015 Greek referendum on the bailout conditions is certainly the most striking example. The government campaigned for the rejection of the program proposed by the memorandum. However, after the voters had followed its advice and had rejected the memorandum with 62.2 percent of the vote, only slightly more than two weeks later, a very similar program was put into place by the very same government. While only few referenda were held regarding the adoption of austerity measures, challengers quite frequently called for them. These attempts, however, remained mostly unsuccessful: They include the 2011 austerity measures in Poland; when trade unions called for a referendum during the first Romanian austerity proposals in 2010; President Hollande's first austerity package, when a broad coalition of radical left parties and trade unions stated that the TSCG could only be adopted by the people's votes; or Latvia in 2009, where trade unions and NGOs demanded a referendum about the dismissal of the parliament. In some cases, opposition parties pushed for a referendum, such as the Hungarian Socialist Party (MSZP) in response to the pension fund nationalization in 2010 that was rejected by the National Election Committee. Italian Prime Minister Matteo Renzi was even challenged from within his own party, the center-left Democratic Party (PD), to hold a referendum on the highly contested Jobs Act in 2014. However, most of these demands remained without any significant impact. Most noteworthy is the Irish Water Tax Episode, in which the "Right2Water campaign" and several groups demanded a referendum. The government subsequently decided to disregard such earlier considerations and finally put the respective policy, capping the water charge, into force.

## DRIVERS OF GOVERNMENT RESPONSIVENESS

Since the 1970s, social scientists have increasingly paid attention to the outcomes of social movements. Building on the theoretical approaches put forward in the pioneering work by Gamson (1975), Piven and Cloward (1977), and Schumaker (1977) recent studies became more systematic in the scope of their analyses, often aiming to offer a comparative framework. In the following, we integrate the seminal theoretical accounts with more recent empirical evidence on the capacity of protest movements to shape policy in their favor, putting the theoretical expectations in the context of our contentious episodes. We have condensed the arguments into three different sets. These are, first, the characteristics of challenger actors; second, the external and domestic economic constraints during the contentious episodes; and third, the pressure posed by public opinion and the internal cohesion of a government. We then shall discuss the operationalization of government responsiveness within the framework of the comparative study of contentious episodes.

There is little consensus in the literature on whether disruption or moderation are more effective strategies for protest movements. While pluralists claim that moderation and bargaining will lead movements to succeed, Gamson's findings show that social movements' willingness to use disruptive actions has a positive effect on their success. The latter's findings are confirmed by some re-analyses of Gamson's data by Steedly and Foley (1979). Various other scholars similarly stress the role of force or disruption for social movements to reach their goals (McAdam 1983; Tarrow 1979; Tilly 1984). Piven and Cloward (1977) emphasize that disruption is especially effective for social movement organizations as they lack resources that are available to parties and interest groups. These accounts suggest that the radicalness of challengers is likely to increase their chances to achieve government responsiveness.

While various scholars have studied the significance that internal factors – characteristics of protest movement such as their organizational capacity – have in shaping policy outcomes, other scholars have emphasized the importance of external factors. These external factors relate to the political environment, the political opportunity structure, and social support for the respective protest agenda (Kitschelt 1986; McAdam 1983; Schumaker 1975). The most important macro condition shaping the political environment in the contentious episodes under study is the Great Recession. The extent to which countries were hit by the crisis varied significantly and divided them into creditor and debtor states (see Chapter 3). External constraints, such as budgetary controls and international debtors, often put states in a dilemma between responsiveness toward their electoral constituencies and domestic challengers on the one hand, and responsibility with respect to the fulfilment of budgetary conditions on the other hand (Mair 2014, 2013). Additionally, the types of episodes and their severity also varied within countries (see Chapter 3). Less severe episodes might offer governments more leeway to react to challengers in a responsive manner, while more severe episodes come with additional external constraints that might hinder any form of government responsiveness. Accordingly, we posit that government responsiveness *should be less likely in episodes that are dominated by international actors and/or involve an I.M.F. intervention*. In addition, the economic situation characterizing the episode under study should have an impact on the potential capacity of governments to respond to challenger demands. Thus, we also hold that those episodes which are marked by *particular economic severity should less frequently result in responsive government action.*

Government responsiveness cannot be conceived of independently from public opinion. Burstein (1999) argues that governments aim to be reelected and are not responsive when the public does not support the challenger's claim. To test this, we included three different variables in our analysis. First, we included *the breadth of the challenger*, as we argue that a broad challenger coalition represents a bigger share of societal forces exerting greater pressure on the government, making the latter more prone to be responsive. Second, we included *government vulnerability*, arguing that a weak position makes a government more likely to react to a challenger's demand. Third, we argued that the *proximity to the previous election* should make it less likely that a government gives in to a challenger. Governments that have just been elected can be confident of having secured widespread popular support among citizens (the "honeymoon period"). Accordingly, this support should work to decrease their incentives to deviate from their legislative endeavors in favor of demands pushed forward by some challenger actors. Finally, we also considered government characteristics. As discussed above, a challenger's success is dependent on the capacity of the government to ignore or repress protest. Lacking this capacity might not only stem from external pressure but also be due to the internal cohesion of governments. Hence, we posit that *internally divided governments are more prone to give in to a challenger's demand*.

## OPERATIONALIZATION OF THE INDEPENDENT VARIABLES

We assessed government responsiveness as a function of variables belonging to the three different sets of theoretical arguments discussed above: *challenger characteristics, external constraints, and government leeway*. In order to assess the differential impact that the characteristics of challengers and their disruptive strategies might have on the outcomes, we used the radicalness of a challenger actor, the breadth of the challenger, and the challenger's degree of contentiousness, as discussed in Chapters 5 and 6.

In addition, we included several explanatory factors related to external constraints that may have an impact on the government's capacity to react to a challenger. Two of these refer to the involvement of international actors. First, we included the share of international actors involved in each episode, including EU, I.M.F., and Eurozone actors, members of the Troika, and other governments and international actors. Moreover, we used the type of episode as introduced in Chapter 3 that identifies whether the central part of a policy proposal is related to an I.M.F. intervention, to a budgetary reform, classical austerity, a bank bailout, or an institutional reform. We operationalized the economic constraints that governments face by using the mean unemployment level over the course of the episode. Additionally, we included the severity of each episode in our empirical tests.

Finally, we assessed whether government responsiveness is a more likely outcome when the government is particularly vulnerable or dependent on public opinion that may go against the government when a challenger contests a government proposal. We did so by measuring the level of public support for the current government: the share of the electorate intending to vote for the government. Further, we included the months that have passed since the last elections to test whether governments were less responsive when elections are held recently, making it unnecessary for them to curry favor with voters. Governments that have just been elected can also be confident to have widespread popular support among the public (the "honeymoon" period). This factor should make them less likely to deviate from their legislative endeavors to accommodate challenger actors. Finally, we considered the polarization of the cabinets to see whether internally divided governments were possibly more responsive to challengers. We operationalized the internal division of governments by relying on a measure of cabinet polarization.

RESULTS

Tables 7.4 and 7.5 present the substantive and procedural government responsiveness during the contentious episodes as a function of the key explanatory variables discussed above. For each independent variable, we compared successful and unsuccessful episodes and provided the means, standard deviations, and the p-value of the t-tests, comparing the corresponding means.

It appears that government responsiveness in the contentious episodes under study is not a function of such predictors that previous accounts have identified as key factors in determining the success of challenger actors to accomplish their demands. The empirical results did not provide us with a clear-cut pattern regarding an association between potential drivers of responsiveness and actual substantive and procedural responsiveness. The difference-in-means and marginal contingencies presented in Tables 7.4 and 7.5 show that the respective variables are not differentially distributed among "success cases," – those episodes that resulted in substantive or procedural responsiveness by governments – and among failure cases, those episodes in which the challenger demands were largely ignored by governments. If we test for the joint impact of each of the three clusters on government responsiveness in a linear regression framework, we find that the cluster of variables relating to external constraints accounts for most of the variance in our data as indicated by the $R^2$ values. Most of the coefficients were insignificant, however, suggesting that government responsiveness was not a linear function of the related predictors. Only the severity of an episode seems marginally to reach statistical significance when

TABLE 7.4. *Substantive government responsiveness: means, standard deviations, and p-values of t-tests comparing the means*

| Dependent: substantive responsiveness | | No | Yes | p |
|---|---|---|---|---|
| Challenger contentiousness | Mean (SD) | 0.4 (0.3) | 0.4 (0.3) | 0.793 |
| Challenger breadth | Mean (SD) | 0.6 (0.5) | 0.8 (0.3) | 0.316 |
| Challenger radicalness | Mean (SD) | 2 (2) | 1.9 (1.7) | 0.663 |
| I.M.F. episode | Yes | 2 (25.0) | 6 (75.0) | 0.405 |
| | No | 21 (40.4) | 31 (59.6) | |
| Share external actors | Mean (SD) | 0.1 (0.1) | 0.1 (0.1) | 0.886 |
| Unemployment | Mean (SD) | 0.5 (0.2) | 0.5 (0.1) | 0.382 |
| Severity | 1 | 5 (50.0) | 5 (50.0) | 0.292 |
| | 2 | 6 (26.1) | 17 (73.9) | |
| | 3 | 12 (44.4) | 15 (55.6) | |
| Electoral honeymoon | Mean (SD) | 17.3 (16.8) | 16.5 (12.8) | 0.727 |
| Cabinet polarization | Mean (SD) | 0.9 (0.9) | 1.3 (1) | 0.109 |
| Vote intention (government) | Mean (SD) | 37.6 (11.3) | 39.4 (12.3) | 0.556 |

TABLE 7.5. *Procedural government responsiveness: means, standard deviations, and p-values of t-tests comparing the means*

| Dependent: procedural responsiveness | | No | Yes | p |
|---|---|---|---|---|
| Challenger contentiousness | Mean (SD) | 0.3 (0.2) | 0.4 (0.3) | 0.221 |
| Challenger breadth | Mean (SD) | 0.6 (0.5) | 0.7 (0.4) | 0.776 |
| Challenger radicalness | Mean (SD) | 1.5 (1.6) | 2 (1.8) | 0.367 |
| I.M.F. episode | Yes | 1 (12.5) | 7 (87.5) | 0.937 |
| | No | 6 (11.5) | 46 (88.5) | |
| Share external actors | Mean (SD) | 0.1 (0.1) | 0.1 (0.1) | 0.215 |
| Unemployment | Mean (SD) | 0.5 (0.2) | 0.5 (0.1) | 0.759 |
| Severity | 1 | 3 (30.0) | 7 (70.0) | 0.140 |
| | 2 | 2 (8.7) | 21 (91.3) | |
| | 3 | 2 (7.4) | 25 (92.6) | |
| Electoral honeymoon | Mean (SD) | 23.4 (18.6) | 15.9 (13.5) | 0.436 |
| Cabinet polarization | Mean (SD) | 1 (0.9) | 1.2 (1) | 0.711 |
| Vote intention (government) | Mean (SD) | 38.1 (16.7) | 38.8 (11.3) | 0.610 |

explaining the variance in procedural responsiveness. It appears that as an episode increased in severity, governments felt forced at least to signal their readiness to negotiate with a challenger. This procedural responsiveness, however, was seemingly only symbolic as it did not result in a substantive responsiveness toward challengers' demands, nor did it prompt actual modifications of the policy proposals in response to heavy contention.

CONCLUSION

What accounts for government responsiveness – and lack thereof – in times of the contentious episodes under study? Building on the seminal account of Gamson (1975), this chapter developed a conceptual tool to study government responsiveness in times of contention. We propose to classify episodes in terms of the nature of responsiveness that governments display towards the demands of challengers and make the case for distinguishing between substantive and procedural responsiveness. Analyzing the individual cases of contention by means of this conceptualization, we have shown that government responsiveness was an exceptional event during the Great Recession. We then proposed to examine the instances of government (non)responsiveness as a function of three different sets of factors to explain when, why, and to what extent challengers have been successful in articulating their demands to the ruling government and in making their opposition toward a policy proposal heard. These factors are: first, the type and characteristics of challengers; second, the external constraints faced by governments, such as international actors putting pressure on them or the domestic state of the economy; and finally, the pressure that governments felt to react toward heavy contention, imposed on them both by public opinion and internal divides within a coalition. Our analysis shows that in episodes characterized by extreme severity, governments at least tried to signal some responsiveness toward the challenger actors. This kind of responsiveness, however, was mostly of a symbolic nature. During the Great Recession, marked by heavy austerity measures and external economic constraints, it appears that governments responded to their domestic challengers only when the economy was not at stake.

PART III

DYNAMICS OF INTERACTION

# 8

# Interaction Dynamics in Contentious Episodes: Path-Dependence, Tit-for-Tat, and Constructive Mediation[*]

Abel Bojar and Hanspeter Kriesi

INTRODUCTION

In the introductory chapter of this volume, we presented our case for studying interaction dynamics between governments, challengers, and third-parties in the "middle ground" because we share Tilly's (2008: 21) view that this level of analysis offers the "opportunity to look inside contentious performances and discern their dynamics" without losing the opportunity to systematically analyze these dynamics in a quantitative framework. In this present chapter, we further develop this middle ground by presenting a novel method for studying these interaction dynamics. We concur with Moore (2000) that most of the literature on the interaction between governments and challengers is based on cross-sectional analyses using national, aggregate yearly data, which is fundamentally inappropriate for the questions raised about the interactions we were studying. To deal with such questions, we need sequential data that allows us to specify how the different actors react to each others' previous actions. Such sequential data not only allows us to causally connect all the actions constituting an episode as we have done in Chapter 6, but it also permits us to take a step further and uncover regularities that occur in the interaction between the protagonists of the conflict. Drawing on the construction of action sequences from Chapter 6, we now focus on the relationship between actions and their triggers and examine some of the main themes and mechanisms in the literature on contention politics through this novel methodological lens. In other words, we shall take the mechanism-centered approach from the narrative tradition and marry it with some of the basic tools of time-series methodology to infuse it

[*] A previous version of this chapter has been published in the *European Journal of Political Research* (Bojar and Kriesi, 2020).

with statistical rigor. This, in essence, is the dynamic aspect of Contentious Politics Analysis that we put forward in this volume.

On the substantive front, we seek to understand the determinants of the action repertoires of the contending actors. In this chapter, we adopt a somewhat stylized approach by asking how the chosen action forms of the contending actors depend on (a) their own past actions, (b) actions of the adversary, and (c) actions of the third parties. To anticipate our main findings, we identify two main stylized nexi of interaction dynamics: one of the adversarial, the other of the cooperative nature. The repression-disruptive mobilization-external legitimation nexus refers to the scenario of challengers undertaking disruptive challenges against the government that in turn responds in kind with repressive acts to subdue the challenge, with third parties providing external support for either side. Alternatively, the interaction can take a cooperative form whereby challengers display cooperative behavior, the government responds in kind by providing concessions, and third parties facilitate the process by mediating between the adversaries. We call this the concession–cooperation–mediation nexus. As it turns out, and somewhat surprisingly, the empirical evidence largely points to this second nexus as better characterizing the interaction dynamics between the actors.

In this approach, we make a number of simplifications to render our data amenable to empirical analysis. First, our analysis is "context-blind" in the sense that we seek to uncover relationships between action forms that hold across space and time in our empirical universe of sixty contentious episodes.[1] Second, we depart from the highly disaggregated ontology of action repertoires and take the analysis to a higher level of aggregation that allows three possible action forms for each actor type. Third, because our primary interest is the action of the contending parties, we do not seek to explain the behavior of third parties as such; we merely study their actions as possible determinants of the behavior of the adversaries themselves.

We shall first present our theoretical considerations and lay out a number of hypotheses on the determinants of action repertoires of governments and challengers. Then, we introduce our data and the operationalization of our basic concepts, relying on the tools derived from the construction of action sequences. In particular, we introduce a novel method for studying interaction dynamics that is based on the notion of *actor-specific action lags* that we shall explain in detail in the third section. In the following two sections, we present our estimation strategy as well as our results. We conclude with a summary, a discussion of the results, and some implications of our methods. We also provide a chapter appendix where we provide some additional empirical exercises for the robustness of our results.

---

[1] The role of context in moderating the relationships that we uncover in this chapter will be the subject of the next two chapters.

## THEORY

As a brief recap of our ontological space, the analysis has three stylized actor types: a government, putting forward a policy proposal; challengers, opposing such proposal; third parties, either taking sides in the debate or mediating between the two adversaries. Each type of actor has a limited set of options for engaging in the interactions within the episodes. Tilly (1986, 1995) has popularized the notion of a limited action repertoire in the social movement literature, but this notion may also extend to the other actors involved in the contentious episodes. In particular, we rely on the aggregated codes for action repertoires presented in the introduction to this volume. The government can either repress its challengers, stick to its proposal, or offer concessions of some form. The challenger can undertake disruptive mobilization against the proposal, engage in nondisruptive opposition to the proposal, or it can cooperate with the government. Third parties can either take the government's side, the challenger's side, or mediate between the two.[2]

The gist of the interaction dynamics within an episode lies of course in the interdependence of these actors. As Beissinger (2011: 27) has observed: "one of the defining features of mobilization – and its greatest challenge for causal explanation – is the high degree of inter-dependence of the actions and reactions involved, both within and across episodes of mobilization. While not a feature characteristic of mobilization alone, it figures so centrally in contentious politics that it is difficult to explain any protest episode without fundamentally addressing this issue." Our model assumes that the actors involved act *retrospectively*, i.e. they react to the actions of the others (see Moore 2000: 121). Even with only three types of stylized actors, there are multiple patterns of possible interactions. In our analysis, we shall have a look at a subset of these possible interactions that are expected to hold across the diverse contexts that we study.

A natural starting point for any dynamic model of contentious politics is how strategic choices taken in the past affect the choices available today. More specifically, we expect for all actors that their past action predicts their current actions in a path-dependent fashion. However, our *path-dependence hypothesis* has two distinct formulations. First, each side has a default strategy to which it tries to adhere throughout the episode. In line with the notion of the action repertoire, each side of the interaction relies on a limited set of strategic options. Actors choose actions that they already know how to perform (Doherty and Hayes 2019: 272) while aiming to choose the least costly option. These costs can be conceptualized in various ways, such as audience costs (Fearon, 1994) – in other words, the loss of credibility that frequent changes in tactics entail – substantive policy costs in the case of significant concessions

---

[2] For all actor types, this somewhat "flat" ontology of action repertoires is derived from a more fine-grained distinction between action types that we presented in Chapter 2.

to the other side or organizational costs when radical actions (repression in the case of government or disruptive mobilization in the case of challengers) induce splits between radical and moderate elements within a given organization. Within the action repertoire of a given actor, there is likely to be a default option that imposes the lowest possible costs on them. For the government this means sticking to its proposal and for the challengers this means opting for a nondisruptive challenge. Ceteris paribus, both sides avoid making costly concessions, and both sides also try to avoid resorting to more repressive or more radical tactics, that is tactics that are likely to increase internal tensions. This is the first aspect of the path-dependence hypothesis.

The second aspect of path dependence refers to episode-specific strategies. As Tilly also consistently stressed, tactics are the result of interaction (Doherty and Hayes 2019: 274): the repertoire does not belong to any one set of actors but is produced through the encounter between different types of actors. Interactions are best understood as the interplay of moves and countermoves. This means that actors may be led to abandon their default strategy in the course of the interaction in a given episode. The neutralization of established challenger tactics by the authorities may, for example, lead to tactical innovation on the part of the challengers (McAdam 1983). Or, more generally, both sides may resort to more costly reactions once it is realized that the default option does not work. If, for whatever reason, the episode-specific tactics start to deviate from the default options, they are also likely to become path dependent: preceding adversarial actions (repression or a disruptive challenge) increase the likelihood of current adversarial actions, while accommodative actions in the past (concessions or cooperation) increase the likelihood of current accommodative actions, both for the government and for challengers. This second form of path dependence may occur as a result of the episode-specific interaction dynamics, but it may also result from external constraints (e.g. the international pressure on the government, or the desperate economic situation on the part of the challengers) that force the adversaries in a given episode to stick to a strategy that is different from their default one.

Having emphasized the importance of the interaction for the actors' tactics, we need to look more closely at the effect of the other actors' choices on the reactions of each stylized actor. Let us begin with the impact of the challengers on the government's actions. Whether or not the government deviates from its default strategy of "sticking" is likely to depend on the costs imposed by the challengers' actions. Protestors imposing few costs can be "innocuous" and disregarded by the government because they pose minimal public nuisances and little threat to the status quo or regime stability (Boudreau 2005, Klein and Regan 2018). When, however, the challenge poses a credible threat, the government will generally employ some form of coercive action to counter or eliminate the threat. This is a highly consistent finding of the literature on repression which Davenport (2007) summarizes as the "law of coercive responsiveness." Earl (2011: 266) reiterates that the most compelling finding in the literature on repression has been that threat is critically important to explain repression, across time, place, and form of analysis. Put simply, the more challengers threaten the government, the more likely they are to face repression. This is the *government's threat hypothesis*: governments facing a disruptive challenge (both in procedural or substantive terms) are more likely to resort to repression.[3] The flipside of the logic underlying this hypothesis is that governments that perceive the challengers as cooperative are more likely to make concessions. In other words, from a game theoretical perspective we expect the stream of interaction to follow a tit-for-tat pattern: While the government tends to reciprocate cooperative behavior by the challengers, a change of challenger tactics to more adversarial action forms is likely to induce the government to respond with repression.

Compared to the impact of the challengers' actions on government repression, the findings for the effect of repression on the challengers' strategic choices have been quite inconclusive, resulting in what Davenport (2007) calls the "punishment puzzle." The expected impact of repression depends on how we interpret its meaning for the challengers. As argued by McAdam and Tarrow (2018), "if we think of repression as the contraction of opportunities, then an increase in repression should typically lead to lower levels of protest or other forms of collective action." In line with this idea, Tilly (1978) had already suggested that "repression works," but, as McAdam and Tarrow also suggest, if we think of repression as a threat, its consequences are more difficult to predict. By now, there is ample evidence that repression of challenger actions may be perceived rather as a threat and induce a radicalization of insurgents (Opp and Rühl 1990; Olivier 1991; Khawaja 1993; O'Brien, 1996; Rasler 1996; Aytaç et al. 2017). This has led Tilly (2005) to abandon his earlier conviction that "repression works" and to conclude that there are no one-size-fits-all rules. We would like to add that in our European context governments seldom repress challengers in such an overtly coercive manner that they disrupt the mobilizing potential of challengers altogether. The soft – sometimes only verbal – repression that is exerted in these countries may be more likely to radicalize challengers. In line with the latter studies and by analogy to the government's threat hypothesis, we formulate the *challenger's threat hypothesis*: the greater the threat exerted by the government's actions, the greater the chances that the challengers will mobilize, often in disruptive forms. In essence,

---

[3] There are two caveats. First, the government's reaction may differ depending on the type of threat that it faces. As Klein and Regan (2018) argue, challengers may cause both concession costs and disruption costs. They show that, contrary to concession costs, which induce the government to repress, disruption costs induce it to adopt accommodating responses. We shall, however, not test this qualification here. Second, this argument, which rests on the "threat-response theory," presumes that governments react to an overt collective challenge by engaging in repressive behavior to control or eliminate challengers. Alternatively, the government may also act in a more forward-looking way, engaging in more covert repression of prospective challengers (Sullivan 2016). We do not take into account such forms of repression.

we expect challengers' behavior to mirror the tit-for-tat logic we put forward for governments.

Next, let us consider the third parties and their impact on the strategies of the two adversaries. The political process approach to social movements suggests in most general terms that open contexts invite moderate strategies on the part of the challengers, while closed contexts have a radicalizing effect (Kitschelt 1986; Kriesi et al. 1995; Lichbach 1998: 55). If institutional access channels are available, challengers will use them, while their absence leads them to resort to more radical means for the articulation of their concerns. Arguably, third-party support constitutes one opening among others. Therefore, one may expect challengers to moderate their tactics if they receive third-party support, while they are likely to radicalize in its absence. This is Piven and Cloward's (1977) perspective: Disruptive action is the weapon of the weak, who have no other way of making themselves heard. Similarly, a government receiving third-party support may feel less threatened by the challengers – which may moderate the government's tactics –while the absence of third-party support may amplify the challengers' threat, inducing the government to resort to repression. This is our *isolation hypothesis*: Isolation radicalizes the adversaries.

However, third-party support may also have the exact opposite effect. Third-party support may provide challengers with additional resources, enabling them to mobilize on a larger scale and reducing the costs of more disruptive action. This is Gamson's (1990: Ch. 6) point of view: Disruptive action is the resort of the powerful. Only powerful challengers have the resources to sustain disruptive action in the face of potential government repression. Arguably, third- party support strengthens the challengers, protects them against government repression, and legitimizes their cause. This may make them more likely to resort to disruptive action. Conversely, governments who receive third-party support may feel less constrained and more legitimate in resorting to repression. This is the *legitimation hypothesis*. Since we are a priori agnostic about the validity and the relative strength of these perspectives, we treated them in the rest of this study as competing hypotheses and let the data adjudicate between them.

Comparatively speaking, we have clearer expectations regarding third parties' efforts to mediate between the two adversaries: Namely, we expect these efforts to bear fruit by fostering cooperation on the part of challengers and concessions on the part of governments. (the *mediation hypothesis*). To be sure, such an effect depends on the way the broker is perceived by the adversaries. Political brokerage is most likely to enhance integration and facilitate compromise when the broker is perceived as an honorable and neutral agent (Shovel and Shaw 2012: 151). In their study of power and trust relations in the Swedish industrial relations system, Svensson and Öberg (2005) show that power and trust relations constitute quite separate coordination mechanisms. Cooperation between the two adversaries in that system – employers and

TABLE 8.1. *Overview of hypotheses*

| Label | Hypothesis summary |
| --- | --- |
| Path dependence | Both actor types tend to stick to their default strategy. Moreover, for each actor, past action predicts current actions. |
| Government's threat | The more challengers threaten the government, the more likely they are to face repression. However, when challengers cooperate, governments are more likely to make concessions. |
| Challenger's threat | The greater the threat exerted by the government's proposal with regard to the challengers' preferences, the greater the chances that they will mobilize (in a disruptive manner). However, when governments make concessions, challengers are more likely to cooperate. |
| Isolation | If left to their own devices while adversaries receive support from third parties, actors lash out against their opponents. |
| Legitimation | Third-party support of a side contributes to the radicalization of that side's strategy |
| Mediation | Third-party mediation induces the two adversaries to cooperate with each other. |

Note that both the government's threat hypothesis and the challenger's threat hypothesis have two parts. If the adversarial part (governments respond to disruptive challenges by repression and challengers respond to repression by radicalization) holds and it is coupled with external support, we can regard this constellation of responses as the repression–disruptive mobilization external-support nexus of interaction. Alternatively, if the cooperative part of both threat hypotheses holds (government concessions are rewarded by cooperative acts from challengers and vice versa) and the actors are aided by mediating acts of third parties, we can think of this as a concession-cooperation–mediation nexus of interaction. When estimating the probabilities of the actor-specific actions in the following empirical exercise, we thus kept these two possible nexi in mind as the overarching logic behind the interaction dynamics.

unions – is only possible because, while distrusting each other, both of them trust the Labor Courts, which fulfill a crucial role as brokers between the two contenders. In line with this result, Fernandez and Gould (1994) find that U.S. government agents in health policy making only gain influence as brokers when they are viewed as impartial. For nongovernment organizations, however, brokerage is positively related to influence regardless of whether they are impartial or not. Given that a predominant share of third-party actors in our sample are external actors – foreign governments or supranational institutions – or domestic state institutions – constitutional courts, local authorities, or independent central banks – we have reason to expect that they satisfy a minimum level of impartiality for the mediation hypothesis to be applicable to their role in the conflict. Table 8.1 summarizes the six hypotheses that we test in this study.

DATA AND OPERATIONALIZATION

Our total dataset consists of the nearly 7,000 individual actions that our team identified according to the procedure we introduced in Chapter 2. The unit of analysis in our inquiry was the action itself. To test the dynamic hypotheses we proposed, however, we needed to reconstruct the preceding chain of actions leading up to any particular action in the episode. To do so, we relied on the action triggers from our codes and the action sequences that we were able to construct relying on the triggers (Chapter 7).

With these sequences in mind, we introduced two distinct conceptualizations of how past actions can influence future actions within an action sequence. Following the conventional notation of time-series methodologies, $action_{it}$ can be a function of the immediately preceding action, $action_{it-1}$, where $t$ does not refer to a fixed temporal unit, such as a day or a week, but simply denotes the chronological order of the action in a sequence, and where $i$ refers to a single action.[4] This generic definition of lags, however, was incomplete for our purposes because our hypotheses are actor-specific, whereas those generic lags correspond to the immediately preceding action in the sequence, irrespective of the actor type that accounts for it. In other words, the generic definition of lags does not take into account that an actor-specific previous action may not be the immediately preceding action in the sequence. For instance, our path-dependence hypothesis predicts that the current action of a given type of actor depends on the last action by the same actor-type in the sequence. This previous action of the same actor-type (e.g. the government), that we shall call a "self-lag," may correspond to the immediately preceding action (i.e. it may correspond to a generic lag), but it may also be the case that the immediately preceding action was an action of another actor type (e.g. a challenger) and the last government action may have occurred earlier in the sequence. We thus needed to introduce a second conceptualization of action lags which we called an *actor-specific*[5] *lag*. According to this conceptualization, $action_{iat}$ is a function of $action_{ibt-1}$ where the subscript $i$ still refers to an individual action and the additional subscripts $a$ and $b$ refer to a particular pair of actor-types, $a$ and $b$, where $a$ is the actor responsible for the current action and $b$ is the actor responsible for the previous action, and $t$ again corresponds to the

---

[4] While it is in principle possible to introduce lag structures that reach back further in the sequence, we limited ourselves to one-unit lags (t-1) in our analyses.

[5] We should highlight at this point that the actor-specific nature of these lags needs to be understood in the context of our stylized use of the term "actor types." Therefore, for instance, it could be the case that the first self-lag of a challenger – in other words the first challenger-specific lag of a challenger action – corresponds to two distinct organizations. An example, using the first Sarkozy–Fillon austerity package, would be the French radical-left protesting in front of the Ministry of Labor on September 20, 2010. While two of the preceding actions triggering this protest were two government actions, the third lag – which is the first challenger-specific lag – was an action by the French unions.

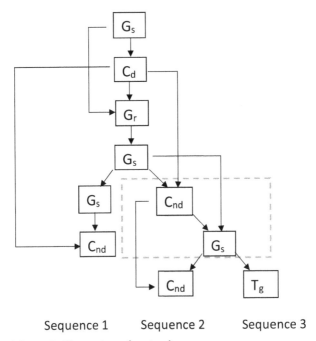

Sequence 1    Sequence 2    Sequence 3

FIGURE 8.1. Schematic illustration of action lags

*Note*: G = government, s = sticking, r = repression; C = challenger, nr = nondisruptive, r = disruptive; T = third party, TG = government support

chronological order of the actions but now refers to the subset of the sequence that involves the pair of actor-types *a* and *b*. While these actor-specific lags constitute the core of our empirical analysis, we were also attentive to their generic lag order as a part of our later robustness checks.

Figure 8.1 serves to illustrate this procedure. The figure distinguishes three stylized sequences that all begin with a government action, Gs (government sticking to its proposal). The solid lines correspond to generic lags, while the dashed lines correspond to non-immediate actor-specific self-lags. When focusing on a set of actions of particular interest indicated by the dashed rectangle containing a nondisruptive challenger action and a government sticking to plans type of action, the lag structures are readily visible from the illustration. The generic lag between the non-disruptive challenger action and the government's sticking to its plans at the same time constitutes an actor-specific lag for the pair challenger$_t$/government$_{t-1}$, with the challenger being actor *b* and the government actor *a*. Another actor-specific lag is the self-lag challenger$_t$/challenger$_{t-1}$, connecting the current nondisruptive challenger action to a previous disruptive challenger action (a pair of actions that contradicts the path-dependence hypothesis). Turning to the government action to be explained within the rectangle (government sticking to plans), its self-lag is another government action (sticking to plans, corroborating the path dependence hypothesis).

In the empirical specifications, both the dependent variable (current actions) and the independent variables (the lagged actions) enter the models in the form of actor-specific categorical variables where the three different strategic options for a given actor are coded as 1, 2, 3 (e.g. concession – sticking to plans – repression for governments). The code 0, which serves as the reference category for the triggering actions in the models, was assigned to instances when no actor-specific lagged action preceded the action in question. For example, if a government action was only preceded by other government actions, the challenger-specific lag variable was coded as 0. Using Figure 8.1 again for illustrative purposes, when seeking to explain the last government action (government sticking to plans), both its government- and its challenger-specific lag would be coded as 2 (government sticking to plans and nondisruptive opposition by challengers). In turn, since no third-party action occurred in the preceding part of the sequence, the third-party-specific lag of this particular government action would be coded as 0.

## ESTIMATION

The empirical investigation to test these hypotheses proceeded in three steps. First, the probability of the occurrence of a particular action form was modeled as a function of its own lags (*path dependence*), then as a function of the lags of the adversary (e.g. challenger actions – *government's threat/tit-for-tat*), and finally as a function of the lags of third-party actions (*legitimation/isolation/ constructive mediation*). Because our dependent variable was a categorical variable that can take on three distinct values for each actor type, we estimated multinomial logistic models, where the probability of occurrence of a particular action form (say, government repression) was estimated relative to an omitted, baseline category. For government and challenger actions, this reference category is concession and cooperation, respectively. The estimated coefficients thus indicate the impact of a past action form on the log odds of a particular outcome relative to concession (for governments) and to cooperation (for challengers). In addition to the lagged action variables, in each model we included a control for the chronological location of the action in a given sequence. The logic behind this control is that certain action types may be more/less likely to occur in early/late phases of the episode. This sequence counter variable was introduced both in a linear and a quadratic functional form to allow for nonlinear effects (for instance, if certain action types occurred at higher frequency during the middle of the episode compared to the beginning and the end, such nonlinear specification would be appropriate).

All models rely on a logit link function whereby action clustering is addressed via clustered errors as well as country-fixed effects in separate models. Although, as we argued earlier, this analysis aims to uncover general patterns of interaction that hold across our broadly comparable contexts, reliable estimates need to be attentive to action clustering in episodes as well as countries. Formally put, the estimated logit models are summarized as follows:

$$Log\left(\frac{p_{iak}}{p_{ial}}\right) = \alpha_0 + \sum_{\beta=1}^{3}\beta_{ab} * X_{iab} + \beta_4 * C_{ia} + \beta_5 * C_{ia}^2 + u + \varepsilon_{ia}$$

Where the left-hand side denotes the log-odds of the probability that a particular action $i$ of an actor $a$ is of action-type $k$ relative to the reference action-type category 1 (e.g. the probability of repression versus concession). On the right-hand side, the set of coefficients $\beta_1$, $\beta_2$, and $\beta_3$ refer to the estimated impact of to $X_{ab}$, the variable containing the action repertoire of actor $b$ where

$$x = \begin{cases} 0 = \text{no government lag} \\ 1 = \text{concession} \\ 2 = \text{sticking} \\ 3 = \text{repression} \end{cases}, \text{ if b = government}$$

$$x = \begin{cases} 0 = \text{no challenger lag} \\ 1 = \text{cooperation} \\ 2 = \text{non–disruptive} \\ 3 = \text{disruptive} \end{cases}, \text{ if b = challenger}$$

$$x = \begin{cases} 0 = \text{no third party lag} \\ 1 = \text{support govt} \\ 2 = \text{mediate} \\ 3 = \text{support chall} \end{cases}, \text{ if b = third party}$$

The double subscript of $X$ follows our notation introduced above, denoting the lagged action specific to actor $b$ that triggers the action of actor $a$. $C_{ia}$ and $C_{ia}^2$ are the action counter variables in linear and quadratic forms explained earlier, $u$ is a country fixed effect for the fixed-effects models and $\varepsilon_{ia}$ is an idiosyncratic error term. We illustrate results via predicted probabilities[6] and refer the reader to all regression output tables in the chapter Appendix, which also includes a table with the distribution of action codes by country and actor type.

RESULTS

## Main patterns

As the first step of the empirical analysis, we began by fitting path-dependence models on both governments and challengers that presume that current action

---

[6] For the calculated probabilities we allowed for one covariate to vary at a time. The predicted probabilities were calculated as averages across all the other covariates in the models.

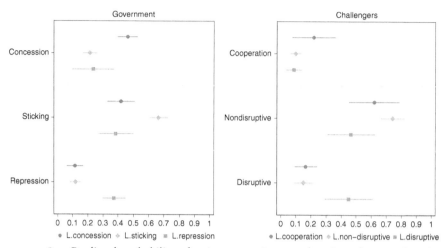

FIGURE 8.2. Predicted probability of action repertoires as a function of past actions by the same actor (predicted probabilities with 95 percent confidence intervals)

forms are exclusively predicted by the past action forms of the same actor. Figure 8.2 captures these predicted probabilities, using the models with clustered errors for illustration. Results for both sides of the contention provide support for the path-dependence hypothesis, albeit the strength of the pattern depends on the side of the contention (government or challenger) as well as on the particular action form under analysis. Starting with the government, its default strategy is sticking to the proposal, in line with the first formulation of our *path- dependence* hypothesis.

Within episodes, however, the government's actions also depend on its preceding strategies. The predicted probabilities for concessions made by the government provide the best illustration for the logic of path dependence: When the previous government action was a concession, the probability of the government following up with another concessionary move was around twice as high (0.46) as for past government actions being sticking (0.21) or repression (0.23). A similar pattern characterizes sticking and repression, both of which are more likely when the same action forms had been chosen by governments in the past.

An example of such path dependence characterizing government repression is readily provided by the most repressive episode in our sample, the constitutional stand-off between Romanian president Traian Basescu and the cross-party left-right parliamentary majority under the leadership of Victor Ponta seeking to impeach him in the summer of 2012. Of the seventy actions constituting the entire episode, fifteen were repressive acts by the government, mostly of a verbal nature. Remarkably, six of the fifteen repressive acts were immediately preceded by other repressive acts, and in six sequences ending with a government repression two further repressive acts had occurred earlier in the sequence.

These action dynamics are mirrored by the challenger-specific models, albeit with somewhat less clear-cut results. In line with our expectations, the challengers' default strategy was nondisruptive opposition to government proposals. Ceteris paribus, this was their action form in around two thirds of the cases. The probability of nondisruptive actions, however, was significantly lower (around 0.5) when challengers had committed to a disruptive action previously. The flip side of this pattern is that when challengers undertook a disruptive action in the past, the likelihood of their following up with another disruptive action increased spectacularly to around 0.4 compared to a rather low probability of around 0.1 under other past scenarios ($p < 0.001$). In other words, while disruptive mobilization is more the exception than the rule, once challengers have had recourse to more disruptive action forms, the likelihood of their following suit with similar actions in the future course of the episode significantly increases. Comparatively speaking, the path dependence for cooperation is less pronounced. Although the point estimates do reveal a considerably higher probability of cooperation following cooperative behavior in the past (0.22 compared to 0.08–0.09 in other scenarios), the estimates were rather imprecise due to the relatively few cases of cooperation, falling short of significance at the 0.05 level.

The logic of interdependence between action strategies points toward the next step in our inquiry that focuses on the patterns of reactions of an actor to the actions of its adversary. Figure 8.3 presents predicted probabilities for governments and challengers as a function of preceding action forms by the opposing party (while controlling for preceding actions of one's own at the same time).

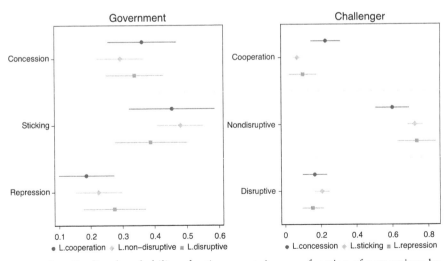

FIGURE 8.3. Predicted probability of action repertoires as a function of past actions by the adversary (predicted probabilities with 95 percent confidence intervals)

Compared to the path dependence models, the patterns of interaction between governments and challengers were considerably weaker and less regular. For the government side, no statistical difference could be discerned between the probabilities of action forms as a function of past action of challengers, although the point estimates pointed in the expected direction. The estimated probability of concession was the highest under past cooperation, the estimated probability of sticking was the highest under past nondisruptive actions, and the probability of repression was the highest under disruptive challenger action in the past. On the challenger side, our models provided partial evidence for this tit-for-tat logic. The probability of cooperation was significantly higher following government concessions. However, this logic of cooperation was not mirrored by the other end of the action repertoire since the probability of disruptive challenger action was largely independent on what the government had done in the past, contrary to the logic of the repression-disruptive mobilization-external legitimation nexus. This null result for disruptive challenger action may possibly be due to variable effects of government repression in different episodes; in some episodes, it may act as a threat, in others it may act more as a closure of opportunities (see Chapter 9).

To illustrate cooperative behavior between governments and challengers, one of the least eventful of our episodes in the sample – thirty-two actions in total – the setting up of the German Bad Bank over the spring and summer of 2019 serves as an interesting example. This especially applies to the challengers' side as three out of the four cooperative acts by challengers were preceded either directly or indirectly by government concessions. One of these cooperative acts concerned Die Linke, the radical-left challenger party with a longstanding opposition to the financial sector in general and to bank bailouts in particular. After overtures by the German government (Finance Minister Steinbruck modified the original plans on the May 4th in response to demands by the grand coalition), Die Linke struck a still critical but nevertheless constructive tone in a position paper they published on May 10.

Proceeding to the impact of third-party involvement, we now investigated which of the two competing perspectives, if either, holds true: Do actors choose more disruptive action forms in response to legitimation from third parties (*legitimation hypothesis*) or, on the contrary, do they engage in disruptive action when they are isolated and feel under pressure to double down (*isolation hypothesis*)? Furthermore, are third parties successful in mediating between the actors, evidenced by a higher likelihood of cooperative behavior on their part? Figure 8.4 provides some answers to these questions. Starting with the government side, neither the legitimation nor the isolation hypothesis received much support from the models since the likelihood of repression was not particularly high in response to third-party actions that provided clear support for one of the adversaries. That said, the estimated probability of repression was somewhat higher (0.14) in the wake of third-party support for challengers compared to scenarios with third-party support for governments (0.08), and the difference

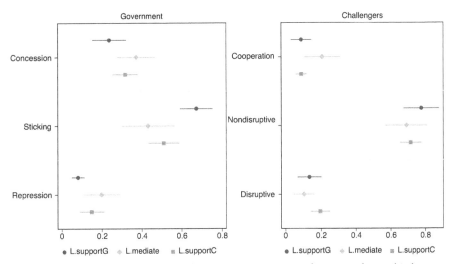

FIGURE 8.4. Predicted probability of action repertoires as a function of past third-party actions (predicted probabilities with 95 percent confidence intervals)

is significant (p = 0.04). This lends (weak) support for the isolation hypothesis on the government side. The stronger pattern, however, concerns the beneficial impact of third-party mediation. In such cases, the probability of governments providing concessions to challengers rose to an estimated 0.4 from the 0.2 to 0.3 range when no such prior mediation occured. In addition, Figure 8.4 also shows an unexpected result: Governments that were supported by third parties were more likely to stick to their guns. As we shall see in the next chapter, for governments, third-party support often meant pressure from international actors to stick to their austerity proposals in the face of domestic resistance.

The beneficial impact of mediating efforts by third parties was mirrored by challengers' action patterns, providing evidence for the concession–cooperation–mediation nexus at play. After a mediating attempt by a third-party actor, the probability of cooperative behavior from challengers was considerably and significantly higher compared to cooperation following other types of third-party actions (around 0.2 compared to less than 0.1, p < 0.05). We can, however, safely reject the isolation hypothesis for challengers, since the likelihood of disruptive mobilization was actually lower following third-party overtures toward governments (although the differences were nonsignificant). The overall findings on third-party involvement thus lent support to the mediation hypothesis, provided only partial and somewhat weak support for the isolation hypothesis (applies only for the government side), and offered no support for the legitimation hypothesis. While it seems that third parties had the power to bring the adversaries to the table, they appeared comparatively powerless to shift the contention in any clear direction.

The beneficial impact of third-party mediation can be illustrated by another example. Shortly after coming to power in spring 2010, the Orban government in Hungary set out its first austerity plans in the summer of 2010 in response to pressure from the European Union to reduce the government's budget deficit in the wake of the economic recession of 2009. The main third-party actors in this debate were the EU and other international actors – the European Commission and I.M.F. officials in particular – attempting to supervise the proposed cuts, while the main challengers were the political opposition parties as well as business associations representing banks and insurance companies who with a new bank levy were to be one of the main targets of the austerity measures. Third-party mediation – typically taking the form of negotiations with the government without clearly siding with either the government or challengers – bore fruit in many instances. Of the eleven challenger actions in this episode, six were preceded by such third-party actions and of these six, three induced challengers to cooperate in the form of a partial acceptance of, or at least willingness to negotiate, the measures. On the governmental side, the impact was even more visible: of the twenty-three government actions, a comparatively high share were concessions of some form (nine in total), and six of these actions were preceded by third-party mediation.

## Robustness Tests

We conducted robustness checks to examine how the patterns we uncovered from the data stood up to scrutiny when restricting the overall sample of contentious actions to theoretically interesting subsets. In particular, we first asked whether the same patterns held when focusing on those episodes characterized by a sufficiently high degree of overall contentiousness. To do so, we used our contentiousness measure from Chapter 4 and reran our models only for those episodes that scored above one on the contentiousness indicator. This left us with thirty-four, slightly more than half of our original episodes. However, since the more contentious episodes also tended to be those with higher overall action counts, this sample restriction implied a loss of only around 25 percent of the original observations. Second, we focused on those actions (across our original sample of sixty episodes) that occurred after a minimal threshold of sequence length to insure that our findings were not driven by isolated actions occurring early in a sequence (and hence unlikely to constitute the core of the broader chain of interaction). In particular, we chose a cut-off point of three to leave room for all three actor types to contribute at least one lagged action to the preceding part of the sequence. Reassuringly, the patterns were quasi-identical for both of these tests (results not shown). Save for minor differences in the predicted probabilities and somewhat larger confidence intervals due to the smaller sample sizes and reduced precision of the estimates, the main effects that we demonstrated earlier held up in these limited subsamples.

Finally, we examined how sensitive the findings are to the temporal characteristics of the lag structure. As a reminder, the independent variables in the models are actor-specific so they are silent on how far removed the lags are from the action, both in terms of their place in the sequence (i.e. the order of their generic lag) and in terms of time. To keep this part of the extended analysis at a manageable level of complexity, we restricted it to the path-dependence models from the previous analysis. In other words, we examined whether the path dependence patterns we uncovered were driven by consecutive actions in the sequence or whether they also held up when the actor-specific lags occurred further back in past.

The only noteworthy difference compared to the baseline results – apart from the lower precision of the estimates because of the restricted sample size – was that the path-dependence logic for challengers was now confined to disruptive, and to some extent nondisruptive, opposition forms. Path dependence in cooperation, by contrast, appeared to be driven by consecutive cooperative actions by challengers.

Replicating this analysis for the temporal dimension, we now restricted the analysis to lags that occurred at least a week before the action. Again, with the exception of cooperative behavior by challengers, path-dependence dynamics seemed to be at work even when actors' previous actions had taken place further back in time. In this sense, path dependence appeared to have a rather long memory.

## CONCLUSION

We have presented a formal analysis of the action repertoires and the interaction dynamics between European governments and their challengers in sixty contentious episodes that took place in the context of the financial and economic crises that shook the European Union in the aftermath of the fall of Lehman Brothers in September 2008. Based on the combination of a new dataset on actor-specific action repertoires and a novel method designed for the dynamic analysis of interaction between these actors (CEA), we tested a number of hypotheses on the patterns that characterize such interaction dynamics. On a general level, our findings underscore the need for a statistical method that allows for an explicit study of interdependence. Contentious actions do not take place in isolation from each other and frequency-based approaches in the epidemiological tradition (such as protest-event analyses or claims analyses) would be hard pressed to uncover the regularities that characterize governments' and challengers' action strategies. The main stakeholders in the policy episodes did, in fact, react to their adversaries as well as to third parties even under severe pressure from the external economic environment as well as from domestic audiences. On the surface, governments may well come across as irresponsive and uncompromising agents of the structural imperatives imposed by global markets, while (some) challengers may equally be seen as opportunistic voices of societal grievances, more interested in their self-serving organizational goals than in policy compromise. Beyond the surface, however, in many instances, a careful analysis reveals interactive strategies rather than a dialogue of the deaf.

Underneath such interdependence, however, we also found strong confirmation for path dependence for all action forms for both adversaries, but the patterns tend to be somewhat stronger on the government side. Governments (and, to a lesser extent, challengers) tended to have their prevailing repertoire to which they stick throughout contentious episodes. Comparatively speaking, the evidence for the tit-for-tat behavior by the contending parties was considerably weaker and was mostly restricted to challengers' cooperative behavior; its likelihood was significantly higher in the wake of concessionary moves by the government. Government behavior was, however, by and large independent of previous challenger actions, although the point estimates for repression did hint in the direction of the expected rank ordering: The more disruptive the challengers' previous actions, the higher the probability of government repression. Although weak, this result was in line with much of the literature, which has consistently shown that disruptive challenging action increases the likelihood of state repression. The fact that this relationship was not stronger is most probably related to the European context of our episodes, where repression and radicalization have generally been rather limited. All in all, the comparatively stronger patterns for path dependence than for tit-for-tat was likely to have been the result of the tightrope that governments had to walk when implementing their austerity plans and related institutional reforms in the face of popular resentment and social grievances. Although, as we shall see in the next chapter that some of the relevant contextual conditions varied from episode to episode, the overall constraints that governments faced tended to push them away from flexibility and compromise.

We did not find any indication at all for the other side of the repression-mobilization nexus – the effect of government repression on the radicalization of challengers – for which the previous literature has found mixed results. In the episodes we have been studying here, repression neither systematically radicalized the challengers, nor did it systematically demobilize them. More detailed analyses will be presented in Chapter 10 to uncover the conditions under which challengers perceive repression as a contraction of opportunities or as a threat to their survival.

Finally, three of our hypotheses referred to the impact of third-party actors on the strategic choices of the two adversaries. In this respect we found little evidence that would support either the legitimation or the isolation perspective. Instead, the gist of the impact of third-party involvement concerned their pressure on governments to stick to their proposals and on their mediating role. For both governments and challengers, third-party attempts to mediate between them tended to be followed by cooperative behavior on the part of the two adversaries. In essence, third parties appeared to be more successful in steering the contending actors toward cooperation via mediation than in decisively settling the debate by firmly taking sides on behalf of either adversary.

Remarkably, the overall results were more supportive of the interdependence of cooperation than of the interdependence of conflict. The repression-disruptive mobilization-external legitimation of conflictive behavior nexus was weaker than the concession–cooperation–mediation nexus. While the literature tends to focus on conflict dynamics, we found that there is a more systematic dynamics of cooperation. Admittedly, this result may crucially depend on the particular contexts we were studying here: for instance, the broadly democratic nature of European political systems. In the present chapter, we have analyzed the "elementary forms" of interaction between the three types of actors independently of context: that is, independently of the type of episode, the characteristics of the proposals, the type of government that presented them, or the country in which the episodes evolved.

To gain a better insight into the asymmetrical outcome of the present study, we need to refine it by more detailed analyses that combine context-specific and interaction-specific considerations in the pursuit of conditional, cross-level questions. Does the path dependence of the government's action repertoire hold in all contexts, or does it systematically vary from one country and/or from one episode to the other? Is the limited responsiveness of governments to challengers' actions a universal phenomenon, or is it specific to particular countries/episodes? Alternatively, does it depend on the kind of challengers that are making their voices heard (e.g. whether they are unions, partisan actors, or social movement organizations)? These are the questions that we shall take up in the next chapter, building on the method we have proposed in the present one.

Let us conclude by pointing out that the novel method we have introduced here is not limited to the specific types of episodes we have studied in this volume. For instance, the method is also applicable to policy episodes when challengers act as initiators by putting a policy proposal on the agenda via protests, petitions, and the usual suspects in their action repertoire. Also, in terms of issue domain, policy episodes related to noneconomic proposals can be studied using the same method. An illustrative example on both counts – a noneconomic policy episode initiated by challengers – is the so-called double-referendum in Hungary in 2004. The referendum was initiated with a petition campaign by a right-wing N.G.O., representing the Hungarian diaspora, demanding the extension of Hungarian citizenship to citizens abroad. Using the scheme of our actor space, this episode thus placed the challengers and their party-political allies – mostly Fidesz and MIEP, the largest Hungarian far-right party at the time – as the actors pushing for a policy change against the left-liberal government, at the end successfully, defending the status quo. With the appropriate fine-tuning of the codes, CEA could then readily be applied to study the interaction dynamics between the actors. On a more general level, the methodological tool kit we propose here will need to be adapted for other researchers' specific goals and designs, but, in our view, it is sufficiently flexible to be operationalized for the specific purposes of other research projects.

# 9

## The Governments' Reactions to Challengers and Third Parties

### Hanspeter Kriesi

### INTRODUCTION

In the previous chapter, we have looked at the interactions between the three types of protagonists, independently of the context in which they interact. In the present chapter, we shall take context characteristics into account in order to identify the extent to which interaction dynamics are context-specific. In doing so, we shall focus on governments and analyze how their reactions to challenger and third-party actions depend on the context. The next chapter will change the perspective and analyze challengers' reactions to government and third-party actions. In focusing on the governments' reactions, we shall build on the analysis of the previous chapter. Concerning the governments' reactions to challengers, the results found in the previous chapter were quite inconclusive. By and large, government behavior appeared to be independent of previous challenger actions, although the results to some extent supported the threat hypothesis with respect to repression. As far as the impact of third parties is concerned, we found some support for the isolation hypothesis: Governments had a higher propensity to repress challengers when they were not supported by third parties. The most important result, however, was the effectiveness of third-party mediation: Governments tended to honor mediation attempts with concessions. In the present chapter, we shall put these somewhat inconclusive results into perspective by taking into account the context-dependence of the governments' reactions. In terms of mechanisms, we introduced environmental mechanisms that condition the relational mechanisms that we studied in a "context-blind" approach in the previous chapter.

The way we think of context in this chapter is in terms of *the actor configurations* characterizing the episodes. Alternatively, one might have considered the overall contentiousness of the episode, the economic context conditions – the problem pressure exerted by the economic crisis, or characteristics of the proposals – such as their substantive targets or their overall severity. As it turns out, these characteristics did have an impact on the governments' reactions, but their impact was generally independent of the challengers' actions. Thus, the reactions by the government were generally more repressive in the more contentious episodes, and they were less repressive in highly severe episodes. Or the governments tended to make fewer concessions when economic problem pressure (indicated by high levels of unemployment) was very high. However, these context characteristics did not condition the effect of challengers' or third-party actions on the governments' reactions across the episodes covered by this study. Instead, the configurations of actors who were involved in the episodes appeared to be the most promising context characteristics to account for the *patterns of interaction* between the governments on one hand, and the challengers and third-party actors on the other.

We consider different actor configurations, allowing us to specify *the impact of the three types of actors* on the interaction dynamics. First, we introduce a simple typology of challenger configurations in order *to specify the threat exerted by challengers* in a given episode. Next, we turn to the composition of the government. We distinguish between center-left and center-right governments in order to analyze whether the greater proximity of center-left governments to unions and civil-society actors more generally had any impact on their reactions to challengers. We also introduce the distinction between popular and unpopular governments, as well as divisions within the governing parties with respect to the challengers, in order to test whether the reactions of governments which were weakened by lack of popularity or internal divisions differed from those securely in power. Finally, we turn to third-party actors and analyze whether and how the governments' reactions to challengers depended on the actors driving the challenge and, in particular, whether or not they were supported by international actors.

This chapter documents that it is possible to put the relational mechanisms into context. It shows how systematically to compare the interactions between the government and its challengers across the sixty episodes covered by our study. As we shall see, however, even the context characteristics that we singled out for the present analysis have a rather limited effect on the interaction patterns under consideration. The surprising context insensitivity of these interaction patterns is most likely attributable to the economic and political constraints under which all the EU member states were operating during the Great Recession.

## CONFIGURATION OF CHALLENGERS

### Three Types of Configurations

The first aspect of the context that we propose to take into account is the configuration of challengers in a given episode. Not all challengers pose the same kind of threat to a government. Following the categorization of actors introduced in Chapter 5, we shall distinguish between three distinct challenger configurations: a partisan challenge, a union challenge, and a challenge by civil-society organizations. We define the three types of challenges based on the relative importance of the corresponding actor type among the challengers in a given episode. Note that the relative preponderance of a given actor type does not mean that the other two types of actors were not also present among the challengers in a given episode. It just means that the actor type in question played a significant role in the corresponding episode.

An episode dominated by a *partisan challenge* poses the least-threatening challenge to a government. A partisan challenge is part of conventional party politics: Opposition parties challenge the government's policy proposal – either the mainstream opposition parties or opposition parties from the radical left or radical right. The opposition might even come from within the government parties themselves. Such challenges are part of conventional party politics and anchored in habitual patterns of interaction. The governments are used to dealing with this type of situation and the threat to the government is usually rather limited. Typically, partisan opposition demanded the withdrawal or at least the modification of the proposal, it verbally attacked (criticized, denounced, or even demonized) the government for its proposed legislation, it boycotted the final vote, or it attempted to influence other governing institutions that have a key role in the decision-making process. Thus, in the Hungarian debate on pension nationalization, the liberal LMP (Hungary's Green Party) accused the government of stealing the people's savings, and the social-democratic MSZP boycotted the final vote declaring that "it did not want to collaborate in such a crime." The case of the Romanian I.M.F. bailout, where the opposition parties sent official letters to the president urging him to refrain from signing up to an I.M.F. loan, illustrates the opposition's seeking support from other parts of the government. Only very rarely did we see more radical actions in this kind of episode.

Roughly one fourth of the episodes in our sample (28 percent) have given rise to predominantly partisan challenges. Table 9.1a presents the list of episodes corresponding to this type. It includes seventeen episodes from ten out of the twelve countries, including all of the German cases. The fact that the German government only faced partisan challenges largely accounts for the finding from Chapter 4 that indicated the low level of contentiousness of the German episodes. Absent from the list are Ireland and Latvia, where no episode involved a predominantly partisan challenge. Note, too, that the list of partisan challenges includes no less than half of the institutional reforms, a finding that also concurs with the earlier reckoning that many of these reforms were not contentious at all.

Almost half of the episodes (47 percent) are characterized by a *union-driven challenge*. In these episodes, unions either challenged the government on their

TABLE 9.1. *Configurations of challengers: list of partisan and civil-society challenges*

(a) Partisan

| Country | Episode | Issue |
|---------|---------|-------|
| France | Hollande 1st austerity pkg. | economic |
| France | Decentralization | institutional |
| Germany | German bank bailout | economic |
| Germany | Bad banks | economic |
| Germany | First bailout Greece | economic |
| Germany | Third bailout Greece | economic |
| Germany | Debt brake | institutional |
| Greece | Third bailout | economic |
| Hungary | 2010 austerity | economic |
| Hungary | Pension nationalization | economic |
| Italy | Judicial reform | institutional |
| Poland | Pension reform | economic |
| Portugal | Muncipal reform | institutional |
| Romania | I.M.F. bailout | economic |
| Romania | Impeachment | institutional |
| Spain | Bankia | economic |
| U.K. | Brexit | institutional |

(b) Civil society

| Country | Episodeid | Issue |
|---------|-----------|-------|
| Greece | Midterm adjustment | economic |
| Hungary | Internet tax | economic |
| Hungary | Media law | institutional |
| Ireland | Bank guarantee | economic |
| Ireland | I.M.F. bailout | economic |
| Ireland | Water tax | economic |
| Ireland | Senate reform | institutional |
| Latvia | 2009 austerity | economic |
| Latvia | Eurozone entry | institutional |
| Poland | Constitutional court | institutional |
| Portugal | I.M.F. bailout | economic |
| Spain | Zapatero 2nd austerity | economic |
| U.K. | 2010 austerity | economic |
| U.K. | Tuition fees | economic |
| U.K. | 2011 austerity | economic |

own or in combination with the mainstream opposition. The unions mainly challenged economic-policy proposals, but they have also mobilized against two institutional reforms – the constitutional reform imposing debt limits in Spain and the TV shutdown in Greece. Union-driven challenges dominated in southern and centraleastern Europe, where they respectively made up two thirds and one half of the episodes, while they were relatively rare in north-western Europe, where they account for only a quarter of the episodes. Among the southern European countries, Italy stands out, where four out of the five episodes gave rise to union-dominated challenges. In Greece, Portugal, and Spain, the challenge was union-driven in three out of the five episodes. The same applies to Latvia, Poland, and Romania, and, uniquely among north-western European countries, to France. This type of challenge was typically articulated in strikes and demonstrations.

The threat posed to the government by a union-driven challenge was also to some extent contained, given that unions are highly institutionalized actors. At least in southern European countries and in France, the government is accus-tomed to being challenged by unions, and the mobilization by unions gives rise to established interaction patterns, even if it is more disruptive than the mobil-ization by parties. Thus, of the eighty-four general strikes counted by Hamann et al. (2013: 1032) in western Europe from 1980 to 2006, thirty-four occurred in Greece, fifteen in Italy, seven each in Spain and France, and two in Portugal. Belgium (a country not studied here) was the only other country where general strikes were rather frequent (eight). Challenges by unions are less usual in centraleastern European countries.

The remaining fifteen episodes (25 percent) were characterized by the mobil-ization of less conventional groups of challengers – social-movement actors that often included students and various N.G.O.s. These are what we call the *civil-society challenges*. Very rarely, this type of actor is alone in mobilizing against the government's proposal. In only two of these fifteen episodes – the Latvian entry into the Eurozone and the Hungarian internet tax, civil-society actors were not joined by more established actors. In all the other cases, civil-society actors joined forces with opposition parties and/or unions. It is the breadth of the opposition in these episodes, as well as the unconventional character of the opposition that arguably posed the greatest threat to the government. Table 9.1b presents the list of these episodes. Four of the Irish and three of the British episodes are associated with this type of broad challenge. In add-ition, three southern European episodes that became famous for their massive mobilization belong to this type:

- the Portuguese I.M.F. bailout in March 2011 that gave rise to the "Geração à Rasca" demonstrations, the biggest demonstrations in Portuguese demo-cratic history;
- the second austerity package of the Spanish Zapatero government that launched the Spanish Indignados movement in May 2011;
- the Greek midterm adjustment program that was at the origin of the mobilization by the Aganaktismenoi, the Greek version of the Indignados, in summer 2011, and which we have already briefly discussed in Chapter 1.

Finally, there are also five centraleastern European episodes in this category:

- the Hungarian internet tax and the Hungarian media law, an institutional reform that was part of a larger process, during which the newly elected Fidesz government used its position to introduce illiberal reforms to constrain the opposition;
- the Polish reform of the constitutional court that was introduced to serve a similar purpose;
- two Latvian episodes – the entry into the Eurozone and the first 2009 austerity package.

This kind of challenge was mainly articulated by demonstrations in the streets, but there were also petition drives and more unconventional actions organized by this configuration of challengers.

In the previous chapter, we have seen that the government threat hypothesis was only weakly supported. In order to test this hypothesis in more detail, we now assume that, depending on the configuration of the challengers, challenger actions incite different types of reactions by the government. According to the government threat hypothesis we would expect government repression to be more likely, the greater the threat to the government posed by the challenger configuration. Arguably, the greatest threat emanates from disruptive action by challengers when civil-society actors join the opposition by unions or parties. In the episodes where the government face such a broad challenge that goes beyond the "usual suspects," the mobilization tends to become particularly intense and unpredictable. Accordingly, we expect the government to react with repressionespecially in this kind of episode, but we do not expect the government to react with repression in the episodes where the opposition is purely partisan. If the challenge is union-driven, repression should be weaker than in the presence of civil-society challengers but stronger than in episodes with purely partisan challenges. We expect this to hold independently of the type of reform that was being challenged: that is, it should not have made a difference whether the government's proposal referred to economic policies or to institutional reforms.

With respect to concessions, however, the type of challenger does at first not seem to make a difference. According to tit-for-tat logic, governments are expected to make concessions to challengers who prove to be cooperative, irrespective of the type of challenger. However, as the previous chapter has shown, this logic does not seem to apply in our episodes. It is conceivable that this logic is suspended by the fact that during the Great Recession, under international pressure and the pressure of the markets, governments were not able to make any significant concessions because of a lack of maneuvering space (see Chapter 7). Under this alternative logic, the type of challenge is also not relevant for concessions to be forthcoming. Whatever the type of challenge, governments simply were not able to respond with substantive concessions. There is, however, a counter-argument suggesting that, even under such an alternative logic, the type of challenge might make a difference with respect to concessions. According to this counter-argument, governments that are exposed to a threatening challenge might revert to a divide-and-rule strategy: They might not only step up repression but also attempt to make some concessions in an attempt to repress the more radical elements among the challengers and to placate the more moderate ones. According to this alternative hypothesis, we would expect some concessions more likely to be forthcoming in the union-driven and the civil society-driven episodes than in the partisan episodes.

## Analysis

In order to test these expectations, we followed the same procedures as in the previous chapter. However, compared to the previous chapter, we reduced the classification of the challenger actions to the simple dichotomy of "challenges" (to include both nondisruptive and disruptive challenges) and "no challenges" (to include cooperative challenger actions and the absence of challenger actions). This simplification is the price to be paid for the introduction of specific context conditions: once we differentiate the context, the number of cases for a specific type of challenger action is considerably reduced. In other words, for our analysis, we face a trade-off between the differentiation of challenger actions and the differentiation of the context in which they take place. Since in this chapter the focus lies on the context conditions, we need to reduce the precision with regard to the type of challenger actions.

Following the procedure introduced in the previous chapter, we estimated multinomial logit models with government reactions as the dependent variable and the lagged challenger actions as the independent variables, controlling for the past government actions and for lagged third-party actions (only main effects). We also controlled for clustering in episodes and in countries (including standard errors clustered by episodes and country fixed effects). We estimated these models both for the economic policy episodes and for all episodes. It was not possible to estimate them separately for the institutional episodes because there were too few of these. We shall only report the results for all episodes taken together, since they do not differ much from the results that we obtained for the economic episodes in particular.

Figure 9.1 presents the predicted probabilities for two types of reactions by the government – repression and concession, depending on the combination of the type of challenger action (no challenge versus challenge) and the type of challenger configuration (partisan versus union versus civil-society challenge). These results are based on the models presented in Table A1, column 1, in the appendix to this chapter. With respect to repression, the left-hand graph of Figure 9.1 shows that the probability of repression increased in reaction to a previous challenge in all three challenger configurations, as we would have expected under the threat hypothesis. The increases were significant for

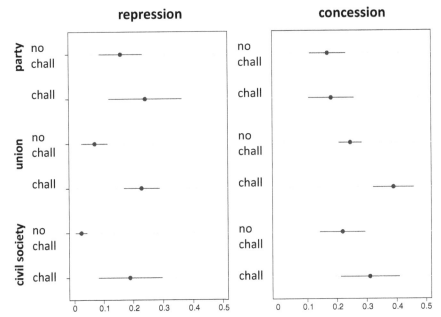

FIGURE 9.1. Government reactions to challenger actions, by configuration of challenger for all episodes: predicted probabilities

union- and civil-society-driven but not for partisan configurations.[1] However, from the point of view of the threat hypothesis, it is more important that the results do not confirm the expected differences between challenges in the three configurations: the point estimates for the repression of challenges were quite similar for all three configurations. Whatever the challenger configuration, the share of repressive reactions to challenges was around 20 percent. Surprisingly, this share was generally rather high in episodes with a partisan configuration, whether there was a challenge (24 percent) or no challenge at all (16 percent). This is a result of our very broad definition of repression, which also includes verbal abuse.

With respect to concessions by the government, in line with the counter-argument, we observed a significant increase in the probability of concessions to challenging actions for episodes with union- and civil-society-driven challenges, but not for those with party-driven challenges.[2] This is shown in the

---

[1] For repression, the Chi2-value of the contrasts between challenges and no challenges in union-driven configurations amounts to 19.13 (1 df, p = 0.000), and to 10.42 (1 df, p = 0.001) in civil society-driven configurations; in partisan configurations, the corresponding value is 1.52 (1 df, p = 0.22).

[2] For concessions, the Chi2-value of the contrasts between challenges and no challenges in union-driven configurations amounts to 15.11 (1 df, p = 0.000), and to 3.76 (1 df, p = 0.053) in civil society-driven configurations.

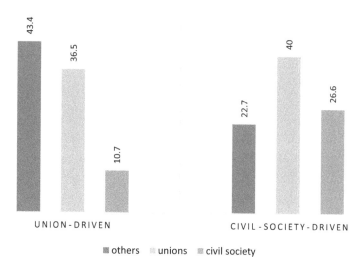

FIGURE 9.2. Concessions in union- and civil-society-driven episodes, in reaction to challenges by unions, civil-society organizations, and other types of actors: percentage shares of government actions

second part of Figure 9.1. In more detailed analyses presented in Figure 9.2, we find some evidence that, in union- and civil-society-driven episodes, the governments indeed applied a strategy of divide-and-rule: thus, in both types of episodes, concessions were more likely to be forthcoming if a union was responsible for the preceding challenging action and not a civil-society actor. In union-driven episodes, other actors (above all mainstream opposition parties) were even more likely to receive concessions than unions, although, compared to unions, they intervened relatively rarely in such episodes. Thus, it was mainstream opposition parties that received procedural concessions in the episode of the 2009 austerity package in Ireland. Upon their intervention, the government was ready to negotiate, although its room for maneuver was rather limited. In civil-society-driven episodes, however, it is the unions who were most likely to get some concessions. Thus, in the Greek midterm adjustment episode, upon the mobilization by the unions, the government considered making substantive concessions. In the case of the Zapatero austerity package that gave rise to the mobilization by the Indignados movement, some concessions to the unions and to the movement had also been forthcoming. Finally, to give a third example, in the episode of the Irish water tax, the government announced that it would consider some substantive concessions to the massively mobilizing civil-society organizations in 2014.

Further analyses of the union-driven configurations showed that unions received fewer concessions in southern Europe, although they mobilized particularly massively in this part of Europe during the Great Recession, and although one might have expected the governments to be more forthcoming, given their proximity to the unions (in all southern European countries, centre-left governments were responsible for a large portion of the austerity policies). In fact, in the case of union-driven challenges, unions received significantly fewer concessions in southern Europe than in the other two regions. We tentatively attribute this relative lack of concessions to unions in southern Europe to the fact that the governments in southern Europe had a particularly limited maneuvering space (see below).

Looking more closely at the kind of concessions the governments made if they were confronted with a challenge, we confirm the finding of Chapter 7 that they often were of a procedural nature: The governments invited the challengers to meetings, intended to open a dialogue with them, organized hearings with groups targeted by the austerity programs to explain their proposed measures, or promised to cooperate more closely with the challengers (the unions) regarding future reforms. Sometimes, as in the examples mentioned earlier, concessions also took the form of substantive promises or more or less vague announcements to consider substantive concessions. In only very few instances, however, did the government proceed to make serious concessions, such as a reshuffle of the cabinet or substantive concessions to the program proposed. It looks as if governments, faced with challenges driven by unions or civil-society organizations, were forced to make some gestures to the challengers without, however, being ready or capable of making real concessions.

TYPE OF GOVERNMENT

As we have observed in Chapter 3, the governments launching an economic policy proposal were both from the center-left and the center-right, five were technocratic governments (Monti in Italy, Papademos and Pikramenos in Greece, Bajnai in Hungary, and Ciolos in Romania, see Table A3.2) and two were grand coalitions (CDU–SPD in Germany). Counting the German grand coalition and the Monti government as center-right, the episodes studied here were dominated by center-right governments. Only sixteen of the sixty proposals (roughly one fourth) were introduced by center-left governments. However, it is important to note that in three of the southern European countries – Greece, Portugal, and Spain – the first austerity proposals were all introduced by governments from the center-left, and even in Italy the key austerity proposals were introduced by a technocratic government that was supported by a broad coalition including the main center-left party. The fact that they were heavily involved in the austerity episodes decisively undermined the center-left mainstream parties in southern Europe (see Hutter and Kriesi 2019; Roberts 2017). In the other regions, the majority of the economic austerity proposals were introduced by governments from the center-right.

Unions are typically closer to center-left parties and the same can be said of civil-society organizations. As we have observed some time ago (Kriesi et al. 1995), when the mainstream left is in opposition, it is a natural ally of the unions and of the new social movements that have dominated the social movement scene in western Europe since the 1970s. However, the situation changes once the mainstream left is in government, because in government it not only faces electoral constraints but also constraints imposed by established policies and by all kinds of stakeholders. These constraints were particularly stringent for center-left governments during the Great Recession. Thus, the center-left governments of the southern European countries that were especially hard hit by the eurozone crisis had to adopt austerity programs that were contrary to their traditional programmatic positions; these cost them dearly in electoral terms. The same applies to center-left governments in other parts of Europe. The point is that the maneuvering space for the center-left governments during the Great Recession was very limited, whether they were the dominant party in government (as in the case of the southern European countries or in the cases of France, Britain, and Hungary); whether they were the minority partner in a grand coalition (as in the case of Germany); or whether they were part of a technocratic government (as in the cases of the Monti government in Italy and the Papademos government in Greece). Given these constraints, we expect center-left governments to have been just as repressive as the center-right governments, and just as little ready to make concessions as center-right governments.

These expectations have been borne out by the data. As it turns out, the reactions of centre-left governments hardly differ from those of centre-right governments. Whatever the configuration of challengers, the two types of governments tended to react similarly. This means that, under the constraints of the crisis, the traditionally greater proximity of centre-left governments to challengers from the unions or civil society did not matter at all (results not shown).

In searching for possible differences between the reactions of the two types of governments to challenges of their austerity policies (and institutional reforms), we have sought to distinguish between popular and unpopular governments from the centre-left and the centre-right. For unpopular governments, challenges to their policies are likely to be more threatening than for popular governments. If a government is popular, it is arguably better able to stick to its policy without having to repress challengers or having to make concessions to them. The government's popularity is a resource that allows it to ignore the challenges to its policy proposals. In contrast, unpopular governments, have a weaker position when facing challengers and are, therefore, more likely to have recourse to repression and/or to make concessions to them. In line with the greater proximity of centre-left governments to the challengers, we might expect unpopular centre-left governments to make more concessions to them, while unpopular centre-right governments, which are generally more distant from the predominant type of challenger, might be more likely to repress them.

Figure 9.3 shows that, in interaction with the type of incumbent, government popularity, indeed, seemed to make a difference. The results presented in this

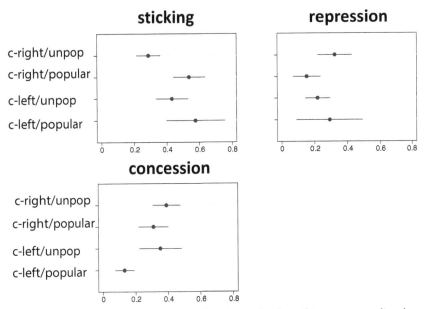

FIGURE 9.3. Government reaction to challenging action by cabinet type: predicted probabilities for unpopular and popular center-left and center-right cabinets

figure are based on the models in Table A9.1, column 2, in the appendix to this chapter. On the one hand, popularity is an asset that helps governments to stick to their proposals. This applies above all to centre-right governments but to some extent also to centre-left governments.[3] On the other hand, as expected, unpopular centre-right governments were more likely to reply with repression to a challenge than popular centre-right governments, while unpopular centre-left governments were more likely to respond with concessions to such a challenge than popular centre-left governments.[4] In the case of centre-left governments, it is striking that they were particularly unlikely to make concessions if they were popular. Examples of unpopular right-wing governments that replied with repressive measures – mainly verbal depreciation of the challengers – include the Greek ND government (in the TV shutdown episode), the

---

[3] For sticking, the Chi2-value of the contrast between unpopular and popular centre-right governments facing a challenge is 13.13 (1 df, p = 0.000). For centre-left governments the corresponding Ch2-value is 2.15 (1 df, p = 0.14). Note that there were many more popular right-wing governments in charge of the episodes we covered than popular left-wing governments. Only two of our episodes were related to proposals of popular centre-left governments (the first Greek bailout and the first Romanian bailout).

[4] For repression, the Chi2-value of the contrasts between unpopular and popular centre-right governments facing a challenge amounts to 6.62 (1df, p = 0.01). For concessions, the Chi2-value of the contrast between unpopular and popular centre-left governments facing a challenge is 12.70 (1 df, p = 0.000).

French Fillon government (in the Sarkozy–Fillon austerity episode), the Romanian Boc government (in the labor regulation episode), or the British Tory government (in the case of Brexit). There are only two popular centre-left governments in our study – the PASOK government at the time of the first bailout and the Romanian Boc government at the time of the IMF bailout, both of which hardly made any concessions at all. Unpopular left-wing governments that reacted with the promise of concessions to challengers include the Greek PASOK government in the case of the midterm adjustment and the second bailout, the Italian PD government under Renzi in the case of the Jobs Act, the Zapatero government in Spain in both of its austerity episodes, and the Hungarian socialist government in the episode of the I.M.F. bailout. These differences between the reactions of unpopular governments suggest that even if the overall approach of the governments was quite similar across all the cases, the type of government was not entirely immaterial for the way challengers were treated during the Great Recession.

## DIVIDED GOVERNMENT

The party-driven German episodes are instances where the government was divided. With the exception of the bank bailout, where the members of the grand coalition agreed, the German government split over the austerity proposals and the institutional reform (the debt brake). Thus, in the episode concerning the ratification of the third Greek bailout, three-fourths of the challenging actions came from within the governing CDU. This is shown in Table 9.2, which, for episodes with divided governments, presents the shares of challenger and third-party actions attributable to actors from the governing parties. Similarly, the third Greek bailout also deeply divided the Greek Syriza government with the intransigent opponents of the bailout eventually splitting off and creating a separate party. Again, no less than three-fourths of the challenging actions were launched by dissidents from the governing party. Two French episodes were instances of a divided government, too. Some members of the governing socialists supported the challengers from the left and announced that they would vote against the President Hollande's first austerity program. In the case of the decentralization reform, it was the regional and local authorities that supported the challengers from the opposition parties. They opposed the reduction of the number of regions and demanded additional financial resources in line with the competences attributed to them.

As Table 9.2 illustrates, there are other episodes where the government was divided, especially among the partisan episodes, but there are also a few notable cases of divided governments among the union-driven episodes. The most notorious case of a divided government was, of course, the case of Brexit, where more than half of all the challenging acts came from members of the governing party. Well known also is the case of the Italian Jobs Act, where the unions were the main opposition forces but where dissidents from the

TABLE 9.2. *Episodes with divided governments: shares of challenger and third-party actions attributable to actors from government parties*

(a) Partisan episodes

| Episode | Country | Shares of challenger actions | Third-party actions |
|---|---|---|---|
| 13. Holland 1st austerity | France | 0 | 24.2 |
| 15. Decentralization | France | 0 | 12.8 |
| 22. Bad banks | Germany | 28.6 | 0 |
| 23. First bailout | Germany | 0 | 19.2 |
| 24. Third bailout | Germany | 76.9 | 0 |
| 25. Debt brake | Germany | 0 | 22.6 |
| 34. Third bailout | Greece | 74.6 | 4.6 |
| 82. Pension reform | Poland | 0 | 5.3 |
| 95. Muncipal Reform | Portugal | 9.7 | 7.0 |
| 105. Impeachment | Romania | 0 | 0 |
| 125. Brexit | U.K. | 56.9 | 2.0 |
| Total | | 43.5 | 7.4 |

(b) Union episodes

| Episode | Country | Shares of challenger actions | Third party actions |
|---|---|---|---|
| 64. Jobs Act | Italy | 0 | 70.9 |
| 72. 2009 austerity | Latvia | 0 | 23.1 |
| 94. 2012 austerity | Poland | 0 | 31.7 |
| 102. 2010 austerity | Romania | 35.5 | 16.0 |
| Total | | 4.9 | 51.1 |

governing party supported the unions' challenge against their own government. Finally, there were two cases of civil-society-driven episodes with divided governments – the second Latvian austerity package in 2009 and the Romanian Constitutional Court reform.

When a government is divided, internal opposition adds to the challenge of its proposal and undermines its position in a particularly threatening way. Therefore, we expect governments that are internally divided to be more repressive than coherent governments, whatever the challengers do. Furthermore, such internally divided governments are expected to be less ready to make concessions than coherent governments. To restore internal coherence, the government leadership needs to assert its authority and to impose itself against the internal opposition. In the episodes we are dealing with, where the government typically faced strong external constraints, it could not afford to give in to internal opposition without losing its standing with other domestic and international stakeholders.

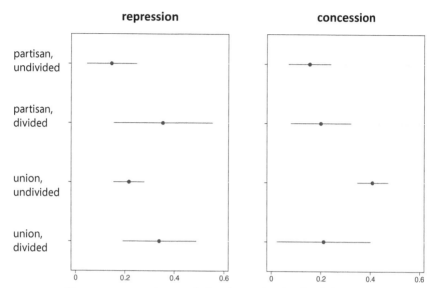

FIGURE 9.4. Government reaction to challenging action by divided government: predicted probabilities for all partisan and union-driven episodes with undivided and divided governments

Figure 9.4 provides the results for the impact of a divided government on the government's response to challenging actions by partisan and union-driven episodes. These results are based on the models presented in *Table A1*, column 3, in the appendix to this chapter. Lacking a sufficient number of cases, the civil-society-driven episodes are not included in this analysis. The first part of the figure refers to repression, the second to concessions. As Figure 9.4 shows, these results go in the expected direction, but the effects are weak. Although divided governments tend to be more repressive than undivided governments in response to challenger actions, the results are not significant.[5] Divided governments also tended to make fewer concessions but then only to union-driven challenges, where the results are significant.[6]

If governments were attacked by partisan challengers, the fact that they are divided did not induce them to make fewer concessions.

The inconclusive result for concessions in the case of partisan episodes can be illustrated by the German episodes, all of which were of the partisan type and all of which, with the exception of the bank bailout, gave rise to important

[5] For repression in union-driven episodes, the Chi2-value of the contrasts between undivided and divided governments facing a challenge amounts to 2.14 (1df, p = 0.144). In partisan episodes, the corresponding Chi2-value of the contrast between undivided and divided governments facing a challenge is 3.52 (1 df, p = 0.061).

[6] For concessions in union-driven episodes, the Chi2-value of the contrasts between undivided and divided governments facing a challenge amounts to 3.90 (1df, p = 0.048).

divisions in the government. The inspection of individual cases reveals that in Germany the configuration of forces was complicated by the opposition between the federal and regional governments, and, furthermore, by international stakeholders, which Germany as the key member-state of the European Union had to take into account. As a result of these complicating factors, the effect of divisions within the government was not as straightforward as posited by the hypothesis we formulated. These additional factors induced the German (centre-right) governments to make some concessions in the economic policy episodes, whether or not the government was divided. Thus, in the bank bailout episode – the only case where the government was not divided, the grand coalition (SPD–CDU), after some reluctance, agreed on a bailout package for the Hypo Real Estate bank to the tune of €26 billion. It also agreed on guarantees for private savings and it showed readiness to compromise regarding the share in the potential losses to be shouldered by the federal member states. In the case of the bad bank scheme, which was designed to allow banks to clean their balance sheets from toxic assets by placing them into so-called bad banks for up to twenty years, the same grand coalition was originally split. While the social-democratic minister of finance insisted on compulsory restructuring of regional banks, the coalition partner, the CDU, insisted that the federal states and not the central government should be responsible for their restructuring. The CDU finally got its way, which was considered to be a concession to the banking sector. In the episode of the first Greek bailout, Chancellor Angela Merkel, heading a center-right coalition, had at first resisted such a bailout altogether. Under international pressure, she eventually came around, supported the bailout in principle, and made additional concessions concerning details (e.g. the question of tax increases). In the case of the third Greek bailout, again under international pressure, the same chancellor, heading by now another grand coalition, urged her party to vote in favor of the bailout. She eventually succeeded in overcoming the internal opposition in her own party (coming mainly from Finance Minister Wolfgang Schäuble) that had favored a temporary Grexit and stopping any further aid to Greece. However, in the case of the German institutional reform, the debt brake, the German grand coalition did not make any concessions and stuck to its proposal throughout, although it was also divided on this point and some members of the governing parties supported the challengers. In this purely domestic case, international stakeholders did not play a role, but regional governments also supported the challengers. In this episode, however, their opposition was not taken into consideration.

THIRD-PARTY ACTORS

Let us now turn to the effect of third parties on government actions in the context of the three challenger configurations. As already pointed out, in Chapter 8 we found that mediation by third parties tends to induce governments to make concessions. Moreover, we found some support for the isolation hypothesis: governments tend to be more repressive when they do not get any third-party support. How do the three configurations of challengers affect the chances of mediation by third parties? We would expect mediation to be easier in situations where the challengers pose less of a threat to the government, as mutual trust relations with third-party brokers are more easily established when the challenge is less threatening. This would suggest that mediation would be more effective in the case of partisan challenges than in the case of broader challenges including civil-society organizations, with union-driven challenges taking a middle position. Accordingly, mediation should induce the most concessions from partisan challenges. For the other two configurations, mediation might not induce concessions, but would at least reduce repression.

Similarly, the variation in the threat exerted by challengers might also influence the impact of third-party support of either of the two adversaries. In line with the expectation formulated for mediation, third-party support of the government was expected to be more effective in less-threatening situations. Accordingly, we can specify the isolation hypothesis. We expect a government that is supported by a third party to be less likely to react in a repressive way if the challenge mainly emanates from conventional party or union politics rather than from civil-society actors. For a greater threat, third-party support of the government might not be effective at all, while support of challengers by third parties increases the threat to the government and is, therefore, likely to enhance its tendency to repress the challengers, especially in the case of the most threatening episodes, those that are civil-society-driven.

To test these expectations, we followed the same procedures as for the government's reactions to the challengers. We used the same models as in the previous analyses, but now added interactions with configurations of challengers for the third-party actions. Figure 9.5 presents the predicted probabilities of repression and concessions in reaction to challenger actions for partisan and union configurations. These results are based on the models presented in Table A1, column 4, in the appendix to this chapter. The expectations are most clearly borne out for the partisan episodes. For such episodes, repression is less likely when the government receives third-party support (govt+), while it is most likely when the challengers receive third-party support (chall+). The effect is weak, but significant.[7] On the other hand, our previous result with regard to mediation fully applies to partisan episodes: Mediation induces concessions in such episodes where conventional partisan challenges prevail.[8]

---

[7] For repression, the Chi2-value of the contrast between governments that are supported by third-party actors when facing a challenge and governments that face a challenger that is supported by third-party actors amounts to 4.16 (1df, p = 0.04) for partisan episodes.

[8] For concessions, the Chi2-value of the contrast between governments that are supported by third-party actors and governments that are facing mediating third-party actors amounts to 7.08 (1 df, p = 0.008).

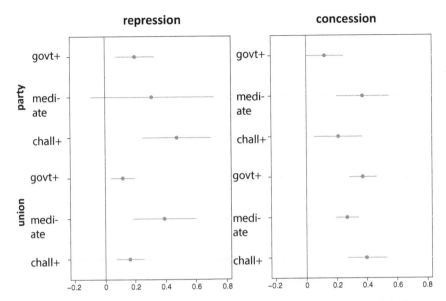

FIGURE 9.5. Government reaction to challenger actions by configuration of challengers and third-party action, for all episodes except for civil-society challenges: predicted probabilities

A conspicuous example of such an effect was the ratification of the third Greek bailout in Germany. From the vantage point of Greece, Germany took a particularly tough stance in this particular instance. However, in spite of the fact that the conditions imposed on the Greeks in return for the bailout were very harsh, indeed, the ratification of the bailout package by the German parliament was not a matter of course. Originally, the German parliament preferred a temporary Grexit or no further financial aid to Greece. Only in reaction to the pressure from other governments, from various EU actors, and from the Troika did it finally give in and accept the arrangement resulting from the negotiations with the Greek government on July 13, 2015. Another case in point is the 2010 austerity package introduced by the first Orban government. This package envisaged the introduction of a bank tax that was to hit foreign banks heavily. The parent banks of six Hungarian banks turned to the I.M.F., asking it to talk the Hungarian government out of introducing the tax. Upon the subsequent intervention of the I.M.F., this tax was slightly modified to ease the burden on more recently established insurance and investment companies. As these cases illustrate once again, even when mediation led to some concessions by the government, the concessions made were quite marginal compared to the stakes involved.

For civil society-driven episodes, third-party actions did not make any difference, which is why the results for civil society-driven episodes are not shown in Figure 9.5. Moreover, for union-driven episodes, third-party actions had a rather unexpected result. As shown in Figure 9.5, in such episodes mediation by third-party actors actually increased government repression and tended to reduce government concessions.[9] The instances of third-party mediation in union-driven episodes mainly refer to the Italian episodes and to the 2009 austerity package in Ireland. In the Irish case, the very severe austerity package was linked to the I.M.F. bailout. Although mediation attempts were undertaken by European actors, these left the government very little maneuvering space and go a long way in explaining why they did not induce the government to make the expected concessions. Thus, in reaction to European mediation attempts, the responsible minister said: "There is an onus on all citizens and all political parties to reflect on these realities," and he repeated the government's commitment to finding the bulk of the €4 billion from spending cuts. In the Italian episodes, mediation was undertaken by some elements of the divided governing parties, but, as we have already seen, in the case of divided governments, repression is rather more likely and may account for the unexpected result.

Overall, we can conclude that the impact of third parties on the government was rather weak. The positive mediation effect that we uncovered in the previous chapter was limited to the least threatening episodes and even there it was at best rather weak. The isolation hypothesis, too, is only confirmed for the partisan configuration. Where the third parties could have had the biggest role to play – in the episodes that involve civil-society actors which are arguably most threatening for the government – we found no effect from third-party actions.

INTERNATIONAL SUPPORT

Finally, we want to check to what extent international support had a more sizeable impact on the government's reaction to the challengers than third-party support in general. We take a closer look at international actors because not only were they a very important category of third-party actors – they make up more than one fourth of this actor type (27.8 percent) – but they are also theoretically crucial. In many of our episodes, they were closely allied with the government and, arguably, constituted the real targets of the challengers. Thus, in the case of the Greek bailouts, the Troika was as much targeted by the challengers as the domestic government. Accordingly, in these episodes, it is somewhat artificial to consider international actors as third parties. We have nevertheless stuck to our parsimonious scheme of actors that treats

---

[9] For repression, the Chi2-value of the contrast between governments that are supported by third-party actors and governments that are facing mediating third-party actors amounts to 8.09 (1 df, p = 0.005) for union-driven episodes. The Chi2-value for the corresponding contrast for concessions is 3.43 (1 df, p = 0.064).

TABLE 9.3. *Episodes with international support of government and challengers*

(a) Support of government (govt+)

| Episode id | Country | Mean | Govt+ | Mediate | Chall+ |
|---|---|---|---|---|---|
| 12. Sarkozy 2nd | France | 0.53 | 77.8 | 11.1 | 11.1 |
| 14. Hollande–Valls | France | 0.21 | 66.7 | 0 | 33.3 |
| 22. Bad banks | Germany | 0.30 | 100.0 | 0 | 0 |
| 31. First bailout | Greece | 0.66 | 93.6 | 0 | 6.4 |
| 32. Midterm adjustment | Greece | 0.42 | 97.7 | 0 | 2.3 |
| 33. Second bailout | Greece | 0.45 | 91.4 | 6.9 | 1.7 |
| 34. Third bailout | Greece | 0.43 | 74.5 | 2.1 | 23.4 |
| 41. I.M.F. bailout | Hungary | 0.39 | 85.7 | 0 | 14.3 |
| 53. I.M.F. bailout | Ireland | 0.30 | 100.0 | 0 | 0 |
| 72. 2009 austerity | Latvia | 0.38 | 80.0 | 20.0 | 0 |
| 75. Eurozone entry | Latvia | 0.80 | 100.0 | 0 | 0 |
| 92. PEC 3 and 4 | Portugal | 0.23 | 88.9 | 0 | 11.1 |
| 93. I.M.F. bailout | Portugal | 0.38 | 76.9 | 7.7 | 15.4 |
| 94. 2012 austerity | Portugal | 0.22 | 77.8 | 22.2 | 0 |
| 101. I.M.F. bailout | Romania | 0.21 | 100.0 | 0 | 0 |
| 111. Zapatero 1st austerity | Spain | 0.25 | 100.0 | 0 | 0 |
| 113. Rajoy austerity | Spain | 0.34 | 81.3 | 12.5 | 6.3 |
| 114. Bankia | Spain | 0.59 | 75.0 | 0 | 25.0 |
| 125. Brexit | UK | 0.25 | 75.7 | 2.7 | 21.6 |

(b) Support of challenger (chall+)

| Episode id | Country | Mean | Govt+ | Mediate | Chall+ |
|---|---|---|---|---|---|
| 35. TV shutdown | Greece | 0.21 | 25.0 | 0 | 75.0 |
| 43. Pension nationalization | Hungary | 0.50 | 0 | 0 | 100.0 |
| 44. Internet tax | Hungary | 0.75 | 16.7 | 16.7 | 66.7 |
| 45. Media law | Hungary | 0.95 | 15.8 | 13.2 | 71.1 |
| 73. 2009 austerity | Latvia | 0.38 | 0 | 0 | 100.0 |
| 74. 2010 austerity | Latvia | 0.80 | 0 | 0 | 100.0 |

international actors as third-party actors. Moreover, as in the previously cited case of the Irish 2009 austerity measures, the international actors put enormous pressure on the government and left it with no alternative but to go ahead with the austerity option.

Nineteen out of the sixty episodes were characterized by an above-average number of interventions by international third-party actors that were, moreover, mainly in favor of the government. These episodes included seven out of the eight I.M.F. cases (including all four economic episodes in Greece), eight of the twenty-four budgetary packages, and two institutional reforms. Table 9.3a presents the list of these episodes. In addition, there were also six episodes with above-average interventions by international third-party actors that were

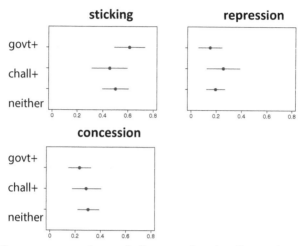

FIGURE 9.6. Government reaction to challenger action, for all episodes with
international actors supporting government, challengers, or neither: predicted
probabilities

mainly in favor of the challengers. These episodes referred to three of the
budgetary packages and three institutional reforms. They are listed in
Table 9.3b.

In most of the episodes listed in Table 9.3a, international support left the
government no option other than to follow the directives of the international
allies. The Troika that imposed the economic austerity policy on the Greek
government is only the most blatant case in point. Accordingly, we expect the
governments to react to international third-party support above all by sticking
to their policies. Second, in line with the isolation hypothesis, we expect
governments to react with repression to challenger actions if the challengers
were supported by international allies. Third, both international support of the
government and international support of the challengers are likely to reduce the
government's concessions; given that international support mostly means international pressure, the government would not be able to make concessions. On
the other hand, international support of the challengers increases the threat to
the government, thereby, according to the isolation hypothesis, making the
government less likely to make concessions.

Figure 9.6 presents the results for the test of these hypotheses about the
interactions between international third parties and the governments' reactions
to challenger actions. They are based on the models presented in Table A1,
column 5, in the appendix to this chapter. We do not distinguish between
different challenger configurations here. The expectations are confirmed for
sticking, even if the effect is rather weak: Governments that are challenged
domestically while being supported by international allies are likely to stick to
their guns in almost two thirds of the cases, while governments faced with a

domestic challenge supported by international allies only do so in half of the cases.[10] This result suggests that governments supported by international actors have less room for maneuver in dealing with domestic challenges than those not supported by such allies.

With respect to repression, we find some support for the isolation hypothesis. If a government faced challengers who are supported by international actors, the likelihood of repression increased from 15 percent – when the government was supported by external allies – to 26 percent when external allies supported challengers.[11] For concessions, international allies did not make a difference. A more detailed analysis reveals, however, that unions received very few concessions when governments were supported by external allies in southern European union-driven episodes. The consequent lack of maneuvering space provides further evidence for governments not making concessions when exposed to a union challenge. It is above all in southern Europe that the governments found themselves under international pressure, and it is in southern Europe that this pressure did not allow the governments to be in any way forthcoming with respect to their "natural allies," the unions. However, international support of challengers does not necessarily make the government less likely to make concessions. For example, the Hungarian internet tax, one of the episodes where the challengers received massive international support (see Table 9.3b), proved to be one of the very few cases where the challengers obtained complete success – the government withdrew the proposed tax in reaction to the challenges (see Chapter 7).

CONCLUSION

In this chapter, we introduced context characteristics that condition the reactions of governments to challenger actions. These characteristics refer to different configurations of the three actor types. First, we distinguished three types of episodes based on the challenger configurations – predominantly partisan, union-driven, and civil-society driven episodes. The intention of this distinction was to specify the intensity of the threat posed by the challengers to the government in the particular episode. Contrary to expectations, the distinction did not provide further evidence in support of the threat hypothesis. While government repression generally increased in reaction to challenging actions, the likelihood of repression following challenging actions did not prove to be higher in the presumably more threatening types of episodes. The distinction

---

[10]  For sticking, the Chi2-value of the contrast between governments that are supported by international allies and governments that face challengers who are supported by external allies amounts to 6.57 (1 df, p = 0.010).

[11]  For repression, the Chi2-value of the contrast between governments that are supported by international allies and governments that face challengers who are supported by external allies amounts to 3.81 (1 df, p = 0.051).

between the three types of configurations proved to be more relevant for concessions. Although we did not find any evidence for tit-for-tat logic, we did find evidence for a divide-and-rule strategy: Governments tended to provide more concessions to less threatening challengers, that is to unions, than to more threatening ones like civil-society organizations.

Second, we classified episodes based on their government composition. Given the limited maneuvering space of governments during the Great Recession, we did not expect government reactions to differ depending on the government's composition. And this is, indeed, what we found at first – overall, the reactions of centre-left and centre-right governments to challenging actions hardly differ. Once we took into account the interaction between the government's composition and its popularity, however, we did find relevant differences in a government's reaction to challengers. In general, popularity proved to be an asset that made a government less vulnerable to challenger actions, whether they were from the centre-right or the centre-left. In contrast, unpopular right-wing governments resorted more frequently to repression, while unpopular left-wing governments tended to make more concessions. This result provided some confirmation for the threat hypothesis. In addition to unpopularity, internal divisions also made governments more vulnerable to challengers. Again, in line with the threat hypothesis, we found that divided governments were more repressive and made fewer concessions than undivided governments. More detailed analyses of the German episodes suggested that the impact of the government's composition was modified by additional factors such as the federalist structure of the state and international pressure, which introduced additional stakeholders.

While we did not systematically analyze the impact of federalist structures or of any other domestic structures for that matter, we did analyze the impact of international pressure with regard to the impact of third-party actors. As it turned out, third-party actors had only weak effects on the interaction patterns between government and challengers. Moreover, the expected effects could be found only in the case of partisan episodes. Thus, the important mediation effect that we uncovered in the previous chapter seems to have been limited to the least-threatening partisan episodes, and even there it was weak at best. For partisan episodes, we also found some support for the isolation hypothesis. In such episodes, repression was less likely when the government received third-party support but most likely when challengers received third-party support. For civil-society-driven episodes, we did not find any effect from third-party actors. For union-driven episodes, surprisingly, we found mediation by third-party actors reduced concessions and contributed to the repression of the challengers. The more detailed analysis of the impact of international actors on a government's reaction to challengers helped to elucidate this surprising result. The support of a government by international allies during the Great Recession was, indeed, a mixed blessing. In many of the episodes, especially in the union-driven episodes in southern Europe, the governments found themselves between Scylla and Charybdis: that is, between a domestic challenge and international pressure. The international "support" typically put the governments under heavy pressure to adopt the austerity proposals as the price to be paid. Such pressure increased the propensity of the governments to stick to their proposal, to make no substantive concessions, and to increase the repression of domestic challengers.

As a result of these forces beyond the control of the governments in the episodes studied, the patterns of government reactions were only weakly related to challenger actions and to third-party interventions. Even if we could specify these patterns to some extent by introducing context characteristics based on the prevailing actor configurations, the resulting effects remain rather weak overall. During the episodes we studied, the constraints imposed on the governments by the economic situation and by international stakeholders were such that they mainly had to stick to their original proposals irrespective of the dynamics of interaction that unfolded in the domestic political arenas – whether in the party arena, the administrative arena, or the protest arena. The most threatening challenger actions were repressed, and concessions – to the extent that they were forthcoming – proved to be mostly symbolic gestures. Had our set of episodes included episodes from different periods in European countries, or episodes confronting governments and challengers in countries with non-democratic regimes, it is quite likely that the context differences would have been more pronounced.

There is also a technical reason why the results of this analysis were not as clear-cut as we might have expected. The technical point refers to the complexity of the context conditions that have to be taken into consideration in an attempt to account for the governments' reactions. In addition to the factors considered in this chapter, there are other domestic structures such as federalism (as in the case of Germany), the division of power between the cabinet and the president (as in the cases of Romania or Latvia), or the influence of courts that have to be taken into consideration as well. With the data at hand, it was, however, impossible to take into account the full configuration of relevant context conditions at one and the same time. Although we can rely on roughly two thousand actions for the analysis of the governments' reactions to challenging actions in our sixty episodes, we quickly hit data limitations once we focused on a specific pair of actions (e.g. government repression versus radical challenger action) in a context characterized by a combination of multiple factors. The number of cases for a given pair-context combination diminishes rapidly. For this reason we chose to reduce the challenging actions to the simple distinction between challenge and absence of challenge, and why we analyzed the various context conditions one-by-one. A more detailed analysis based on a larger number of data points would allow us to test the various hypotheses in a more adequate way than was possible in the present chapter.

# 10

# The Effect of Repression on Protest

Katia Pilati

## INTRODUCTION

On May 5 and 6, 2010 Greece witnessed extensive protests including a forty-eight-hour nationwide strike and demonstrations in major cities. Protests were provoked by the passing of three austerity measures by the Greek parliament in February 2010, in March 2010, and finally in May 2010. The measures were part of the conditions for the €110 billion first EU bailout, acquired in order to solve the Greek government debt crisis. These events ended with clashes between the police and anti-austerity protesters, during which the police made widespread use of tear-gas and flash bombs, and made multiple arrests. Three people died when some individuals set fire to a bank branch with Molotov cocktails, and tens of people were injured. One year later, the police once again made use of violence against protesters at the May 11 demonstrations. This was a few days before the Greek Indignant Citizens Movement on May 25, 2011 started to protest in major cities across Greece. In June 2011, in concomitance with the government discussions on the midterm adjustment program and additional austerity measures (the adjustment program was later passed on June 29, 2011), police clashed with demonstrators numerous times – again, making excessive use of tear-gas.

In France in 2010, between October 14 and 18 more than three hundred students protesting against the Sarkozy–Fillon austerity package, were arrested and injured by the police. These events saw the occurrence of many accidents, such as that of a student who was severely injured by a flash ball.

In Spain, in July and August 2011, during Zapatero's negotiations on the second bailout, the Spanish national police collided with the 15-M movement, named after the beginning of the demonstrations on May 15, 2011, the Indignados, and dismantled their camps in Las Palmas, Santa Cruz de Tenerife, Palma de Mallorca, Manacor, Badajoz, and Castellón. Police actions were also reported in the Sol camp in Madrid.

Repressive measures such as those listed above touched most European countries affected by the crisis where anti-austerity protests developed. However, systematic empirical evidence on the effects of repressive measures adopted by governments against anti-austerity protesters during the Great Recession – namely, on their repertoire of actions – is still lacking (for single case studies however, see Sotirakopoulos and Sotiropoulos 2013; Portos Garcìa 2016).

While in Chapter 9 we examined government repression as a response to challengers' actions, in this chapter, by acknowledging that the repression – dissent nexus is two-sided, we analyze the other side of the relationship. We investigate how anti-austerity protesters in European countries reacted to the governments' repressive measures to suppress their challenges during the Great recession. This chapter thus aims to answer the following research questions: What were the effects of government repressive measures on the challengers' responses? Did the challengers' repertoire of actions change accordingly? Did repressive measures silence protests, did they lead to violent reactions or to an increase in peaceful and nonviolent political debates and interactions?

We shall explore the sequence of interactions, broadly examined in Chapter 8, by taking a closer look at the impact of repression on diverse forms of mobilization, and examining in greater depth the challengers' forms of mobilization presented by Gessler and Hutter in Table 4.2.[1] We contend that the link between repression and protests depends on the specific form of action considered and on the type of challengers engaged in protests. We shall also argue that the repression–protest nexus is conditional on certain context characteristics – based on the concept of political opportunity structure (POS) as expressed in the literature. By studying such dynamics, this chapter aims to clarify crucial issues related to the democratic functioning of European countries. Repression threatens democracy, to the degree that it aims to contain and hinder the possibilities for a multiplicity of civil-society organizations – unions as well as oppositional political parties – to participate in protests and thus to engage fully in the political sphere. In this framework, our first contribution is to uncover how repression has an impact on shifts in challengers' repertoire of actions. Second, we shall examine this relationship using CEA, thereby overcoming the limitations of large-N studies as well as those of single-case studies and narrative approaches. We can, in fact, focus on a large number of cases related to various forms of government repression and challengers' protests in a way similar to the epidemiological approaches Tilly used (Tilly 2008: 206). Furthermore, we are able to reconstruct the particular interactions within a specific time sequence. Thus, when focusing on a large-N empirical dataset, we will not lose out on what actually occurs during such interactions since we are able to trace them back to specific actors and to the specific action repertoires.

---

[1] The variables used for identifying forms of mobilization in Table 4 and in this chapter differ slightly. Table 4 lists forms of mobilization solely involving procedural actions. Whenever they are mentioned in our sources, the variable in this chapter refers to all forms of mobilization.

## EXPLAINING CHANGES IN CHALLENGERS' REPERTOIRE
## OF ACTIONS THROUGH REPRESSION

In addressing the question of what accounts for changes in challengers' repertoire of actions, and under what circumstances changes in the character of
contention occur, Tilly (2008) argues that performances and repertoires vary as
a result of the influence of a given campaign – successful or not – on the next
campaign.[2] This kind of influence operates through alterations in three channels: the political opportunity structure (POS), available models, and connections among potential actors. We focus on changes occurring through
alterations of the POS, positing that a campaign can transform the POS and
therefore alter the subsequent campaign. As Tilly (2008) argues, the POS is
affected by previous campaigns in diverse ways: by bringing new actors into the
regime; by establishing new alliances between challengers and holders of
power; by changing a regime's repressive policy. The latter was the main focus
of Chapter 9. In this chapter, we study how the repertoire of actions has been
modified by examining the impact of changes in the POS implied in the use of
repressive measures by governments. Repression is considered as "any action
by another group which raises the contender's cost of collective action" (Tilly
1978: 100) and, therefore, it closes, limits, and hinders challengers' opportunities to mobilize in the political sphere.[3] Forms of repression include nonviolent
state actions such as sanctions, restrictions of liberties, as well as forms of
control such as arrests, tear gas, and shootings. Next to these actions, scholars
have emphasized that government threats and negative evaluations of challengers may further contribute to the closing of opportunities to mobilize, given
that they represent forms of symbolic repression. Discursive frames by elites
and institutional actors define a cultural set of opportunities referred to as a
*discursive opportunity structure* (DOS) (Koopmans et al. 2005); this shapes the
challengers' political actions by attributing to them and/or denying them political legitimation and recognition.

   As already mentioned in Chapter 8, the way that repression affects protests
is still largely debated in the literature, despite its study having long informed
the analysis of contentious politics in several social science areas of study,
including social movements, revolutions, ethnic conflicts, civil wars, and civil
resistance. Researchers have proposed various hypotheses on the repression–
dissent nexus. However, they have been divided with regard to the direction of

---

[2] Campaigns are defined by Tilly (2008) as coordinated series of episodes involving similar claims
on similar or identical targets.
[3] In this case, repression is thought of as a contraction of opportunities. As mentioned in Chapter 9,
this claim was reformulated later, by Tilly himself (2005), who argued that the effect of repression
is less straightforward. When repression is perceived as a threat, it may also induce a radicalization of insurgents.

the repression effect, and have only to a limited extent succeeded in offering coherent and consistent interpretative patterns (Earl 2011). As Lichbach has observed (1987: 271) "what is unknown is how repression both escalates and deters dissent." Following rational action theories, researchers claim that harsh repression depresses protest mobilization. From this perspective, engagement in action is determined by careful cost-benefit calculations by potential participants. Individuals are likely to participate if the benefit from participating is greater than its costs (Oberschall 1973). In contrast to this hypothesis, others emphasize that harsher coercion accelerates protests. Under such circumstances, a core of the opposition group might become dedicated to organizing reactive protests (Lichbach 1987: 270). Researchers have also put forward a nonlinear link between repression and protest mobilization, suggesting a convex U-shaped relationship (Lichbach and Gurr 1981). Under this model, both low and high levels of repression lead to high levels of protest, whereas protest is at its lowest levels during medium-level repression. Other authors have suggested a concave or inverted U-shaped relationship: Gurr (1970: 238) argues that the threat and severity of coercive violence may increase the anger of dissidents and intensify their opposition. Yet, this occurs up to some threshold beyond which fear predominates. Under very repressive regimes, the costs and risks associated with protest and rebellion instill fear, terror, and distress in the population and therefore prevent the open display of dissent. Following this reasoning, protesters can be mobilized best under semi-repressive regimes.

## The Link between Repression and Protests: Considering Forms of Protests and Types of Challengers

Past studies on the policing of protests in Italy and Germany in the 1970s claimed that repression hinders peaceful protests while it intensifies violent protests (della Porta 1995). In the increasingly repressive context of Italy in the 1970s, mass protests and peaceful demonstrations decreased after reaching a peak in 1971, while political violence increased throughout the 1970s (Tarrow 1989). Along the same line of reasoning, Lichbach (1987: 285) proposed that "an increase in a government's repression of nonviolence will reduce the nonviolent activities of an opposition group but increase its violent activities." According to this argument, repression radicalizes protests, and therefore has a positive effect on the use of political violence. Political violence is, however, only one form of action within the broader repertoire of contention that challengers may engage in. Under authoritarian regimes, protesters often redirect their activities toward more moderated repertoires of action, since these are often perceived as less threatening. Challengers may also turn to transnational actions outside their country, or use strategies aimed to self-contain their protests (Pilati 2016). In many countries of the Middle East and North Africa, as a response to the prohibition of protests, activists often chose itineraries of deradicalization by committing themselves to forms of social, cultural, intellectual, and artistic activities (Duboc 2011). Following these studies, we can expect repression to have an effect on the repertoire of action, an effect that is likely to depend on the type of action deployed by the challenger. On one hand, we follow the simplest hypothesis and suggest that repression is likely to remove the challengers' opportunities to mobilize. This is in line both with the POS perspective – arguing that closing opportunities dampens protests – and with a rational choice model, given that repression implies higher costs for challengers to engage in protests. We therefore expect that repression reduces most forms of protest (*repression works hypothesis*). On the other hand, we expect repression to polarize protests: that is, to increase both the challengers' engagement in moderate and conventional forms of actions and in violent action forms (*polarization hypothesis*).

Following the argument in the previous chapter, we also expect that repression has a different effect depending on which actors challenge the government's proposals. The contentious episodes analyzed in this book involve diverse actors, with varying degrees of institutionalization, the most institutional being international and government bodies and political parties, and the least being civil-society organizations (CSOs), including social-movement organizations. We expect that repression has a stronger dampening effect on the protests by the least institutionalized actors – CSOs or even trade unions – and a weaker dampening effect on protests by more institutional actors, such as political parties or governmental actors. In particular, as proposed in Chapter 9, we expect repression to be harsher when contentious episodes are driven by the least institutionalized actors, such as civil-society organizations, than when they are mainly driven by more institutionalized actors, such as political parties (*civil- society organizations hypothesis*).[4] Institutional actors, beside being more likely to be involved in electoral politics, are perceived as more legitimate, even if they intervene in the protest arena. Furthermore, they are likely to perceive governmental repression as less intimidating and/or threatening compared to the least institutionalized actors.

In contrast to this hypothesis, we may also expect that the most institutional actors are used to adopting routine actions and interact more often in the parliamentary and electoral arena than in the protest arena. Consequently, we expect that if they resort to protest, which is "unusual" for them, and meet with governmental repression, they will quickly retreat from such activities. In other words, we expect that the dampening effect of repression on protest is stronger when political parties are the dominant challengers, as they are used to engaging in institutional politics and are less prepared to interact and respond to government repression in the protest arena (*political-party hypothesis*).

---

[4] In the previous statement, the focus was on single actors, while here the focus is on the episode-level actors' configurations as in Kriesi's Chapter 9.

## The Role of the Context in Moderating the Relationship between Repression and Protests

Preexisting context conditions may also affect the way repression has an impact upon challengers' opportunities to engage in protests. In those countries where challengers are accustomed to repressive measures, in less democratic regimes, challengers may anticipate the adoption of repressive measures by the governments, in contrast to challengers operating in contexts where governments tend to promote negotiations, dialogue, and cooperation with challengers. Likewise, governments that are perceived as untrustworthy, or political systems that are unstable, may equally provoke different reactions by challengers responding to government repression, compared to responses by challengers operating in more trustworthy and stable contexts.

Considering the context, we first examined the effect of repression on protests for the Greek case in particular, given that Greece was the country where the most anti-austerity protests took place (Kriesi et al. 2020). Second, we analyzed the moderating effect of two of the least stable dimensions of the POS – the political orientation of the cabinet in charge and elite alliance.[5] The literature has widely acknowledged the effects of the political orientation of the cabinet on protests. Left cabinets are expected to stimulate the participation of groups in politics, given that they will appeal to constituencies of the civil society to build as broad an electoral coalition as possible and facilitate challengers' mobilization.

When, however, left cabinets are in power, the need for mobilization may decrease because of anticipated possibilities of reform in their favor (Kriesi et al. 1995: 59–60). Depending on whether government orientation is left or right, challengers may also react differently to repression. With left cabinets in power, challengers may perceive repression as less threatening, and they may consider governments as possible allies. This may be even more true for challengers engaged in anti-austerity protests during the Great Recession, given that many of them were driven by leftist ideologies. We therefore expected that the dampening effect of repression on protests might be weaker under left cabinets (*left cabinet's reinforcing hypothesis*). Alternatively, because challengers may not anticipate repression from left cabinets and, consequently, may be caught off guard when such governments nevertheless resort to repression, the dampening effect of government repression on protests might actually be stronger under left cabinets than it would be under right cabinets from whom repression is more expected (*left cabinet's dampening hypothesis*).

---

[5] Next to these dimensions, we have also tested the conditional impact of both more-stable dimensions of the POS – namely, the type of democracy – and of other less stable dimensions of the POS, such as the degree of political stability and the type of electoral system, specifically testing whether a higher degree of proportionality or a more majoritarian system had some moderating effect. However, neither of these dimensions had a significant moderating effect or models did not provide reliable estimates.

The second dimension of the POS that we examined refers to alliances. In particular, when national governments build ties with international actors, they may be reinforced in their original plans. Thus, in the case of anti-austerity protests, international actors have often been perceived as having been at the origin of many austerity measures themselves. This was the case in Greece, where the European Commission (E.C.), the European Central Bank (E.C.B), and the International Monetary Fund (I.M.F.), the so-called Troika, imposed austerity programs on the Greek government. Under such circumstances, the dampening effect of repression on protests was likely to be stronger, since challengers were likely to perceive more constraints on protest mobilization (*constraint hypothesis*). The situation is likely to be very different when international actors ally themselves with challengers, as in the case of supranational institutions building coalitions with opposition parties against national governments. Under such circumstances, coalitions between challengers and international actors are likely to be perceived as numerically strong, and worthy to be listened to; international actors may heighten challengers' legitimacy and symbolic recognition, overall improving challengers' WUNC – *worthiness, unity, numbers, and commitment* (Tilly 2006: 53). Alliances with international actors, endowed with many symbolic and material resources, are therefore likely to provide challengers with an easier access to politics, thanks to the provision of resources that challengers may lack. We thus expected challengers' alliances with international actors to affect the impact of repression on protests by opening opportunities. Consequently, repression would have a lower dampening effect on protests when challengers ally themselves with international actors (*international ally hypothesis*). Since in our episodes international actors were mostly institutions, we expected repression most likely to have a dampening effect on the most conventional forms of protest actions rather than on other forms of protest, given that institutional actors are more likely to engage in conventional actions (*conventional actions hypothesis*).

METHODS

## Dependent Variables

In the subsequent analysis, the dependent variable consists of the various forms of protest mobilization. In our first step, we investigated challengers' engagement in any form of protests. Next, we delved into the analysis of four specific forms of protests: conventional actions, strikes, demonstrative actions, and the most disruptive forms of actions – confrontational and violent actions – which we refer to as radical actions. The category of conventional actions includes direct democratic actions, such as legal procedures, proposals to change the legislation, initiations of referenda, and public consultations. Together with petitions these actions made up the majority of institutional forms of protest. Nondisruptive and disruptive protests, referred to in Chapters 8 and 9, were disaggregated into specific types of protests. In particular, we disaggregated disruptive actions and distinguished radical actions (confrontational and violent actions) from demonstrations. All the dependent variables are binary variables (1 = challenger action takes the form in question; 0 = other challenger action). We examined how repression affects the different forms of protest mobilization, including both outright actions and verbal statements.[6]

## Main Independent Variables

Our main independent variable is government repression. Following the previous two chapters, we considered the lagged actions by government, using a binary variable focusing on repression (1 = government repression; 0 = other government action). Examples of repressive actions included the use of legal provisions against challengers, police clashes, and arrests of demonstrators. Repressive verbal statements were claims aimed demonizing, depreciating, or not recognizing challengers, including denouncing specific party decisions or criticizing workers such as public employees who resist wage cuts.

The conditional effects of the POS variables on the repression–protests link were tested by adding interactions between repression and POS variables. The latter are country- or episode-specific. Interactions were added separately, one in each model.

Control variables included in the models are the following: lagged actions by third parties, a binary variable (1 = third parties supported challengers; 0 = did not do so); challengers' lagged actions, a binary variable (1 = challengers' lagged action is of the same type; 0 = it is not of the same type);[7] country fixed effects; sequence length and squared sequence length.

## Models

To test our hypotheses, we followed the same procedures as in the previous chapters. Given that our dependent variables are binary variables, we estimated logit models with challengers' reactions (different types of protests) as the dependent variables and the lagged government actions – repression – as the main independent variable. We estimated logit regression models that take into account the multistage research design, and the correlation of data within episodes and countries. While the research design has a four-level structure

[6] This simplification of the analysis is imposed by the lack of data. As in the previous chapter, we quickly met the limits of the number of cases once we distinguished between different action forms and/or introduced context characteristics into the analysis. While the previous chapter chose to reduce the number of action forms, the focus on action forms in this chapter imposed another type of simplification.

[7] The model predicting the probabilities of engaging in any type of protest form includes the variables on challengers' lagged actions as coded in Chapters 8 and 9.

(with actions at level 1, nested within sequences at level 2, within episodes at level 3, and countries at level 4), we used a cluster option, with the clustering variable accounting for the episode.[8] We estimated the models, pooling all episodes together. Models first tested the effect of repression on different types of protests, thus testing the *repression works hypothesis* and the *polarization hypothesis;* second, models considered different types of challengers, thus testing *the civil society organizations hypothesis* and the *political party hypothesis*. Then, models tested the interaction effects, addressing the *left cabinet's reinforcing* and the *left cabinet's dampening*, as well as the *constraint*, the *international ally*, and the *conventional actions hypotheses*. Before turning to hypotheses testing, however, we shall describe levels and types of protests used by challengers across European countries between 2008 and 2016.

## RESULTS

### Protests during the Great Recession: Levels and Forms

Table 10.1 focuses on challengers' forms of mobilization. It illustrates the distribution of challengers' actions or verbal statements, focusing on those in which a specific form of protest mobilization has been explicitly mentioned.

The table shows that approximately half of challengers' actions and verbal statements involved some form of protest mobilization. While Greece and Ireland show the highest number of challengers' claims, Greece, Portugal, and France were the countries in which at least 60 percent of all challengers' claims implied some form of protest mobilization. Considering the absolute number of protests, and confirming previous studies, Greece, Portugal, Spain, and Ireland were the countries showing the largest number of forms of protest mobilization, while Germany was the country with the smallest number of protests.

Most forms of protest mobilization were public demonstrations and strikes, accounting, respectively, for 18.4 and for 11.7 percent of all claims by challengers. Fewer challengers engaged in more conventional channels of participation: 11.2 percent of all political claims were conventional actions, of which 2.0 percent were petitions. While in most European countries challengers mainly engaged by demonstrating in the streets, in France and Greece challengers mostly engaged in strikes. The latter include the pension reform strikes that occurred in September and October 2010 in France, involving both the public and private sectors, and the two-day general strike staged by trade unions in Greece on June 28 and 29, 2011 against the midterm adjustment program, a

---

[8] We used the vce (cluster clustvar) STATA option that indicates that the actions were independent across the episodes and countries but were not necessarily independent within those groups. This option specifies that the standard errors allow for intragroup correlation, relaxing the usual requirement that the observations be independent.

TABLE 10.1. *Challengers' engagement in different forms of protest mobilization across countries (row %)*

| Country | Other actions | Conventional actions | Protest (actions and threats) | | | | | Total % | n (Protest and other actions)[a] | n (Protest only)[b] |
|---|---|---|---|---|---|---|---|---|---|---|
| | | | Strikes | Demonstrations | Confrontational | Violent actions | | | |
| Greece | 34.8 | 5.5 | 28.4 | 19.1 | 10.8 | 1.5 | 100.0 | 472 | 308 |
| France | 40.0 | 1.1 | 34.4 | 17.8 | 5.6 | 1.1 | 100.0 | 90 | 54 |
| Portugal | 40.8 | 21.0 | 15.7 | 22.3 | 0.3 | 0 | 100.0 | 319 | 189 |
| Poland | 43.4 | 31.9 | 0 | 24.8 | 0 | 0 | 100.0 | 113 | 64 |
| Romania | 48.8 | 21.5 | 9.9 | 18.6 | 1.2 | 0 | 100.0 | 172 | 88 |
| Hungary | 51.5 | 22.0 | 5.3 | 21.2 | 0 | 0 | 100.0 | 132 | 64 |
| Germany | 56.1 | 43.9 | 0 | 0 | 0 | 0 | 100.0 | 41 | 18 |
| Spain | 57.1 | 3.5 | 5.2 | 32.9 | 1.3 | 0 | 100.0 | 231 | 99 |
| Latvia | 57.3 | 15.5 | 3.6 | 21.8 | 1.8 | 0 | 100.0 | 110 | 47 |
| Ireland | 75.0 | 5.5 | 4.8 | 14.6 | 0.2 | 0 | 100.0 | 440 | 110 |
| Italy | 77.2 | 2.3 | 8.2 | 9.6 | 0.5 | 2.3 | 100.0 | 219 | 50 |
| U.K. | 78.7 | 7.9 | 2.8 | 8.8 | 0.9 | 0.9 | 100.0 | 216 | 46 |
| Total | 55.5 | 11.2 | 11.7 | 18.4 | 2.7 | 0.6 | 100.0 | 2,555 | 1,137 |

[a] includes all challengers' actions
[b] includes conventional actions, strikes, signatures, demonstrations, confrontational, and violent protests

199

new package of deeply unpopular austerity measures that was passed at the end of the month.

In contrast, in Germany conflict between challengers and authorities was both much more limited and restricted to the most conventional channels of participation. Conflict there largely took place in the institutional and partisan arena through actions such as handing in complaints to the constitutional court or voting against government initiatives. Challengers' actions included, for instance, a petition by the populist and Eurosceptic Alternative for Germany, AfD, in July 2015 against the EU's planned bailout of Greece. Neither strikes, nor demonstrations, nor more radical actions were ever observed in Germany during the economic crisis as far as the selected episodes are concerned.

Only 3.3 percent of all public claims making involved radical actions: that is, either confrontational or violent actions. More specifically, violent actions only represented 0.6 percent of all 2,555 challengers' claims. In other words, only fifteen violent protests were reported during the contentious interactions that occurred in the twelve European countries from 2008 to 2016.[9] Considering that we have examined contentious interactions that occurred during sixty episodes that concerned key policy proposals related to the great economic crisis – essentially austerity packages – we can claim that anti-austerity protests were definitely nonviolent actions. Confrontational actions were more present than violent actions during the contentious episodes, although still representing quite limited and sporadic events, accounting for 2.7 percent of all challengers' claims. Almost half of the violent actions occurred in Greece; likewise, three quarters of the confrontational actions occurred in Greece.

Given the exceptional characteristics of the Greek case, we propose to have a closer look at the contentious episodes in Greece. Figure 10.1 shows the daily count of protests and repressive measures during the five episodes in Greece.[10] Considering the pattern of protests, the figure suggests that the five episodes were part of a single wave of contention. In particular, as argued by Kriesi et al. (2020: ch. 4), the three first episodes in Greece (the first bailout, the midterm adjustment, the second bailout) mark three different phases of the Greek wave of contention. The first, focusing on economic issues, occurred in 2010, mostly staged by unions and the radical left ; the second occurred in summer 2011 in

---

[9] This figure only concerns the percentage of violent actions that were actually reported by the media outlet used as sources of our data. Given that violent acts tend to find considerable public resonance and to be reported by newspapers more frequently than the least contentious forms of protests, it is unlikely that these percentages are underestimated. Furthermore, the peak of violent events in southern Europe, where most of the protests took place, occurred in the early phase of the crisis that is not included in our episodes. Specifically, in Greece it occurred at the end of December 2008 in the aftermath of the shooting of a teenager by the police (Kriesi et al. 2020: chs. 4 and 5).

[10] The daily count of protests is only a rough measure and does not take into account important details such as the number of participants in the events.

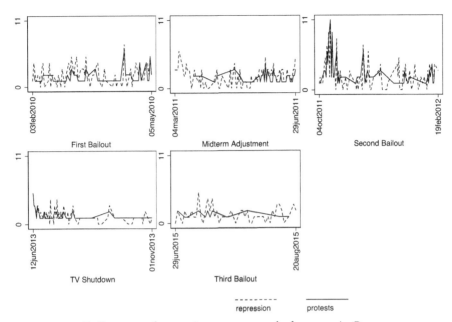

FIGURE 10.1. Daily count of repressive measures and of protests in Greece across contentious episodes

concomitance with the appearance of the Greek Indignant Citizens Movement and was characterized by semi-spontaneous and innovative forms of protests; the third, between October 2011 and February 2012, marked a continuation of the previous wave and was characterized by the intensification of low-level unions actions (see Chapter 12 for an in-depth analysis of the Greek case). The demobilization phase of the Greek wave of contention unfolded during the last two episodes examined, the ERT TV shutdown and the third bailout, during which the number of daily actions clearly diminished.

During the second bailout, next to demonstrations and strikes, the repertoire of actions expanded and protests included some radical actions (as shown in Figure 10.2). In our episodes, most violent actions occurred at the end of the second bailout negotiated between early October 2011 and February 2012. The protests during this period resulted in violent confrontations between anarchists and the police. The clashes with the police erupted after the demonstrations in February 2012 by the General Confederation of Greek Workers (GSEE) and the Civil Servants' Confederation (ADEDY) (see in Figure 10.2 the peak of confrontational/violent actions at the end of the episode concerning the second bailout). Considering confrontational actions, a few occurred during the first bailout in May 2010, concerning, inter alia, the occupation of the Acropolis by members of the Greek Communist Party (KKE). Most confrontational actions

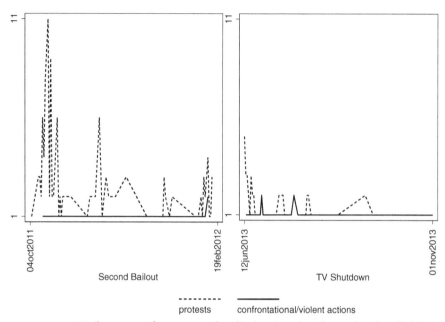

FIGURE 10.2. Daily counts of protests and radical actions (confrontational and violent actions) during the second bailout and the TV shutdown in Greece

were employed during two episodes, the second bailout (October 2011–February 2012) and the ERT TV shutdown (June–November 2013). During the second bailout in January 2012 protesters occupied Syntagma Square and other public buildings, such as the law school. Most occupations, however, occurred during the shutdown by the Greek parliament of the country's public broadcasting service, ERT, in June 2013 that led to a reshuffling of the cabinet. The shutdown was a major event among others in summer 2013. During this period, in addition to the ERT TV shutdown, the country witnessed the passage of reforms related to yet another austerity package, imposed by the ongoing EU–I.M.F. bailout. In particular, the first reform was approved by the Greek parliament on April 28, 2013 and the second one on July 17, 2013. In this context, the occupation of ERT headquarters by its employees started in the middle of June 2013 and ended in early November 2013. These events also triggered the implementation of broadcasting activities on alternative platforms, and prompted Syriza M.P.s to confront the police in their effort to enter the ERT headquarters. The two peaks in the otherwise flat line in the right-hand graph of Figure 10.2 precisely signal the presence of occupations during the TV shutdown.

Turning to the actors engaged in protest forms of mobilization in Europe between 2008 and 2016, analyses (not presented here) show that, with the exclusion of conventional actions, trade unions coordinated, organized, or participated in more than 60 percent of all the forms of protest observed. Trade unions were especially active in France, where they represented around 70 percent of all challengers' forms of protest mobilization, in line with the historically strong class cleavage in this country, and in Greece, where they represented the main challenger in more than 65 percent of all forms of protests. As expected, trade unions were the main actors involved in the most notable and traditional form of action in the labor field, strikes, as they accounted for around 92 percent of the strikes that occurred after 2008. Trade unions, however, also widely engaged in demonstrations throughout the crisis, and after classic civil-society organizations represent the second actor mainly engaged in demonstrations. This suggests an engagement of trade unions beyond workplace mobilization and is in line with studies that have highlighted the presence of broad coalitions during the Great Recession. These networks were active in demonstrations, and in open public spaces such as streets, squares, and parks, and focused on cross-cutting issues and cross-border initiatives such as social exclusion and austerity measures (Ancelovici 2011; della Porta 2015).

## Repression during the Great Recession

Governments had various options for interacting with challengers in the contentious episodes examined. These options spanned from repressing challengers to fully engaging in negotiations with them. As shown in Table 4.2, 7.2 percent of government procedural actions were repressive measures. If we also consider threats related to repression, the same table shows that 32.0 percent of government's procedural claims depreciated challengers, and 7.1 percent failed to recognize them. If we compare the most extreme forms of actions by challengers and by governments – that is, violent actions and repression, respectively – the latter makes up a far larger share of government actions than violence in relation to challenger actions. Considering all countries, outright repressive measures included a limited number of actions in absolute terms as compared to other actions adopted by governments (43 repressive actions), while most repressive measures consisted in threats (232 threats including both depreciating and not recognizing challengers). As Table 10.1 demonstrates, in addition to Greece, only in Italy, France, and the U.K., were violent actions ever reported. These included the outbreak of disorder across the U.K. in November 2010 during student demonstrations against the government's higher-education plans and in Italy the violent contestations in early 2012 against the so-called Fornero pension reform (named after the Italian minister of labour, social policies, and gender equality), which was part of the austerity measures known as the "Save Italy" decree passed in December 2011.

In contrast, except for Hungary, some form of repression was present in all countries. The country employing the most number of repressive actions was Greece, where 32.6 percent of all repressive actions took place (fourteen actions and thirty-seven threats). Repression included violent police clashes with anti-austerity protesters, arrests, use of tear gas, and the eviction of protesters occupying public buildings.

The empirical analysis of the effects of repression on protest focuses on repression that preceded the challengers' protest mobilization within a sequence of interactions. To clarify, we only selected instances of repression–protest interactions such as the one that occurred during the 2013 ERT TV shutdown in Greece. On June 29, 2013 the police removed the ERT transmitter in Ymittos, a suburb of Athens, and clashed with demonstrators by arresting nine protesters. As a response to such repressive action, on June 30, ERT employees, ANTARSYA (the Front of the Greek Anti-Capitalist Left, a coalition of radical-left political organizations in Greece), and SPITHA (a political movement led by Mikis Theodorakis, a composer) engaged in protests against the ERT closure.

In most cases, repressive measures were not connected with protests in a sequence of interactions and, consequently, cannot directly represent factors associated with protest mobilization. The absence of protest by challengers after repression suggests that challengers may organize a reaction to counter repression through actions that may not explicitly and purposefully address a specific repressive measure or which take a long time for their organization and, consequently, may not be reported as directly linked to repression.

As shown by Figure 10.1, the pattern of daily protests and of lagged repressive measures used by governments in the Greek case partly overlap. This was clearly visible during some periods, such as during the end of the episode concerning the first bailout, at the end of the midterm adjustment, and at the beginning of the second bailout, where the peaks of the lines evidently overlap, suggesting that repression may have had some effect on protests. The next section will unfold this issue more clearly.

## Repression and Types of Protests

We shall first specifically examine how repressive measures impact upon different forms of protest (*repression works* and *polarization hypotheses*), explore whether the impact changes depending on the type of challenger involved (*civil-society organizations* and *political party hypotheses*), and then analyze whether the effect changes depending on specific conditions of the context in which protests emerge (*left cabinet's reinforcing, left cabinet's dampening hypotheses, and constraint, international ally,* and *conventional actions hypotheses*).[11] For each model we calculated the predicted probabilities of protesting when

---

[11] The following analyses examine the impact of repression on all forms of protest mobilization, thus including actions and verbal threats or menaces. As already mentioned, we also examined protest actions only and show the results when significant.

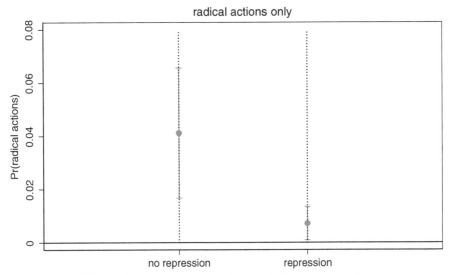

FIGURE 10.3. Effects of government repression on challengers' radical actions

governments repress and when they don't, and report the results in Figures 10.3 to 10.7.[12]

Figure 10.3 shows that with the exception of radical actions, most forms of protest mobilization were not affected by government repression. The figure shows, however, that there is a significant and negative, although small, effect of government repression if radical, including violent, forms of protest mobilization have been observed.

More specifically, when focusing only on actions, repression decreases radical actions by 3.3 percentage points (Figure 10.3), suggesting that the effect of repression depends on the form of protest considered, and the *repression works hypothesis,* which stipulates an overall dampening effect of repression on any form of protest, was not confirmed. Our findings also fail to confirm the expectations formulated in the *polarization hypothesis* suggesting that repression polarizes protests. Repression adopted during the Great Recession had neither a radicalizing nor a moderating impact on the action repertoire. This means that, despite the use of repression by governments, anti-austerity protesters did not ultimately adopt more violent and confrontational actions, while challengers adopted a peaceful repertoire of action throughout the contentious episodes analyzed, even after government repression. This result underscores the finding in Chapter 8 that the probability of disruptive challenger action is

[12] From now on, we only show the figures when interaction terms are significant. For the full models based on which we calculated the predicted probabilities shown in the Figures, the reader may turn to the author.

largely independent of what the government has done previously (see Figure 8.3). Once we distinguish between violent and confrontational actions on one side, and demonstrations on the other, we do find an effect of government repression. As suggested by these results, the slightly negative effect of repression on violent and confrontational actions is likely to be suppressed by the lack of a corresponding effect for (the much more numerous) demonstrations.

## Repression and Type of Challengers

The *civil-society organizations hypothesis* and the *political party hypothesis* maintain that repression may have different effects on protests depending on the type of challenger. We tested these hypotheses by classifying episodes according to the prevailing type of challenger engaged in the interactions with governments within each episode. Following Chapter 9, we categorized challengers according to their level of institutionalization and specifically looked at the effect of protests when parties, trade unions, or civil-society organizations were the main challengers in the contentious episodes examined. Figure 10.4 shows that government repression significantly decreased engagement in any protests by the most institutionalized actors – parties, but not when trade unions or CSOs were the main challengers. When political parties drove

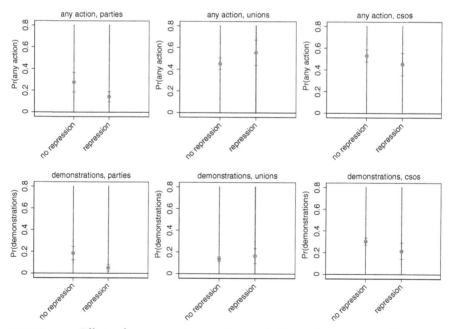

FIGURE 10.4. Effects of government repression on challengers' protests, considering episodes classified according to actors' configurations

contentious episodes, repression reduced their protests, above all the demonstrations they organized, by 13 percentage points. These results confirm the *political party hypothesis*: There is a stronger dampening effect of repression on protests, particularly on demonstrations, in those episodes where the most institutional actors were the prevailing challengers, than in those episodes where other actors predominated. Figure 10.4 also shows that there was a dampening effect of repression on demonstrations when CSOs were the prevailing challengers, thus confirming the *civil-society organization hypothesis* as well (the effect is significant in the model).

## The Conditional Impact of Context on the Effect that Repression Has on Protests

We shall delve further into the analysis by focusing on how the effect of repression on protests may change depending on the context in which challengers operate. First, we shall look at the Greek case in more depth. As we already mentioned, it was in Greece that protest was most intense. Results for the Greek case (Figure 10.5) confirm that repression dampens radical actions (when considering actions only). Although findings were only marginally significant, radical actions diminished by around 10 percentage points due to repression. These results mainly concern trade unions, which engaged in more than 60 percent of all forms of protest mobilization examined in Greece and in more than 75 percent of all radical actions examined. Given the propensity of trade unions to engage in strikes, the traditional form of protest mobilization by trade

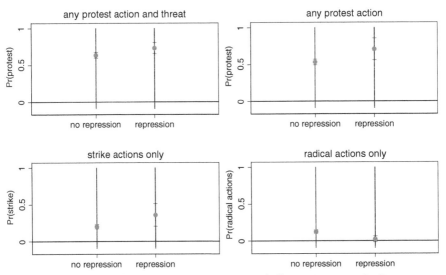

FIGURE 10.5. Effects of government repression on challengers' protests in Greece

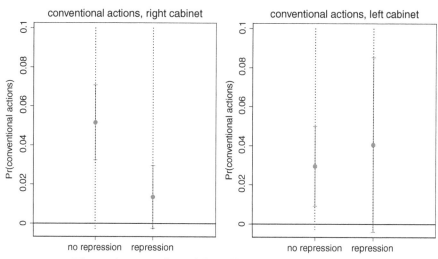

FIGURE 10.6. The moderating effect of the different political orientation of cabinets

unions, any form of repression by governments easily contained their engagement in more radical actions. In addition, Figure 10.5 shows that repression in
Greece increased the challengers' overall protests by around 10 percentage
points (by 17.5 percentage points when actions only are considered) and, more
specifically, strike actions by 15 percentage points (the effects are significant in
the models).

The analyses of the Greek case partly responded to our query about a
moderating effect of the context in shaping the relationship between repression
and protests. As it turned out, the repression–protest nexus was especially
significant for the Greek case, whereas in most other countries challengers
engaged far less in protests, generally, and rarely engaged in radical actions.[13]

We shall next turn to examine whether the context dependency of the
repression–protests nexus is related to some specific dimensions of the POS.
Figure 10.6 shows the moderating effect of the political orientation of the
cabinet on the impact that repression has on protests. The graph on the left
shows that there was a higher dampening effect of repression on conventional
actions in countries where right-wing cabinets were in power in comparison to
governments where there were left-wing cabinets. Repression decreased the
challengers' conventional actions by around 4 percentage points when a
right-wing cabinet was in power, in comparison to the change in the predicted
probability when left-wing cabinets were in power that, in contrast, was
positive (only slightly significant in the model). The *left-wing cabinet's*

[13] Due to the limited number of cases when considering protests in individual countries, we have
limited the analysis of the effect of repression on protests to the Greek case.

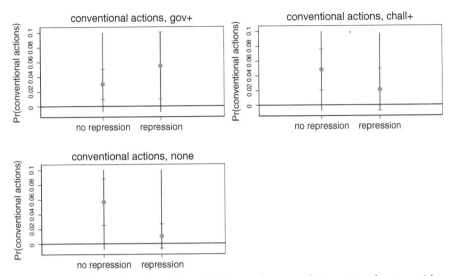

FIGURE 10.7. The moderating effect of different alliances of international actors with challengers (chall+) and governments (gov+) on the impact that repression has on protests

*reinforcing hypothesis* (but not the *left-wing cabinet's dampening hypothesis* ) is thus confirmed, supporting the idea that the dampening effect of repression on protests is weaker under left-wing cabinets. However, this holds only for those moderated forms of protests, such as conventional actions, including petitions.

Figure 10.7 also shows that the effect of repression on protest actions was also moderated by the presence of international allies, but not in the direction we expected. In particular, the *constraint hypothesis* – on a stronger dampening effect of repression on protests when international actors ally with governments – was not confirmed, nor was the *international ally hypothesis* – on a weaker dampening effect of repression when challengers ally with international actors since the effect is not significant. The effects of repression on protests when either elites or challengers ally with international actors were not significant, but there was a stronger dampening effect of repression on conventional actions when no such alliances exist. Repression decreased the challengers' conventional actions by around 4.5 percentage points when no alliances existed. This result is in line with the *conventional actions hypothesis*.

## CONCLUSIONS

In this chapter we examined the effects of repression adopted by European governments on the protests which occurred in Europe from the beginning of the Great Recession in 2008 up to 2016. While most of the contentious episodes considered were peaceful, and violence basically nonexistent, all the governments adopted some degree of repressive measures. Repression, however, did not significantly alter the repertoire of actions, which tended to remain moderate without showing any form of radicalization throughout the episodes. Anti-austerity protests were largely nonviolent actions and, despite the use of repression by governments, challengers did not respond by adopting more violent and confrontational actions. They engaged in a peaceful repertoire of actions throughout the contentious episodes analyzed, even after government repression.

The only changes in the forms of protest mobilization due to repression concerned radical actions that were slightly reduced due to repression. This occurred especially in Greece, where repression decreased the likelihood of occupations by trade unions and induced trade unions to engage more in strikes. The effect of repression changed across types of challengers and also across specific dimensions of the context. Results also show that repression mainly affected institutional actors such as political parties, whose participation in protests significantly decreased. This was partly linked to the institutional nature of parties, and their tendency to engage in other political arenas such as electoral or parliamentary ones. The same was true for CSOs engaging in demonstrations. These findings thus suggest that repression hampers democracy to the extent that it decreases engagement by institutional actors and CSOs in the protest sphere, reducing their level of political participation – a crucial dimension of democracy.

The impact of government repression on protests also depended upon some conditions of the contexts where governments and challengers interacted. Besides country-level differences, illustrated by the effect of repression in the Greek case, the contingent conditions of the political system examined, namely the political orientation of the cabinet and alliances with international allies to some extent, affected the degree to which repression shaped challengers' repertoire of actions. In particular, for specific forms of protests, namely conventional actions, repression had a stronger dampening effect under right-wing governments. It is thus especially under right-wing governments that repression hampers democracy, specifically by decreasing levels of participation in conventional actions such as petitions. Finally, the effect of repression was a matter of isolation. Repression dampened protests when no international actors intervened in domestic politics, thus suggesting that repression works when government – challengers interactions are confined to the domestic and national arena of interactions.

# 11

# Turning Points

Abel Bojar

## INTRODUCTION

The previous chapters on interaction dynamics, the central aspect of the second part of this volume, have investigated the determinants of various action forms of the contending parties as a function of preceding action types or contextual features of the episodes. One particular feature of these dynamics, however, has remained unexplored. The flow of interaction between the contending parties does not proceed in a smooth, linear fashion – with one action triggering a reaction that in turn triggers a counter-reaction – as a stylized understanding of contentious politics might suggest. As we have shown earlier in Chapter 6 on the construction of action sequences, the empirical reality paints a more complex picture. While some actions indeed trigger one and only one further action and move the episode forward in that stylized fashion, others trigger two or more reactions, while still others put an end to a sequence and trigger no further actions at all. In other words, some actions have turned out to be considerably more consequential for the remaining part of the episode than others. Our first aim in this chapter is to highlight one type of such actions, in particular those with a heightened capacity to trigger an outstanding number of reactions, and seek to understand the regularities that characterize these actions. We shall refer to these actions as *points of opening,* inspired by the intuition that they open up contentious episodes to different threads of contention.

In terms of timing, episodes were also characterized by varying levels of intensity. While at some periods multiple sequences ran parallel to each other, other periods were characterized by more focused, unidirectional dynamics where interactions ran in a central thread for an extended period of time. The second broad goal of this chapter is to understand when such phases set in, to identify those actions that close off alternative avenues of contention and channel the interaction in that central thread. We shall label these actions as *points of closure.*

The broad theoretical frame we adopted for this exercise was borrowed from Abbot's notion of turning points (2001:249) that can be thought of as events that "give rise to changes in overall direction or regime, and do so in a determining fashion." The particular meaning of what these regimes are, of course, largely depends on the particular field that adopts and applies the concept. Their natural home, life course studies, for instance refer to events as turning points when they mark a clear separation of certain key characteristics – such as employment trajectories, family status, or even the evolution of friendship networks (Becker et al., 2009) – of individuals' lives before and after the event. A particularly fertile research area of the concept is criminology, where researchers probe the type of event that leads delinquents to abandon their criminal past (Carlsson, 2011; Sampson and Laub, 2005; Teruya and Hser, 2010). Closer to home, an implicit example of a turning point is the notion of critical elections and realignment (Aldrych, 1999; Key, 1955) that separate two periods marked by relatively stable patterns of party competition. Note that in all these applied examples, a turning point does not refer to any particular direction of change, merely a more or less permanent switch from one state to another.

The empirical literature on social movements has, of course, long recognized that the time periods during which a contentious episode unfolds are "punctuated by decisional moments that engage actors' agency and they have the capacity to channel the direction of subsequent events" (Ermakoff 2015: 72). This insight closely resonates with the political opportunity structure perspective. Meyer and Minkoff (2004) for instance regard the passage of the Civil Rights Act in 1964 as such a key event in accounting for the mobilization dynamics of black civil rights activists in the United States. In a similar vein, Alimi (2016) focuses on the Israeli pullout from the Gaza strip in 2005, and offers a relational analysis of the Jewish settler movement before and after the pullout. Likewise, Ramos (2008) uses the term "critical events" to account for the ebbs and flows of aboriginal mobilization in Canada. In his account, these events need not mark something as dramatic as a strategic military decision provided by the previous empirical example; they can take the form of something as routine and institutionalized as the release of a policy brief, or a "White Paper" on the status of aboriginals. What these events share in common is not their substantive content but the fact that they changed the course of issue-specific mobilization by the parties involved, whether it was black civil rights activists, Israeli settlers, or Canadian aboriginals. Therefore, only with the passage of time can one retrospectively tell whether an event can be considered a turning point as per our conceptualization in the context of contentious episodes.

Note, moreover, that the type of contention that the empirical literature engages with typically spans multiple years or even decades. For our purposes of understanding interaction in more narrowly defined and temporally concentrated contentious episodes, we shall revert back to the terminology of sequence analysis and focus on on the day-to-day flow of events to identify the relevant turning points. A natural place to start conceptualizing them is defining the relevant states of contention. To do so, we have built on the notion of complexity (see Chapter 6) that captures the extent to which a contentious episode was focused in a narrow channel of interaction or moved forward in divergent patterns along multiple sequences. To use our tree metaphor that we introduced in Chapter 2, at any given point in time, the episode can move forward along a single trunk or branch – in which case the contention is focused; or it proceeds along multiple branches or leaves at the same time – in which case contention is unfocused. With these two stylized states in mind, we can thus differentiate between two types of points that mark the transition either from a focused to an unfocused state, or from an unfocused to a focused one. We shall refer to the first type of turning point as a *point of opening*, since it opens up contention to various directions. In contrast, we shall refer to the second type of turning point as a *point of closure* by inverse logic: a point where contention narrows down to a central thread for an extended period of time. Figure 11.1 offers a stylized illustration of what the two turning points look like.

In this stylized example, the actions are listed in a chronological order from top to bottom, and arrows indicate the triggers. Two turning points can be readily identified based on the definitions given earlier. Uniquely among the actions, action 3 triggers more than two further actions, so in this particular scheme it can be safely regarded as a point of opening. Action 12, however narrows down the contention in one single thread (running from action 12 to action 15) since no other sequence continues beyond that point in time. It thus serves as a perfect example of a point of closure.

One of our main contributions in this chapter is methodological. We offer a systematic and replicable tool for identifying turning points in political conflict where the criterion for pinpointing a turning point is not merely its substantive importance (e.g. a passage of legislation, or a violent confrontation in the streets) but also a numerical, comparable, and transparent threshold. Did it in fact trigger a great many actions as its substantive importance would suggest, or did it turn out to be just one of multiple actions in the course of events? Did it in fact close down alternative threads of contention and focus the further course of the debate in a narrow thread, or did those alternative threads continue to move forward by triggering further actions? Providing a simple answer to these questions is a relatively straightforward exercise given the nature of our data and, as such, offers great potential in the identification of turning points in various forms of policy debates.

However, relying on either the narrative approach or the epidemiological approach to study turning points would be ridden with difficulties. While the former is well suited for studying the mechanism through which a potential turning point shifts one state of contention into another, it is less well equipped

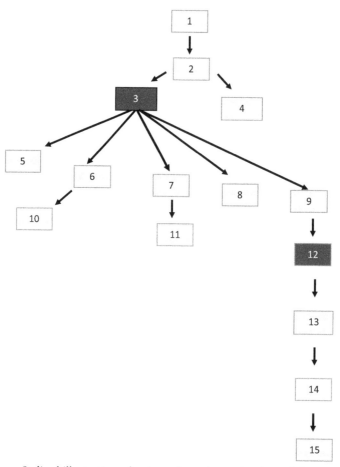

FIGURE 11.1. Stylized illustration of points of opening and points of closure

to pinpoint what the turning point actually was among all the alternatives occurring around similar times. On the other hand, the epidemiological approach is constrained by a well-known limitation that we have emphasized at various points in this volume. Lacking an explicit way to connect individual actions, it could merely rely on the change of action frequencies over time without the necessary reassurance that a surge (or sudden decline) of action counts after a particular action is actually causally linked to the prior action. In other words, it could only provide an "educated guess" on what the turning points might be. Our first and main task in this chapter is therefore to circumvent the weaknesses of these alternative approaches and leverage the strength of Contentious Episode Analysis (CEA) to identify turning points at a higher level of certainty.

Beyond this somewhat admittedly mechanistic exercise, however, we also aim to attribute substantive meaning to turning points. Our next empirical task therefore will be to characterize the turning points themselves in terms of the main actors responsible for them, their timing, and the type of action forms that are more or less likely to become turning points. Furthermore, we shall examine the changes in some of the relevant aspects of contention from the state before to the state after these turning points occurred in terms of the main actors involved and the most prevalent forms of actions in the respective states. In other words, in this chapter we sought to predict both the determinants of turning points as well as their impact, and our dataset was uniquely well suited to accomplish this dual task.

Providing a systematic operationalization of these turning points along with a descriptive summary of their distribution across episodes is the subject of the next section. Next, we shall lay out our theoretical expectations on two fronts. First, we shall theorize which particular actions are more or less likely to become turning points. Second, we shall put forward two further hypotheses on how the shape of contention changes substantively from one phase of the episodes to another, separated by the turning points. After that, we shall present our empirical results from both angles, based on a large-n statistical analysis of our entire sample of sixty episodes. Before we conclude, we shall follow this with a short case study of the Sarkozy–Fillon austerity and pension-reform episode in France to illustrate some of the empirical patterns in action.

## IDENTIFYING TURNING POINTS

Against the backdrop of the clear intuitive appeal of the two types of turning points introduced above, the empirical reality in a cross-episode perspective is not as clear-cut as the stylized illustration might suggest. For instance, long episodes that are rich in actions are by nature more likely to contain actions that trigger a large number of further actions. With regard to points of closure, episodes rarely end in a single thread of contention with no further bifurcations occurring, except at the very end of the episodes. To get around these empirical limitations, we propose an operational rule for turning points that takes into account the total action count of the episode.

In the case of points of opening, this means that in order to become a turning point, an action has to trigger a high enough number of further actions *relative* to the total action count in an episode. For convenience, we put this threshold at 10 percent of the total action count. In other words, if an action triggers at least 10 percent of total actions of the episode, we consider it as a turning point. For the most action-rich episodes, such as the Water tax episode in Ireland or the Brexit episode in the United Kingdom, this put the threshold at around thirty. For episodes with few total actions, such as the Internet tax in Hungary or the German debt brake, three triggered actions sufficed. However, we argue that this relative understanding of points of opening is preferable to using a fixed threshold because an action triggering a few further actions carries a very different meaning depending on how "noisy" and crowded the overall action field is. In sum, we define those actions as points of opening that *trigger at least 10 percent of all actions in an episode*.

To get around the problem posed by the lack of points of closure in the stylized sense presented above, we also use this 10 percent operational threshold but now we apply it to the length (measured in action count) of the narrowing to occur. In particular, we stipulate that an action was considered to close off other avenues of contention *if the next n actions in the chronological order of the episode were all triggered by that action* (or, in other words, if the action at hand and subsequent ones all lay on the same sequence) where n was the rounded integer of 10 percent of the total count of the episode. Note that in some cases, an action could be both a point of opening and of closure if by triggering a large enough number of actions, it also closed off alternative threads of contention. In such cases, for practical considerations to ensure a roughly even distribution of the two kinds of turning points, we coded these actions as closures rather than openings.

With these definitions in mind, we are now well placed to provide a quick empirical overview of the frequency of the two kinds of turning points. Figure 11.2 shows the number of points of opening and closure by episodes as well as by episode types in our sample.

The distribution by episodes shows that both types of turning points moved in a similar range between 0 and 7 (Berlusconi's second austerity period in Italy had six points of closure while the second Portuguese austerity package had seven points of opening), but a fair number of episodes, such as three of the Irish episodes or the Brexit episode in the United Kingdom had either only points of openings or only points of closure, but not both.

The overall sample mean for the number of openings and closures is very similar, with slightly more openings occurring (just above two on average) in the episodes than closures (1.6). A natural point to raise is whether the frequency of the two types of turning points is really just the two sides of the same coin; after all, the more points of opening that occur in an episode, the more difficult it becomes to narrow the action space in a central thread of contention. Indeed, the Pearson correlation coefficient between the frequencies was -0.45, suggesting that episodes that are characterized by a high number of openings tended to have fewer points of closure. However, the strength of this correlation is far from overwhelming, assuaging concerns that the occurrence of openings mechanistically prevents the occurrence of subsequent closures.

When comparing the distribution across episode types, the average number of both kinds of turning points move in a relatively narrow range. Budgetary consolidations stand out with a relatively high average number of openings (2.5), while institutional episodes tend to have just above one opening on average. Bank bailouts have relatively few points of closures (one) while

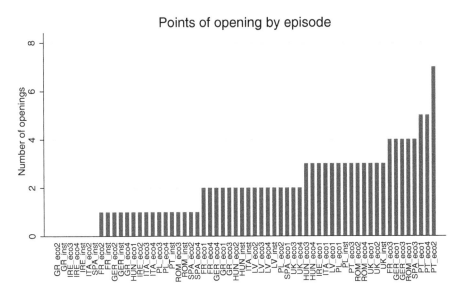

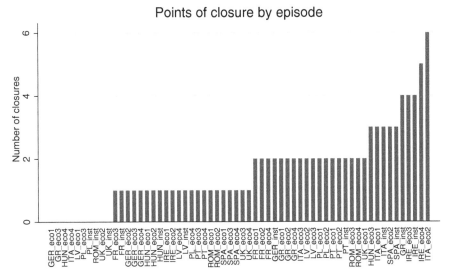

FIGURE 11.2. Number of points of opening and closing

institutional reforms and structural reforms have a somewhat more average number of closures than the rest (1.7 on average). All in all, however, it is fair to say that the key issues around which contention revolves – in other words, the type of episodes – did not fundamentally determine the frequency of turning points in an episode.

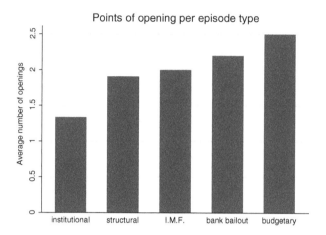

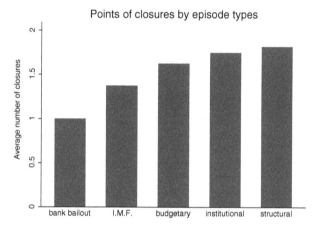

FIGURE 11.2. *(cont.)*

## THEORIZING TURNING POINTS AND THEIR IMPACT

The theoretically more interesting domain of investigation, however, points beyond the frequency of turning points in a given episode. In the rest of this chapter we shall examine the determinants of individual turning points themselves as well as their impact on the subsequent evolution of the episodes. We shall start by asking which of our three stylized actor types' actions were likely to become turning points.

Given the nature of our episodes – policy proposals at risk – the natural candidate for the actor type most likely to undertake actions that become turning points was the government itself. Although as we have seen earlier, the total number of coded actions was roughly evenly divided between governments, challengers, and third-party actors, the probability of such actions serving as triggers for further actions is likely to be unevenly distributed. The main reason for this is that more often than not, the status quo is on the government's side, in the sense that once a policy proposal has been made, it is likely be adopted and become law barring reactions from other parties. Those seeking modification of the proposal, therefore, must react to it. The reverse, however, is not true. The government is forced, in *sensu stricto*, to respond to challengers' or third-parties' actions only to the extent that its policy preferences have been threatened or it has perceived that it would run electoral risks by not responding. The same consideration applies to further stages of the policy-making process as the government follows up with policy details, announces amendments, puts forward formal documents on the reform, passes the legislation in the relevant bodies and so on. Such moves by a government have a heightened potential to act as points of opening since they are likely to draw new actors into the conflict or prompt existing participants to respond.

Moreover, while government actions – the policy proposal itself, subsequent follow-ups, concessions, negotiations etc. – are likely to involve multiple stakeholders, such as trade unions, opposition parties, or external third parties, actions by individual challengers are less likely to involve actors other than the government. For instance, any individual trade union is much less likely to respond to an action by another trade union than to the actions of the government. For these reasons, we expect government actions, more than challenger or third-party actions, to become points of opening by triggering a large number of further actions by all contending parties.

A similar logic can be put forward regarding points of closure. Following from the definition provided earlier, points of closure imply that an action occurs which closes off alternative avenues of contention and focuses attention on a narrower stream of interaction. Again, we expect that the government's actions have much greater potential to achieve this narrowing because they could make alternative avenues of contention irrelevant. To provide a stylized example: If various challengers object to the government's insistence on its proposal and these objections prompt the government to grant a concession, it is likely to satisfy at least some of these challengers, closing off certain parts of the contention space and focusing subsequent actions in a narrower channel. Integrating these two considerations in a single hypothesis, we put forward the *government-centred hypothesis* regarding turning points:

*H1: Government actions are more likely to become turning points – both openings and closures – than challenger or third- party actions.*

In addition to the actors responsible for turning points, another important question to ask relates to the temporal dimension. Did turning points occur early or late in the episodes? To lay out our expectations, we must differentiate here between the two types of turning points. With regard to points of opening, it is important to consider that in the early phases of the episodes, more options are available, more actors are yet to have their say, and less information is publicly available on the government's determination to push the proposal through or its willingness to compromise on it. In that sense, more avenues of contention are likely to open up simply because actors operate in a world characterized by a higher level of uncertainty. Actions occurring in the early phases of the episodes, by any of the contending parties, are therefore more likely to become points of opening.

Mirror logic characterizes points of closure. After a while, certain avenues of contention run their natural course either because demands have been satisfied, compromise has been found, or the actors have realized that further dialogue is futile and there is simply nothing left to be said or done. The likelihood of such a termination of sequences is considerably higher with the passage of time, when the information set is restricted to narrower options and only a central thread is yet to be resolved. Therefore, in contrast to the government-centric hypothesis, the *temporal hypothesis* yields opposing expectations regarding the two types of turning points:

H2: *While points of opening are more likely to occur in earlier phases of episodes, points of closure are more likely to occur later.*

Finally, turning points are also likely to depend on the types of actions by the contending parties. In particular, we highlight two action types that we borrow from our earlier chapters. One end of the contention spectrum is characterized by highly disruptive actions on the part of challengers, such as violent demonstrations and other confrontational forms of resistance, and repressive reactions, such as police crackdowns, on the part of governments. At the other end, we observe actions of cooperation among the actors, or what we referred to in Chapter 8 as the "concession-construction mediation – cooperation nexus." We shall collectively refer to the first broad action type – disruptive mobilization by challengers and repression by government – as disruptive actions, while we refer to actions belonging to the aforementioned nexus as cooperative actions.

In terms of our expectations, disruptive actions are more likely to serve as points of opening. While a government sticking to its proposal in a conventional manner would be unlikely to elicit responses beyond those from direct stakeholders, a brutal police repression would be more likely to draw other parties into the game, such as third parties condemning the violence. Acts of cooperation, however, tend to be targeted at a given organization – a government indicating willingness to negotiate with unions for instance - and hence unlikely to trigger responses by wider audiences. When challenger organizations cooperate, it usually means that they bring contention back to the routine, institutionalized channels of conflict resolution, obviating the need for other parties – third-party mediators for instance – to intervene. Therefore our third hypothesis, the *contention-cooperation hypothesis (a)* can be stated as follows:

*H3: Disruptive actions are more likely and cooperative actions are less likely to serve as points of opening.*

Turning to our expectations for points of closure, mirror logic characterizes disruptive and cooperative actions. Disruptive actions are unlikely to narrow down the action space to a single thread for the same reasons they are more likely to act as points of opening. If multiple stakeholders respond to a disruptive action, the probability that some of these responses will trigger further reactions increases, reducing the scope for any narrowing to occur. In contrast, disruptive actions are more likely to achieve that effect because concessions by the government, mediation efforts by third parties, and cooperative action forms by challengers are likely to reveal the part of the policy proposal that is worth fighting over (challengers) or further engaging with (government). In that sense, when such a cooperative move is made by any of the contending parties, the likelihood of narrowing to occur increases. Formulating these considerations under our fourth hypothesis, the *disruption-cooperation (b)* hypothesis:

*H4: Disruptive actions are less likely and cooperative actions are more likely to serve as points of closure.*

Once these turning points do occur, the next task is to analyze whether they mark a change in the course of an episode in substantive terms. To do so, we first divide up each episode into three parts. The first part of the episode is the initial phase, before the first point of opening occurs (in instances where there are multiple points of opening). We label this phase the *opening phase*. Once the first point of opening occurs, a new phase kicks in, that we call the *main phase*. Although this phase might be interspersed with multiple points of further openings and closures, we regard the last point of closure as the start of the final phase of the episode, the *closing phase*. Overall, the bulk of the actions are concentrated in the main phase of the episodes (47 percent of total actions), whereas the remaining actions are roughly evenly divided between the opening and the closing phases (26 and 27 percent, respectively).

We first inquire about the main actors involved in the different phases. The clearest theoretical expectation concerns the government: that is likely to be the most active in the opening phase because that's the time when the first announcements are made and details of the policy proposal come to light. At the same time, challengers need first to constitute and come up with a response strategy before they launch a challenge at all. Therefore, they are likely to become more active in later phases of the episode. Third parties are expected to occupy an intermediate role; while they also need to wait for the policy details to emerge before they decide to intervene, they are also unlikely to be the protagonists in the closing phase of the episode once they have had their say and taken sides in the debate. Their action intensity is more likely to take an inverted U-shape, peaking in the main phase of the episode, after the first opening but before the last closure. To capture these considerations in a testable hypothesis, our *actor-displacement hypothesis* can be stated as follows:

*H5: Governments tend to be the most active in the early phases of the episode, challengers get more active over time, while third parties tend to concentrate their efforts in the middle.*

Second, we consider the evolution of action forms over the different phases of the episodes. We dinstiguish between the same aggregated action forms as we did for the identification of turning points and we seek to predict when the different forms are more or less likely to occur. For disruptive forms, we build the notion of radicalization in social movement studies (Alimi et al, 2015; Della Porta, 2018). In particular, we rely on the central insight of how radicalization tends to unfold over time. While in the beginning, contention is driven by wider coalitions of moderates, these elements gradually taper off as their demands are partially satisfied ,or they are not willing to undertake costlier actions to fight for their demands (De Nardo, 1985: 6). On the other hand, radicals tend to persevere until the bitter end, and with no moderates holding them back, their demands are more likely to erupt in confrontational action forms toward the end. In a similar spirit, Tarrow's work (1989) on protest cycles highlights the notion of competition among different movement groups over time, with some turning to institutionalization and moderation while other were engaging in increasingly sectarian actions (see also Koopmans, 2004 for an overview). To translate this into our episode phases, we would thus expect that the likelihood of contentious actions – disruptive mobilization by challengers and repressive government responses – would increase with time and peak at the closing phase of the episode. In contrast, we expect cooperative actions to occur earlier, especially in the main phase where demands have already been made – contention is already under way but the moderate elements in challenger organizations still leave room for dialogue and cooperative dynamics. To formulate it as a testable hypothesis, our *escalation hypothesis* can be stated as:

*H6: While disruptive actions are most likely to occur in the final phase of the episodes, the likelihood of cooperation tends to peak in the main phase.*

We summarize our six hypotheses in *Table 11.1*.

TABLE 11.1. *Summary of our hypotheses*

**Part I Determining the probability turning points**

| | |
|---|---|
| *Government-centered hypothesis* | The main actor responsible for turning points is the government |
| *Temporal hypothesis* | Points of opening tend to occur early; points of closure tend to occur late |
| *Disruption-cooperation hypothesis (a)* | Disruptive actions are more likely; cooperative actions are less likely to become points of opening |
| *Disruption-cooperation hypothesis (b)* | Disruptive actions are less likely;cooperative actions are more likely to become points of closure |

**Part II Estimating the impact of turning points on different phases of episodes**

| | |
|---|---|
| *Actor-displacement hypothesis* | Governments dominate in the opening phase, challengers in the closing phase, and third parties in the middle. |
| *Escalation hypothesis* | Contentious actions tend to occur later; cooperation tends to occur earlier. |

EMPIRICAL ANALYSIS

Predicting Turning Points

In the first part of our empirical analysis, we seek to predict the probability of the occurrence of the two kinds of turning points – points of opening and points of closures – separately. We run binary choice logit models with episode fixed effects to take into account the varying number of turning points in episodes. The independent variables are the dummy variables for actor types (with government as the omitted reference category), a standardized time variable that measures the relative time that has elapsed in the course of an episode as a fraction of the total duration of the episode, and two dummy variables taking on the value of 1 for disruptive actions: government repression or disruptive mobilization by challengers; and cooperative actions – government concessions and challengers' cooperative behaviour, respectively.

Table 11.2 and Figure 11.3 show the results for the points of opening model. The hypotheses receive mixed support. As for the government-centric hypothesis, the differences between the predicted probabilities indeed show a marked contrast between the government and the other two actor types. According to the calculated probabilities,[1] points of openings occurred with a probability of around 0.13 for government actions, while they were barely above 0 (around 0.5 percent) for challengers and third parties. This offers clear support for our first hypothesis, suggesting that challengers and third parties

[1] The predicted probabilities were calculated for the middle of the episode in terms of relative number of days and noncontentious actions.

*Abel Bojar*

TABLE 11.2. *Logit models of points of opening*

| DV | Openings | Openings | Openings | Openings |
|---|---|---|---|---|
| Challenger | −5.292** | | | −5.476** |
| | (5.25) | | | (5.41) |
| Third party | −4.335** | | | −4.751** |
| | (6.04) | | | (6.55) |
| Relative number of days | | −4.073** | | −4.029** |
| | | (8.64) | | (8.33) |
| Contention | | | −0.426 | −0.777* |
| | | | (1.22) | (2.01) |
| Cooperation | | | −0.521 | −1.562** |
| | | | (1.74) | (4.76) |
| Constant | −2.794 | −2.000 | −3.947 | −0.277 |
| | (3.84) | (2.69) | (5.52) | (0.34) |
| N | 53 | 53 | 53 | 53 |
| n | 5,613 | 5,603 | 5,613 | 5,603 |
| Pseudo R2 | 0.3 | 0.15 | 0.07 | 0.4 |
| AIC | 948.29 | 1121.79 | 1221.88 | 827.89 |
| BIC | 1313.1 | 1479.87 | 1586.68 | 1212.49 |

$^*p <0.05$; $^{**}p <0.01$

were very unlikely to open up contention to various directions. The temporal patterns are also in line with our expectation. For instance, when calculating probabilities for the occurrence of points of opening when the actor type is a government and its action is nonrepressive, there is a clear downward trend with the passage of time. While in the early phases of the episode this probability moves between 0.15 and 0.25, it approached 0 toward the end of the episode. Finally, the data contradicted our expectations regarding contentious action types serving as the most likely candidates for points of opening. As the coefficient estimates show, though nonsignificant if anything, radical action types appear to reduce the estimated probability of points of opening.

Turning to predicting points of closure (Table 11.3), the models fare considerably worse as the pseudo $R^2$ statistics are considerably lower. Our hypothesis on actor types is confirmed for points of closures as well. Similar to points of openings, governments are also the primary actors responsible for this kind of turning point (see predicted probabilities in Figure 11.4). While the probability of any particular government action becoming a point of closure is around 0.05, the same probability of the other two actor types was barely above 0. As for the timing of their occurrence, although on average points of closures tend to occur later than points of opening, they are not concentrated in the later parts of the episode. It would be more accurate to characterize their occurrence as fairly evenly spread out in time, with a constant probability of occurrence somewhat below 0.02. Finally, again in a similar fashion to points of openings,

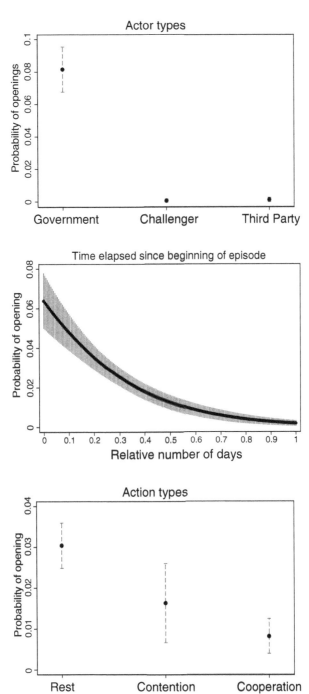

FIGURE 11.3. Predicted probabilities of points of opening*

*Probabilities were the calculated averages over the values of the other covariates in the merged model.

TABLE 11.3. *Logit models for points of closure*

| DV | Closure | Closure | Closure | Closure |
|---|---|---|---|---|
| Challenger | $-3.668^{***}$ | | | $-3.693^{***}$ |
| | (6.16) | | | (6.20) |
| Third party | $-2.445^{***}$ | | | $-2.587^{***}$ |
| | (6.77) | | | (7.07) |
| Relative number of days | | $-0.265$ | | $-0.106$ |
| | | (0.98) | | (0.28) |
| Contention | | | $-0.511$ | $-0.652$ |
| | | | (1.22) | (1.51) |
| Cooperation | | | 0.267 | $-0.538$ |
| | | | (0.94) | (1.81) |
| Constant | $-2.893$ | $-3.902$ | $-4.052$ | $-2.553$ |
| | (3.99) | (22.23) | (5.65) | (3.31) |
| N | 50 | 50 | 50 | 50 |
| n | 5,514 | 5,506 | 5,514 | 5,506 |
| Pseudo R2 | 0.21 | 0.06 | 0.06 | 0.22 |
| AIC | 868.02 | 909.78 | 1009.4 | 868.84 |
| BIC | 1212 | 916.9 | 1353.34 | 1232.59 |
| Fixed effects | Yes | Yes | Yes | Yes |

* $p <0.05$; ** $p <0.01$

points of closures are also somewhat less likely to take the form of contentious or cooperative actions (around 0.012) compared to other action forms (around 0.02), although the coefficient estimates for the action form dummies are nonsignificant in the model.

   In sum, this preliminary empirical exercise has shown a number of interesting findings, especially with regard to points of opening. In particular, in line with our expectations, both points of opening and points of closure were usually undertaken by governments. While openings occur typically in the early phases of the episodes, points of closure are fairly evenly spread out in time. Somewhat surprisingly, and partly against our expectations, both disruptive and cooperative actions are somewhat less, rather than more, likely to become turning points although the coefficient estimates are significant only for points of opening. Therefore, we receive only partial confirmation for both formulations of the *disruption-cooperation hypothesis*: cooperative actions do indeed tend to reduce the probability of points of openings, and disruptive actions tend to (somewhat) reduce the probability of points of closures.

   If neither type of turning points tend to take the form of disruptive or cooperative actions: that is, the two opposite poles of the contention spectrum, then a natural question to raise is What form do they typically take? Combining the findings on actor-types and action forms given earlier, the short answer is that governments sticking to plans is the most common source of turning

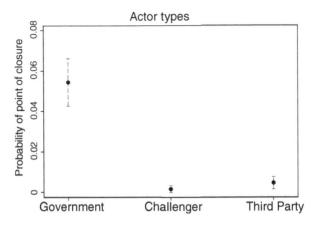

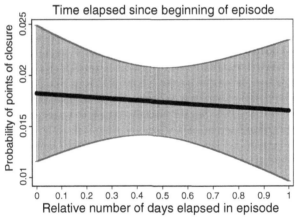

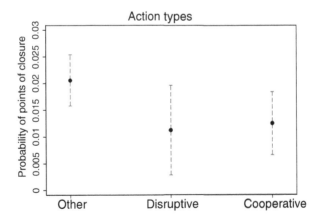

FIGURE 11.4 Predicted probabilities of points of closure as a function of actor types and relative number of days since beginning of episode*

*Probabilities are the calculated averages over the values of the other covariates in the merged model.

points. These actions, however, refer to a highly generic overall stance of the government vis-à-vis the proposal and its adversaries, and it can include a wide variety of actions in practice. As a brief extension to our empirical analysis, we thus took a step further and coded tuning points according to the institutional arena in which they occurred. Accordingly, we distinguish between (a) legislative actions – legislative organs deliberating, debating, passing, or voting down acts related to the proposal; (b) governmental decisions – governments putting forward or formally adopting specific measures related to the proposals; (c) judicial decisions; (d) mobilization by challengers; (e) international interventions (by external third parties); (f) other procedural actions –resignations, reference to constitutional courts, publishing official documents etc.; and (g) public statements by any of the contending parties. The bulk of these actions fell under the broad category of "government sticking to plans."

As Table 11.4 reveals, government decisions and public statements make up the lion's share of turning points, collectively responsible for more than 70 percent of them. Legislative decisions also turn out to be a fairly frequent source of turning points, just above 15 percent of both openings and closures. Comparatively speaking, the other forms of actions are few and far between, with the only partial exception of other procedural actions making up more than 10 percent of points of closures. Consistent with our previous finding that both types of turning points are predominantly undertaken by governments, mobilizations and external third-party interventions correspond to only very few turning points, three and eight, respectively.

While the particular content of government decisions relating to a policy proposal is fairly straightforward, public statements might take a wide variety of forms and could theoretically correspond to multiple actor types. We thus further disaggregated these statements according to their content. Of the seventy-two turning points that took the form of such statements, the most common form (38 percent) is a government defending its own policy proposal

TABLE 11.4. *Turning points and their types (percent of total)*

| Types of turning points | Opening | Closure | Total |
|---|---|---|---|
| Government decision | 43.9 | 32.3 | 38.8 |
| Public statements | 33.3 | 32.3 | 32.9 |
| Legislation | 16.3 | 15.6 | 16 |
| Other procedural actions | 4.1 | 10.4 | 6.9 |
| External intervention | 1.6 | 6.3 | 3.7 |
| Mobilization | 0.8 | 2.1 | 1.4 |
| Judicial decisions | 0 | 1 | 0.5 |
| Total percentage (%) | 100 | 100 | 100 |
| Total N | 123 | 96 | 219 |

against criticism. The second-most common form (17 percent) is the government setting the policymaking timetable by indicating the specific timeframe for the introduction of the measures or the legislative agenda. Two further forms of public statements (both corresponding to 11 percent of all public statements that become turning points) are expressions of opposition to the adversaries and the announcement of (or at least hinting at) new measures or policy details. Other types of statements that featured rarely among turning points are specific demands made on the adversary (or the proposal) beyond simple opposition (8 percent), statements indicating hesitation regarding the previous action path chosen (8 percent), and specific promises made to the adversary (6 percent).

All in all, the particular actions that became turning points varied greatly, both in their institutional form and particular content. The most common forms to highlight, however, are formal steps in the policy agenda (government decisions and legislative measures), as well as accompanying public statements defending the policy in the face of criticism against it.

### Predicting the Impact of Turning Points on the Phases of Episodes

Turning to the tests of the *actor-displacement* and the *escalation* hypotheses, we seek to predict the prevalence of the three stylized actor types as well as the occurrence of the two opposite action forms – contentious actions and cooperation – in the various phases of the episodes, as defined earlier. In other words, we investigate whether turning points marked changes not only in a mechanical (numerical) sense of the episodes but also in a substantive one. We run multinomial logit models with episode fixed effects, and to ease the interpretation of the estimates, we again provide predicted probabilities for each actor type and action form in the three respective stages (Figure 11.5).[2]

For the models predicting the prevalence of the three actor types, we indeed discern clear differences in line with our expectations. Governments, by far, are the most active in the opening phase, with a predicted probability of any action in this phase being a government action close to 0.4, compared to less than 0.3 in subsequent phases, whereas challengers tend to increase their efforts throughout the episode, culminating in a probability of any particular action being a challenger action at 0.46 in the closing phase of the episode, compared to less than 0.3 in the opening phase. Still in line with our hypothesis, the highest predicted probability of any particular action being a third-party action corresponding to the main phase, although this estimate is statistically indistinguishable from the opening phase (but significantly above the probability corresponding to the closing phase. Therefore, in line with our expectations,

---

[2] The regression output from the multinomial logit models predicting actor types and action types in the various phases are provided in the chapter Appendix.

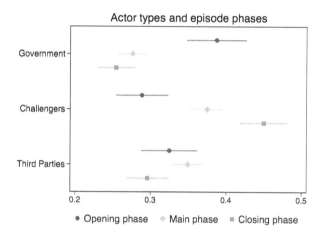

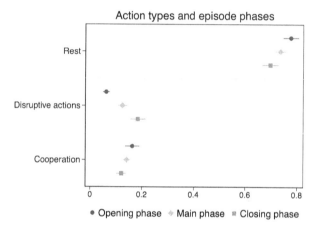

FIGURE 11.5. Predicted probabilities of actor types and action forms in different phases of the episodes

third parties indeed tend "to exit the show" toward the end of an episode, leaving the adversaries to their own devices.

In contrast to actor types, the patterns are somewhat less clear-cut with regard to the two opposite action forms, contention and cooperation. In line with our expectations (*escalation hypothesis*) the probability of contentious actions indeed increases with time and peaked at around 0.2 in the closing phases of the episodes, where the radical elements of challenger organizations tend to make their last stand against the proposals (and governments occasionally repressed them). However, the likelihood of cooperation tends to be higher in earlier phases of the episodes, although the differences are considerably smaller than the differences between the probabilities of contentious actions.

The main patterns concerning the differences between the phases of the episodes, as defined by the first point of opening and the last point of closure, can thus be summarized as follows. In the opening phase, governments tend to predominate as they put forward their initial proposals. In this phase, few contentious actions and a relatively high number of cooperative actions are forthcoming. Proceeding to the main phase, third parties and challengers enter the fray and cooperation gradually gives way to contention. In the closing phase, governments and third parties tend to withdraw from the debate and challengers remain as the main actors involved, with an increased frequency of contentious action forms.

## TURNINGS POINTS IN ACTION: A CASE STUDY

To illustrate these turning points in action, we invite the reader to refer back to our illustrative case of austerity that we presented in the methodological overview of our book in Chapter 2 (see Figure 2.2): the first French austerity episode, or what we call the Sarkozy–Fillon austerity package. This episode can be seen as a paradigmatic case of austerity during the Great Recession. Occurring in the early phases of our study period at the height of the economic malaise afflicting the continent, it is a fairly contentious episode type, including both a three-year public-spending freeze and a pension reform (a two-year increase in the statutory retirement age).

In some respects, the episode is highly illustrative of the dynamics noted earlier, while in other respects it has important idiosyncrasies as well. For instance, somewhat unusually, the first turning point was a point of closure and the first opening occurred only around halfway through the episode (calculated by calendar days) in the summer of 2010. Subsequently, another opening occurred on October 10, while October 22 marked the final turning point, a point of closure.

When focusing on these four turning points, it is readily apparent that all four were government actions and took neither the form of disruptive or of cooperative action. Instead, they were all "government sticking to plans" actions and, more specifically, they all marked stages of the policy-making process, two in the form of government decisions, two in the form of legislation. Starting with the early point of closure, on June 15, the French government presented the first draft of the reform, including the rise in the retirement age from sixty to sixty-two. This presentation of the draft proposal (a government decision) indeed narrowed contention to what can be considered as the main thread of events, while an alternative thread related to the earlier announcement of the public spending freeze in May was closed off. Shortly afterward, directly triggered by this draft proposal, the government adopted the draft legislation for the pension reform on the July 13, making it ready for submission to parliament. The draft legislation confirmed the postponement of the national retirement age and no concessions were offered regarding the issue of working conditions as demanded by an alliance of challengers, the CGT and CFDT, two union confederations. This adoption of the draft legislation constituted the first point of opening, triggering fifteen further actions, easily passing the episode-specific relative threshold to qualify for a point of opening. Interestingly, seven of these fifteen actions were challenger actions by the unions, but they only occurred after the summer recess. It is likely that the government timed the release of this draft legislation just before the recess to give itself some breathing space before contentious actions would gather steam in the autumn. As the first point of opening of the episode, the draft legislation also marked the transition from the initial phase to the main phase. After a successful passage through the National Assembly in September, the second point of opening occurred on October 10, when the government actually promulgated the pension reform, triggering seventeen further reactions. Twelve days later, October 22 marks the final turning point of the episode, when the last legal hurdle fell: The reform passed the senate. With this passage, an alternative thread of contention that had started in response to the earlier draft proposal was closed off and the episode entered its closing phase.

What do these phases look like in terms of the main actors involved and the types of actions they undertook? In terms of distribution of the action count by the phases, the episode more or less reflects the distribution in the overall sample. Of the 120 total actions, only thirty-four (28 percent) occurred in the opening phase despite its relatively long duration in terms of calendar days. Seventy-two actions (60 percent) occurred in the main phase and fourteen (12 percent) occurred in the closing phase. When analyzing the preponderance of the actors involved in the respective phases, it is important to point out that this episode was comparatively rich in challenger actions because of the frequent protests by the unions: Close to half (48 percent) of all actions were attributed to challenger organizations.

Against this backdrop, in the initial phase of the episode, before the first point of opening occurs, the government played a comparatively more active role with more than 35 percent of actions attributed to it (compared to only 28 percent for the entire episode). Many of these actions were highly tentative statements on the future of the pension reform, including communication and calls for negotiation with social partners and party-political actors. It is noteworthy that in this initial phase, the French government signaled a great deal of willingness to take union demands on board, especially those from the moderate CFDT. At the same time, while unions were already fairly active in this phase, only two of their actions were coded as contentious. On April 15, they called for a large-scale mobilization for the 1st of May, marking a scale shift in the course of their challenge and the actual mass mobilization they successfully organized across the country, two weeks later on Labor Day.

At the same time, third-party actors tended to stay on the sidelines in the opening phase (with only six actions attributed to them). This drastically changed after the first point of opening occurred: Third-party actors were responsible for nineteen actions in the main phase of the episode. Most of these actions were undertaken by mainstream opposition parties (the French socialists) who tended to side with the challengers by opposing the pension reform throughout the summer of 2010. Only in rare instances, such as the National Assembly's social affairs commission on July 22, did these third parties provide explicit support for the government. As for challengers, they also stepped up their effort against the government proposal during this phase, and they did so under an umbrella of a fairly wide challenger coalition. In addition to unions, students and the radical-left opposition also mobilized with ten disruptive actions overall, including blockades of schools and oil refineries. In response to such challenges, the government also ramped up its repressive repertoire with no less than seven repressive actions – some verbal, some coercive repression. While in the beginning of this phase the government attempted to continue the cooperative strategy it had pursued in the opening phase, as the conflict escalated it gradually abandoned such overtures and increasingly relied on its coercive apparatus.

Entering the closing phase of the episode, after the passage of the reform in the senate, the patterns we indicated in the statistical analysis earlier are clearly discernible. Of the fourteen final actions occurring after this last turning point, ten were by challengers, three by third parties, and only one by the government. Although only two of the ten challenger actions were coded as disruptive, including the very last action in the form of a massive demonstration at the end of November, all ten were union actions, including the radical fringe of the union movement, the CGT. Of the three third-party actions, two were by the mainstream opposition socialists, who attempted to erect a final obstacle to the reform by referring it to an (ultimately unsuccessful) constitutional review. This stands in contrast to the main phase of the episode when the mainstream parliamentary opposition took a more vocal stand against the government and on various occasions offered explicit support for the challengers.

Overall, this brief account of the Sarkozy–Fillon austerity episode provides a helpful illustration of turning points at work. The episode began with a low level of intensity, with a relatively dominant government and various attempts to appease challenger demands. While such attempts continued in the beginning of the main phase after the adoption of the draft legislation (the first point of opening), the conflict quickly escalated, with challengers resorting to more contentious tactics on the back of third-party support by the mainstream opposition – which then prompted the government to turn to more coercive tactics. Eventually, in the closing phase of the episode, the challenger coalition made its final stand, while third parties by and large withdrew from the contention.

CONCLUSION

With the benefit of hindsight and in light of the final outcome, it is often tempting to pinpoint particular actions as turning points in an episode without actually observing the day-to-day flow of events that followed from one action or another. Only with a systematic reconstruction of the action sequences is it possible, however, to tell, with a degree of certainty, which action triggered the highest number of reactions or closed off already unfolding interactions for that matter. We found that governments were mostly responsible for turning points of both types. It is government decisions that open up the interaction dynamics, and also close them down to more focused exchanges. For instance, as we have shown in the French case, these turning points coincided with some of the milestones of the policy-making process in the form of government decisions and legislative acts. In others, they simply took the form of public statements, at times of a defensive and at other times of a proactive, accusatory nature. Somewhat surprisingly, however, they were unlikely to be highly disruptive actions, such as mobilization by challengers or repression by governments. Nor did they tend to take the form of dialogue between the adversaries in the form of government concession, mediation of third parties, or cooperative acts of challengers. Most turning points tended to be in the "gray zone" between the two polar ends of the contention spectrum, or what we referred to as "government sticking to proposal" throughout this volume.

Importantly, therefore, turning points often tend to occur where one would least expect. Though it is tempting to retrospectively assign crucial importance to some of the most dramatic flashpoints in the course of political conflict, a careful reconstruction of the causal chain of events reveals that they are no more likely to serve as turning points than some of the routine steps in the policy-making process. In particular, 44% of all points of opening in our sample were government decisions, including confirmations, clarifications, amendments, and updates of the policy proposal under discussion within the routine, institutional channels of policy-making in the ministries and other state bureaucracies.

Once we located these turning points in the respective episodes, we proceeded to investigate their impact on the subsequent evolution of contention. We broke up an episode into three parts, the first lasting until the first point of opening and the last beginning at the last point of closure, with the middle phase – or what we called the main phase – bridging the two. Because of the highly uneven occurrence of turning points in time, the length of these phases greatly varied in episodes and not all episodes could be broken up into three phases. With these caveats, however, we have shown that the prevalence of the three actor types systematically varies throughout the phases, with governments predominating in the opening phase and third parties concentrating their efforts in the main phase. Challengers were often left to their own devices in the closing phase, with governments and third parties withdrawing from the fray by that time. Moreover, we have also seen that episodes tend to escalate over time, with cooperation gradually giving way to conflict. In the illustrative case of the Sarkozy–Fillon episode, we have indeed seen a high number of government concessions in the opening phase and to some extent in the beginning of the main phase, but, later on, the increasingly disruptive forms of challenger actions prompted the government to respond in kind. All in all, these findings reveal that turning points are not merely statistical artefacts directly following from the rules we used to identify them: They mark real forms of departure from one state of contention to another, with the dominant type of actions and actors alternating between them.

Although our attempts to provide a systematic reconstruction of turning points in contentious episodes produced some interesting results largely in line with the extant literature and theoretical expectations we derived from it, some limitations warrant further research based on the tools of contentious episode analysis (CEA). First, we restricted ourselves to a limited set of variables, both to predict turning points as well as to examine their impact. Beyond actor types, action forms, and timing, another interesting aspect to look at is how the constellations of actors produce (or fail to produce) turning points. Building on the central idea from the previous chapters, it may not only be the characteristics of individual actions that determine the probability of turning points but also the dynamic relationship – for example, path-dependence or tit-for-tat dynamics – between actions and reactions that steers episodes into a new phase. Likewise, turning points may exert their impact not only via the actors and action forms that predominate in the various phases but also via the pace of actions, or the breadth of challenger coalitions and other aspects of the episodes that we have derived earlier in this book.

Finally, we must note that the very definition of turning points (and their corresponding operationalization) may be subject to debate and dissent. Our underlying premise defining the "states" of contention was based on a somewhat mechanistic understanding of how complex the episode is at any given point in time. We, accordingly, defined points of opening and points of closure with the idea of branching out and closing off in mind. However, alternative definitions of the states of contention, such as their average pace, might be equally plausible candidates for defining turning points in general and *points of acceleration* or *points of deceleration* in particular. Moreover, we argued for a relative operationalization of turning points by taking the overall action count of an episode into account to set a threshold for how many actions are needed for a trigger or for how long the narrowing needs to persist. Setting these thresholds is inevitably an arbitrary endeavor, and our results may be highly sensitive to the particular threshold chosen. While explicitly addressing alternative conceptualizations of turning points and examining their sensitivity to operational choices lies beyond the scope of this chapter, we encourage scholars to take up this challenge in their future research agenda.

# 12

# The Greek Case

## Argyrios Altiparmakis

### INTRODUCTION

This chapter departs slightly from the previous chapters and attempts to treat the contentious episodes of one country not only as separate units of analysis but as parts of an evolving chain of contention of a larger campaign that unrolled during the years Greece was under the bailout. In doing so, this chapter delves deeper not into the quantitative aspects of contentious episodes but proceeds in a qualitative fashion and utilizes the contentious episodes as a structured backbone upon which to build a narrative of Greek contention.

The rationale behind doing a case study is therefore to showcase an alternative use of contentious episodes in a more qualitative, mixed, and "richer" narrative rather than as a branch of sequence analysis. Additionally, the chapter explores perhaps the most deviant case in our data. As we have repeatedly seen in previous chapters, Greece is a particular outlier, a country battered by an unparalleled wave of protest within the context of the Great Recession.

The main objectives of the chapter therefore are twofold. First, the aim is to present and describe the evolution of Greek contention, focusing on the Greek "economic" episodes – those covering the bailout – and their links to each other. I am including four episodes in the narrative of this chapter: the first bailout taking place in spring 2010; the midterm adjustment of the first bailout taking place from March to July 2011; the second bailout covering October 2011 through February 2012; and the third bailout from June to August 2015. Second, my aim is also to propose some mechanisms through which this evolution of contention interacted with institutional politics, based on combining study of contentious episodes with a deeper, open-content analysis of newspaper and parliamentary archives during this period.

## THE GREEK OUTLIER

Compared to other contentious episodes, the Greek episodes emerge as outliers, not only in terms of protest but also in terms of the type of interactions between government and challengers and the role of international actors. The first three episodes are the most egregious in this respect. In their intensity, radicalism, duration, and breadth (see Chapters 5 and 6), they stand apart from most other episodes coded in this dataset. There were more participants in contentious acts, more violent confrontations, more protracted standoffs, and more frequent interactions between government, challengers, and other parties than almost anywhere else, on a relative and often absolute scale. Events in Greece comprise 20 percent of all the events coded in our contentious episodes database, which includes twelve countries. As shown in Table 12.1, Greece corresponds to most of the codes in almost all categories.

Greece has the second-largest number of government actions and the largest number of actions where the government ignores or represses challengers, despite continued protest. Continuous protest may be an understatement, as Greek protest was overwhelmingly more frequent and possibly more massive than in most countries. The plurality of demonstrations and strikes (34 percent) occurred in Greek contentious episodes, along with the vast majority of violent and confrontational protest events. While the government did not concede much, the challengers were also unrelenting; as shown in Table 13.1, Greece was home to 29 percent of the entire European mobilization during this period. Similar only to Spain in this respect, almost 66 percent of the challenger events

TABLE 12.1. *Greek contentious episodes in comparison*

| Case | Challenger mobilization (%) + | Strikes/ demos | Diversity of actors* | International actors | Government persistence (%) ** |
|------|------|------|------|------|------|
| Greece | 65.6 | 184 | 17.2 | 239 | 84.8 |
| Average, excl. GR | 43.2 | 32 | 13.2 | 37 | 71.9 |
| Maximum, excl. GR | 66.2 (ES) | 78 (ES) | 17.4 (IE) | 69 (HU) | 87.4 (ES) |
| Of total (Rank) | 28.9 (1) | 34.6 (1) | – (2/IE) | 37.2 (1) | 19.0 (1) |

+ Challenger mobilization is the share of challenger events in which the challenger explicitly mobilizes, rather than threatening to do so.

* Diversity of challengers is measured by the inverse Simpson index, a measure similar to the effective number of parties, essentially measuring the effective number of actors, based on the counts of their events and the probability that any two events in the dataset are performed by the same actor.

** Government persistence is simply the share of government actions in which the government states that it will stay the course and implement its policy plan.

are about challenger mobilization, in contrast to other countries where threats, negotiation, concessions, withdrawals, and other challenger behavior is more prominent.

The outlier characteristics do not end here. Greece famously became a European battleground during the Eurozone crisis, the epicenter of the fight over austerity. The incidence of coded actions by third actors is also at its highest here and the bulk of those actions concern statements, reactions, and nudges by international actors (i.e., foreign governments, European institutions, the I.M.F. or all of them together as "the Troika"). In fact, other civil-society agents, such as N.G.O.s, business and professional associations etc. were as likely to appear as challengers in Greece as they were to appear in our codes as third parties. It is the preponderance of international actors that inflates the diversity of actors in Greece.

As shown in Chapter 6, Greek episodes, particularly the first two bailouts and the midterm adjustment, are the ones with the fastest pace and highest complexity compared to all other episodes in our database. As such, sequences tend to be longer, with more "tit-for-tat" action occurring; faster, occurring in shorter timespans; and wider, involving a large variety of actors responding to the government. Similar to the Irish bailout discussed in Chapter 6, the time constraints and involvement of international actors in the Greek bailouts caused them to be highly contentious, quickly evolving, and inclusive in terms of actor diversity. However, the high contentiousness and radicalness across all episodes compared to the rest of Europe obscures the significant variation of actions, claims, and actors as the campaign against successive bailouts escalated from one episode to the next. In the following section, I shall describe the evolution of the anti-bailout campaign and try to show that while we describe the different contestations of bailouts as distinct, independent units, in fact they are linked, successive steps in a wider campaign that transformed and changed as the stakes were raised.

## THE GREEK ANTI-BAILOUT CAMPAIGN, 2010–2015

I want to describe the evolution of the Greek campaign in terms of three variables – actors, protest forms ,and claims – and one parameter, the mode of conflict, which I am calling a parameter because it is essentially not varying throughout this campaign.

I slightly reorganize the challenger-actors into categories that differ from those used in previous chapters in order to provide an image of Greek contention that is more relevant to the specific context of Greece. Thus, actors are classified as belonging to parties or organizations of the radical left (Syriza, Communist Party), government rebels – M.P.s or party executives from government parties who disobey the government whip – peak associations: that is, top-level unions that are composite associations of workplace/sectoral unions ("base" unions), professional associations (unions of lawyers, judges, engineers etc.), and finally Indignados – mostly internet-based or/and grassroots actors whose assemblies and occupations occurred semi-spontaneously and with limited institutional support or guidance. I am not including the breakdown between government and third-party actors because it is much less varied. Government actors were predominantly the government, speaking through ministers, spokesmen, or the prime minister (97 percent of government actions), while third parties are split between either international actors (EU partners, the I.M.F. – 46 percent of third-party actions) and institutional actors, such as opposition parties (32 percent of third-party actions). Compared to the relative stability of the composition of government and third-party actors throughout the episodes, the composition of challengers presents much more variety and is more interesting for understanding the successive waves of contention as shown in Table 12.2.

Meanwhile, Table 12.3 presents the variation of different types of mobilization across the Greek contentious episodes, focusing on the variation over time. This table only takes into account actual mobilizations, rather than threats or announcements of mobilization; hence the different action counts compared to Table 12.2.

TABLE 12.2. *Comparison of challengers across Greek contentious episodes*

| Actor type (%) | 1st Bailout | Midterm | 2nd Bailout | 3rd Bailout | Average |
|---|---|---|---|---|---|
| Rad. Left | 20.2 | 15.5 | 0 | 0 | 10.3 |
| Gov. rebels | 3.9 | 16.4 | 4.9 | 74.6 | 18.3 |
| Peak assoc. | 30.8 | 15.5 | 10.8 | 10.9 | 17.8 |
| Base unions | 30.8 | 20.7 | 49.0 | 0 | 28.1 |
| Professionals | 14.4 | 0 | 21.4 | 3.6 | 10.3 |
| Indignados | 0 | 31.9 | 13.7 | 10.9 | 15.1 |
| Total | 100.0% | 100.0% | 100.0% | 100.0% | |
| N (% of all eps) | 104 (27.6) | 116 (30.8) | 102 (27.1) | 55 (14.6) | 377 (100) |

TABLE 12.3. *Comparison of mobilization forms across all Greek contentious episodes*

| Mobilization (%) | 1st Bailout | MidTerm | 2nd Bailout | 3rd Bailout | Average |
|---|---|---|---|---|---|
| Strikes | 70.9 | 30.4 | 67.3 | 6.7 | 53.6 |
| Demonstrations | 16.3 | 62.3 | 7.1 | 66.7 | 29.1 |
| Confrontational | 5.4 | 1.4 | 8.2 | 0 | 5.0 |
| Violent | 1.8 | 1.4 | 6.1 | 0 | 3.4 |
| Other | 5.4 | 4.3 | 11.2 | 26.7 | 7.2 |
| Total | 100.0% | 100.0% | 100.0% | 100.0% | |
| N (% of all eps.) | 55 (23.2) | 69 (29.1) | 98 (41.4) | 15 (6.3) | 237 (100) |

As Tables 12.2 and 12.3 reveal, the face and repertoire of contention shifts significantly among the different episodes. When Papandreou's government asked for its first bailout in April 2010, opposition was first and foremost *institutional*. The predominant mode of reaction was the strike, accompanied by a large demonstration (often turning into a riot) in front of parliament. The main actors were the unions and parties of the left, particularly the Communist Party and its associated union organizations. The leading unions – GSEE, representing workers in the private sector, and ADEDY, representing public sector employees – called for three successive general strikes in February, March, and May in the build-up to the legislation for the first bailout. The claims of those initial protests were mostly focused on economic grievances: on the demand to cancel the impeding cuts imposed by the proposed bailout and the austerity packages that preceded it. There were hints of what was to come in certain slogans ("the thieves should pay"), but in general, the actor profile, repertoire, and claims were a direct continuation of Greek patterns of contention as they had existed before the crisis: leading unions declaring a general strike, joined by workplace/sectoral unions, producing a massive challenge to the government in the streets and hoping for some concessions. Attempted pension reforms in 2001 and 2007 (Matsaganis 2007; Sotiropoulos 2018) had been contested in the same mode by the unions who achieved significant concessions.

While the protests against the first bailout therefore produced the repetition of a traditional pattern of contestation, this first step in the Greek wave of anti-bailout contention still needs to be noted for three reasons: First, the protests against the government's plans were massive, gathering at the final general strike hundreds of thousands in the streets to oppose the proposed bailout legislation (Rüdig and Karyotis 2014; Karyotis and Rüdig 2018). While the actors and claims were of the pre-bailout variety, the unions arranged the convergence and coordination of disparate groups and activists under their umbrella in successive demonstrations, allowing for the formation of an "informal coalition" against the bailout, as argued by Kanellopoulos et al. (2017). The second characteristic of this mode of contention was the creation of a network of S.M.O.s, N.G.O.s, parties, and unions opposing the bailout, facilitated by successive strikes and demonstrations against it. Finally, its third characteristic is that the government responded to it with hard repression, a recipe that was to be followed in the successive episodes as well, as shown in Table 12.4. Whereas unions had managed to achieve concessions in previous rounds of mobilizations, they were completely thwarted by the government in this one, achieving only engagements in hand-to-hand confrontations with the riot police. Intransigence and repression were characteristic of the government's actions, evidenced by the extremely low number of government cooperative actions, and the constant amount of government and challenger conflictual action throughout all episodes. The Greek mode of interaction between government and challengers in this period was extremely one-sided, containing

TABLE 12.4. *Action typology: distribution of action types*

| Action (%) | 1st Bailout | MidTerm | 2nd Bailout | 3rd Bailout | Total |
|---|---|---|---|---|---|
| Government, conflictive | 22.5 | 22.3 | 21.2 | 20.1 | 21.6 |
| Third party, pro-government | 28.6 | 16.1 | 27.9 | 28.7 | 25.0 |
| Government, cooperative | 2.0 | 5.6 | 4.5 | 1.4 | 3.6 |
| Third party, mediating | 0 | 0 | 3.9 | 1.4 | 1.3 |
| Challenger, cooperative | 1.7 | 1.6 | 1.6 | 0.5 | 1.4 |
| Third party, pro-challenger | 11.6 | 18.0 | 9.9 | 22.0 | 14.8 |
| Challenger, conflictive | 33.7 | 36.4 | 31.1 | 25.8 | 32.2 |
| Total | 100.0% | 100.0% | 100.0% | 100.0% | 100.0% |
| N | 294 | 305 | 312 | 209 | 1,120 |

only one type of relationship, that of conflict. Pressured by external actors and impeding bankruptcy, the Greek government gave no ground, nor did its challengers.

The 2010 round of protests ended as the bailout was legislated despite an unprecedented, even by Greek standards, round of general strikes and massive mobilizations. In the last and most massive strike, riots enveloped the Athenian capital. As Molotov cocktails were being thrown around indiscriminately, a bank building caught fire killing three people inside. The somber mood created by those deaths and the government's narrative of an "irresponsible and violent" response to its measures gaining traction – along with the bailout's legislation – ended this first round of mostly institutionalized protest. The government appeared to have decisively defeated the challengers, since its popularity remained high and its polling percentages were undented by the bailout legislation. The challenger response, despite its massiveness, was deemed as ineffective.

Significant protest ceased for almost a year, as shown in Figure 12.1,[1] until the government's fiscal targets were not met, and it had to "amend" the first bailout program and implement more austerity. This triggered another round of contestation, only this time its characteristics were almost the polar opposite of the previous round.

---

[1] The only other protest peak and exception was in December 2010, when there were some well-covered riots on the second "anniversary" of the murder of a youth by police in the central square of Exarcheia.

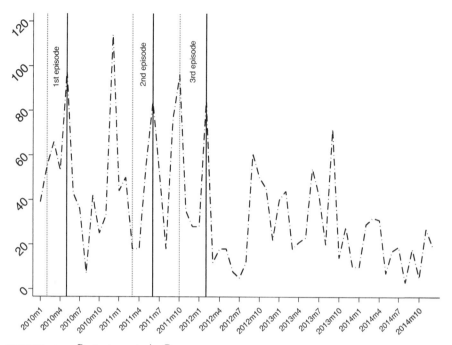

FIGURE 12.1. Protest events in Greece, 2010–2012.
*Source*: POLCON Protest Event Analysis.
*Note*: The solid lines are months in which major austerity laws or legislation was passed.

The summer of the Greek Indignados, that started with the announcement of the midterm adjustment, is treated as an episode distinct from the mobilization of the first bailout, but in many ways emerged out of it. It built on the network of unaffiliated activists and independents, many of whom had attended the previous round of mobilization but were dismayed by the narrow economic claims of the unions, their ineffective challenge to the government, and the eruption of violence as demonstrations ended. The success of the previous round in drawing massive crowds and the failure of the unions and parties leading it to represent and achieve the objectives of this crowd led directly to the transformation of almost all facets of contestation.

This second round was much more bottom-up, spontaneous, nonviolent, and participatory. Unlike the first and the second bailout, in this one, demonstrations rather than strikes were the most frequent protest. Starting on May 24, with an anonymous call for action on Facebook that went viral, inspired by the Spanish Indignados, the so-called Greek Indignados would converge on the central squares of almost all major urban centers and occupy them, holding direct-democracy assemblies and deliberative sessions aimed at examining and resolving the country's conundrum (Aslanidis and Marantzidis 2016; Diani and Kousis 2014; Kanellopoulos et al. 2017; Petropoulos 2014; Simiti 2015).

Therefore, as shown in Tables 12.2 and 12.3, strikes gave way to demonstrations as union-led, top-down mobilization was displaced by Indignados-style, bottom-up mobilization. Furthermore, the claims of those demonstrations far exceeded the narrow economic perspective of the last round. As Petropoulos (2014) observes, the Greek Indignados focused much more on "political" themes, voicing loudly (and sometimes rudely) their dissatisfaction with the political class, their anger at their representatives and the system of bipartisanism that they considered responsible for the country's near-bankruptcy and decline. Chants such as "thieves, thieves," rude gestures directed toward parliamentarians, and demands to burn down parliament were often heard, particularly in the "upper" part of Syntagma Square, which hosted the more apolitical, right-leaning faction of the Greek Indignados.

In tune with this shift toward more "political" grievances, the period of the Greek Indignados was associated with the emergence of another type of protest repertoire, a "disruptive" repertoire that aimed to confront politicians and hold them accountable in their daily, personal, and institutional routines and to disrupt the functions of the state. There are abundant examples of attacks,[2] booing, and eggs thrown at ministers, government, and party officials throughout this episode, when routine speeches of ministers and international meetings were hijacked by protesters and turned into a demonstration of indignation against the political class.

The transformation of all aspects of contestation in this new round of protests initially numbed and successively spooked the government. At first, the protests were welcomed as a departure from the more confrontational conflicts; with unions, left organizations, government M.P.s, and ministers in early May attempting to appeal, to woo, and offer their sympathies to the Greek Indignados. An important turning point, however, was on June 1, when the Greek Indignados surrounded the parliament building, blocking all its exits while M.P.s were discussing the new measures inside. M.P.s trapped in the building were eventually forced to evacuate it with the help of the fire brigades who provided them with ladders to escape through the dark alleyways of the national garden behind the building. The eerie feeling of being besieged by protesters and their souring mood led to expressions of nervous breakdown by M.P.s, such as the one provided below by Maria Theochari, a PASOK M.P.:

God ... I will quit everything. I never imagined I would need the help of firefighters, policemen, and torchlights to leave parliament ... I left through the National Garden, within the darkness as if I was being hunted; I strained my foot. (Xasapopoulos 2011; author's translation)

---

[2] Most of those examples were not "tracked" initially via the more conventional focus of the contentious episode keywords but were only picked up later by a more in-depth open content analysis of newspaper archives, demonstrating the limits of comparative and somewhat generic CEP coding through non-context-specific keywords.

As the numbers of the Greek Indignados surged from an initial demonstration of 20,000 to a daily occupation numbering hundreds of thousands, such expressions of panic became widespread among PASOK M.P.s. Unlike during the first episode, the party was now slipping in the polls, having lost 12 percentage points since the first episode, with its social and electoral base outside parliament protesting and threatening its M.P.s who could no longer go on about their daily lives unperturbed. While the unions initially reacted to the Greek Indignados with perplexity and reluctance, the bourgeoning numbers of protesters motivated them to enter the fray and two general strikes were called, culminating in demonstrations that converged with the Greek Indignados crowd. The expanding crowd spooked government M.P.s, who, as if in a chorus, started demanding amendments and changes to the proposed measures and the formation of a more inclusive government that would alleviate the burden that was placed solely on PASOK's shoulders.

Despite the efforts by the PASOK government to change the austerity mix in negotiations with creditors and to lure the institutional opposition of New Democracy into the governing coalition, not much progress was achieved by any of them. Eventually, the PASOK government, facing the prospect of bankruptcy, felt obliged to legislate the midterm adjustment alone, ending the stalemate and the efforts at appeasement of the Greek Indignados. The new austerity package was voted in at the end of June. After the eclipse of violent actions for the month by the Greek Indignados, new riots erupted, and repression was again utilized as the standard response by the Greek government to this wave of protest.

As shown in Figure 12.1, while the Greek Indignados fizzled slowly throughout the summer, it would not be until the next austerity legislation of austerity – and the beginning of our third episode – in October that the movement would recover and once again challenge the government in the streets. Although passage of the legislation of the mid-term adjustment effectively put an end to the Greek Indignados, they nevertheless had bequeathed an important legacy to the anti-austerity movement: quantitative and qualitative expansion. The numbers of those joining the anti-bailout movement surged yet again, spurring demonstrations with half a million protesters, and their claims expanded as well, directly blaming the PASOK government, depending on who spoke, for its ineptitude in its negotiations, its conspiracy with creditors, and its responsibility for all the practices that led to bankruptcy. Rather than making a simple plea to avert austerity, as was characteristic of the first round, the Greek Indignados initiated a period of distributing political accountability and offering more general advice about how to deal with Greek political dysfunction, generally requiring that the bankrupt bipartisan system be abandoned. Additionally, in combination with poll slippage, the Greek Indignados opened the first cracks within PASOK, as its M.P.s began hesitating when faced with increasing societal pressure against the bailout, looking for ways to dodge the criticism directed at them. At the end of the episode, the finance minister associated with the first bailout, Papakonstantinou, was sacrificed to appease the protesters, as the only way for the government to defuse the pressure.

Consequently, during our third episode, which began when a new austerity bill was due to pass in October 2011, the legacy of the Greek Indignados remained strong: The disruptive repertoire that had started during the summer of 2011 persisted and further expanded, eventually subsiding when the second bailout was passed. In this third episode, this disruptive repertoire was fully deployed. When the new austerity bill, including liberalization, privatizations, and cuts was presented in early October, state employees began more persistently, and in an organized fashion, to sabotage state functions and routine operations. While this was not captured in our original coding – which counted the strikes and demonstrations – going back to the newspaper archive revealed an extensive disruptive set of actions embedded within those strikes recorded in our coding. For example, the power company union proceeded to stage periodical blackouts in different parts of the capital by way of protest throughout October. Treasury employees occupied the state Central Accounting Unit blocking the disbursal of funds, and waste was not collected throughout the capital in a showdown between the government and municipal employees. In a "hot autumn," a wave of strikes unrolled, as shown in Table 12.3, spearheaded by workplace/sectoral unions completely paralyzing the country, as key state organizations protested against an unrepresentative government that was ignoring the public will as expressed in squares and demonstrations.

As Papandreou yet again passed a new austerity bill, aimed at achieving the missed targets of the first bailout, despite protest and internal turmoil, on October 20, he was not afforded any reprieve. On October 26 he attended a European summit where it was finally decided to provide the Greek government with a haircut on its debt, conditional however on further, unspecified austerity in the future. While Papandreou returned to Greece in a triumphant mood, satisfied at having achieved some debt forgiveness, in the public imagination the prospect of further austerity was far more tangible resulted in a small eruption. Two days later, on October 28, the planned parades to honor resistance to the Axis in World War II had to be canceled in multiple cities as an assortment of Greek Indignados, radical left organizations, and various activists and social-movement organizations staged a disruptive intervention, blocking the parading units from marching and hounding the attending politicians. In Thessaloniki, the second-largest city, the president of the Republic was attending the parade there in person. After protesters broke through the police cordon sanitaire and threatened to overtake the podium where the officials stood, the parade was canceled and the building evacuated. With rhythmic chants of "traitors, traitors" made to escaping politicians, the impression was one of total state breakdown. The state was not able to perform even a celebratory, symbolic function, nor to protect its figurehead from the wrath of protesters.

Shocked by the surprise expansion of the disruptive repertoire into such rudimentary state functions, the political personnel reacted with panic. The prospect of another austerity deal, the fear of a return of the Greek Indignados, the personal persecution of M.P.s and the polling collapse of PASOK, which by that time was scraping the low twenties in polls, led to an uncoordinated but immediate reaction by M.P.s, who pleaded to avoid the situation of PASOK voting alone for another deal. As the opposition and the streets were piling the pressure on PASOK, Papandreou attempted to solve this conundrum faced by PASOK by holding a referendum. However, in events well documented elsewhere (Spiegel 2011), he was forced to call off the referendum under domestic and foreign pressure and to resign in favor of a technocratic government.

The technocratic government of Papademos, installed shortly after on November 10, 2011, and supported also by the major opposition, was initially well received by creditors and public opinion, but its honeymoon ended prematurely. As it negotiated the second bailout, the bickering of the parties that formed it, the attempts to dodge responsibility and the realization that another deal would not be much better than the previous one despite the cooperation of all Greek mainstream parties, quickly resulted in the final round of contestation which shared many of the features of the first one. In February 2012, as the second bailout was voted, a general strike by key unions fused the previous waves of protest, allowing for the convergence of almost half a million protesters, once again at Syntagma Square. As the bill passed with the support of both major parties, the protest quickly devolved into an uncontrolled riot that burnt multiple historic buildings of the capital.

In this third wave of contention, we had one major departure from before. What had previously been a confrontation between institutional and extra-institutional actors – the government, ministers, and M.P.s versus street protesters, unions, and leftists – was now turned, through the imposition of the technocratic government and the collapse of PASOK, into a clash *within* the institutional actors. As shown in Table 12.2, the actions belonging to government rebels were fewer than in the midterm adjustment, and they were far more decisive – another unappreciated aspect if we treat our data in a purely quantitative way. In the midterm adjustment, government rebels, dissenting M.P.s, and party officials, protested, warned, and threatened the government. In this episode, such actions were relatively fewer, dwarfed by a barrage of strikes and occupations, but they were far more significant: At the vote for the second bailout, forty-three M.P.s abandoned the two major parties, many of them joining the more radical, fringe and opposition parties. What was before perceived as a faultline that separated government and opposition, now pitted a nefarious "establishment," composed of the two major parties, against those heeding the calls of protesters: the radical opposition, the dissenters, the rebels, and the Greek Indignados. It is in this final act of two-party convergence and expulsion of dissenting M.P.s that the divide that was to politically manifest itself in the earthquake elections of 2012 became apparent for the first time – the confrontation between the pro-bailout and anti-bailout sides.

The intermediate years between this episode and the last one, the third bailout, were when this divide became institutionalized, left the streets, and entered parliament, embodied in the confrontation between Syriza and New Democracy. The gap between this episode and the last one was punctuated by three electoral contests in which the anti-bailout side, represented by Syriza and other parties, constituted itself as an institutional force, continually gaining seats and representation in parliament. From its shocking rise as the main opposition to New Democracy in the twin elections of 2012, Syriza eventually launched a successful bid for power that was completed in 2015, as the party grew in those contests from 4 percent in 2009, to 16, 26, and 36 percent in the three successive elections in May 2012, June 2012, and January 2015, respectively (see Chapter 3).

It is only with the last episode that this divide was finally overcome and the issue settled, as Syriza, the representative of the street opposition during the anti-bailout campaign was forced to concede a bailout of its own, leaving the anti-bailout movement without political representation once again.

This final episode, taking place in the summer of 2015, is notable for its lack of contention compared to the previous ones. There were only a few demonstrations, attended by a mere few thousands since the main arena of contention, as shown in Table 12.2, shifted from the streets to parliament. Indeed, almost three quarters of all actions against the bailout were attributed to government rebels, that is, institutional forces. Rather than a renewed confrontation in the streets, it appeared as if the opposition to the bailout had been reduced to the internecine war within Syriza, as a faction of the party refused to support the government in its new path and sabotaged its legislative proposals, without, however, clearly abandoning the party. The fraction of Syriza that would eventually splinter before the next September elections, Popular Unity, consisting of its most-left-leaning M.P.s, challenged each phase of the bailout in parliament, filibustered parliamentary procedures stubbornly but eventually failed to muster or accompany this institutional activity with any kind of street mobilization during the last summer of the bailout saga. Instead, the streets emptied as the country was drawn to the parliamentary spectacle of everyday clashes and divisions within the governing elite, waiting to see the outcome of this tussle. Eventually, as the faction loyal to then Prime Minister Tsipras prevailed relatively easily, the shock of the sudden turnaround of Syriza, the summer lull, and the exhaustion and frustration of having to potentially restart the whole cycle of challenge to the bailout led to the absence of protest. As Syriza handily won the elections of September 2015, the era of protest spearheaded by the anti-bailout movement was essentially over.

MECHANISMS OF INTERACTION BETWEEN CONTENTIOUS
AND INSTITUTIONAL POLITICS

Without being able to do it full justice, I have now briefly outlined the evolution
of the anti-bailout movement between the four episodes covered in this case.
There are many more details and interesting points about this movement, but
in the following section, I want to develop a theory of how contentiousness
interacted with institutional politics, a theory that springs from the close
scrutiny of the chains of interactions highlighted by our contentious episode
data. This will hopefully highlight how contentious episodes can be used in a
broader fashion. If we only analyzed the cycle of government–challenger–
government actions and reactions, we would only produce a relatively
uninteresting account of repetitive rounds of challenger intransigence meeting
government repression. However, by treating the bailout episodes as part of
an evolving campaign that unfolded over time, we can trace some
interesting mechanisms through which contentious politics interacted with
institutional ones.

## Elite Breakdown/Resignation

The first such mechanism refers to the gradual paralysis of the state apparatus
and government-political personnel as the anti-bailout movement expanded.
The division of elites, a similar theme, is one of the most common mechanisms
identified in the literature for showing how social movements influence institutional dynamics, typically an integral part of POS literature (Giugni 2009;
Kriesi et al. 1992; McAdam et al. 1996). Elite division is usually understood,
however, as a more active process, with the focus being on the actual splintering
and factionalism within elite organizations. Thus, McAdam and Tarrow (2013)
provide the example of a split in parties or split in a class coalition. The elite
breakdown I describe in Greece bears some resemblance but is not an exact
match with the processes described by other scholars.

Its most critical part lies in the legislative-procedural system. It concerns the
relationship between government and supporting M.P.s. This is a relationship
that degraded over time, as increasingly more M.P.s became less tied to government parties and manifested centrifugal tendencies. The rupture was not
primarily one between the ruling elite and other elites (which also happened), as
in Skocpol (1979), but one *within* the political class itself, more akin to
Goldstone's (1998) tale of the collapse of the U.S.S.R., where elites gradually
lost faith in their own project. I want to emphasize not so much division in the
sense of factionalism and splits over the direction of the government's policy
but a sort of breakdown – a paralysis – an inability of the government to
discipline its M.P.s and motivate them to stay the course. Additionally, there
was the spectacle of increasing resignation in the face of mounting pressure

from international actors and social movements, especially as the latter expanded their repertoire and started targeting M.P.s personally.

This paralysis manifested itself in gradually sharpening tones. Whereas in the first bailout, PASOK already faced the loss of four M.P.s who decided to vote against the government, the rest of their parliamentary group held the line and did not protest too much against the first bailout. As is shown in Table 12.2, government rebels were not a prominent part of the first bailout. However, government rebels became a much more important facet of opposition to the government's plans in the second bailout, as even ministers threatened to resign, fearful of the rising tide of indignation and the continued attacks on politicians. Already there was a jump of 13 percent in actions by government rebels between the first and second episode. Beyond the mere number of these actions, it is important to understand the increasing frequency with which government M.P.s also demanded other changes to government policy or status, such as the formation of a government of national unity, or the holding of elections in the fear that the electoral base of the party was dissipating. Several characteristic quotes from government M.P.s immediately following the Greek Indignados or October 2011 parade events that appeared in newspaper articles at the time revealed their fear and reluctance to shoulder the bailout burden.

Half of PASOK voters are depressed and the other half in the squares...imagine voting for the measures with a million people outside. (Kroustalli 2011; Nedos 2011)

It's gone...We will not make it through October. PASOK is collapsing, the government is sinking, the political system is being dismantled and society out there is boiling. (Mpourdaras 2011)

National consensus or a government of emergency or elections. Enough. (Mpourdaras 2011)

The evolution of contention was closely paralleled by an ongoing paralysis and centrifugal tendencies in the governing party/parties. In the first episode four MPs left, in the second episode there was a reshuffle and the sacrifice of the finance minister and eventually even the prime minister was required to quiet M.P. unrest, while in the third episode the whole thing finally unraveled, as the PASOK majority was definitely lost and a bipartisan, technocratic government was formed. The passage of the second bailout came with a huge majority but also at the cost of the largest rebellion in Greek parliamentary history, as forty-three M.P.s finally cracked and dissented.

The sense of a loss of control, admitted by Papandreou when he reminisced about the October 2011 events (Spiegel 2011), permeated the ranks of PASOK's M.P.s and gradually led many of them to conclude that the cost they bore for the government and the purported salvation of the country was too high personally and politically. The firm majority of PASOK at the beginning of this period dwindled, as more and more of its M.P.s became paralyzed and abandoned the bailout project, preferring to return to their privacy or preserve their remaining political capital for another day. It is no coincidence that the first major cracks in the edifice appeared as the Greek Indignados rose and the disruptive repertoire expanded, making politicians feel impotent and threatened. This was not, however, the only explanation for their paralysis, since the polling collapse of PASOK and wider civil-society disobedience should be taken into account, too. The decline of the power of the government's whip is well correlated with the successive episodes of contention.

## Expansion of Political Conflict

While the gradual decay in the government–M.P. relationship was already apparent in the number and type of government rebel reactions recorded in our codification of contentious episodes, a deeper analysis of our data is required to unveil the second mechanism, that of the expansion of political conflict. Although we did not record claims per se in our analysis, a more thorough reading of the articles coded and a return to the archives after the timeline was structured by the contentious episode codification reveals an interesting pattern. Specifically, in between mobilization in 2010 and demobilization after 2012, the most interesting development relating to social movements in Greece in the bailout age was the expansion of protest themes and claims from a narrow economic dimension toward more multidimensional claims that incorporated political and nationalist themes. This is somewhat akin to one of the ways McAdam and Tarrow (2010) observe that movements interfere in the institutional scene: by introducing innovations and discursive patterns into it – innovations that are then taken up by political entrepreneurs – or to the ways protest waves and cycles typically unfold (Koopmans 2007; Tarrow 1993). Aslanidis and Marantzidis (2016) have also suggested the expansion of conflict as a mechanism underlying the effect of social movements on political discourse in the Greek case, particularly pertaining to the way Syriza adopted the language and claims of the Greek Indignados.

In my view, something slightly more extensive in scale and somewhat different in nature was going on: The social movements partially introduced but mostly solidified and foregrounded – an underlying theme of the bailout years – that of the indignation about the political class and elites.[3] I presented the ways in which this thematic expansion of the bailout occurred through the intervention of social movements, specifically through the rise of the Greek Indignados, who introduced the issues of the political class's incompetence,

[3] This is similar to Bremer et al.'s (2020) hypothesis that social movements function as a "signal" of political grievances and blame attribution.

greediness, and callousness. Rather than by the actions of political entrepreneurs (Aslanidis and Marantzidis 2016; De Vries and Hobolt 2012), the addition of a political dimension to the bailout issue was triggered by social movements. Social movements in Greece in the bailout era had the effect of expanding the anti-bailout issue to include anti-political/anti-elitist claims and cement those as constitutive elements of the "anti-bailout" coalition and position in the political space.

This was quite significant because imbuing the bailout with these connotations gave it the potential to realign and disturb the contemporary political equilibrium. The bailout was one of those sporadic instances in which mass social movements invaded the political agenda and reinterpreted it, expanding the political conflict (Schattschneider 1960). If opposition to the anti-bailout changed from a narrower economic conception to a wider one that included opposition to political elites and tinges of nationalist calls for sovereignty, the result was that the way political conflict was perceived, and parties categorized, changed as well. Categories of left and right became less relevant, while the separation between "old" parties and practices (the parties responsible for the crisis and the practices that led to it), and "new" ones (untainted by government) acquired a clearer and more concrete meaning. When the mainstream parties were forced, by their European partners, to take a position on the bailout, at the same time the meaning of the bailout, with the help of protest, became associated with a wider list of grievances that enabled the expansion of the coalition of the aggrieved to incorporate a wider circle than the typical leftist, unionized audience that had promulgated the first round of protest.

In the end, as developed elsewhere in more detail (Altiparmakis 2019), Syriza benefited from those effects, not so much in terms of a direct transfusion of personnel and resources from the Greek Indignados to the party, but by successfully claiming the legacy, the vocabulary, and the demands of the movement, uniquely combining the strand of economic resistance and anti-establishment politics in its 2012 campaigns. Eventually the party identified a causal link between economic crisis and the bankruptcy of the "old political parties and class" that adequately expressed the will of the participants and sympathizers of the Indignados to see both a change of economic policy and a change of guard and the political marginalization of those considered responsible for the Greek debacle.

Finally, it must be noted that the process of expanding political conflict was not only evident in the expansion of protest claims to incorporate indignation at the political class but was also manifest in the expansion of protest into more radical action forms, and particularly into the personal hounding of political agents seen as responsible for the bailout situation. Political conflict was therefore expanded both in the sense of the meanings and connotations that the bailout issue incorporated but also in the sense of increasing radicalization of actions and civil-society disobedience and disruption, which directly contributed to the mechanism of elite breakdown.

CONCLUSIONS

To conclude, this chapter served three main functions. First, it provided a glimpse into perhaps the most anomalous and most contentious case in our entire database, that of Greece. Throughout the book, Greece has been shown to be a significant outlier and the only case comparable to famous incidents of contentious turmoil in the past. In this chapter, we tried to shed some light on why this was so, showing the particularity of the context but also the ways in which the severe downturn led to contentious action that, in turn, infiltrated the institutional scene and produced a wholesale collapse of the Greek political system. The mechanisms through which protest infected Greek politics were probably unique to this case in our dataset, or at least to such a degree, and provide a plausible account of the outlier status of Greece. Indeed, the Greek anti-bailout movement was more reminiscent of other, more tumultuous incidents of contention and of Tilly's notion of a full-fledged campaign (Tilly 2004), engaging multiple new claims, groups of claimants, and the wider Greek public.

The second function of the chapter was to showcase the potential of our contentious episode approach to be deployed in a less formal and more qualitative way. In this chapter, I have used our dataset not for the purposes of analyzing sequences, tipping points, or other aspects of contentiousness in quantitative terms but with the aim of creating a structure for a narrative. The interactions present in the Greek case were reassessed, embedded in a wider context that included more thorough archival research and memoirs and primary sources from the age of the bailout to make sense of the ways contention influenced mainstream politics. While such a task was impossible to complete for all our cases in the dataset, it was useful to demonstrate that at least in the case of Greece, the dataset was able to provide a point of reference that guided our research intuitions and hypotheses.

Finally, the chapter also demonstrated possible future expansions of datasets. I have paid a significant amount of attention to substantive claims in this chapter, a variable almost completely absent from our original coding. Whereas I reconstructed claims from primary and secondary sources, in the future contentious episode coding could include them more rigorously and systematically, providing further empirical evidence for our hypotheses and narratives. The same more or less applies to actors, where the data was there but had to be significantly recoded for this chapter. It thus becomes evident that the dataset utilized here could be modified productively to fit other cases but that it is also modular enough to be transformed and redeployed when the research requires it.

PART IV

CONCLUSION

# 13

# Conclusion

## Abel Bojar and Hanspeter Kriesi

At the outset of this volume, we situated our approach between two main paradigms prevailing in the field of contentious politics, taking up the challenge that Tilly (2008) put forward more than a decade ago. One, epitomized by the "narrative" approach, focuses on conventional storytelling, where explanation takes the form of an unfolding open-ended story. The other, protest event analysis (PEA) (see Hutter, 2014 and Koopmans and Rucht, 2002 for reviews), or what we called the epidemiological approach, focuses on a narrower set of action types: namely, instances of popular mobilization in the streets, and primarily relies on statistical techniques to explain the temporal regularities of protest actions or protest waves (Lorenzini et al, 2020). We aimed to accomplish this task by drawing on the programmatic Dynamics of Contention (McAdam et al. 2001) with an eye on preserving the conceptual depth of the former infused with the methodological rigor of the latter. In addressing "the middle ground" favored by Charles Tilly, we applied an analytical approach to the study of the dynamics of contention that allows for the systematic comparative analysis of causal patterns across individual narratives.

Such ambition, of course inevitably comes down to a set of trade-offs that the researcher faces, and the main task is ultimately a balancing act between the two competing goals outlined above. We do not claim to have found the magic formula that fully satisfies the most vocal advocates of either paradigm. What we did achieve, however, is the successful implementation of a novel method (Contentious Episode Analysis) that we hope can move the two camps closer to each other, both in terms of their methodological inclinations and in terms of their substantive reach. In particular, we hope to convince researchers working in the narrative-based tradition that building systematic datasets relying on human coders is a fruitful exercise inasmuch as it allows for a systematic and transparent way to collect and document all actions related to a particular contentious episode and that these datasets can serve as rich empirical material to refine the narratives they wish to tell their readers, even if they stop short of the sort of quantitative approach we propose.

On the flipside, we hope to have shown a way forward to scholars working in the PEA tradition and convince them that there is much more to contentious episodes than popular mobilization and immediate government responses to it. Thus, more than half (55.5 percent) of all actions we coded for challengers related to fairly routine and institutionalized forms of political actions vis-à-vis governments or third parties – for instance, verbal claims on governments, different forms of negotiation with governments or third parties and so on. In this sense, our approach sides with the main thrust of political claims analysis (Eggert and Giugni, 2015; Koopmans and Statham, 1999): we agree that the PEA tradition can be greatly enriched by explicitly incorporating these forms of non- protest-related actions in the action repertoires it studies because their lower visibility does not make them any less relevant for a general understanding of political conflict. Having incorporated this wider set of action types in their datasets, they can of course apply the same statistical techniques as they see fit for their particular purposes using this broader action repertoire as their empirical base.

On this optimistic note, in this concluding chapter we wish to summarize both our methodological and our substantive contribution to the field. In the next section, we discuss some of the main methodological choices we have made in the spirit of Chapter 2, where we have introduced the issues in question, including their limitation. We shall now examine these choices through the lenses of the empirical exercises presented in the subsequent chapters of the present volume and evaluate them according to the empirical experience. In the following section, we provide an overview of our substantive contribution via a quick recap of the main findings between Chapters 4 and 12. Finally, we wish to leave the reader with a note of encouragement and we dedicate our final section to some tentative thoughts on how our novel approach can travel across space, time, and context.

## CORNERSTONES AND MAIN CONTRIBUTIONS

As a quick reminder of the most important building blocks of our approach, the main methodological novelty and ambition we offer is to focus on the action component of contentious episodes and to capture the vast empirical universe of actions and actors with a limited set of codes. The most vexing challenge when constructing these codes was that they had to be diverse enough to cover the universe of codable actions, but they had to be limited and clear in their scope for human coders to interpret and assign them to all political actions that were relevant to our study. To facilitate this task, we decomposed both the actions and the actors into different components. For the actions, we distinguished between their substantive and procedural dimensions, and for a subset of them where popular mobilization was involved, we also coded the type of mobilization. For the actors, we started from a stylized three-way typology of governments–challengers–third parties and complemented it with an institutional taxonomy of actors that permits the specification of the tripartite typology but does not fully overlap with it. For instance, opposition parties can be both challengers and third parties, while government parties can act as governments, third parties, and sometimes even as challengers. According to our assessment, with this comprehensive and yet flexible coding scheme, our coders – after multiple rounds of exchanges with the core research team – were able to assign all relevant actions and actors to the appropriate categories and we ended up with one of the largest and most diverse cross-national datasets to date on contentious policy episodes.

Second, we aimed to strike the right balance between cross-episode variation in the relevant contextual conditions as outlined in detail in Chapter 3 and some basic level of ontological commonality in terms of the scope conditions of our selected cases. One such important commonality was the requirement that all our selected episodes begin with a government proposal and the policy debate that revolves around it. Another is that, given our focus on contentious episodes during the Great Recession, our cases were mostly economic policy episodes (plus some institutional reforms as control cases). Other politically highly salient policies contested along the cultural (Norris and Inglehart, 2019) or the integration-demarcation cleavage-line (Hutter and Kriesi, 2019; Kriesi et al, 2008) were left outside our purview for now. With these caveats, however, the cases we studied offered a wide range of contextual conditions: such as the type of economic policies on the table (bank bailouts, sovereign bailouts, fiscal adjustment episodes, structural reforms as well as institutional reforms); the depth of the economic and political crisis that the countries of the study experienced at the time of the policy proposals; the governments' electoral standing in the polls; the quality of the prevailing set of democratic institutions; macro-political attitudes of the population; and a host of other episode-specific variables that we presented in detail in Chapter 3. Such variation makes us fairly optimistic that our proposed approach is applicable for a wide variety of contexts and travels beyond the ones that we have focused on in this volume.

Third, our highly detailed coding scheme in a large number of cases – sixty episodes in total – allowed us to undertake cross-sectional analyses on some of the key dimensions of contentious politics. Based on the conceptual building blocks, we created a set of theoretically informed indicators to encompass the gist of each episode. Thus, we attempted to quantify the various aspects of *contentiousness* of the episodes by taking into account the frequency and type of actions by the contending actors involved. Moreover, we were able to analyze coalition dynamics by classifying the challengers by their institutional type – such as unions, social-movement organizations, opposition parties etc. – and to characterize episodes by the *breadth or diversity* of the challenger coalition opposing the government's policy proposal. We also sought to characterize the structure of contention in terms of time and the multiplicity of different threads of contention that run parallel throughout the conflict. Accordingly, we constructed variables on the average *pace* of the conflict – measured by the average number of days that elapsed between an action and the action that it triggered – as well as on the overall *complexity* of the episode, measured by the average number of action sequences running parallel to each other and their average length. Finally, we classified episodes in terms of outcomes, according to the nature of *government responsiveness* to challenger demands. In particular, we distinguished between the substantive and procedural responsiveness of the government to challenger demands, building on Gamson's framework (1975). Overall, the indicators we derived allowed us to characterize each episode by substantively important and empirically well-grounded features that future scholars can build upon for their particular purposes.

Fourth, perhaps the most innovative aspect of our study is the way our approach allowed us to study the dynamics of contention (Part III, Chapters 8–11 of the book). As we alluded to above, one of the crucial aspects of our approach was to identify for each action the so-called *trigger events* in the preceding part of the episode to which the action under analysis was a direct response. With the help of these triggers, we constructed *action sequences* that allowed us to undertake a dynamic analysis of contention, building on the logic of time series analysis. Instead of exclusively relying on the chronological ordering of events we also introduced lagged variables at various lag orders, allowing us to distinguish between the *actor-specific lags* of each event. The actor-specific lags, in essence, differentiate between the past actions in the sequence according to the three stylized actor types that undertook them. As our analysis documents, this actor-specific construction of lags is crucial to test, in a quantitative framework, various hypotheses that we find in the literature on contentious politics.

Our fifth empirical contribution was provided in the penultimate empirical chapter (Chapter 11) of the book. Our detailed coding scheme allowed us to trace varying patterns of contention over time and identify *turning points* that mark the transition from one state of contention to another. Our strategy for identifying turning points offers a more systematic and generalizable method than most of the empirical literature, which relies on detailed case studies. Accordingly, we identified two types of turning points, points of opening and points of closure, according to the extent they open up or close off (narrow down) contention.

The last empirical chapter, Chapter 12, illustrates the final contribution of our approach. As this chapter shows, the quantitative reconstruction of contentious episodes can also serve as a structured backbone upon which to build a narrative of a series of interlinked contentious episodes. The detailed analysis of the Greek case illustrates the potential for our contentious episode analysis to be deployed in a less formal and more qualitative way. In this chapter, the quantitative data were not used to analyze sequences, turning points, or other aspects of contentiousness quantitatively but to create a structure for a narrative. The interactions present in the unique Greek episodes were re-assessed, embedded in a wider context that included more thorough archival research and the memoirs and primary sources of the period covered to make sense of the ways in which contention influenced mainstream politics. While such a task was impossible to complete for all our cases, it was useful to demonstrate that at least in the case of a country in which we had a specific interest, our approach was able to provide a point of reference that guides our research intuitions and hypotheses.

## MAIN SUBSTANTIVE RESULTS

Having recapped the main contributions of our approach, it is time to take stock of what we have learned in substantive terms from this volume. As a reminder, we systematically studied the most important economic episodes, as well as a few institutional reforms, designed to come to terms with the adverse effects of the Great Recession in Europe. Although the crisis, as we know, affected all EU countries in one way another, we have revealed significant variation in the way individual countries suffered from crisis as well as in the type of response different governments provided. The variation in the countries' responses to the Great Recession and in the overall characteristics of the contentious episodes they unleashed is the first aspect we would like to demonstrate in our discussion of the substantive results. Next, we shall summarize our results with respect to the interaction dynamics of the episodes, followed by a consideration of the impact of specific actions on their overall development and the outcomes of the episodes.

### Variation in the Responses to the Great Recession and in the Contention They Unleashed

To come to terms with the variation in government responses, we cataloged the type of economic policies proposed by governments, with fiscal adjustment measures and structural reforms being the most common forms. Some of these fiscal adjustment measures came on the back of international sovereign bailouts orchestrated by the infamous Troika – the European Commission, the Eropean Central Bank, and the I.M.F. – and, as we saw in subsequent chapters of this volume, it is the episodes linked to international bailouts that experienced some of the most sustained forms of contention. Other types of episodes, namely bank bailouts and institutional reforms, were typically followed by more muted societal reactions, although one needs to keep in mind the Brexit referendum, an institutional reform, out of all our episodes, that turned out to have the most lasting impact on subsequent events.

The type of policy episodes on offer was closely related to the economic and political context in which the countries found themselves. Accordingly, we systematically mapped the relevant contextual conditions, both descriptively (Chapter 3) and as predictors of substantively important determinants of various features of contention (Chapters 4–7). We showed a fairly large variation in the extent to which the twelve countries were exposed to the crisis, both objectively, proxied by the unemployment and the annual G.D.P. growth rate, and subjectively, in terms of economic sentiment. At one extreme, one can place Greece, and to some extent Spain, with skyrocketing unemployment rates and a deep and prolonged recession, while Poland at the other extreme uniquely escaped recession almost completely with an unemployment rate that barely budged.

While the depth of the crisis and the pressure it exerted on the respective governments was, of course, crucial for the timing and the type and severity of the governments' responses, it was only partly, if at all, related to the overall prevalence of political grievances among Europeans and to the subsequent development of the contentious episodes unleashed by the governments' responses. Political factors proved to be more important for the key characteristics of the episodes, such as their contentiousness. Among these factors, we highlighted the role of a country's quality of democracy. In fact, the quality of democratic institutions showed great variation among our countries, both on the input (participatory democracy index) and the output (state effectiveness) side as measured by expert surveys from the Varieties of Democracies project (Coppedge et al., 2019). While some countries performed relatively well on both counts (such as France, Germany, and the U.K.), others proved susceptible to elite closure and ineffective state bureaucracies (such as Greece, Hungary, and Romania). This variation is important because these institutions played a crucial role in processing the claims and conflicting demands of the political world. Beyond institutions that were relatively fixed and stable, we also highlighted important variations in terms of the governments' composition (center-left or center-right) and popular attitudes, both in the sense of diffuse (satisfaction with democracy, trust in government) and of specific (electoral standing of the government) support. Although the fluctuation in these variables was partly attributed to the timing of the policies, both in the crisis period but also along the electoral cycles, they were important because they had the potential to expose or shelter governments from popular pressure. Accordingly, while some governments, such as the Merkel's in Germany, Cameron's in the U.K., or Orban's in Hungary, had considerable political leverage in enacting their policies, others, such as the Greek governments before Tsipras and the PDL-led governments in Romania were severely constrained by lack of popular support.

It was this variation in the economic and political context that one needs to keep in mind when we summarize the results of Part II of our book: where we derive indicators on the nature of political conflict that emerged in our chosen episodes, and attempt to explain their variation through a cross-sectional study design by taking episodes as the units of analysis. Chapters 4 and 5 take up this task by focusing on two key features of our episodes: how contentious they were as indicated by the intensity (frequency of actions)and the disruptiveness of challengers, and the alignment patterns of third-party actors vis-à-vis governments or challengers. The multiple components of our contentiousness indicator allowed us to classify episodes according to which actor type drove the contention. Accordingly, we grouped episodes as low-intensity (most of the German ones); bottom-up episodes characterized by high levels of challenger but low levels of government/third-part contentiousness (such patterns were typical of Portugal); top-down episodes with repressive government actions but lacking highly disruptive challenger tactics (e.g. the German bank bailout); and, finally, episodes that saw full-fledged contention from all parties with the Greek bailout being the paradigmatic example for them.

In a closely related manner, we also described the diversity of actor coalitions, relying on a redundant word detailed institutional taxonomy of actor types that went beyond the stylized government–challenger–third party trichotomy. The challenger coalition could be narrow or diverse, depending on whether only a narrow set of actors challenged governments (such as in France, where unions were the predominant types of challengers) or government proposals were under attack from multiple fronts, such as in most British episodes, where civil-society actors, opposition parties, and even government actors joined the fray. Adding third parties to the mix, we could differentiate between episodes where third parties tended to support governments and those where they joined the challenger coalition. Examples of the former are Greek and Spanish episodes where international third parties tended to stand behind the governments' austerity and reform plans. In those episodes, the international actors were closely allied with the government and, arguably, constituted the real targets of the challengers. Thus, during the Greek bailouts, the Troika was targeted by the challengers as much as the domestic government. Accordingly, in these episodes, it was somewhat artificial to consider international actors as third parties. We nevertheless stuck to our parsimonious scheme of actors that treats international actors as third-party actors. Examples of the latter were found in Hungary and Ireland, where third parties (many of them domestic) were part and parcel of the challenger coalition against the government.

How did we account for such variation, relying on the contextual conditions outlined above? With regard to contentiousness, we attempted to explain both challenger contentiousness and the overall contentiousness of the episodes. The most robust predictor turned out to be the democratic quality of the countries, with higher-quality institutions being associated with lower levels of contentiousness. As a tentative explanation, we proposed that limited access to democratic channels pushed challengers into a corner, triggering a cycle of contention between them and the government. Moreover, the two indicators we derived also closely relate to each other, with the diversity of the challenger coalition positively and significantly associated with both the overall level of contentiousness of the episode and the contentiousness of the challengers themselves. While we cannot make definitive claims on the particular mechanism driving this relationship, we can safely conclude that episodes that drew in a wide institutional spectrum of challengers also tended to make them act in a more disruptive manner.

Understanding the drivers of such disruptive challenger behaviour is one of the themes that emerge from what we called a "dynamic analysis" of contentious episodes. We laid the ground for this analysis in Chapter 6 where we decomposed episodes into their constituent sequences: chronologically ordered sets of actions connected via their trigger actions. We then focused on two key characteristics of these sequences: their average pace (the average number of days between two consecutive actions) and the complexity of their overall structure within an episode (i.e. the product of their average length and width). Similar to our construction of types of contentiousness, we mapped the distribution of our pace and complexity indicator to locate episodes in different clusters according to whether they scored high or low on these dimensions.

As it turned out, while episodes that move forward quickly could take both complex and simple forms, those that are slow in pace were always of limited complexity. Slow-moving episodes did not develop the momentum necessary for complex interactions between a government and its challengers. When focusing on an episode cluster that included the most rapid and most complex types of interactions, we showed that they are more likely to occur when fueled by high economic and political grievances, especially when coupled with the involvement of external third parties. I.M.F. bailouts, as exemplified in our comparison of two Irish episodes in the chapter, tended to fit the pattern. With a heavy involvement of external third parties (by definition), I.M.F. conditionality tended to result in highly severe policy packages coupled with a widespread sense of loss of control over the democratic process. As a result, action sequences that followed in their wake tended to take the form of rapid "ping-pong" interactions along multiple threads of the conflict, putting the episode in the high-pace–high-complexity end of the spectrum.

## Patterns of Dynamic Interaction

While analyzing episodes in terms of their constituent action sequences was an innovative aspect of our approach in its own right, this also offered us the potential to test and substantiate some of the insights of the social movement literature on the interdependence of actions between governments and challengers. Although the extant literature abounds with propositions on such empirical regularities (e.g. the "law of coercive responsiveness" (Davenport, 2007) or "repression works"), most findings are highly context-specific. Lacking the sort of large-n systematic dataset we have provided, they are inherently incapable of offering generalizable patterns of action dynamics. In Part III of this volume we thus attempted to overcome this limitation by focusing on the particular relationship between the actions of the contending parties, relying on the action sequences and the notion of actor-specific action lags that we constructed and utilized for statistical analysis.

Unsurprisingly, we indeed found that what emerged as a statistical relationship in the full set of cases turned out to be highly contingent on episode-specific characteristics. Chapter 8 investigated these relationships in the full sample of episodes. We found that in addition to a fairly robust path-dependence dynamics guiding the behavior of the adversaries with a given action strategy likely to be followed by similar action strategies in the future, governments and challengers also responded to the cooperative overtures of the opposing side by themselves turning to more cooperative action forms. When all this was aided by explicit attempts to mediate between the adversaries by third parties, what we called a "concession–cooperation–constructive mediation" nexus emerged from the data, surprisingly suggesting a more cooperative form of interdependence than much of the literature that focuses on the dynamics of conflict. In contrast, the notion of threat that permeates much of the literature received-comparatively weaker support. Although our statistical point estimates did suggest that governments tended to ramp up their repressive repertoires in response to threat by challengers (operationalized as disruptive mobilization forms), in general the estimated differences were nonsignificant and we hardly found evidence of a generalized tit-for-tat pattern of reciprocal responses.

When examining particular subsets of cases, we showed that the regularities in the interdependence of actions largely depended on contextual conditions in general, and on actor configurations in particular. In Chapter 9 we focused on the governmental side of the equation by examining how governments react to the threats posed by the challengers depending on the type of challenger organizations that the government faced and on the partisan composition of governments. We found that the cooperative behavior of governments in the form of concessions that we uncovered in Chapter 8 was largely restricted to episodes dominated by the kind of adversaries they were most familiar with – parties and trade unions – and therefore were likely to have found the most effective ways for coping. We called this kind of government behaviour a "divide-and-rule" strategy because governments may strategically choose those adversaries to whom they grant concessions in an attempt to put a wedge within the challenger coalition. Moreover, these concessions were also more likely to be extracted from left-wing (but not from right-wing) governments when they fared poorly in the polls. Also, beneficial third-party mediation effects that we uncovered in the general analysis of the previous chapter only applied to partisan episodes – and even in these episodes they turn out to be weak. Therefore, what emerged as a cooperative nexus between governments and challengers was heavily contingent on a complex relationship between the type of challenger, partisan composition, and electoral prospects.

The same applies to the notion that the governments responded to increasing threat by stepping up repression. Thus, it was only right-wing but not left-wing governments that tended to resort more frequently to repression when facing electoral threat. In addition to unpopularity, internal divisions also made governments more vulnerable to challengers. Accordingly, divided governments tended to be more repressive and make fewer concessions than undivided governments. More detailed analyses of the German episodes suggested that the impact of the government's composition was further modified by factors such as the federalist structure of the state and international pressure, which introduced additional stakeholders.

Third-party actors generally had only a limited effect in the episodes we studied, but some of the effects were actually quite unexpected. Thus, surprisingly, we found for union-driven episodes that mediation by third-party actors actually contributed to the repression of challengers and to the limitation of concessions. As a more detailed analysis clarified, it was above all the support of the government by international allies that turned out to be a mixed blessing during the Great Recession. Especially in the union-driven episodes in southern Europe, the governments found themselves between Scylla and Charybdis, i.e. between a domestic challenge and international pressure. The international "support" typically put the governments under heavy pressure to adopt the austerity proposals that were the price to be paid for international support. Such pressure increased the governments' propensity to stick to their proposal, to make no substantive concessions at all, and to increase the repression of domestic challengers.

We observed similar context-conditionalities on the other side of the government–challenger interaction dynamics: the action repertoire of challengers in response to government tactics. Chapter 10 focused on the effect of government repression – in the relatively rare cases it occurred – on the propensity of challengers to radicalize or, for that matter, deradicalize. In a sense, this set-up provided a mirror logic to the notion of challenger threats. In the same way that a disruptive mobilization was seen as a threat to a government's sense of stability and electoral viability, government repression might threaten the cohesion and the organizational integrity of challenger groups as the prospect of violence (or simply legal or verbal stigmatization) might have deterred some of the members from participating.

In fact, the most visible patterns emerged in the usual suspect of Greece and pointed towards deradicalization in line with the "repression works" perspective. In response to police repression, Greek challengers gradually shifted toward less violent action forms. More generally, and similar to the findings from Chapter 9, we found that actor characteristics play a mediating role between government repression and challenger responses. More institutionalized types of challenger organizations, namely opposition parties, tended to disengage from the protest arena and revert back to their routine, institutional channels to voice their opposition when facing repression. As for the partisan composition of the government, repression under center-right cabinets (but not under center-left cabinets) tended to have a dampening impact on certain challenger mobilization forms, such as petitions and other direct-democratic channels. Overall, therefore, the impact of the action repertoire of one party in the contention spectrum on the action repertoire of its adversary was heavily contingent on the type of challenger organizations and the type of government involved in a debate.

## Milestones and Outcomes

Inevitably, our statistical analysis of interaction dynamics among governments, challengers, and third parties treated all actions as equal. When it comes to understanding the key milestones and the ultimate outcome of these episodes, however, one must be attentive to some of the key actions that determine the flow of events and the final outcome of the policy debate. Two of our chapters took up this task: Chapter 7 focused on government responsiveness and Chapter 11 focusing on turning points. To understand government responsiveness, we placed government concessions at the center of our analysis but we made a distinction between substantive concessions (i.e. policy concessions) and procedural concessions that signify a government's actions toward recognizing challengers as relevant and legitimate interlocutors. Although one may be understandably sceptical about the practical relevance of such procedural concessions, it is important to keep in mind that such symbolic victories by challengers may make or break their very viability as organizations.

Accordingly, we built on Gamson's (1975) framework to characterize episodes according to whether substantive or procedural responsiveness (or neither or both) occurred. A complete withdrawal of the policy proposal occurred in only one of our episodes. Somewhat paradoxically, the self-proclaimed standard-bearer of European illiberalism, the Orban government withdrew its "Internet Tax" proposal in response to popular mobilization on the streets of Budapest. That said, the share of episodes where the government did not display any form of responsiveness was also rare (six episodes, four of which were institutional ones). The typical government behavior was therefore partial recognition of challenger demands, which, however. rarely touched upon the core of the policy debate. We referred to this type of responsiveness on the margin as "window-dressing." Among the tools that the challenger organizations used – with varying success – to obtain concessions from the government were referenda (such as the Brexit episode in the U.K. and the Impeachment episode in Romania) and constitutional review by the courts, as in the case of the 2009 Latvian austerity measures. In accounting for the episode-specific correlates of outcomes, we highlighted episode severity as a determinant of responsiveness: in highly severe episodes, governments were under pressure to provide procedural responsiveness to challengers. However, these highly severe episodes also tended to be those under high external constraints (market pressure, international creditors etc.), so whatever goodwill the government attempted to signal toward the challengers was unlikely to go much beyond the "window-dressing" outcome, with few substantive concessions granted.

In addition to government concessions, which may or may not indicate substantive changes in the policy proposal, we also focused on another set of key actions that changed the overall nature of contention, either by opening up the debate to various directions or by narrowing multiple threads of conflict in a central one. Drawing on Abbott's (2001) work on sequence analysis in the context of life course studies in sociology, we referred to these actions in Chapter 11 as turning points. According to the two types outlined above, we differentiated between points of opening and points of closure. We found that an overwhelming majority of these turning points were government actions – by way of governments sticking to their policy without either repressing challengers or granting concessions to them. Such actions often occurred via the formal steps in the policy-making process (cabinet decisions, legislative steps, etc.). We have also shown that these turning points not only changed the structure of contention (by definition), but they could also be used to demarcate various phases of the episodes in an empirically well-grounded manner. As we statistically showed – and qualitatively illustrated via the Sarkozy–Fillon episode in France – the phases indeed differed in terms of the most prevalent actors and the type of actions they undertook. Interestingly, we discovered a pattern of escalation throughout the episodes, with cooperation gradually giving way to conflict from one phase to another.

Finally, as we already indicated above, the last chapter of our volume (Chapter 12) provided an example of how our dataset could be used by scholars predisposed toward the narrative tradition. It demonstrated how our approach could be applied to the analysis of a single case. In doing so, it went beyond our most basic conceptualization of our empirical universe as a series of policy episodes and connected them via what we referred to as the continuous and sustained anti-bailout campaign between the years of 2010 and 2015. By revealing the interconnectedness of the Greek episodes, not just in terms of the policy content but also in the composition and tactics of the challenger coalition, this chapter showed that nothing in our approach prevents the analyst from linking individual episodes in a more encompassing narrative. Based on this single case, Chapter 12 illustrated many of our findings in more detail than any of the previous chapters could have possibly done. Most importantly, it showed how the mutual perception of threat between governments and challengers that formed the backbone of the dynamic analyses in Chapters 8–10 was not represented merely by the individual actions of the contending actors but culminated in a series of events, or in what we defined as two key mechanisms in line with the DoC tradition (McAdam et al, 2001): elite breakdown (as in Goldstone 1998) and conflict expansion (as in Schattschneider, 1960).

## WHERE DO WE GO FROM HERE?

At the end of this volume, it is well to recall the scope conditions of our results. We were studying austerity policy episodes (plus some institutional reforms) during the Great Recession in Europe. These policies were especially drastic redundant and most challenged in southern Europe (see Kriesi et al. 2020). Within southern Europe, Greece stood out as the country with the most imposing protest wave and, as we have confirmed in the present study, with the most contentious episodes of all the European countries. While the south of Europe in general, and Greece in particular, were special in terms of overall amount of contention and in the contentiousness of the challenges addressed to the government, the patterns of interaction uncovered in our analyses and the outcome of the challenges was basically similar across Europe. We generally found rather civilized interaction patterns, little violence on the part of the challengers, and limited repression on the part of the governments. The challengers were mainly conventional political actors – unions above all but also political parties – and in terms of the action repertoires that the two adversaries applied, it was largely "business as usual" (see also Kriesi and Wueest 2020).

In terms of the outcomes of the episodes of contention, it was largely a lack of success by the challengers. The governments overwhelmingly stuck to their original proposals. The defining moment of the whole period took place in summer 2015 in Greece: on July 5, the Greek voters in a referendum, following the advice of their own government, rejected the bailout conditions imposed by the international creditors by a majority of 61 to 39 percent. Within a week, however, on July 13, the very same government that had recommended a "No" vote, signed the bailout with even harsher conditions than those rejected by the voters. As this crucial series of events (which were part of the fourth Greek economic policy episode) made more than clear for public audiences across Europe, the maneuvering space for the national governments during the Great Recession was highly constrained indeed.

During this period, as a result of forces beyond the control of the governments, the patterns of government reactions were only weakly related to challenger actions and third-party interventions. Even if we could have specified these patterns to some extent by introducing context characteristics based on the prevailing actor configurations, the effects we found are far from overwhelming. During the episodes we studied, the constraints imposed on the governments by the economic situation and by international stakeholders were such that they mainly had to stick to their original proposals irrespective of the dynamics of interaction that unfolded in the domestic political arenas – whether in the party arena, the administrative arena, or the protest arena. The most threatening challenger actions were repressed, and concessions, to the extent that they were forthcoming, proved to be mostly symbolic gestures. Similarly, challenger actions evaporated eventually and third-party actors' interventions, with the exception of the interventions by international actors, tended to be inconsequential as well. We attribute the absence of strong results in terms of the key interaction patterns and of the episodes' outcomes above all to our having chosen to study economic policy episodes during this particular period in the European context, thereby limiting the scope of the patterns of interaction covered. While we have shown that our approach worked for this particular set of episodes, we believe that the episodes we studied constituted a particularly "hard case" for what we are proposing. It is likely that our approach will provide stronger results for episodes that are more open-ended and less dominated by conventional actors, fought out in less conventional action repertoires, and under less democratic regimes.

In addition to the limitation of the scope of the episodes covered, there is also an inherent substantive limitation to the generalizability of the results of this type of analysis. As we have pointed out before, the generalizability of inter-action patterns between governments and their challengers finds its limitation in the complexity of the context conditions that have to be taken into consider-ation in an attempt to account for them. In addition to the factors considered in our different chapters, there were other domestic structures such as federalism (as in the case of Germany), the division of power between the cabinet and the president (as in the cases of Romania or Latvia), or the influence of courts (which ruled in favor of the government's policy reforms in several cases, but which at times also turned against the governments as in the case of the 2009 Latvian austerity measures) and referenda (as in the case of Brexit) that have to be taken into consideration as well. With the data at hand, we were not able to systematically include the full range of relevant context conditions in our analyses. Although we could rely on more than 2,000 actions per actor-type for the analysis of the different interaction patterns in our sixty episodes, we quickly hit the limits of the data once we focused on a specific pair of actions (e.g. government repression versus radical challenger action) in a context characterized by a combination of multiple factors. The number of cases for a given pair-context combination diminishes rapidly; for this reason we had to make some hard choices with regard to the number of variables and categories per variable included in a given analysis. A more detailed analysis based on a larger number of data points would enable testing the various hypotheses in a more encompassing way than was possible here.

Limitations due to the scope of the episodes covered and data constraints can be overcome in future research, assuming it can rely on the resources (access to native-language media, availability of native-language coders etc.) necessary to provide the relevant data. For the time being, our approach is rather resource intensive, which limits its applicability. Technical progress in terms of data collection may make it easier to implement and allow for overcoming the limits we have indicated here.

There are other types of limitations of our approach that, we believe, can be more easily overcome, however. Perhaps most importantly, as mentioned above, we selected a very particular subtype of policy episode with the govern-ment's policy proposal serving as a conceptual anchor for the unfolding of the contentious episode it triggered . When extending our scheme to other types of cases, the codes might need to be adapted to the possibility that there might not be any government policy proposal to begin with and it would be challenger demands that would form the conceptual pillar of the codebook. For instance, in the case of bottom-up outbursts of popular mobilization over recent years, such as Extinction Rebellion, FridaysforFuture and related protests in general with Swedish climate activist Greta Thunberg as a common figurehead, there is no underlying government proposal to speak of. If anything, it is governments' inaction that the climate change protests were targeted against and, as such, challenges were proactive rather than reactive. One way the coding scheme could incorporate this setup is that instead of the government proposal, challenger demands would serve as the reference point. Instead of "government sticking to proposal," "government dismissing challengers' demands," "challengers insisting on demands" could reflect continuity in the protagonists' action strategies ,while government concessions would now take the form of promised actions against climate change instead of stepping back from earlier proposals according to our original scheme.

Furthermore, our three-way typology between governments, challengers, and third parties need not be set in stone because other relevant actor types might have an autonomous role in the episode. For instance, in the context of the Black Lives Matter movement that dominated the headlines at multiple flashpoints over the last few years in the United States and beyond, it might be justified to treat state authorities, as distinct from the federal or even local governments, with their own action repertoire set . A similar case could be made for separating out the coercive apparatus as a separate actor type in cases of popular uprisings against political regimes, as most recently evidenced in the streets of Minsk and other Belarussian cities in the wake of the widely alleged electoral fraud in the 2020 presidential elections in Belarus. Whatever set of stylized actor types researchers choose to work with, they need to pay special attention to specifying them in a way that is both exhaustive and parsimonious. When designing the list of action repertoires, researchers should ask themselves whether a graduate student in a political science or related stream could easily assign any relevant action they encounter in the media under one of the action categories.

Another important adjustment that may be necessary when applying our scheme to other contexts concerns timing. The reader may recall that we applied a transparent rule in terms of both the beginning (first announcement of measures) and end (passage of legislation or winding down of contention for an extended period of time) of the policy episode. These criteria work less well in examples sited above, where certain key events proved to be the catalyst. For instance, the recent resurgence of the Black Lives Matter movement can clearly be traced back to the tragic murder of George Floyd by a police officer in Minnesota. Likewise, the Belarusian protests were obviously ignited by the fraudulent election itself. The matter of timing is less clear-cut in the case of environmental protests, where the original trigger is less obvious. In such instances where no universal rule can be conveniently applied, researchers should proceed on a case-by-case basis and try to identify events that served as a reference point during the first steps of mobilization. Although some of these adjustments to our scheme may require substantial prior work, they are a worthy investment in order to extend Contentious Episode Analysis to other, otherwise comparable contexts.

Yet another limitation we need to reckon with concerns one of the important simplifications we decided to introduce: the assumption that actor identity remains constant in terms of the three-way categorization of actors into government, challenger, and third-party categories throughout the entire episode. In particular, the classification criterion hinged on whether a particular actor undertook nonroutine challenges at least once during the episode. While this rule worked well for coding purposes and made the analysis significantly easier to interpret, it is admittedly problematic in the light of the nature of contentious politics. Some actors' identity in fact changes in the course of an episode. While they may act as challengers in the initial phases of the episode, they may shift to the mediating role of third parties later on (or vice versa). Even government actor identities may not be fixed in cases of internal splits in the government or the state. To return to one of the examples above on popular uprisings, when coercive forces defect from the regime and switch sides, they automatically join the challenger coalition themselves. Relaxing our "fixed actor identity" rule could thus be a welcome step forward in future research projects.

Finally, what we consider as one of the main strengths and most important contributions of our method is also its weakness. The construction of actor-specific lags constitutes a key step in the dynamic analysis presented in Part III of the book. The lag construction, however, is a fairly involved process resulting in a sequence file with a complex structure including (in our case) more than 2,000 variables, taking into account all the lags of all the main variables in the core file (the action file). While most of these variables are auxiliary in the sense that they are not used in the dynamic analysis, it is important for researchers wishing to construct similar datasets to acquaint themselves with the logic of a sequence file. Also, it is important to recognize that the lag construction process crucially hinges on the proper identification of the action triggers in a recursive manner. In other words, only with a proper identification of the triggering event of each action can we accurately derive the entire action sequences. In addition to a great deal of labor that needs to be invested to this end, incomplete and often less than explicit references to the triggering actions in the text corpus inevitably necessitate a deep and detailed understanding of the policy episode and occasional informed judgements by the coders. Paradoxically, perhaps, the systematic reconstruction of the sequence of events of a given contentious episode is only possible based on a detailed preliminary understanding of the narrative chronology of the episode in question. Addressing some of these limitations of our proposed middle-ground approach would thus be a most welcome step forward for future scholarship in the study of contentious politics.

# APPENDICES

## Appendix I Detailed description of the policy proposals

Three of the eight international bailouts concern Greece. The first Greek bailout was a memorandum of understanding between Greece and the E.C.B.–EU–I.M.F. Troika, devised to help Greece overcome its debt crisis. In exchange for a rescue loan, Greece committed to adopt fiscal and other structural reforms in the labor market, the product market, and the financial sector. Overall, the program foresaw €30 billion in spending cuts and tax increases. Characteristic of this episode were the sluggish progression of the adoption of the austerity measures, the incapacity of the Greek government to contain the crisis, and the high degree of uncertainty of a European response. The Greek government's announcements of reforms were not only heavily opposed by an array of internal challengers but also continuously undermined by financial speculation and the incessant downgrading of Greece by international rating agencies.

After the midterm adjustment program, required by Greece's creditors to achieve the goals of the first bailout and that we classify as a fiscal reform, the second bailout intervened. This episode included an update of the first bailout in the form of a "multi-law bill," as well as the first steps toward a second bailout between the new technocratic Papademos government (which was installed during this episode) and the creditors. This episode also included negotiations about debt relief and the haircut to privately held Greek bonds. The third Greek bailout phase started with the announcement of the bailout referendum on June 27, 2015. It included the voting of the agreement with the creditors and ended on August 21, 2015 with the announcement of snap elections, one week after the parliament passed the third bailout.

In Portugal, the international bailout constituted the third episode. Following the socialist prime minister's resignation in spring 2011, the caretaker government called for new elections to be held in June and ushered the bailout memorandum through parliament, with the joint agreement of all major parties. In the short term, the memorandum agreement was received with scarcely any public contestation, since public protest was channelled into the June 2011 elections. The latter strongly punished the incumbent socialist government and gave an absolute majority to the centre right. The new government promised to honor the terms of the bailout agreement and adopted the requisite additional severe austerity measures.

The three cases of international bailouts in eastern Europe concern Hungary, Latvia, and Romania. Hungary was one of the first countries to feel the full impact of the financial crisis in 2008. As early as October 2008, its socialist government had to turn to the EU and the I.M.F. for help. The international bailout constituted the first Hungarian episode. In return for the bailout, the government had to adopt austerity measures, the most prominent features of which were cuts to the thirteenth-month salary of public servants and restrictions to thirteenth-month pensions. These early cuts were followed by additional measures in spring 2009, including an increase to personal income tax, tax cuts for employers, increases to VAT and corporate taxes, and the raising of the retirement age to sixty-five. Prime Minister Ferenc Gyurcsány eventually resigned over the unsuccessful management of the austerity measures and the crisis in general.

Not much later, the government in Latvia, after protracted negotiations, had to agree to an I.M.F. rescue deal centered on maintaining the exchange rate peg to the euro in December 2008 – the first episode considered for this country. The deal implied the restructuring of the Latvian banking system and the adoption of a series of austerity measures. The latter included severe cuts in public spending that, among other things, reduced salaries in the public sector by some 25 percent over a period of two years. Particularly painful was the issue of old-age pensions, which the I.M.F. believed were excessively high and in need of trimming down. The proposed budget cuts reinvigorated the protracted political crisis, and the Latvian prime minister was forced to resign in February 2009 – the first "victim" of the international bailouts in Europe.

The first two Romanian episodes covered the international bailout, which occurred in summer 2009, and the measures linked to it. The I.M.F. and EU agreement gave Romania a €20 billion line of credit. The main points of contention referred to the conditions imposed on Romania by the bailout. Labor unions and opposition parties strongly opposed the bailout decision and the requisite budgetary adjustments. The fiscal measures imposed by the I.M.F. bailout made up the second episode. These measures included a 25 percent reduction in salaries and a 15 percent reduction in pensions and were adopted in May 2010.

Apart from Iceland, Ireland was the only northwestern European country that had to accept an international bailout. The Great Recession hit Ireland fast and hard: The country entered into recession in fall 2008, while most O.E.C.D. countries did so only in 2009. The Irish crisis evolved in four acts: from a banking crisis that was largely caused by the structural problems of the pre-crisis Irish growth model to a fiscal crisis (as a result of the fateful bank guarantee that marked the first key event of the Irish story); from a fiscal crisis to a public-debt crisis (leading to the Irish bailout); and from the public debt crisis to a domestic political crisis (see Salo 2017). The financial crisis immediately affected Irish finances and imposed the bank bailout and a series of austerity measures that were passed in October 2008. While the Irish state saved its banks, the E.C.B.–EU–I.M.F. Troika saved Ireland – with harsh conditions. After much denial, Ireland formally requested financial support from the E.F.S.F. (European Financial Stability Facility) and the I.M.F. in November 2010. On November 28, the Troika and the Irish government agreed to a €85 billion rescue deal.

## BANK BAILOUTS

We have already mentioned the Spanish bailout, the only bank bailout in southern Europe, and the Irish bank bailout. The other bank bailouts took place in the U.K. and in Germany. The British bank bailout was a potentially large operation. It was announced by the Labour government on October 8, 2008 and involved a rescue package totaling some £500 billion (approximately €590 billion). It was designed to restore market confidence and help stabilize the British banking system. The remaining three bank bailouts refer to three *German* episodes: The first one was triggered by the Hypo Real Estate crisis and again included a large bailout package to the tune of €480 billion to guarantee domestic bank losses. The German and the British initial bailouts were both assessed as of medium severity because neither was imposed by international agencies, nor accompanied by public budget cuts. The second German episode, in May 2009, was the "bad bank scheme," which would allow banks to cleanse their balance sheets of toxic assets by placing them into so-called bad banks for up to twenty years. The third German bank bailout episode related to the financial consequences for Germany of the third Greek bailout.

As we have already seen, the Irish bank bailout was part of the first Irish episode, but this episode also included a cluster of highly severe fiscal measures, which is why we classified it among the fiscal measures. The episode started during the night of September 29–30, 2008 with the fateful decision by the Irish government to issue a blanket guarantee covering all liabilities of five Irish financial institutions. This decision, which implied that all bank creditors were underwritten by the government, opened the Irish state to estimated potential liabilities of €400 billion. Hypothetical at first, the costs of the rescue mounted as the banks' losses grew, creating a gigantic hole in Irish public finances that had to be plugged eventually by the international bailout.

## FISCAL MEASURES

Fiscal measures, as we have already observed, were the most widespread measures. In southern Europe, they were particularly stringent. In Greece, the case in point was the midterm adjustment, which intervened in the aftermath of the first bailout, and that we introduced in some detail in Chapter 1. In Portugal, fiscal measures included three austerity packages – the PECI-II and

PECIII-IV of the socialist government, and the austerity package of the PSD–CDS–PP government. In Spain, the Rajoy government adopted an austerity package in 2012 that introduced the harshest cuts in recent Spanish history, reducing spending by the order of €65 billion over two years. All these packages were very severe. Other fiscal measures included two packages of medium severity: Zapatero's more limited 2010 austerity package and the equally limited clutch of austerity measures adopted by the Italian Berlusconi government shortly before its fall in 2011.

In northwestern Europe, fiscal measures included three of the four French, British, and Irish episodes, and one German episode. In France, two successive governments struggling with the same crisis together introduced a series of four austerity packages: two by Sarkozy's and two by Hollande's government. Since the first Sarkozy–Fillon austerity package in 2010 was focused on the pension reform, we classified it as a structural reform. The other three packages, however, were classified as fiscal measures, two of which were very severe, while Hollande's first package was much less incisive and classified as of low severity. The three British episodes all refer to the spending review of the Conservative–Liberal government that took office in May 2010. They included the new coalition government's June 2010 austerity package, the measure concerning university tuition fees in October 2010, and the adoption of welfare reform legislation, the Welfare Reform Act in February 2012. Except for the measure regarding tuition fees, which was considered as low severity, these measures were classified as highly severe. The one German episode among the fiscal measures refers to the first Economic Adjustment Program for Greece, which consisted of €110 billion. The German share amounted to €22.4 billion in the form of an interest-bearing and repayable loan provided by the development bank KfW (Kreditanstalt für Wiederaufbau). In connection with the loan for Greece, the German government also proposed budget cuts in Germany that were passed by the Bundestag in September 2010, and which is why this package was classified as very severe.

Two of the three Irish fiscal measures were highly severe and were linked to the bank bailout and the international bailout. The third, less severe, measure concerned the water charge. The bank bailout austerity measures passed in October 2008 included an increase to VAT, as well as tax increases on petrol (gasoline, alcohol, and tobacco; the ending of automatic entitlement to a medical card for people over seventy; an income levy for workers; severe cuts in healthcare and education; a reintroduction of third-level university fees; and a tax on nonprincipal private residencies. As predictions for further increases in the budget deficit were put forward, the emergency budget passed in April 2009 introduced new austerity measures. The second austerity package refers to the 2010 budget, which was delivered immediately after the announcement of the international bailout. The budget introduced cuts to decrease the national deficit by €4 billion. The main measures concerned a 4 percent cut in social welfare payments (excluding old-age pensions); decreases in child benefit and jobseekers' allowance; 5–10 percent cuts in public-sector pay; the intro-duction of a carbon tax, as well as a series of additional measures including a cut in the prime minister's salary. The third Irish austerity proposal concerned the water tax, which has been a constant element in Irish politics for decades. The commitment to charge once again for water (free in Ireland since 1997) was included in the memorandum signed by Ireland and its international lenders in 2010. Then, the Fianna Fail-led government promised to have water charges in place by 2013 and to shift responsibility from local authorities to a new water utility. The new FG/Labour government taking office in March 2011 kept this promise (despite Labour's electoral pledge to take it back). The controversy became more intense in 2014 when the Commission for Energy Regulation announced the exact figures for the water charge.

In central and eastern Europe, there were three fiscal packages in Latvia, and two fiscal packages each in Hungary and in Romania, but no such measures were introduced in Poland. Just as in the case of Ireland, the global financial crisis brought Latvia's preexisting vulnerabilities to a head. Years of unsustain-ably high growth and large current account deficits coalesced into a financial and balance-of-payments crisis. All four Latvian economic episodes dealt with the management of this crisis. After the initial bailout by the I.M.F., which intervened in December 2008, the next three episodes followed in rapid succes-sion, with all involving the adoption of fiscal packages linked to the payment of installments to the I.M.F. The latter included severe cuts to public spending that, among other things, reduced salaries in the public sector by some 25 per-cent over a period of two years in 2009–2010. Particularly painful was the issue of old-age pensions, which the I.M.F. believed to be excessively high and in need of trimming down (Ikstens 2010: 1043). The first set of measures was classified as of high, the remaining two of medium severity.

Similarly, the two Romanian fiscal measures were closely linked to their I.M.F. bailout. The first set of fiscal measures imposed by the I.M.F. was also very severe and included a 25 percent reduction of salaries as well as a 15 percent reduction in pensions. It was adopted in May 2010. The next set of measures followed immediately and focused on the additional I.M.F. loan that the government was forced to accept in July 2010. This loan came attached with additional austerity measures of medium severity. In contrast, the two Hungarian fiscal measures were not imposed by the I.M.F. They were both taken by the Fidesz government that had come to power in April 2010. The first set of measures refers to Orban's first economic "action plan," which consisted of twenty-nine items of overall medium severity. The most controversial parts of Orbán's plan were public-sector salary caps and the so-called bank tax, which was opposed by the I.M.F. and the E.U and led to Hungary's break with the I.M.F. when the contract concluded by the previous government expired. The second measure (of low severity) refers to the so-called internet tax that Orban attempted to introduce once he was reelected in June 2014, but was withdrawn after the tax met the biggest wave of protest since 2006.

## STRUCTURAL REFORMS

Finally, there is the category of structural reforms. These concern either the pension systems or the labor code of the respective countries or both. All four Polish episodes fall into this category, as well as three of the Italian episodes, plus one episode each from Hungary, Romania, Spain, and France. Overall, structural measures were the least severe of the measures adopted to counteract the economic crises. Only one of these reforms has been considered of high severity, all the others were of either low or medium severity. These measures were not backed by international pressure and met with strong domestic resistance from the targeted groups. These factors may explain why they were generally less severe than the bailouts and the fiscal measures linked to them. Pension reforms were implemented in Poland (twice), Hungary, Italy, Spain, and France. Exceptionally, the Italian pension reform was considered as high severity. This reform had been introduced by the technocratic Monti government as part of a wider package. The Monti government, which came to power in November 2011, essentially adopted two main policy packages: the Salva-Italia (Save Italy) decree and the Cresci-Italia (Grow Italy) decree. These two packages, introduced respectively on December 5, 2011 and January 20, 2012, had the objective of recovering the state of public finances and of the economy. The Salva-Italia decree was introduced very quickly due to economic emergency. It put more emphasis on the public finances and was essentially an austerity package, whose most important aspect was pension reform ("legge Fornero"), while the Cresci-Italia decree put more emphasis on the liberalization of the economy. The policy process of the second decree was comparatively slower, and there were many more negotiations and summits between the government and the various interest groups (employer organizations, trade unions, etc.). Importantly, the second decree also contained measures aiming at reforming the labor market. The final act in Monti's reform effort came in March 2012, when he presented his proposals for the liberalization of the labor market. A softened version of the proposal was adopted in June 2012. From that point on, austerity no longer dominated the agenda of Italian politics. The reform of the labor market, however, has remained a key issue of Italian politics. Two of the other Italian episodes were also concerned with the reform of the labor market – one under the Berlusconi, and the other under the Renzi government (the famous "Jobs act").

As already mentioned, Poland managed exceptionally well through the crisis. Its quick recovery, with declining unemployment rates from 2011 onward, was a result of painful measures of external devaluation implemented by the national government (Walter 2016). None of the four Polish episodes was considered as high severity. Two of them – the first and the fourth – mainly concerned the labor market and were classified as low severity, while the other two focused on pensions and were rated as medium severity. The labor market measures were aimed at greater flexibility for labor contracts (a similar set of measures was also adopted in Romania), while the pension reforms were designed to alleviate the fiscal pressure. A first set of "technical" measures changed the pension system to alleviate budgetary problems; a second set, which was part of the austerity measures introduced immediately after the second Tusk government took office in fall 2011, raised the retirement age from sixty-five to sixty-seven.

The restructuring of Hungary's pension system, announced by Orbán in October 2010, resembles the "technical" restructuring of the Polish system. It amounted to the transfer of the mandatory private pension-fund contributions to the state to allow the Orbán government to reduce the central budget deficit to the 3 percent threshold necessary to obtain Hungary's removal from the EU's Excessive Deficit Procedure. The French pension reform mainly amounted to increasing the retirement age by two years, from sixty to sixty-two. In addition to this pension reform, the first Sarkozy–Fillon austerity package in 2010 included the freezing of public spending for three years.

## THE INSTITUTIONAL REFORMS

The bulk of the institutional reforms were of medium severity. Only two were assessed as low severity – the German debt brake and the Spanish constitutional amendment; another two as highly severe – the Brexit referendum and the reform of the Polish Constitutional Court. The case of the Brexit referendum refers to the first phase of the protracted Brexit process that amounts to the most important institutional change for the entire EU during the period covered. The beginning of the events that eventually led to the decisive referendum in June 2016 can be traced back to 2012, when Prime Minister David Cameron dismissed the demands for a referendum, yet indicated that a referendum could be held in the future. In a speech in 2013, he promised that if the Conservative Party were to win the next general election (2015), the government would renegotiate the terms of the U.K. membership of the EU, and then ask the people whether, under these new conditions, they wanted the U.K. to stay or leave. Once the Conservatives had won the general election in 2015, the renegotiations took place in late 2015/early 2016, and the British obtained some limited concessions from the EU in the areas of economic governance, competitiveness, sovereignty, and immigration. The episode we look at for Brexit covers the period from February 2016, when the European Council adopted the arrangement with the U.K., to the immediate aftermath of the referendum vote on June 23, 2016.

The other institutional reforms were highly diverse. Three reforms were more or less directly related to the management of the economic crises. They include the German debt brake (*Schuldenbremse*) adopted in 2009, the Spanish constitutional amendment adopted by the Zapatero government in summer 2011 that enshrined the obligation for all levels of government to adjust their conduct to the principle of budgetary stability, and Latvia's entry into the

Eurozone in July 2013 that occurred in spite of a lack of popular enthusiasm. It was made possible because the established ethnic and anti-corruption divisions effectively rendered economic policy alternatives politically unrealistic (Eihmanis 2018).

Two cases of institutional reform were directly imposed by the Troika, and one represents a disguised attempt to achieve similar goals without foreign pressure. The cases imposed by the Troika concerned the shutdown of ERT, the Greek public broadcaster, which implied the firing of 2,650 employees in June 2013, and the municipal reform in Portugal, resulting from the memorandum agreement with the Troika aimed at reducing the costs of local administrations. The most contentious aspect of the reform was the reduction in the number of parishes. The disguised attempt to reduce the national deficit without foreign intervention refers to the French decentralization reform. This reform, undertaken by the PS (Socialist Party) government, started in April 2013 and took roughly two years. It aimed at extending some of the competences of local authorities, while centralizing the allocation of financial resources, thereby allowing reductions in public spending.

Two cases concerned illiberal constitutional reforms in Hungary and in Poland. The Hungarian case refers to the reform of the media law that was part of a larger process, during which the new Fidesz government, which had gained a two-thirds majority in the 2010 elections, used its new position to adopt a new constitution in 2011 and to cow the media. The Polish case concerns the reform of the constitutional court by the newly elected PiS government that, in December 2015, attempted to control the constitutional court by making its own appointments to the court, arguing that the previous government's appointments of five judges were unconstitutional.

Two cases of reforms – the Italian and the Romanian – were undertaken in relation to the wheelings and dealings of key political leaders. In Italy, the judicial reform concerned mainly the legal problems of Prime Minister Silvio Berlusconi at the time. Throughout the entire period of the fourth Berlusconi government (from May 2008 to November 2011), judicial reform was repeatedly announced by the government, and just as repeatedly became a source of conflict between political and judicial actors. After numerous delays, the reform bill arrived in the parliament but did not reach the end of the approval process due to the fall of the government. The only part of the reform that was approved concerned the so-called Lodo Alfano, which guaranteed the postponement of Berlusconi's judicial trials. The Romanian case covered the referendum about the impeachment of President Basescu in summer 2012. As part of the conflict between the center-right president and the center-left government in the semi-presidential system of Romania, the parliament voted in favor of impeaching President Basescu, triggering the holding of a referendum within a month. The quorum for the referendum vote was not sufficient, the president refused to resign, and the Constitutional Court eventually decided to invalidate the impeachment referendum and to reinstate Basescu as president.

Finally, the Irish abolition of the senate, the second chamber of Ireland's parliament, was an anodyne reform unrelated to the crisis. It was proposed by the newly elected FG Labor government to increase government effectiveness in March 2011, and was eventually rejected in a referendum held in October 2013.

# Appendix II Additional information on policy episodes

TABLE A3.1. *Coding rules for severity measurement*

| Episode type | Criteria | Coding rule |
|---|---|---|
| Fiscal measures (with or without Troika bailouts) | Aimed spending/revenue/deficit reduction (as a % of GDP) – small or large? | High severity if 3 of 5 criteria satisfied |
| | Was it an across the board cut (or did it just target a particular social group/ program)? | Medium severity if 1 or 2 satisfied |
| | Was it imposed by external creditors? | Low severity if none satisfied |
| | Was it coupled with structural reforms (e.g. privatization, liberalization etc.)? | |
| | Did the bulk of the measures fall on socially vulnerable groups? | |
| **Structural reforms** | | |
| *Labor market* | Did it imply a **significant** reduction in job security? | High severity if 2 satisfied |
| | Did it imply a reduction in unemployment protection generosity? | Medium severity if 1 satisfied |
| | Did it imply a constitutional amendment? | Low severity if none satisfied |
| *Pension market* | Did it imply a rise in the statutory pension age? | High severity if 3 satisfied |
| | Did it imply a reduction in pension payments (changed indexation rules, replacement rates, etc.) | Low severity if none satisfied |
| | Did it imply a paradigmatic change in the pension system with direct costs for existing stakeholders? | |
| | Did it curtail early retirement? | |
| Bank and international bailouts | Was a significant amount of public money actually spent (or only guaranteed/other measures)? If so, please specify amounts. | High severity if 2 satisfied |
| | Was it coupled with immediate cuts in the public budget? | Medium severity if one satisfied |
| | Were international creditors involved? | Low severity if none satisfied |

TABLE A3.1. *(continued)*

| Episode type | Criteria | Coding rule |
|---|---|---|
| Institutional reforms | Did it **fundamentally** change the constitutional order of things? | High severity if 3 satisfied |
| | Did it impose **direct costs** on a **sizeable** group of stakeholders? | Medium severity if 1 or 2 satisfied |
| | Did it imply a concentration of power in the hands of the government? | Low if none satisfied |
| | Did it restrict fundamental human rights? | |

TABLE A3.2. *List of governments in the twelve countries during the period covered*

| Country | Start date | Cabinet name | Party name | Left or right | Episode |
|---|---|---|---|---|---|
| France | 18 Jun-07 | Fillon II | UMP | right | 1 |
| France | 14 Nov-10 | Fillon III | UMP | right | 2 |
| France | 15 May-12 | Ayrault I | Socialist Party | left | 3 |
| France | 18 Jun-12 | Ayrault II | Socialist Party | left | inst/4 |
| France | 31 Mar-14 | Valls I | Socialist Party | left | |
| Germany | 22 Nov-05 | Merkel I | CDU-SPD | grand coal | 1/inst/2 |
| Germany | 28 Oct-09 | Merkel II | CDU-FDP | right | 3 |
| Germany | 17 Dec-13 | Merkel III | CDU-SPD | grand coal | 4 |
| Greece | 1 Oct-07 | Karamanlis Kos II | New Democracy | right | |
| Greece | 6 Oct-09 | Papandreou G | PASOK | left | 1/2/3 |
| Greece | 11 Nov-11 | Papademos | no party affiliation | technocratic | |
| Greece | 16 May-12 | Pikramenos | no party affiliation | technocratic | |
| Greece | 20 Jun-12 | Samaras I | New Democracy | right | |
| Greece | 25 Jun-13 | Samaras II | New Democracy | right | inst |
| Greece | 27 Jan-15 | Tsipras I | Syriza | left | 4 |
| Greece | 21-Sep-15 | Tsipras II | Syriza | left | |
| Hungary | 2 May-08 | Gyurcsany III | Hungarian Socialist Party | left | 1 |
| Hungary | 14 Apr-09 | Bajnai | no party affiliation | technocratic | |
| Hungary | 29 May-10 | Orban II | Fidesz | right | 2/3/inst |
| Hungary | 10 May-14 | Orban III | Fidesz - | right | 4 |
| Ireland | 7 May-08 | Cowen | Fianna Fail | right | 1/2/3 |
| Ireland | 9 Mar-11 | Kenny I | Fine Gael | right | inst/4 |

*(continued)*

TABLE A3.2. *(continued)*

| Country | Start date | Cabinet name | Party name | Left or right | Episode |
|---|---|---|---|---|---|
| Italy | 8 May-08 | Berlusconi IV | The People of Freedom | right | inst/1/2 |
| Italy | 16 Nov-11 | Monti | technocratic | technocratic | 3 |
| Italy | 27 Apr-13 | Letta I | Democratic Party | left | |
| Italy | 18 Nov-13 | Letta II | Democratic Party | left | |
| Italy | 22 Feb-14 | Renzi | Democratic Party | left | 4 |
| Latvia | 20 Dec-07 | Godmanis II | Latvian First Party+ | right | 1 |
| Latvia | 26 Feb-09 | Dombrovskis I | New Era | right | 2/3 |
| Latvia | 17 Mar-10 | Dombrovskis II | New Era | right | 4 |
| Latvia | 3 Nov-10 | Dombrovskis III | Unity | right | |
| Latvia | 25 Oct-11 | Dombrovskis IV | Unity | right | inst |
| Latvia | 22 Jan-14 | Straujuma I | Unity | right | |
| Latvia | 5 Nov-14 | Straujuma II | Unity | right | |
| Poland | 16 Nov-07 | Tusk I | Civic Platform | right | 1/2/3 |
| Poland | 18 Nov-11 | Tusk II | Civic Platform | right | 4 |
| Poland | 22 Sep-14 | Kopacz | Civic Platform | right | |
| Poland | 16 Nov-15 | Szydlo | Law and Justice | right | inst |
| Portugal | 12 Mar-05 | Socrates I | Socialist Party | left | |
| Portugal | 26 Oct-09 | Socrates II | Socialist Party | left | 1/2/3 |
| Portugal | 15 Jun-11 | Passos Coelho I | Social Democratic Party | right | inst/4 |
| Portugal | 30 Oct-15 | Passos Coelho II | Social Democratic Party | right | |
| Portugal | 26 Nov-15 | Costa | Socialist Party | left | |
| Romania | 5 Apr-07 | Popescu-T. III | National Liberal Party | right | |
| Romania | 22 Dec-08 | Boc I | Democratic Liberal Party | right | 1 |
| Romania | 23 Dec-09 | Boc II | Democratic Liberal Party | right | |
| Romania | 19 May-10 | Boc III | Democratic Liberal Party | right | 2/3 |
| Romania | 9 Feb-12 | Ungureanu | Democratic Liberal Party | right | 4 |
| Romania | 7 May-12 | Ponta I | Social Democratic Party | left | inst |
| Romania | 21 Dec-12 | Ponta II | Social Democratic Party | left | |
| Romania | 4 Mar-14 | Ponta III | Social Democratic Party | left | |

TABLE A3.2. *(continued)*

| Country | Start date | Cabinet name | Party name | Left or right | Episode |
|---------|-----------|--------------|-----------|---------------|---------|
| Romania | 15 Dec-14 | Ponta IV | Social Democratic Party | left | |
| Romania | 10 Nov-15 | Ciolos | technocratic | technocratic | |
| Spain | 12 Apr-08 | Zapatero II | PSOE | left | 1/2/inst |
| Spain | 21 Dec-11 | Rajoy I | People's Alliance Party | right | 3/4 |
| Spain | 20 Dec-15 | Rajoy II | People's Alliance Party | right | |
| U.K. | 27 Jun-07 | Brown | Labour | left | 1 |
| U.K. | 11 May-10 | Cameron I | Conservatives | right | 2/3/4 |
| U.K. | 8 May-15 | Cameron II | Conservatives | right | inst |

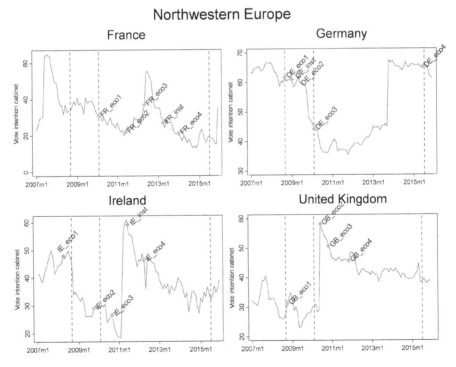

FIGURE A3.1. Government popularity and timing of the episodes (2007–2015), by country and region

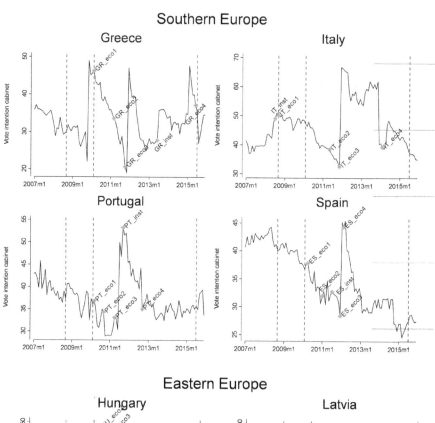

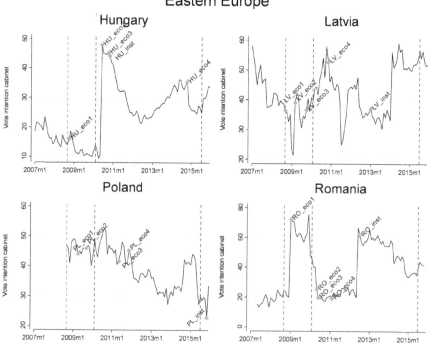

# Appendix III Additional information on action sequences (Chapter 6)

TABLE A6.1. *List of contentious episodes by clusters according to their sequence types*

|  | Slow-simple | Fast-simple | Fast-complex |
|---|---|---|---|
|  | FR_eco1 | FR_eco2 | GER_eco1 |
|  | FR_inst | FR_eco3 | GR_eco1 |
|  | IRE_inst | GER_eco2 | GR_eco2 |
|  | ITA_eco1 | GER_eco3 | GR_eco3 |
|  | ITA_inst | GER_eco4 | GR_eco4 |
|  | PL_eco2 | GER_inst | GR_inst |
|  | PL_eco3 | HUN_eco1 | IRE_eco2 |
|  | PL_eco4 | HUN_eco2 | IRE_eco3 |
|  | PL_inst | HUN_eco3 | IRE_eco4 |
|  | PT_inst | HUN_eco4 | IT_eco3 |
|  |  | HUN_inst | IT_eco4 |
|  |  | IRE_eco1 | PT_eco2 |
|  |  | ITA_eco2 | ROM_eco1 |
|  |  | LV_eco1 | ROM_eco2 |
|  |  | LV_eco2 | ROM_eco4 |
|  |  | LV_eco3 | SPA_eco3 |
|  |  | LV_eco4 | UK_inst |
|  |  | LV_inst |  |
|  |  | PL_eco1 |  |
|  |  | PT_eco1 |  |
|  |  | PT_eco3 |  |
|  |  | PT_eco4 |  |
|  |  | ROM_eco3 |  |
|  |  | ROM_inst |  |
|  |  | SPA_eco1 |  |
|  |  | SPA_eco2 |  |
|  |  | SPA_eco4 |  |
|  |  | SPA_inst |  |
|  |  | UK_eco1 |  |
|  |  | UK_eco2 |  |
|  |  | UK_eco3 |  |
|  |  | UK_eco4 |  |
| Median pace | 53.54 | 9.21 | 3.73 |
| Median complexity | 2.59 | 7.93 | 40.55 |

TABLE A6.2. *Multinomial logistic regression on the determinants of episode-clusters* □

| | | | Model I | Model II | Model III | Model IV | Model V |
|---|---|---|---|---|---|---|---|
| **Economic grievances** | FS vs. SS | Unemployment | 0.09 (0.98) | | | | |
| | | CCI | 0 (0.12) | | | | |
| | | High severity | 1.94+ (1.72) | | | | 1.45 (0.87) |
| | FC vs. SS | Unemployment | 0.15 (1.49) | | | | |
| | | CCI | −0.03 (0.86) | | | | |
| | | High severity | 3.01* (2.46) | | | | 2.78 (1.60) |
| **Macro-political attitudes** | FS vs. SS | Trust in govt | | 0.48 (0.13) | | | |
| | | Democracy satisfaction | | −3.33 (1.28) | | | −3.73 (0.88) |
| | FC vs. SS | Trust in govt | | −6.16 (1.33) | | | |
| | | Democracy satisfaction | | −5.21+ (1.70) | | | −7.72+ (1.74) |
| **Actor characteristics** | FS vs. SS | Center-left | | | 1.84 (1.60) | | 2.35 (1.62) |
| | | Chal. diversity | | | 1.03 (1.08) | | −0.04 (0.02) |
| | FC vs. SS | Center-left | | | 2.20+ (1.81) | | 2.68+ (1.72) |
| | | Challanger diversity | | | 2.18+ (1.90) | | 0.42 (0.23) |

| Macro-constraints | | (1) | (2) | (3) | (4) | (5) |
|---|---|---|---|---|---|---|
| FS vs. SS | Urgency | | | | $-0.89$ (0.85) | |
| | Ext. pressure | | | | $93.76^*$ (2.17) | $102.53^+$ (1.65) |
| | Govt. control | | | | $5.99$ (0.99) | |
| FC vs. SS | Urgency | | | | $0.46$ (0.44) | |
| | Ext. pressure | | | | $92.03^*$ (2.13) | $98.28$ (1.58) |
| | Govt. control | | | | $6.05$ (0.97) | |
| | Constant | $-3.10^*$ (2.18) | $4.30^{**}$ (2.70) | $-1.58$ (1.58) | $-2.65^+$ (1.76) | $0.38$ (0.16) |
| | N | 60 | 60 | 60 | 60 | 60 |
| | Aic | 117.73 | 119.46 | 122.52 | 102.60 | 102.26 |
| | Bic | 134.48 | 132.03 | 135.09 | 119.35 | 127.40 |
| | Pseudo R2 | 0.14 | 0.09 | 0.06 | 0.27 | 0.34 |

$^+$ $p < 0.1$; $^{**}$ $p < 0.05$; $^{***}$ $p < 0.01$; $^{****}$ $p < 0.001$

□ SS (omitted baseline category): slow-simple

FS: fast-complex FC: fast-complex

# Appendix IV Additional information on dynamic analysis of contentious episodes (Chapter 8)

TABLE A8.1. *Distribution of action codes by country and actor-type*

| | FR | GER | GRE | HUN | IRE | ITA | LV | POL | PT | ROM | SPA | U.K. | Total |
|---|---|---|---|---|---|---|---|---|---|---|---|---|---|
| **Government** | | | | | | | | | | | | | |
| Sticking | 18.9 | 15.8 | 17.7 | 14.2 | 18.8 | 18.5 | 24.7 | 12.9 | 11.6 | 23.0 | 25.4 | 13.6 | 17.9 |
| Repression | 2.2 | 3.2 | 3.9 | 8.4 | 3.8 | 5.9 | 2.6 | 3.0 | 1.9 | 7.9 | 1.2 | 3.9 | 4.0 |
| Concession | 7.1 | 12.0 | 3.9 | 13.4 | 9.0 | 11.2 | 15.6 | 8.9 | 6.9 | 7.2 | 3.8 | 2.8 | 7.6 |
| **Challenger** | | | | | | | | | | | | | |
| Non-disruptive | 19.2 | 10.7 | 23.2 | 29.9 | 27.1 | 23.4 | 24.4 | 33.2 | 36.6 | 29.1 | 27.2 | 33.9 | 26.6 |
| Disruptive | 6.2 | 0 | 10.7 | 4.9 | 4.6 | 3.1 | 8.0 | 12.9 | 10.6 | 6.5 | 15.9 | 2.5 | 7.2 |
| Coope-ration | 1.6 | 2.2 | 1.7 | 3.5 | 4.6 | 3.9 | 6.9 | 8.4 | 4.0 | 4.0 | 3.4 | 1.8 | 3.5 |
| **Third Parties** | | | | | | | | | | | | | |
| Support govt | 16.7 | 16.4 | 21.6 | 6.7 | 8.2 | 12.3 | 5.5 | 6.9 | 8.7 | 10.5 | 14.5 | 26.9 | 14.0 |
| mediate | 1.2 | 9.5 | 1.4 | 4.4 | 3.4 | 5.0 | 3.3 | 5.0 | 3.5 | 3.5 | 2.2 | 1.6 | 3.2 |
| Support challenger | 26.9 | 30.3 | 16.1 | 14.5 | 20.5 | 16.8 | 9.1 | 8.9 | 16.2 | 8.4 | 6.4 | 13.1 | 16.1 |
| Total n | 323 | 317 | 1,325 | 344 | 1,210 | 715 | 275 | 202 | 623 | 430 | 497 | 566 | 6,827 |
| Total % | 100 | 100 | 100 | 100 | 100 | 100 | 100 | 100 | 100 | 100 | 100 | 100 | 100 |

TABLE A8.2. *Government path-dependence models*

| DV: log odds of government action forms | Sticking vs. concession | | Repression vs. concession | |
|---|---|---|---|---|
| L.concession | −1.070 | −1.001 | −0.636 | −0.660 |
|  | (3.34)*** | (2.84)*** | (1.41) | (3.01)** |
| L.sticking | 0.171 | 0.102 | 0.166 | 0.107 |
|  | (0.54) | (0.34) | (0.46) | (0.52) |
| L.repression | −0.480 | −0.685 | 1.222 | 0.956 |
|  | (1.00) | (1.47) | (3.12)** | (2.44)* |
| sequencelength | −0.025 | −0.021 | 0.022 | 0.029 |
|  | (0.55) | (0.55) | (0.53) | (0.77) |
| sequencelength2 | 0.001 | 0.001 | −0 | −0.001 |
|  | (0.78) | (0.67) | (0.30) | (0.77) |
| Constant | 1.008 |  | −0.911 |  |
|  | (4.21)*** |  | (2.78)** |  |
| N | 2045 | 2045 | 2045 | 2045 |
| AIC | 3876.45 | 3672.37 | 3876.45 | 3672.37 |
| BIC | 3977.67 | 3739.85 | 3977.67 | 3739.85 |
| Pseudor2 | 0.055 | 0.102 | 0.055 | 0.102 |
| Fixed Effects | N | Y | N | Y |

\* $p < 0.05$; \*\* $p < 0.01$; \*\*\* $p < 0.001$

TABLE A8.3. *Challenger path-dependence models*

| DV: log odds of challenger action forms | Nondisruptive vs. cooperation | | Disruptive vs. cooperation | |
|---|---|---|---|---|
| L.cooperation | −1.156 | −1.476 | −1.023 | −1.437 |
|  | (2.19)* | (3.11)** | (2.24)** | (3.56)*** |
| L.nondisruptive | −0.167 | −0.107 | −0.307 | −0.248 |
|  | (0.72) | (0.35) | (0.95) | (0.67) |
| L.disruptive | −0.523 | −0.647 | 0.913 | 0.730 |
|  | (1.28) | (2.03)* | (2.05)* | (1.65) |
| sequencelength | 0.010 | 0.052 | −0.069 | −0.023 |
|  | (0.14) | (1.32) | (0.87) | (0.61) |
| sequencelength2 | 0.001 | −0.001 | 0.003 | 0.001 |
|  | (0.29) | (0.39) | (1.11) | (1.01) |
| Constant | 2.000 |  | 0.956 |  |
|  | (6.77)*** |  | (2.99)** |  |
| N | 2555 | 2555 | 2555 | 2555 |
| AIC | 4033.33 | 3821.5 | 4033.33 | 3821.5 |
| BIC | 4138.56 | 3891.65 | 4138.56 | 3891.65 |
| Pseudor2 | 0.029 | 0.077 | 0.029 | 0.077 |
| Fixed effects | N | Y | N | Y |

\* $p < 0.05$; \*\* $p < 0.01$; \*\*\* $p < 0.001$

TABLE A8.4. *Government threat models*

| DV: log odds of government action forms | Sticking vs. concession | | Repression vs. concession | |
|---|---|---|---|---|
| **Government self-lag** | | | | |
| L.concession | -0.998 (2.97)** | -0.897 (3.70)*** | -0.696 (1.51) | -0.740 (2.03)* |
| L.sticking | 0.218 (0.66) | 0.136 (0.65) | 0.073 (0.20) | -0.025 (0.08) |
| L.repression | -0.373 (0.77) | -0.599 (1.91)* | 1.133 (2.68)** | 0.889 (2.25)* |
| **Challenger cross-lags** | | | | |
| L.cooperation | -1.034 (3.61)*** | -1.285 (4.65)*** | 0.441 (1.05) | 0.481 (1.31) |
| L.nondisruptive | -0.760 (3.62)*** | -0.932 (6.27)*** | 0.848 (2.25)* | 0.795 (3.81)*** |
| L.disruptive | -1.134 (3.97)*** | -1.676 (7.22)*** | 0.912 (2.36)* | 0.646 (2.33)* |
| sequencelength | 0.029 (0.58) | 0.052 (1.63) | -0.042 (0.81) | -0.032 (0.71) |
| sequencelength2 | 0.000 (0.08) | -0.001 (0.77) | 0.001 (0.68) | 0.001 (0.41) |
| Constant | 0.976 (4.01)**** | | -0.926 (2.77)** | |
| N | 2,045 | | | |
| AIC | 3761.04 | 3598.77 | 3761.04 | 3598.77 |
| BIC | 3912.86 | 3936.16 | 3912.86 | 3936.16 |
| Pseudor2 | 0.088 | 0.144 | 0.088 | 0.144 |
| Fixed Effects | N | Y | N | Y |

* p <0.05; ** p <0.01; *** p <0.001

TABLE A8.5. *Challenger threat models*

| DV: log odds of challenger action forms | | Nondisruptive vs. cooperation | | Disruptive vs. cooperation | |
|---|---|---|---|---|---|
| **Challenger self-lags** | | | | | |
| L.cooperation | | −0.503 | −0.945 | −0.350 | −0.913 |
| | | (0.84) | (1.76)* | (0.69) | (2.16)* |
| L.nondisruptive | | 0.011 | 0.017 | −0.102 | −0.112 |
| | | (0.05) | (0.05) | (0.28) | (0.28) |
| L.disruptive | | −0.302 | −0.464 | 1.197 | 0.960 |
| | | (0.69) | (1.45) | (2.54)* | (2.39)* |
| **Government cross-lags** | | | | | |
| L.concession | | −1.614 | −1.899 | −1.413 | −1.640 |
| | | (3.52)*** | (4.15)*** | (3.37)*** | (4.37)*** |
| L.sticking | | −0.194 | −0.602 | 0.039 | −0.386 |
| | | (0.39) | (1.27) | (0.10) | (0.85) |
| L.repression | | −0.573 | −0.845 | −0.664 | −0.928 |
| | | (1.29) | (1.51) | (1.55) | (2.15)* |
| sequencelength | | 0.041 | 0.080 | −0.041 | 0.003 |
| | | (0.70) | (1.98)* | (0.55) | (0.07) |
| sequencelength2 | | −0 | −0.001 | 0.002 | 0 |
| | | (0.22) | (1.06) | (0.78) | (0.30) |
| Constant | | 2.301 | | 1.066 | |
| | | (5.09)*** | | (3.03)** | |
| N | | 2555 | 2555 | 2555 | 2555 |
| AIC | | 3971.27 | 3753.89 | 3971.27 | 3753.89 |
| BIC | | 4129.11 | 3824.04 | 4129.11 | 3824.04 |
| Pseudor2 | | 0.048 | 0.094 | 0.048 | 0.094 |
| Fixed effects | | N | Y | N | Y |

* p < 0.05; ** p < 0.01; *** p < 0.001

TABLE A8.6. *Government–third-party models*

| | Sticking vs. concession | | Repression vs. concession | |
|---|---|---|---|---|
| **Government self-lag** | | | | |
| L.concession | -0.964 (3.17)*** | -0.886 (3.63)*** | -0.723 (1.58) | -0.754 (2.06)* |
| L.sticking | 0.128 (0.44) | 0.071 (0.34) | 0.075 (0.21) | -0.014 (0.04) |
| L.repression | -0.342 (0.80) | -0.579 (1.83) | 1.120 (2.59)** | 0.860 (2.17)* |
| **Challenger cross-lag** | | | | |
| L.cooperation | -1.244 (4.34)*** | -1.466 (5.17)*** | 0.347 (0.80) | 0.395 (1.05) |
| L.nondisruptive | -0.876 (4.28)*** | -1.070 (6.97)*** | 0.800 (2.08)* | 0.762 (3.55)*** |
| L.disruptive | -1.300 (4.41)*** | -1.846 (7.70)*** | 0.840 (2.07)* | 0.492 (1.73)* |
| **Third-party cross-lag** | | | | |
| L.supportG | 0.073 (0.27) | -0.237 (1.34) | -0.605 (1.72) | -0.941 (3.48)*** |
| L.mediate | -0.918 (2.83)** | -0.756 (3.15)*** | -0.098 (0.31) | -0.018 (0.06) |
| L.supportC | -0.553 (2.40)* | -0.629 (3.69)*** | -0.254 (0.75) | -0.370 (1.59) |
| sequencelength | 0.062 (1.28) | 0.090 (2.65)** | -0.020 (0.37) | -0.007 (0.14) |
| sequencelength2 | -0.001 (0.49) | -0.002 (1.62) | 0.001 (0.43) | 0.000 (0.05) |
| Constant | 1.054 (4.95)*** | | -0.901 (2.63)** | |
| N | 2045 | | 2045 | |
| AIC | 3728.79 | 3577.54 | 3728.78 | 3577.54 |
| BIC | 3931.22 | 3965.54 | 3931.21 | 3965.54 |
| Pseudor2 | 0.1 | 0.154 | 0.1 | 0.154 |
| Fixed effects | N | Y | N | Y |

* $p < 0.05$; ** $p < 0.01$; *** $p < 0.001$

TABLE A8.7. *Challenger–third-party models*

| | Nondisruptive vs. cooperation | Disruptive vs. cooperation | Disruptive vs. cooperation | Nondisruptive vs. cooperation |
|---|---|---|---|---|
| **Challenger self-lags** | | | | |
| L.cooperation | −0.640 | −0.675 | −1.152 | −1.026 |
| | (1.18) | (1.29) | (2.60)** | (1.81) |
| L.nondisruptive | −0.103 | −0.293 | −0.323 | −0.109 |
| | (0.52) | (0.81) | (1.05) | (0.41) |
| L.disruptive | −0.404 | 0.970 | 0.750 | −0.518 |
| | (1.04) | (1.93) | (1.88) | (1.32) |
| **Government cross-lags** | | | | |
| L.concession | −1.526 | −1.320 | −1.495 | −1.764 |
| | (3.31)*** | (3.08)** | (3.68)*** | (3.81)*** |
| L.sticking | −0.189 | 0.003 | −0.297 | −0.518 |
| | (0.41) | (0.01) | (0.65) | (1.06) |
| L.repression | −0.407 | −0.488 | −0.740 | −0.656 |
| | (0.96) | (1.09) | (1.55) | (1.30) |
| **Third party cross-lags** | | | | |
| L.supportG | 0.061 | −0.499 | −0.379 | 0.092 |
| | (0.16) | (1.33) | (1.36) | (0.33) |
| L.mediate | −0.962 | −1.667 | −1.149 | −0.798 |
| | (2.60)** | (3.65)*** | (1.95) | (1.79) |
| L.supportC | −0.027 | −0.108 | −0.543 | −0.214 |
| | (0.11) | (0.36) | (2.33)* | (0.78) |
| sequencelength | 0.062 | 0.002 | 0.045 | 0.100 |
| | (1.22) | (0.03) | (1.18) | (2.07)* |
| sequencelength2 | −0.001 | 0.001 | −0.001 | −0.002 |
| | (0.65) | (0.37) | (0.63) | (1.65) |
| Constant | 2.275 | 1.051 | | |
| | (4.96)*** | (2.86)** | | |
| N | 2555 | 2555 | 2555 | 2555 |
| AIC | 3958.62 | 3958.62 | 3734.03 | 3734.03 |
| BIC | 4169.07 | 4169.07 | 3804.18 | 3804.18 |
| Pseudor2 | 0.056 | 0.056 | 0.099 | 0.099 |
| Fixed effects | N | N | Y | Y |

* p <0.05; ** p <0.01; *** p <0.00

Appendix VI Regression output table on government responses to challengers (Chapter 9)

TABLE A9.1. *Government reaction to challenger actions by configuration of challenger, cabinet composition, divided governments, and third-party actors, for all episodes: mlogit model parameters, t-values, and significance levels*

| | (1) Three types of configurations | (2) Cabinet composition-popularity | (3) Divided government | (4) Third-party actors/three types of configurations | (5) International third-party actors |
|---|---|---|---|---|---|
| **Repression** | | | | | |
| no government lag | | | | | |
| lag: concession | 0.263 | 0.170 | 0.260 | 0.329 | 0.272 |
| | (0.559) | (0.380) | (0.542) | (0.739) | (0.575) |
| lag: sticking | -0.071 | -0.133 | -0.071 | -0.003 | -0.123 |
| | (-0.176) | (-0.341) | (-0.167) | (-0.009) | (-0.306) |
| lag: repression | 1.217** | 1.171** | 1.174** | 1.319** | 1.401** |
| | (2.858) | (3.028) | (2.581) | (3.233) | (3.224) |
| partisan union-driven | -0.875* | | | -0.173 | |
| | (-2.005) | | | (-0.394) | |
| civil-society-driven | -2.116*** | | -2.238** | -0.925 | |
| | (-3.442) | | (-3.009) | (-1.557) | |
| challenge (international) | 0.621 | 2.161*** | | 1.731*** | 1.604*** |
| | (1.365) | (4.762) | | (5.766) | (4.701) |
| partisan##challenge | | | | | |
| unions ## challenge | 1.307* | | 2.238*** | | |
| | (2.501) | | (3.509) | | |
| smos # challenge | 2.038*** | | 2.972*** | | |
| | (3.339) | | (4.727) | | |
| no third party | | | | | |
| govt+ | -0.805** | -0.706** | -0.766** | -0.922* | |
| | (-3.071) | (-2.661) | (-2.685) | (-2.135) | |

| | (1) | (2) | (3) | (4) | (5) |
|---|---|---|---|---|---|
| mediate | 0.569 | 0.637 | 0.618 | 0.414 | |
| | (1.058) | (1.343) | (1.122) | (0.358) | |
| chall+ | 0.112 | 0.075 | 0.083 | 0.860 | |
| | (0.444) | (0.282) | (0.332) | (1.806) | |
| sequence lengh | −0.034 | −0.058 | −0.036 | −0.068 | −0.029 |
| | (−0.631) | (−1.197) | (−0.685) | (−1.240) | (−0.524) |
| sequence length squared | 0.000 | 0.001 | 0 | 0.001 | −0 |
| | (0.160) | (0.585) | (0.262) | (0.666) | (−0.127) |
| c-right, unpopular | | | | | |
| c-right, popular | | −0.068 | | | |
| | | (−0.136) | | | |
| c-left, unpopular | | −1.673* | | | |
| | | (−2.507) | | | |
| c-left popular | | −1.736** | | | |
| | | (−2.728) | | | |
| c-right, popular#challenge | | −1.439* | | | |
| | | (−2.479) | | | |
| c-left, unpopular#chall | | 0.793 | | | |
| | | (1.128) | | | |
| c-left, popular#challenge | | 0.835 | | | |
| | | (1.808) | | | |
| divided | | | −0.469 | | |
| | | | (−0.809) | | |
| challenge#divided | | | 1.950** | | |
| | | | (3.114) | | |
| unions # divided | | | 0.332 | | |
| | | | (0.443) | | |

(continued)

TABLE A9.1. (*continued*)

| Repression | (1) Three types of configurations | (2) Cabinet composition-popularity | (3) Divided government | (4) Third-party actors/three types of configurations | (5) International third-party actors |
|---|---|---|---|---|---|
| smos # divided | | | -12.916*** (-10.487) | | |
| chall#union#divided | | | -1.551 (-1.662) | | |
| chall#civil society#divided | | | 10.915*** (8.372) | | |
| union#govt+ | | | | -0.046 (-0.076) | |
| unions # mediate | | | | 0.339 (0.266) | |
| unions # chall+ | | | | -1.291* (-2.079) | |
| civil society # govt+ | | | | 1.034 (1.571) | |
| civil society#mediate | | | | -0.988 (-0.713) | |
| civil society#chall+ | | | | -0.459 (-0.657) | |
| chall+ international | | | | | 0.871* (2.428) |
| neither international | | | | | 0.484 (1.091) |
| Constant | -2.042* (-2.411) | -2.220*** (-4.120) | -1.704 (-1.827) | -2.390** (-2.998) | -2.919*** (-3.921) |

| Concession | (1) Three types of configurations | (2) Cabinet composition-popularity | (3) Divided government | (4) Third-party actors/three types of configurations | (5) International third-party actors |
|---|---|---|---|---|---|
| no government lag | | | | | |
| lag: concession | 0.974*** | 0.959** | 0.924** | 1.104*** | 0.963** |
| | (3.294) | (3.288) | (2.966) | (3.792) | (3.223) |
| lag: sticking | −0.058 | −0.083 | −0.043 | 0.054 | −0.152 |
| | (−0.209) | (−0.293) | (−0.153) | (0.202) | (−0.545) |
| lag: repression | 0.608 | 0.462 | 0.541 | 0.801* | 0.518 |
| | (1.513) | (1.114) | (1.330) | (2.045) | (1.153) |
| partisan | | | | | |
| union-driven | 0.369 | | 0.415 | 0.766* | |
| | (1.186) | | (1.146) | (2.110) | |
| civil society-driven | 0.119 | | 0.147 | 0.350 | |
| | (0.310) | | (0.320) | (0.793) | |
| challenge (international) | 0.254 | 1.600*** | −0.174 | 0.946*** | 0.880*** |
| | (0.710) | (6.527) | (−0.447) | (6.225) | (5.380) |
| partisan##challenge | | | | | |
| unions ## challenge | 0.947* | | 1.404*** | | |
| | (2.511) | | (3.365) | | |
| smos # challenge | 0.638 | | 1.165* | | |
| | (1.387) | | (2.213) | | |
| no third party | | | | | |
| govt+ | −0.007 | 0.221 | −0.032 | −0.689 | |
| | (−0.033) | (0.992) | (−0.152) | (−1.146) | |

(continued)

TABLE A9.1. (*continued*)

| Concession | (1) Three types of configurations | (2) Cabinet composition-popularity | (3) Divided government | (4) Third-party actors/three types of configurations | (5) International third-party actors |
|---|---|---|---|---|---|
| mediate | 0.535 | 0.691* | 0.620 | 1.381** | |
| | (1.443) | (2.018) | (1.635) | (3.221) | |
| chall+ | 0.394 | 0.436 | 0.438 | 0.769 | −0.008 |
| | (1.709) | (1.960) | (1.953) | (1.276) | (−0.168) |
| sequence length | −0.036 | −0.051 | −0.025 | −0.054 | 0 |
| | (−0.802) | (−1.120) | (−0.540) | (−1.248) | (−0.334) |
| sequence length squared | 0 | 0.001 | 0 | 0.001 | |
| | (0.211) | (0.528) | (−0.079) | (0.672) | |
| c-right, unpopular | | | | | |
| c-right, popular | | 0.061 | | | |
| | | (0.194) | | | |
| c-left, unpopular | | −0.217 | | | |
| | | (−0.733) | | | |
| c-left popular | | −0.411 | | | |
| | | (−1.121) | | | |
| c-right, popular#challenge | | −1.019** | | | |
| | | (−3.176) | | | |
| c-left, unpopular#chall | | −0.348 | | | |
| | | (−0.884) | | | |
| c-left, popular#challenge | | −1.523*** | | | |
| | | (−5.111) | | | |
| divided | | | −0.087 | | |

| | |
|---|---|
| | (−0.201) |
| challenge#divided | 0.916 |
| | (1.487) |
| unions # divided | −0.249 |
| | (−0.519) |
| smos # divided | 0.045 |
| | (0.061) |
| chall#union#divided | −1.513 |
| | (−1.661) |
| chall#civil society#divided | −17.907*** |
| | (−17.580) |
| union#govt+ | 0.769 |
| | (1.210) |
| unions # mediate | −1.197 |
| | (−1.892) |
| unions # chall+ | −0.439 |
| | (−0.643) |
| civil society # govt+ | 0.806 |
| | (0.900) |
| civil society#mediate | −0.853 |
| | (−0.918) |
| civil society#chall+ | −0.483 |
| | (−0.718) |
| chall+ international | 0.542 |
| | (1.824) |
| neither international | 0.491 |
| | (1.697) |

*(continued)*

TABLE A9.1. (*continued*)

| Concession | (1) Three types of configurations | (2) Cabinet composition-popularity | (3) Divided govern-ment | (4) Third-party actors/three types of configurations | (5) International third-party actors |
|---|---|---|---|---|---|
| constant | −1.588** | −1.266** | −1.649** | −1.841*** | −1.568** |
| | (−2.849) | (−2.629) | (−2.904) | (−3.338) | (−2.949) |
| observations | 2010 | 2010 | 2010 | 2010 | 2010 |
| AIC | 3359.12 | 3346.52 | 3349.21 | 3374.18 | 3404.89 |
| BIC | 3639.41 | 3632.42 | 3679.96 | 3699.32 | 3629.13 |
| r2 | 0.12 | 0.13 | 0.13 | 0.12 | 0.10 |

# Appendix VI Regression output table from turning point analysis (Chapter 11)

TABLE AII.I. *Multinomial logit models on actor- and action-types across the episode phases*

|  |  | Actor types | Action types |
|---|---|---|---|
| Challenger vs. Govt | Main Phase | 0.634 (4.58)*** | |
|  | Closing Phase | 0.920 (5.94)*** | |
| Third Party vs. Govt | Main Phase | 0.428 (3.12)*** | |
|  | Closing Phase | 0.332 (2.15)** | |
| Disruption vs. Rest | Main Phase | | 0.841 (4.01)*** |
|  | Closing Phase | | 1.365 (5.84)*** |
| Cooperation vs. Rest | Main Phase | | −0.093 (0.66) |
|  | Closing Phase | | −0.198 (1.16) |
|  | Constant | −0.474 (1.74)* | −1.430 (5.16)*** |
| N | | 60 | 60 |
| n | | 6,889 | 6,889 |
| Pseudo R2 | | 0.06 | 0.11 |
| AIC | | 14473.22 | 9294.52 |
| BIC | | 15321.09 | 10142.39 |
| Fixed Effects | | Yes | Yes |

* p <0.1; ** p <0.05; *** p <0.01

# References

Abbott, Andrew. 1983. "Sequences of Social Events: Concepts and Methods for the Analysis of Order in Social Processes." *Historical Methods* 16(4): 129–147.

 1995. "Sequence Analysis: New Methods for Old Ideas." *Annual Review of Sociology* 21:93–113.

 2001a. "On the Concept of the Turning Point," pp. 240–260 in *Time Matters. On Theory and Method*, edited by Andrew Abbott. Chicago: University of Chicago Press.

 2001b. *Time Matters: On Theory and Method*. Chicago: The University of Chicago Press.

Accornero, Guya and Pedro Ramos Pinto. 2015. "'Mild Mannered'? Protest and Mobilisation in Portugal under Austerity, 2010–2013." *West European Politics* 38(3):491–515.

Aldrich, John Herbert. 1999. "Political Parties in a Critical Era." *American Politics Quarterly* 27(1):9–32.

Alimi, Eitan. 2016. "The Relational Context of Radicalization: The Case of Jewish Settler Contention before and after the Gaza Pullout." *Political Studies* 64 (4):910–929.

Alimi, Eitan Y., Lorenzo Bosi, and Chares Demetriou. 2012. "Relational Dynamics and Processes of Radicalization: A Comparative Framework." *Mobilization* 17 (1):7–26.

Almeida, Paul D. 2003. "Opportunity Organizations and Threat-Induced Contention: Protest Waves in Authoritarian Settings." *American Journal of Sociology* 109 (2):345–400.

 2007. "Defensive Mobilization: Popular Movements against Economic Adjustment Policies in Latin America." *Latin American Perspectives* 34(3):123–139.

 2014. *Mobilizing Democracy. Globalization and Citizen Protest*. Baltimore: Johns Hopkins University Press.

Altiparmakis, Argyrios. 2019. "The Age of the Bailout. Contention, Party-System Collapse and Reconstruction in Greece, 2009–2015." PhD thesis, Department of Political and Social Sciences, European University Institute, Florence.

Ancelovici, Marcos. 2011. "In Search of Lost Radicalism. The Hot Autumn of 2010 and the Transformation of Labor Contention in France." *French Politics, Culture & Society* 29(3):121–140.

Armingeon, Klaus. 2012. "The Politics of Fiscal Responses to the Crisis 2008–2009." *Governance* 25(4):543–565.

Aslanidis, Paris, and Nikos Marantzidis. 2016. "The Impact of the Greek Indignados on Greek Politics." *Southeastern Europe* 40 (2): 125–157.

Aytaç, Erdem S., Luis Schiumerini, and Susan Stokes. 2017. "Protests and Repression in New Democracies." *Perspectives on Politics* 15(1):62–82.

Baumgarten, Britta. 2013. "Geração à Rasca and Beyond: Mobilizations in Portugal after 12 March 2011." *Current Sociology* 61(4):457–473.

Baumgartner, Frank R., Christian Breunig, and Emiliano Grossman, eds. 2019. *Comparative Policy Agendas: Theory, Tools, Data*. Oxford: Oxford University Press.

Baumgartner, Frank R. and Bryan D. Jones. 1993. *Agendas and Instability in American Politics*. Chicago, IL: University of Chicago Press.

Becker, Jennifer. A. H., Amy.Janan Johnson, Elizabeth.A.Craig, Eileen.S.Gilchrist, Michel.M. Haigh, and Lindsay T. Lane. 2009. "Friendships Are Flexible, Not Fragile: Turning Points in Geographically-Close and Long-Distance Friendships." *Journal of Social and Personal Relationships* 26(4): 347–369.

Beissinger, Mark. 2002. *Nationalist Mobilization and the Collapse of the Soviet State*. Cambridge: Cambridge University Press.

2011. "Mechanisms of Maidan: The Structure of Contingency in the Making of the Orange Revolution." *Mobilization* 16(1):25–43.

Bermeo, Nancy and Larry M. Bartels. 2014. "Mass Politics in Tough Times," pp. 1–39 in *Mass Politics in Tough Times: Opinions, Votes and Protest in the Great Recession*, edited by N. Bermeo and L. M. Bartels. Oxford: Oxford University Press.

Bernburg, Jón Gunnar. 2015. "Economic Crisis and Popular Protest in Iceland, January 2009: The Role of Perceived Economic Loss and Political Attitudes in Protest Participation and Support." *Mobilization* 20(2):231–252.

Biggs, Michael. 2002. "Strikes As Sequences of Interactions: The American Strike Wave of 1886." *Social Science History* 26(3):583–617.

Bishara, Dina. 2015. "The Politics of Ignoring: Protest Dynamics in Late Mubarak Egypt." *Perspectives on Politics* 13(4):958–975.

Blanchard, Philippe. 2011. "Sequence Analysis for Political Science". APSA Annual meeting paper. Available at https://papers.ssrn.com/sol3/papers.cfm?abstract_id=1902086

Bloom, Joshua. 2015. "The Dynamics of Opportunity and Insurgent Practice: How Black Anti-Colonialists Compelled Truman to Advocate Civil Rights." *American Sociological Review* 80(2):391–415.

Boudreau, Vince. 2005. "Precarious Regimes and Marchup Problems in the Explanation of Repressive Policy," pp. 33–57 in *Repression and Mobilization*, edited by Christian Davenport, Hank Johnston, and Carol Muelle. Minneapolis, MN: University of Minnesota Press.

Boydstun, Amber E., Shaun Bevan, and Herschel F., Thomas. 2014. "The Importance of Attention Diversity and How to Measure It." *Policy Studies Journal* 42(2):173–96.

Bremer, Björn, Swen Hutter, and Hanspeter Kriesi. 2020. "Electoral Punishment and Protest Politics in Times of Crisis," pp. 227–250 in *Contention in Times of Crisis:*

*Recession and Political Protest in Thirty European Countries*, edited by Bruno Wüest, Hanspeter Kriesi, Jasmine Lorenzini, and Silja Hausermann. Cambridge: Cambridge University Press.

Bremer, Björn and Guillem Vidal. 2018. "From Boom to Bust: A Comparative Analysis of Greece and Spain under Austerity," pp. 113–140 in *Living under Austerity: Greek Society in Crisis*, edited by Evdoxios Doxiadis and Aimee Placas. New York: Berghahn Books.

Burden, Barry C. and Amber Wichowsky. 2014. "Economic Discontent as a Mobilizer: Unemployment and Voter Turnout." *The Journal of Politics* 76(4):887–898.

Burstein, Paul. 1999. "Social Movements and Public Policy," pp. 3–21 in *How Social Movements Matter*, edited by Marco Giugni, Doug McAdam, and Charles Tilly. Minneapolis, MN: University of Minnesota Press.

Carlsson, Christoffer. 2011. "Using 'Turning Points' to Understand Processes of Change in Offending." *British Journal of Criminology* 52 (1):1–16.

Carmines, Edward G. and James A. Stimson. 1993. "On the Evolution of Political Issues," pp. 151–168 in *Agenda Formation*, edited by William H. Riker. Ann Arbor: University of Michigan Press.

Carvalho, Tiago. 2018. "Contesting Austerity: A Comparative Approach to the Cycles of Protest in Portugal and Spain under the Great Recession (2008–2015)". PhD thesis, Cambridge University.

Coppedge, Micheal, John Gerring, and Carl Henrik Knutsen. 2019. "The Methodology of "Varieties of Democracy" (V-dem)." *Bulletin of Sociological Methodology* 143 (1): 107–133.

Cunningham, Kathleen Gallagher. 2013. "Understanding Strategic Choice: The Determinants of Civil War and Non-Violent Campaign in Self-Determination Disputes." *Journal of Peace Research* 50 (3):291–304.

da Silva, Frederico Ferreira and Mariana S. Mendes. 2019. "Portugal – A Tale of Apparent Stability and Surreptitious Transformation," pp. 139–164 in *European Party Politics in Times of Crisis*, edited by Swen Hutter and Hanspeter Kriesi. Cambridge: Cambridge University Press.

Dahlberg, Stefan and Sören Holmberg. 2014. "Democracy and Bureaucracy: How Their Quality Matters for Popular Satisfaction." *West European Politics* 37(3):515-37.

Davenport, Christian. 2007. "State Repression and Political Order." *Annual Review of Political Science* 10:1–23.

Davenport, Christian and D.A. Armstrong II. 2004. "Democracy and the Violation of Human Rights: A Statistical Analysis from 1976–1996." *American Journal of Political Science* 48(3):538–554.

De Haan, Jakob and Jeroen Klomp. 2013. "Conditional Political Budget Cycles: A Review of Recent Evidence." *Public Choice* 157 (3):387–410.

della Porta, Donatella. 1995. *Social Movements, Political Violence, and the State: A Comparative Analysis of Italy and Germany*. New York: Cambridge University Press.

2015. *Social Movements in Times of Austerity: Bringing Capitalism Back into Protest Analysis*, Cambridge: Polity Press.

2018. "Radicalization: A Relational Perspective." *Annual Review of Political Science* 21:461–474.

della Porta, Donatella and Dieter Rucht. 1995. "Left-Libertarian Movements in Context: A Comparison of Italy and West Germany, 1965–1990," pp. 229–272 in *The Politics of Social Protest: Comparative Perspectives on States and Social Movements*, edited by J. Craig Jenkins and Bert Klandermans. London and New York: Routledge.

della Porta, Donatella, and Mario Diani. 2006. *Social Movements. An Introduction.* Oxford: Blackwell Publishing.

della Porta, Donatella, Joseba Fernandez, Hara Kouki, and Lorenzo Mosca. 2017b. *Movement Parties against Austerity*. Cambridge: Polity Press.

della Porta, Donatella, Massimiliano Andretta, Tiago Fernandes, Francis O'Connor, Eduardo Romanos, and Markos Vogiatzoglou. 2017a. *Late Neoliberalism and its Discontents in the Economic Crisis: Comparing Social Movements in the European Periphery*. Basingstoke: Palgrave Macmillan.

De Nardo, James. 1985. *Power in Numbers. The Political Strategy of Protest and Rebellion*. Princeton, NJ: Princeton University Press.

De Vries, Catherine E., and Sara B. Hobolt. 2012. "When Dimensions Collide: The Electoral Success of Issue Entrepreneurs." *European Union Politics* 13 (2): 246–268.

de Wilde, Pieter, Anna Leupold, and Henning Schmidtke. 2016. "Introduction: the Differentiated Politicisation of European Governance." *West European Politics* 39(1):3–22.

Diani, Mario. 2013. "Organizational Fields in Social Movement Dynamics," pp. 145–168 in *The Future of Social Movement Research: Dynamics, Mechanisms, and Processes*, edited by Jacquelien van Stekelenburg, Conny M. Roggeband, and Bert Klandermans. Minneapolis, MN: University of Minnesota Press.

2015. *The Cement of Civil Society: Studying Networks in Localities*. Cambridge: Cambridge University Press.

Diani, Mario and Ivano Bison. 2004. "Organizations, Coalitions, and Movements," *Theory and Society* 33 (3–4):281–309.

Diani, Mario and Maria Kousis. 2014. "The Duality of Claims and Events: The Greek Campaign Against the Troika's Memoranda and Austerity, 2010–2012." *Mobilization: An International Quarterly* 19(4): 387–404.

Doherty, Brian and Graeme Hayes. 2019. "Tactics and Strategic Action," pp. 271–288 in *The Wiley Blackwell Companion to Social Movements*, new and expanded version, edited by David A. Snow, Sarah A. Soule, Hanspeter Kriesi, and Holly J. McCammon, Oxford: Wiley.

Duboc, Marie. 2011. "Egyptian Leftist Intellectuals' Activism from the Margins: Overcoming the Mobilization/Demobilization Dichotomy," pp. 61–79 in *Social Movements, Mobilization, and Contestation in the Middle East and North Africa*, edited by J. Beinin and F. Vairel, Stanford,CA: Stanford University Press.

Earl, Jennifer, Andrew Martin, John D. McCarthy, and Sarah A. Soule. 2004. "The Use of Newspaper Data in the Study of Collective Action." *Annual Review of Sociology* 30: 65–80

Earl, Jennifer. 2011. "Political Repression: Iron Fists, Velvet Gloves and Diffuse Control." *Annual Review of Sociology* 37:261–284.

Easton, David. 1975. "A Re-Assessment of the Concept of Political Support." *British Journal of Political Science* 5 (4):435–457.

Edelman, Murray Jacob. 1985. *The Symbolic Uses of Politics*. Champaign, IL: University of Illinois Press.

Eggert, Nina, and Marco Giugni. 2015. "Migration and Social Movements," pp. 159–172 in *Oxford Handbook of Social Movements*, edited by Donatella Della Porta and Mario Diani. Oxford: Oxford University Press.

Eihmanis, Edgars. 2018. "Cherry-Picking External Constraints: Latvia and EU Economic Governance, 2008–2014." *Journal of European Public Policy* 25 (2), 231–249.

Ermakoff, Ivan. 2015. "The Structure of Contingency". *American Journal of Sociology* 121(1):64–125.

Fearon, James D. 1994. "Domestic Political Audiences and the Escalation of International Disputes." *American Political Science Review* 88(3):577–592.

Fernandez, Roberto M. and Roger V. Gould. 1994. "A Dilemma of State Power: Brokerage and Influence in the National Health Policy Domain." *American Journal of Sociology* 99(6):1455–1491.

Ferree, Myra Marx, William A. Gamson, Jürgen Gerhards, and Dieter Rucht. 2002. *Shaping Abortion Discourse. Democracy and the Public Sphere in Germany and the United States*. Cambridge: Cambridge University Press.

Flesher Fominaya, Cristina. 2017. "European Anti-Austerity and Pro-Democracy t Wake of the Global Financial Crisis." *Social Movement Studies* 16(1):1–20.

Franklin, James C. 2009. "Contentious Challenges and Government Responses in Latin America." *Political Research Quarterly* 62(4):700–714.

Franzese, Robert J. 2002. "Electoral and Partisan Cycles in Economic Policies and Outcomes." *Annual Review of Political Science* 5:369–421.

Franzese, Robert J. and Karen L. Jusko. 2006. "Political-Economic cycles," pp. 545–564 in *Oxford Handbook of Political Economy* edited by D. Wittman and B. Weingast, Oxford: Oxford University Press.

Gamson, William A. 1975. *The Strategy of Social Protest*. Homewood, Il: Dorsey Press. 1990. *The Strategy of Social Protest*. Belmont, CA: Wadsworth Publishing Company.

Gamson, William A. and David S. Meyer. 1996. "Framing Political Opportunity," pp. 275–290 in *Comparative Perspectives on Social Movements. Political Opportunities, Mobilizing Structures, and Cultural Framings*, edited by Doug McAdam, John D. McCarthy, and Mayer N. Zald. Cambridge: Cambridge University Press.

Giugni, Marco. 1999. "Introduction," pp. xiii–xxxiii in *How Social Movements Matter*, edited by Marco Giugni, Doug McAdam, and Charles Tilly. Minneapolis , MN: University of Minnesota Press.

2009. "Political Opportunities: From Tilly to Tilly." *Swiss Political Science Review* 15 (2):361–368.

Goldstone, Jack Andrew. 1998. "The Soviet Union: Revolution and Transformation." in Dogan, Mattei, and John Higley. *Elites, Crises, and the Origins of Regimes*. Lanham, MD: Rowman & Littlefield Pub Inc.

Goldstone, Jack A. and Charles Tilly. 2001. "Threat (and Opportunity): Popular Action and State Response in The Dynamics of Contentious Action," pp. 179–194 in *Silence and Voice in the Study of Contentious Politics*, edited by Ronald R. Aminzade, Jack Goldstone, Dough McAdam, Elizabeth J. Perry, William H. Sewell, Sidney Tarrow, and Charles Tilly. Cambridge: Cambridge University Press.

Goodwin, Jeff and James M. Jasper. 1999. "Caught in a Winding, Snarling Vine: The Structural Bias of Political Process Theory." *Sociological Forum* 14(1):27–92.

Grasso, Maria and Marco Giugni. 2016. "Protest Participation and Economic Crisis: The Conditioning Role of Political Opportunities." *European Journal of Political Research* 55(4):663–680.

Green-Pedersen, Christoffer and Stefaan Walgrave, eds. 2014. *Agenda Setting, Policies, and Political Systems: A Comparative Approach.* Chicago and London: The University of Chicago Press.

Greskovits, Bela. 2015. "The Hollowing and Backsliding of Democracy in East Central Europe." *Global Policy* 6(1):6–37.

Griffin, Larry J. 1993. "Narrative, Event-Structure Analysis, and Causal Interpretation in Historical Sociology." *American Journal of Sociology* 98(5):1095–1133.

Gross, Neil 2018. "The Structure of Causal Chains." *Sociological Theory* 36 (4): 343–367.

Gurr, Ted. 1970. *Why Men Rebel?* Princeton, NJ: Princeton. University Press.

Hall, Peter A. 2013. "The Political Origins of Our Economic Discontents: Contemporary Adjustment Problems in Historical Perspective," pp. 129–149 in *Politics in the New Hard Times. The Great Recession in Comparative Perspective,* edited by Miles Kahler and David A. Lake. Ithaca, NY and London: Cornell University Press.

Hamann, Kerstin, Alison Johnston, and John Kelly. 2013. "Unions against Governments: Explaining General Strikes in Western Europe, 1980–2006." *Comparative Political Studies* 46(9):1030–1057.

Heaney, Michael T. and Fabio Rojas. 2015. *Party in the Street: The Antiwar Movement and the Democratic Party after 9/11.* Cambridge: Cambridge University Press

Hedström, Peter and Petri Yilikoski. 2010. "Causal Mechanisms in the Social Sciences." *Annual Review of Sociology* 36: 49–67.

Heise, David R. 1989. "Modeling Event Structures." *Journal of Mathematical Sociology* 14 (2–3) 139–169.

Hernández, Enrique and Hanspeter Kriesi. 2016. "The Electoral Consequences of the Financial and Economic Crisis in Europe." *European Journal of Political Research* 55(2):203–224.

Hirschman, Albert O. 1970. *Exit, Voice, and Loyalty: Responses to Decline in Firms, Organizations, and States.* Cambridge,MA: Harvard University Press.

Hooghe, Liesbet and Gary Marks. 2009. "A Postfunctionalist Theory of European integration: From Permissive Consensus to Constraining Dissensus." *British Journal of Political Science* 39(1):1–23.

Hunger, Sophia and Lorenzini, Jasmine. 2019. "All Quiet on the Protest Scene? Repertoires of contention and protest actors during the Great Recession," pp. 75–146 in *Contention in Times of Crises: Comparing Political Protest in 30 European Countries, 2000–2015,* edited by H. Kriesi, J. Lorenzini, B. Wueest, and S. Häusermann. Cambridge: Cambridge University Press.

Hutter, Swen. 2014. "Protest Event Analysis and Its Offspring," pp. 335–367 in *Methodological Practices in Social Movement Research* edited by D. Della Porta. Oxford: Oxford University Press

Hutter, Swen, Edgar Grande, and Hanspeter Kriesi, eds. 2016. *Politicizing Europe: Integration and Mass Politics.* Cambridge: Cambridge University Press.

Hutter, Swen and Hanspeter Kriesi, eds. 2019. *European Party Politics in Times of Crisis,* Cambridge: Cambridge University Press.

   2019. "Politicizing Europe in Times of Crisis." *Journal of European Public Policy* 26 (7): 996–1017.

Hutter, Swen, Hanspeter Kriesi, and Guillem Vidal. 2018. "Old versus New Politics: The Political Spaces in Southern Europe in Times Of Crises." *Party Politics* 24 (1):10–22.

Ikstens, Jánis. 2010. "Latvia." *European Journal of Political Research* 49:1049–1057.

Isaac, Larry W., Debra A. Street, and Stan J. Knapp. 1994. "Analyzing Historical Contingency with Formal Methods: The Case of the "Relief Explosion" and 1968." *Sociological Methods & Research* 23(1): 114–141.

Kanellopoulos, Kostas, Konstantinos Kostopoulos, Dimitris Papanikolopoulos, and Vasileios Rongas. 2017. "Competing Modes of Coordination in the Greek Anti-Austerity Campaign, 2010–2012." *Social Movement Studies* 16 (1): 101–118.

Karyotis, Georgios, and Wolfgang Rüdig. 2018. "The Three Waves of Anti-Austerity Protest in Greece, 2010–2015." *Political Studies Review* 16 (2): 158–69.

Kerbo, Harold R. 1982. "Movements of 'Crisis' and Movements of 'Affluence.'" *Journal of Conflict Resolution* 26(4):645–663.

Key, Valdimer Orlando. 1955. "A Theory of Critical Elections." *The Journal of Politics* 17(1):3–18.

Khawaja, Marwan. 1993. "Repression and Popular Collective Action: Evidence from the West Bank." *Sociological Forum* 8 (1):47–71. X

Kitschelt, Herbert. 1986. "Political Opportunity Structures and Political Protest: Anti-Nuclear Movements in Four Democracies." *British Journal of Political Science* 16 (1):57–85.

Klein, Graig R. and Patrick M. Regan. 2018. "Dynamics of Political Protests." *International Organization* 72 Spring:485–521.

Koopmans, Ruud. 2004. "Protest in Time and Space: The Evolution of Waves of Contention," pp. 19–46 in *The Blackwell Companion to Social Movements*, edited by David H. Snow, Sarah A. Soule, and Hanspeter Kriesi. Oxford: Blackwell Publishing.

2007. "Protest in Time and Space: The Evolution of Waves of Contention." Availablse at https://doi.org/10.1002/9780470999103.ch2.

Koopmans, Ruud and Dieter Rucht. 2002. "Protest Event Analysis," pp. 231–259 in *Methods of Social Movement Research*, edited by Bert Klandermans and Suzanne Staggenborg. Minneapolis, MN: University of Minnesota Press.

Koopmans, Ruud, and Paul Statham. 1999. "Political Claims Analysis: Integrating Protest Event and Political Discourse Approaches." *Mobilization* 4 (2):203–221.

2010. "Theoretical Framework, Research Design, and Methods," pp. 34–59 in *The Making of a European Public Sphere. Media Discourse And Political Contention*, edited by Ruud Koopmans and Paul Statham, Cambridge: Cambridge University Press.

Koopmans, Ruud, Paul Statham, Marco G. Giugni, and Florence Passy, eds. 2005. *Contested Citizenship: Immigration and Cultural Diversity in Europe*. Minneapolis, MN: University of Minnesota Press.

Kriesi, Hanspeter. 1985. *Bewegungen in der Schweizer Politik: Fallstudien zu politischen Mobilisierungsprozessen in der Schweiz*. Frankfurt am Main: Campus.

2004. "Political Context and Opportunity," pp. 67–90 in *The Blackwell Companion to Social Movements*, edited by D. A. Snow, S. A. Soule, and H. Kriesi. Oxford: Blackwell.

2015. "Political Mobilization in Times of Crises: The Relationship Between Economic and Political Crises," pp. 19–33 in *Austerity and Protest: Popular Contention in Times of Economic Crisis*, edited by Marco Giugni and Maria Grasso. Burlington, VT: Ashgate.

Kriesi, Hanspeter, Edgar Grande, Romain Lachat, Martin Dolezal, Simon Bornschier, and Timotheos Frey. 2008. *West European Politics in the Age of Globalization*. Cambridge; New York: Cambridge University Press.

Kriesi, H., R. Koopmans, J. W. Duyvendak, and M. Giugni. 1992. "New Social Movements and Political Opportunities in Western Europe." *European Journal of Political Research* 22 (2): 219–44.

Kriesi, Hanspeter, Ruud Koopmans, Jan Willem Duyvendak, and Marco G. Giugni, eds. 1995. *New Social Movements in Western Europe*, Minneapolis, MN: University of Minnesota Press.

Kriesi, Hanspeter, Jasmine Lorenzini, Bruno Wüest, and Silja Häusermann (eds.) 2020. *Contention in Times of Crisis. Recession and Political Protest in 30 European Countries*. Cambridge: Cambridge University Press.

Kriesi, Hanspeter and Bruno Wüest. 2020. "Conclusion," pp. 276–291 in *Contention in Times of Crises*, edited by Hanspeter Kriesi, Jasmine Lorenzini, Bruno Wüest , and Silja Häusermann. Cambridge: Cambridge University Press.

Kroustalli, Dimitra. 2011. "PASOK troubled over the measures and protest." *To Vima*, May 30, 2011, sec. Politics.

Lichbach, Mark I. 1987. "Deterrence or Escalation? The Puzzle of Aggregate Studies of Repression and Dissent." *The Journal of Conflict Resolution* 31(2):266–297.

1998. *The Rebel's Dilemma*. Ann Arbor, MI: The University of Michigan Press.

Lichbach, Mark. 2005. "How to Organize Your Mechanisms: Research Programs, Stylized Facts, and Historical Narratives," pp. 227–243 in *Repression and Mobilization*, edited by Christian Davenport, Hank Johnston, and Carol Muelle. Minneapolis,MN: University of Minnesota Press.

Lichbach, Mark I. and Ted R. Gurr. 1981. "The Conflict Process a Formal Model." *Journal of Conflict Resolution* 25(1):3–29.

Lupu, Noam. 2014. "Brand Dilution and the Breakdown of Political Parties in Latin America." *World Politics* 66(4):561–602.

Mair, Peter. 2013. "Smaghi Versus the Parties: Representative Government and Institutional Constraints," pp. 143–168 in *Politics in the Age of Austerity*, edited by Wolfgang Streeck and Armin Schaefer. Cambridge: Cambridge Polity Press.

2014. "Representative Versus Responsible Government," pp. 495–512 in *On Parties, Party Systems and Democracy*, edited by Peter Mair. Colchester: ECPR Press.

Malet, Giorgio and Hanspeter Kriesi. 2019. "Economic Shocks and the Cost of Ruling: Evidence From Italy." *Journal of Elections, Public Opinion and Parties* 30 (1):22–41.

Manin, Bernard. 1997. *The Principles of Representative Government* (Cambridge: Cambridge University Press).

Matsaganis, Manos. 2007. "Union Structures and Pension Outcomes in Greece." *British Journal of Industrial Relations* 45 (3):537–555. https://doi.org/10.1111/j.1467-8543.2007.00627

McAdam, Doug. 1983. "Tactical Innovation and the Pace of Insurgency." *American Sociological Review* 48(6):735–754.

1996. "Conceptual Origins, Current Problems, Future Directions," pp. 23–40 in *Comparative Perspectives on Social Movements: Political Opportunities, Mobilizing Structures, and Cultural Framings*, edited by D. McAdam, J.D. McCarthy, and M.N. Zald. Cambridge: Cambridge University Press.

McAdam, Doug and Hilary Boudet. 2012. *Putting Social Movements in Their Place: Explaining Opposition to Energy Projects in The United States, 2000–2005*, Cambridge: Cambridge University Press.

McAdam, D., and S. Tarrow. 2010. "Ballots and Barricades: On the Reciprocal Relationship between Elections and Social Movements." *Perspectives on Politics* 8 (2):529–542.

McAdam, Doug and Sidney Tarrow. 2011. "Introduction: Dynamics of Contention Ten Years on." *Mobilization* 16(1):1–10.

McAdam, D. and S. Tarrow. 2013. "Social Movements and Elections: Toward a Broader Understanding of the Political Context of Contention," pp.325–346 in *The Future of Social Movement Research: Dynamics, Mechanisms, and Processes*, edited by J. Van Stekelenburg, C. Roggeband, and B. Klandermans. Minneapolis, MN: University of Minnesota Press.

2018. "Political Contexts," pp. 19–42 in *Wiley-Blackwell Companion to Social Movements* (2nd ed.), edited by David Snow, Sarah Soule, Hanspeter Kriesi, and Holly McCammon. Oxford: Blackwell.

McAdam, Doug, John D. McCarthy, and Mayer N. Zald, eds. 1996. *Comparative Perspectives on Social Movements: Political Opportunities, Mobilizing Structures, and Cultural Framings*. Cambridge: Cambridge University Press.

McAdam, Doug, Sidney Tarrow, and Charles Tilly. 2001. *Dynamics of Contention*. New York: Cambridge University Press.

Meyer, David S. and Debra C. Minkoff. 2004. "Conceptualizing Political Opportunity." *Social Forces* 82(4):1457–1492.

Moore, Will H. 2000. "The Repression of Dissent. A Substitution Model of Government Coercion." *The Journal of Conflict Resolution* 44(1):107–127.

Mpourdaras, Giorgos. 2011. "MPs Close to Nervous Breakdown." *Kathimerini*, 2011, sec. Politics. Available at https://doi.org/10.1017/S0007123413000112.

Nedos, Vassilis. 2011. "Rift in PASOK Because of the New Measures." *Kathimerini*, March 6, 2011, sec. Politics. Available at www.kathimerini.gr/428240/article/epi kairothta/politikh/rhgma-sto-pasok-logw-twn-newn-metrwn.

Norris, Pippa, and Ronald Inglehart. 2019. *Cultural Backlash: Trump, Brexit, and Authoritarian Populism*. Cambridge: Cambridge Core.

O'Brien, Kevin J. 1996. "Rightful Resistance." *World Politics* 49(1):31–55.

Oberschall, Anthony. 1973. *Social Movements and Social Conflict*. Englewood Cliffs, NJ: Prentice-Hall.

Olivier, Johan. 1991. "State Repression and Collective Action in South Africa, 1970-84." *South African Journal of Sociology* 22:109–117.

Opp, Karl-Dieter and Wolfgang Rühl. 1990. "Repression, Micromobilization and Political Protest." *Social Forces* 69 (2)) 1–47.

Petropoulos, P. Nicholas. 2014. "A Sociopolitical Profile and the Political Impact of the Greek Indignados: An Exploratory Study." pp. 342–394 in *The Debt Crisis in the Eurozone: Social Impacts*, edited by P. Nicholas Petropoulos and O. George Tsobanoglou. Newcastle upon Tyne: Cambridge Scholars Publishing.

Pilati, Katia. 2016. "Do Organizational Structures Matter for Protests in Non-Democratic African Contries," pp. 46–72 in *Contention, Regimes, and Transition – Middle East and North Africa Protest in Comparative Perspective*, edited by E. Y. Alimi, A. Sela, and M. Sznajder. Oxford: Oxford University Press.

Piven, Frances Fox and Richard A. Cloward. 1977. *Poor People's Movements: Why They Succeed, How They Fail*, New York: Vintage Books.

Pontusson, Jonas and Damian Raess. 2012. "How (and Why) Is This Time Different? The Politics of Economic Crisis in Western Europe and the United States." *Annual Review of Political Science* 15:13–33.

Portos, Martin. 2017. "Keeping Dissent Alive under the Great Recession: No-Radicalisation and Protest in Spain After the Eventful 15M/Indignados Campaign." *Acta Politica* 54(1):45–74.

Portos, Martín and Tiago Carvalho. 2019. "Alliance Building and Eventful Protests: Comparing Spanish and Portuguese Trajectories under the Great Recession." *Social Movement Studies*. Available at https://doi.org/10.1080/14742837.2019.1681957

Portos García, Martin. 2016. "Taking to the Streets in the Context of Austerity: A Chronology of the Cycle of Protests in Spain, 2007–2015". *Partecipazione e conflitto* 9(1):181–210.

Quaranta, Mario. 2016. "Protesting in 'Hard Times': Evidence from a Comparative Analysis of Europe, 2000–2014." *Current Sociology* 64(5):736–756.

Ramos, Howard. 2008. "Opportunity for Whom? Political Opportunity and Critical Events in Canadian Aboriginal Mobilization, 1951–2000." *Social Forces* 87 (2):795–823.

Rasler, Karen. 1996. "Concessions, Repression and Political Protest." *American Sociological Review* 61:132–152.

Roberts, Kenneth M. 2013. "Market Reform, Programmatic (De)alignment, and Party System Stability in Latin America." *Comparative Political Studies* 46 (11):1422–1452.

2017. "State of the Field. Party Politics in Hard Times: Comparative Perspectives on the European and Latin American Economic Crisis". *European Journal of Political Research*, 56(2):218–233.

Rucht, Dieter. 2004. "Movement Allies, Adversaries, and Third Parties," pp. 197–216 in *The Blackwell Companion to Social Movements*, edited by David A. Snow, Sarah A. Soule, and Hanspeter Kriesi. Oxford: Blackwell Publishing.

Rüdig, Wolfgang, and Georgios Karyotis. 2014. "Who Protests in Greece? Mass Opposition to Austerity." *British Journal of Political Science* 44 (3): 487–513.

Salo, Sanna 2017. The Curious Prevalence of Austerity: Economic Ideas in Public Debates on the Eurozone Crisis in Ireland and Finland, 2008–2012. Phd-Thesis, Florence: European University Institute.

Sampson, Robert. J and John H. Laub. 2005. "A Life-Course View of the Development of Crime." *Annals of the American Academy of Political and Social Science* 602:12–45.

Schattschneider, E.E. (1960[1975]). *The Semi-Sovereign People: A Realist's View of Democracy in America*. New York: Holt, Rinehart and Winston.

Schumaker, Paul D. 1977. "Policy Responsiveness to Protest-Group Demands." *The Journal of Politics* 37(2):488–521.

Simiti, Marilena. 2015. "Rage and Protest: The Case of the Greek Indignant Movement." *Contention* 3 (2): 33–50.

Skocpol, Theda. 1979. *States and Social Revolutions: A Comparative Analysis of France, Russia and China*. Cambridge: Cambridge University Press.

Snow, David A., Sarah A. Soule, and Hanspeter Kriesi. 2004. *The Blackwell Companion to Social Movements*. Available at https://onlinelibrary.wiley.com/doi/book/10.1002/9780470999103.

Sotirakopoulos, Nikos and Georg Sotiropoulos. 2013. " 'Direct Democracy Now!': The Greek Indignados and the Present Cycle of Struggles." *Current Sociology* 61 (4):443–456.

Sotiropoulos, Dimitri A. 2018. "Political Party–Interest Group Linkages in Greece before and after the Onset of the Economic Crisis." *Mediterranean Politics*, 1–21. Available at https://doi.org/10.1080/13629395.2018.1428149.

Spiegel, Peter. 2011. "How the Euro Was Saved." *Financial Times*, May 2011, sec. The Long Read

Steedly, H.R., and J.W. Foley. 1979. "The Success of Protest Groups: Multivariate Analysis." *Social Science Research* 8:1–15.

Stovel, Katherine and Lynette Shaw. 2012. "Brokerage." *Annual Review of Sociology* 38: 139–158.

Sullivan, Christopher M. 2016. "Undermining Resistance: Mobilization, Repression, and the Enforcement of Political Order." *Journal of Conflict Resolution* 60 (7):1163–1109.

Svensson, Torsten and Perola Öberg. 2005. "How are Coordinated Market Economies Coordinated? Evidence from Sweden." *West European Politics* 28(5):1075–1100.

Tarrow, Sidney. 1979. *Power in Movement*. Cambridge: Cambridge University Press.

   1989. *Democracy and Disorder: Protest and Politics in Italy, 1965–1975*. New York and Oxford: Clarendon Press.

Tarrow, S. 1993. "Cycles of Collective Action: Between Moments of Madness and the Repertoire of Contention." *Social Science History* 17(2): 281–307.

Taylor, Verta. 1989. "Social Movement Continuity: The Women's Movement in Abeyance." *American Sociological Review* 54(5):761–775.

Teurya, Cheryl and Yih-Ing Hser. 2010. "Turning Points in the Life Course: Current Findings and Future Directions in Drug Use Research." *Current Drug Abuse Reviews* 3(3):189–195.

Tilly, Charles. 1978. *From Mobilization to Revolution*. Reading, MA: Addison-Wesley.

   1984. "Social Movements and National Politics," pp. 297–317 in *Statemaking and Social Movements*, edited by Charles Bright and Susan Harding. Ann Arbor,MI: University of Michigan Press.

   1986. *The Contentious French*. Cambridge, MA: Harvard University Press.

   1995. *Popular Contention in Great Britain, 1758–1834*. Cambridge, MA: Harvard University Press.

   2002. "Event Catalogs as Theories." *Sociological Theory* 20 (2): 248–254).

   2004. *Social Movements, 1768–2004*. Paradigm Publishers. Available at https://books.google.gr/books?id=TentAAAAMAAJ.

   2005. "Repression, Mobilization, and Explanation," pp. 211–226 in *Repression and Mobilization*, edited by Christian Davenport, Hank Johnston, and Carol Mueller, Minneapolis, MN: University of Minnesota Press.

2006. *Regimes and Repertoires*. Chicago and London: University of Chicago Press.

2008. *Contentious Performances*. Cambridge: Cambridge University Press.

Tilly, Charles, Doug McAdam, and Sidney Tarrow. 2001. *Dynamics of Contention*. Cambridge: Cambridge University Press.

Tooze, Adam. 2018. *Crashed. How a Decade of Financial Crises Changed the World*. Bristol, UK: Allen Lane.

Vandaele, Kurt. 2016. "Interpreting Strike Activity in Western Europe in the Past 20 Years: The Labour Repertoire Under Pressure." *Transfer: European Review of Labour and Research* 22(3):277–294.

Vidal, Guillem, and Irene Sánchez-Vítores. 2019. "Spain – Out with the Old: The Restructuring of Spanish Politics," pp. 75–94 in *European Party Politics in Times of Crisis, edited by Swen Hutter and Hanspeter Kriesi*. Cambridge: Cambridge University Press.

Walgrave, Stefaan and Rens Vliegenthart. 2012. "The Complex Agenda-Setting Power of Protest: Demonstrations, Media, Parliament, Government, and Legislation in Belgium, 1993–2000." *Mobilization* 17(2):129–156.

Walter, Stefanie. 2016. "Crisis Politics in Europe: Why Austerity Is Easier to Implement in Some Countries Than in Others." *Comparative Political Studies* 49(7):841–873.

Weber, Beat and Stefan W. Schmitz. 2011. "Varieties of Helping Capitalism: Politico-Economic Determinants of Bank Rescue Packages in the EU during the Recent Crisis." *Socio-Economic Review* 9:639–669.

Yuen, Samson and Edmund W. Cheng. 2017. "Neither Repression Nor Concession? A Regime's Attrition against Mass Protests." *Political Studies* 64(3):611–630.

Xasapopoulos, Nikos. 2011. "The Nocturnal Experiences of Blockaded Parliamentarians." *To Vima*, January 6, 2011, sec. Politics.

# Index

*Index*

Books in the Series (*continued from p.ii*)

Ingram Content Group UK Ltd.
Milton Keynes UK
UKHW010701250423
420667UK00009B/30

9 781009 002011